Sugar Confectionery Manufacture

Edited by

E.B. JACKSON
Technical Service Manager,
Confectionery Industries,
Cerestar, UK

Blackie
Glasgow and London

Van Nostrand Reinhold
New York

Blackie and Son Ltd
Bishopbriggs, Glasgow G64 2NZ
and
7 Leicester Place, London WC2H 7BP

Published in the United States of America by
Van Nostrand Reinhold
115 Fifth Avenue
New York, New York 10003

Distributed in Canada by
Nelson Canada
1120 Birchmount Road
Scarborough, Ontario M1K 5G4, Canada

16 15 14 13 12 11 10 9 8 7 6 5 4 3 2 1

© 1990 Blackie and Son Ltd
First published 1990

British Library Cataloguing in Publication Data

Sugar confectionery manufacture.
1. Sugar industries & trade
I. Jackson, E. B. (E Brian)
338.1736

ISBN 0-216-92794-3

Library of Congress Cataloging-in-Publication Data

Sugar confectionery manufacture / [edited by] E.B. Jackson.
p.   cm.
Includes bibliographical references (p.).
ISBN 0-442-30285-1
1. Confectionery.   I. Jackson, E.B. (E. Brian)
TX783.S87   1990   89-29392
664'.15--dc20   CIP

Phototypesetting by Thomson Press (India) Ltd., New Delhi
Printed in Great Britain by BPCC Wheatons Ltd, Exeter

Preface

This book is written for food scientists and technologists in the sugar confectionery manufacturing industry, and will also serve as a useful source of reference for ingredient suppliers and equipment manufacturers and those working in academic and research institutions. It complements the book *Industrial Chocolate Manufacture and Use*, edited by S.T. Beckett (Blackie, 1988). The authors have been carefully chosen and are recognised as experts in their subjects. They are from both manufacturing industry and academic research, and have been working in the field of sugar confectionery for many years. I would like to thank them for the care that they have taken to provide a varied and instructive compilation of chapters. I also wish to thank Cerestar UK Ltd for their help and support, my wife and family for their forbearance during preparation of the manuscript, and the publishers for giving me the opportunity to edit this book.

EBJ

Acknowledgements

Thanks are expressed, for help, information and permission to use material, to: *APV Baker*, Westfield Rd, Peterborough, PE3 6TA, UK; *A/S Kobenhavns*, Pektinfabrik DK 4623, Lille Skensved, Denmark; *Bramigk & Co. Ltd*, 2A Towcester Rd, London E3 3ND, UK; *Bulmers H.P. Limited*, Hereford HR4 0LE, UK; *Cerestar (UK) Ltd*, Trafford Park, Manchester M17 1PA, UK; *The Biscuit, Cake, Chocolate and Confectionery Alliance*, London, UK; *Clextral SA*, BP10, 47202 Firminy, Cedex, France; *Iranex*, 4 Rue Frederic-Passey, BP13, 92205 Neuilly-sur-Seine, France; *Kelco International Ltd*, Westminster Tower, 3 Albert Embankment, London, SE1 7RZ, UK; *Kenman Foods*, Melbourne, Australia; *New Zealand Milk Products*, PO Box 80816, Petaluma, CA 94975-8016, New Zealand; *NID Pty Ltd*, PO Box 38, Alexandria 2015, Sydney, Australia; *Asser-Oakes Asser Engineer Ltd*, Chesterton, Staffordshire, ST5 9JB, UK; *PB Gelatins*, Division of Tessenderlo Chemie, Marius Duchestraat 260, 1800 Vilvoorde, Belgium, *Nestlé-Rowntree plc*, Haxby Rd, York, YO1 1XY, UK; *Sanofi Bioindustries*, 15 Avenue D'Eylau, 75116 Paris, France; *Sollich/GmBH Co. Kg*, Siemensstraße 17–23, Postfach 629 D-4902, Bad Salzuflen, West Germany; *TEMEC*, Societé des Téchniques Méchaniques et Chimiques, 25 Rue Singer, 75016 Paris, France.

Contents

10 Gums and jellies   190
E.T. BEST

11 Liquorice paste, cream paste and aerated confectionery 218
E.B. JACKSON

12 Tablets, lozenges and sugar panning 236
J. BEACHAM

13 Medicated confectionery and chewing gum   258
C.S. CUMMINGS

14 Centers, fondants, marzipan and crystallized confectionery   280
M.S. JEFFERY

20 Sugar confectionery in the diet

E.M.S. EDMONDSON

Appendix: Glossary

Index

Contributors

B. Beacham *Givaudan Co. Ltd, Godstone Road Whyteleafe, Surrey CR3 0YE*
Barry Beacham was educated at King Edward's High School, Birmingham, and Birmingham College of Further Education where he studied chemistry. In 1948 he commenced a 5 year apprenticeship in the Quality Control Laboratory at Cadbury Bros Ltd. He joined Beecham Foods at Brentford in 1956 working in the Product Development Department on Murray Confectionery products. In 1965 he moved to become Chief Chemist of W.S. Shuttleworth Ltd. In 1972 he joined Givaudan Flavours as Manager of the Technical Centre at Mitcham, responsible for application, creation, legislation and health and safety. At present he is Technical Controller of Givaudan Flavours at Whyteleafe, responsible for the growing areas of food legislation, labelling and health and safety. He represents Givaudan on the Technical Committee of the British Essence Manufacturers Association (BEMA) and is a member of the Institute of Food Technology (Chicago), the Institute of Food Science and Technology (UK), the Institute of Packaging, and the Royal Society of Health.

J. Beacham *George Payne plc 5 Percy Road, Mitcham Junction, Surrey CR4 4JW*
Jayne Beacham started her career in food technology in 1976 when she joined the Food Research Association at Leatherhead. For seven years her work involved research into the properties and applications of raw materials in a variety of areas including oils and fats, general food analysis and confectionery. Her work included the development of new products for the UK and overseas clients and as a secondary role, researching specific client problem areas and advising accordingly in a 'trouble-shooting' capacity. Following one year at Tunnel Refineries Ltd setting up confectionery application facilities, Jayne became the Product Development Technologist with George Payne and Co. Ltd in 1983. Her duties extended to the improvement of existing products, including the application of new raw materials with emphasis on both quality and cost aspects.

E.T. Best, MFC, C.Chem., FRSC, FIFST *Nestlé-Rowntree plc, PO Box 204, York Y01 1XY*
Eric Best started work in the colour, fibre, frozen, pharmaceutical and grocery food manufacturing areas before becoming Senior Scientist in confectionery. Roles included Research and Development Manager, Chief Confectioner, and Technical Services Manager at various locations throughout Europe. He achieved one of the first HNDs in Food Technology. Part-time education continued and he became an Honours Chemistry Graduate and was later awarded the fiirst Masters degree in Food Control. On the way, he also gained a Graduate Diploma in Food Science (Credit) and was a pupil on the Confectioners Diploma course at Solingen, West Germany. He has served on innumerable European trade, administrative, legislative, research and professional councils and committees.

I.M. Billcliff *Thorntons Ltd, Derwent Street, Belper, Derbyshire DE5 1WP*
Ian Billcliff is presently Technical Manager of Thorntons plc. His career started in the Quality Control laboratories of Glaxo plc, and he was mainly concerned with pharmaceutical analysis until he entered the confectionery industry in 1971 as Works Chemist with Hall Bros. (Whitfield) Ltd. He became Chief Chemist with Smith Kendon Ltd (subsequently Callard & Bowser Group) in 1976, before taking up his present position in 1985. He is a Charted Chemist and Member of the Royal Society of Chemistry, and obtained a Diploma in Management Studies from Manchester Polytechnic in 1975. At the time of publication he is Secretary of the Food & Drink Sector Committee of the British Quality Association and also serves on the Legislative Standards Committee of the Biscuit, Cake, Chocolate and Confectionery Alliance.

Raymond David Bullock *Thorntons Ltd, Derwent Street, Belper, Derbyshire DE5 1WP*
David Bullock is Laboratory Services Manager for Thorntons plc. He joined the Company in

1966 as Quality Assurance Manager and installed their first laboratories. Previously, he was Works Chemist for Diversey (UK) Ltd having started his career as an assistant analyst with Boots Pure Drug Co. Ltd. He was educated at Swanwick Hall Grammer School, and Nottingham and District Technical College, where he studied Chemistry and Advanced Analytical Techniques. He is a Licentiate of the Royal Society of Chemistry and a Member of the Institute of Food Science and Technology. He is a Committee member of the Confectionery Panel of the Leatherhead Food Research Association and has served on the Scientific Committee and the Legislative Standards Committee of the Biscuit, Cake, Chocolate and Confectionery Alliance.

C.S. Cummings   *Hall Bros (Whitefield) Ltd, Morris Street, Dummers Lane, Radcliffe, Manchester M26 9QT*
Colin Cummings has been New Products Development Manager for Hall Brothers Limited (an affiliate of the Warner Lambert Company) since 1980. His responsibilities include product regulatory compliance for all markets and product registrations. For the previous fourteen years he was Quality Assurance Manager for the same company, including a period as Production Manager. His earlier confectionery experience was with the Barker & Dobson Group and in the starch and glucose industry with CPC Ltd (now Cerestar). He gained food manufacturing experience with James Keiller & Sons (Crosse & Blackwell/Nestlé) and food and drug analytical experience with a Public Analyst.

R. Early   *Dairy Crest Foods, Development Centre, Crudgington, Telford, Shropshire TF6 6HY*
Ralph Early qualified as a Dairy Technologist at Seale-Hayne Agricultural College and subsequently obtained a BA (Science and Technology) degree from the Open University. Prior to joining Dairy Crest Foods in 1980, he gained experience in cheese, yogurt and chocolate crumb manufacture. He is currently Project Manager responsible for Dairy Crest Food industrial product development. He has delivered a number of lectures on various aspects of dairy technology, and in particular, recombination technology with which he has much experience. He also holds a patent for a cream powder. A member of the Institute of Food Science and Technology, he is also UK representative and chairman of the International Dairy Federation Group (B39) for Spray Drying, as well as UK and Ireland representative on the Technical Working Group of the Association of Lactose Manufacturers.

E.M.S. Edmondson   *Mars Confectionery, Division of Mars UK Limited, Dundee Road, Slough SL1 4JX*
Maureen Edmondson graduated from Queens University Belfast in 1971 with a B.Sc. (1st Hons) in Food Science followed by a Ph.D. in Agricultural and Food Bacteriology in 1974. She worked in University and Government positions in the UK and Australia before joining the Mars Corporation, where she is currently Scientific Affairs Manager for Europe. Maureen is chairman of the Health and Nutrition Sub-Committee of the Biscuit, Cake, Chocolate and Confectionery Alliance (BCCCA).

I. Fabry   *ZDS, Zentralfachschule der Deutschen Sußwarenwirtschaft, De-Leuw-Strasse 3/4, D5650 Solingen-Grafrath, West Germany*
Ivan Fabry has 35 years' experience in sugar and chocolate confectionery technology. From 1955 to 1968 he worked for Chocolaterie Jacques, Eupen in Belgium, where he was master of the candy department. In 1969 he joined the Zentralfachschule der Deutschen Sußwarenwirtschaft (Central College of the German Confectionery Trade) as teacher for confectionery. Since 1983 he has been Technical Director of ZDS Solingen and responsible for the organisation of seminars and practical courses as well as research and development activities. He is co-author of *Le Guide Technologique de la Confiserie Industrielle* Published by Sepaic, Paris.

J.N.S. Hancock, B.Sc., Ph.D., FIFST.   *Anglia Oils Limited, King George Dock, Hull HU9 69*
John N.S. Hancock trained as a physicist at Sir John Cass College, London and at Reading University. He joined Rowntree Mackintosh as a research scientist where he worked initially on the physical properties of confectionery raw materials and products. As manager of the Oils and Fats Section, he developed a keen interest in fat based systems and led a team of technologists working on the processing of chocolate and couvertures. He later became Chief Chemist for the

York factory of Rowntree Mackintosh. Dr Hancock is currently Technical Director of Anglia Oils Limited, who supply a full range of refined oils and fats for the food industry.

R.D. Howling   *Cerestar UK Ltd, Trafford Park, Manchester M17 1PA*
David Howling obtained his degree in Chemistry at the University of Loughborough. He began his career in the pharmaceutical industry in new product development at Boots. He spent three years working in enzyme research at the Unilever laboratory at Colworth House during which time he obtained his Ph.D. Following a period of production management experience at Procter Gamble he joined CPC (UK) Ltd (now Cerestar UK Ltd) as technical development manager. He is responsible for all the technical aspects of the Cerestar business in the UK including quality assurance, new product development and technical service. Dr Howling has spoken widely on the subject of starch and its derivatives in Europe and US, including the Interpack Symposium at Solingen. He is a fellow of the Royal Society of Chemistry.

E.B. Jackson   *Cerestar UK Ltd, Trafford Park, Manchester M17 1PA*
Brian Jackson has 40 years' experience in the confectionery industry. He qualified in Food Science at Manchester Polytechnic and Salford Technical College, and later in Nutritional Studies and Cocoa Sugar Confectionery. He spent two years in the Royal Air Force as Instructor, Food and Nutrition, four years at RHM, and six years at CWS in Product Research & Development. He has worked in India concerned with the production of chocolate and chocolate products, in West Germany at three or four different factories, and had a period of time in Scandinavia doing technical work. Brian Jackson is at present employed by Cerestar UK Ltd in the capacity of Technical Adviser in Food and Sugar Confectionery Industries. Over the last 29 years this job has embraced the United Kingdom and Europe. Brian has 21 years of teaching experience at the Solingen School and has presented more than 35 technical papers at this establishment. He has also been a part-time lecturer at Salford Technical College, the Leatherhead Food Research Association and the South Bank Polytechnic, London. He has addressed the Interpack Symposium, IFF Cambridge (1984), PMCA, Lancaster, USA (1986) and FIE London (1988). He has been a panel member of Leatherhead Food Research Association for 25 years and a committee member for 4 years; he is a member of the American Association of Candy Technologists, and a Founder Member, IFST. He was co-author of *Sugar Confectionery and Chocolate Manufacture* (Leonard Hill, 1973).

D. James, B.Sc., ARCS, C.Chem, FIFST, FRSH.   *Tate & Lyle, Plaistow Wharf, London E16 2PG*
Douglas James is Senior Food Technologist at Tate & Lyle Sugars, London. He qualified in chemistry at Imperial College and entered the food industry with J. Lyons & Co. He spent more than 20 years in the confectionery industry with E.S. Morton Ltd and Clarnico Ltd, where he was Chief Chemist and Technologist. Employed now by Tate & Lyle Sugars he works on food product and process development. He has been a member of the Leatherhead Food Research Association Confectionery Panel for over 30 years and has lectured and written articles on sugar and sweet making.

M.S. Jeffery   *Jeffery Associates, 319 Thomaston Road, Connecticut 06795, USA*
Maurice Jeffery is President of Jeffery Associates, Consultant to Hershey Foods Corporation and to the Chocolate Confectionery Industry. Formerly, he spent 30 years with the Cadbury Company, 20 years of which were in England with Cadbury Ltd in various technical capacities, as Group Process Development Manager. In 1979 at the takeover of Peter Paul he transferred to the USA, as Director of R&D/QA. He was responsible for the Cadbury North American Operation for all research and quality matters. He obtained an Honours Degree from the University of London. He is an Associate of the Royal Institute of Chemistry and Fellow of the American Institute of Chemistry. He is currently Chairman of the American Cocoa Research Institute and Chocolate Manufacturers Association Scientific Committee, as well as being Chairman of the PMCA Research Committee.

C.J. Knewstubb, B.A., MIFST   *Overseal Foods Ltd, Swains Park, Burton-on-Trent. Staffordshire DE12 6JX*
Conrad Knewstubb studied chemistry at Cambridge University, from where he qualified in 1964.

After a short period spent in the Quality Control department for a major food/pharmaceutical company, he transferred to food product development. In 1976 he moved into Technical Services, specialising in colourants, vitamins and nutritive sweeteners for the food industry. He is currently Technical Sales Manager at Overseal Foods Limited.

R. Lees *38 St Vincent Road, Walton-on-Thames, Surrey*
Ronald Lees is Superintendent, Planning, Marketing and Services Division, Laboratory of the Government Chemist, in Teddington. Formerly, he has been in the Department of Industry, the Department of Trade and Industry, and the Ministry of Technology. He is a member of the Royal Society of Chemistry, a Fellow of the Royal Society of Health, and an Associate of the Institute of Food Science and Technology. Ronald Lees has been associated with the sugar and chocolate industry for more than 30 years. His career has involved development, management, quality control, research and 'trouble-shooting'.

D.F. Lewis *Leatherhead Food Research Association, Leatherhead, Surrey KT22 7RY*
David Lewis received a B.Sc., and Ph.D. degree in Food Science from the Procter department of University of Leeds. This has been followed by nearly twenty years studying the microscopy of food and its practical application to the food industry at the Leatherhead Food Research Association, where he currently manages the Microscopy and Trace Organics Sections. He is a member of the editorial board of the Journal of Food Microstructure.

P. Murphy *Rowntree PLC, York, YO1 1XY*
Pauline Murphy graduated in Food Science from Reading University. She has spent 15 years in the confectionery industry and has been involved in product development in the UK and Europe. She is currently Product Development Manager for Rowntree Mackintosh Confectionery Ltd.

C. Nelson *Cerestar UK Ltd, Trafford Park, Manchester M17 1PA*
Charles Nelson is currently a Manufacturing Executive working within the Fox's Biscuits Division of the Northern Foods Grocery Group, responsible for implementation of a number of special projects. Prior to this, he fulfilled a number of roles within the Barker and Dobson Confectionery Division, including Factory Management, Special Projects and finally, as Divisional Technical Manager, he was involved in many aspects of product, process and packaging developments. He spent the early part of his career working with Nabisco Brands, working on chocolate moulding lines and on the development of coatings and processes in various operational/technical functions.

T. Pepper *Finn Sugar Xyrofin (UK) Ltd, 41–51 Brighton Road, Redhill, Surrey RH1 6YS*
Tammy Pepper obtained both her B.Sc. and Ph.D. degrees in the Department of Food Technology at the University of Reading. She began her career at the Leatherhead Food Research Association as a Research Scientist in the Confectionery Section. She subsequently joined Lyons Maid Ltd as Senior Food Technologist, where she gained experience in ice-cream technology. She commenced employment with Xyrofin (UK) Ltd in 1983 as Technical Services Manager, co-ordinating applications research and advising customers on the use of bulk sweeteners. In this capacity she has presented papers on the properties and applications of sweeteners at several international symposia including the Solingen Interpack Seminar, AACT, Behr's Seminar and Food Ingredients Europe. She is currently Vice-President, Scientific and Technical Services.

P.B. Rayner, LRSC, MIFST, MRIPHH, M.Bl.M. *Overseal Foods Ltd, Swains Park,*
Burton-on-Trent, Staffordshire DE12 6JX
Peter B. Rayner has spent his working life within the food industry in a range of disciplines including product development, quality assurance, production, technical sales and service. He has worked in flavours, confectionery, functional ingredients and colours. He is currently Project Manager for Overseal Foods Limited.

A. Rix *Burton's Gold Medal Biscuits, Quality House, Vicarage Lane, Blackpool, FY4 4NQ*
Alan Rix graduated in Chemistry and Physiology from the University of Sheffield in 1968. After a short spell in the paper industry he joined Rowntree Mackintosh in their Edinburgh factory where he eventually became Deputy Chief Chemist and gained wide experience of a range of chocolate

and sugar confectionery products. After 12 years with Rowntree, he joined Barker & Dobson Ltd as Group Chemist where he was involved in the development and production of a wide range of gum and jelly products, toffees and boiled sweets under the Keiller, B&D, Benson and Fryers brand names. In 1987 Alan joined Burton's Biscuits Ltd at their Blackpool factory as Technical Manager, where a range of biscuits and confectionery products, including mallows and Liquorice Allsorts, are manufactured. In addition to his experience in product development, Alan has a special interest in Quality Assurance, BS 5750 and Food Legislation.

D. Stansell   *United Biscuits, Waterton Industrial Estate, Bridgend, Mid Glamorgan, CF31 3DJ*
Derek Stansell started his career as a chemist but has spent nearly 40 years in confectionery production and research. Fifteen years in industry were followed by eight years at the Leatherhead Food Research Association and since then he has been development manager with Callard & Bowser, now part of Terry's group. He is currently chairman of the Food Research Association Confectionery Panel Committee.

P.D. Whitehead   *Dairy Crest Foods, Development Centre, Crudgington, Shropshire TE6 6HY*
Paul Whitehead qualified as a chemist and he is a Member of the Institute of Food Science and Technology. He joined Cavenham Confectionery Limited (now Elizabeth Shaw Limited) in 1973. He was principally involved in sugar confectionery product and process development, until 1982 when he moved to the company's Bristol site to work on chocolate development. In 1985 he joined Specialist Dairy Ingredients, working in the development and application of lactose hydrolysed whey concentrates, with particular reference to confectionery. He is currently a Project Leader with Dairy Crest Foods engaged in industrial product development, primarily for the confectionery industry but also for other sectors of the food industry.

D.J. van Zuilichem   *Agricultural University, Biotechnion, Wageningen, Netherlands*
Dick J. van Zuilichem is Professor at the Agricultural University of Wageningen, the Netherlands. He has been performing research work on food extrusion technology in the Department of Food Processing Engineering since 1969 and he has published numerous papers in the field of cooking extrusion. Since 1976 he has been part of a team of lecturers which has travelled internationally to give one-week courses in food extrusion technology. His other research interests are in the field of food process engineering, especially the heat treatment of food and food logistics. He received his process engineering degree at Delft University of Technology in 1963.

1 Sugar

D. JAMES

1.1 Introduction

Sugar is in fact a generic name referring to a host of carbohydrates, but it has become common usage for it to refer to one particular substance—sucrose. Sucrose is produced in vast quantities throughout the world and it is *the* basic ingredient for classical sugar confectionery. Indeed, the whole confectionery industry has been built around the physicochemical properties of sucrose and their modification by other traditional sweeteners. In this chapter, the use of the word 'sugar' will imply sucrose.

Sugar occurs very widely in the vegetable world, in the roots and stems of grasses and root vegetables and in the sap of many trees. It also appears in the juices of many fruits. Commercially, however, it is extracted from sugar cane, which is grown in tropical areas, and from sugar beet, which is grown in temperate climates. World sugar production is upwards of ninety million tonnes a year, of which roughly 60% is cane and 40% is beet.

1.2 Production of cane sugar

The harvested sugar cane is crushed and the juice is squeezed out. The juice is heated and treated with lime to remove many of the impurities, after which it is evaporated until the sugar crystallises. The resulting mixture of crystals and mother liquor (often called *massecuite* or *masse*) is centrifuged to produce raw cane sugar and the mother liquor which is spun off is reboiled to produce another crop of raw sugar. The second mother liquor is boiled for a third time. The third mother liquor is economically (but not chemically) exhausted of sugar and is called *factory molasses*.

Raw sugar contains about 97% sucrose, the remainder being molasses which has clung to the sucrose crystals. At the refinery, the white sugar is extracted as follows:

Affination   The raw sugar is mingled with a saturated sugar syrup
(affination syrup), which softens the molasses film. The masse
is centrifuged to give affined sugar.

Dissolution	The affined sugar is dissolved in water and weak recovered sugar syrups.
Carbonatation	The syrup is treated with lime, followed by carbon dioxide (from boiler flue gas). The precipitated chalk carries down much of the impurities.
Filtration	The carbonatated sugar is filtered, usually through plate presses under pressure.
Decolorisation	The clarified liquor is percolated through a decolorising medium (such as bone charcoal and/or resin) to remove dissolved coloured impurities.
Boiling	The decolorised liquor is evaporated under vacuum until it crystallises.
Centrifugation	The masse is centrifuged and the crystals are lightly washed with distilled water. The mother liquor is reboiled to produce further crops of sugar. A fourth boiling produces an off-white sugar (industrial granulated), after which the impurity level is too high to produce more sugar. Some of the syrup is used to make blends of flavoursome syrups for sale. As much sugar as possible is extracted from the remainder in a recovery process and is added to the raw sugar at the start of the process. The residual final syrup, from which it is considered uneconomical to extract further amounts of sucrose, is sold as *refinery molasses*.
Drying	The damp granulated sugar is dried in a current of hot air.

1.3 Production of beet sugar

A cane sugar refinery operates throughout the year, drawing its raw sugar supplies from different parts of the world. Beet sugar factories, which draw their supplies of beet from nearby growers, produce sugar only from about October to January. Whilst raw beet sugar can be produced, it is usual to avoid this step and the normal process is as follows:

Extraction	The harvested beets are washed and sliced into *cossettes* (about $3'' \times \frac{1}{4}'' \times \frac{1}{8}''$). These are fed into a continuous diffuser and extracted with water.
Carbonatation	The raw juice is carbonatated, filtered, recarbonatated and refiltered.
Decolorisation	Normally, double carbonatation is sufficient but, if required, active carbon can be added during carbonatation.
Evaporation	The 'raw' or 'thin' juice is evaporated to about 60%

concentration to give 'thick' juice and then further evaporation takes place in vacuum pans until it crystallises.

Centrifugation   After centrifuging the masse and washing the crystals, white sugar is produced. The mother liquor is reprocessed but the sugar has too much colour for whites and is redissolved and added to the thick juice. The second mother liquor is again reboiled and the spun sugar is taken back to the first carbonatation stage. The final mother liquor is beet molasses.

Drying   The damp granulated sugar is dried.

1.4 Types of sugar

1.4.1 *Granulated*

This is marketed in several grades.

1.4.1.1 *Mineral water*. This is the purest grade of sugar which is commercially available. It has a lower colour and ash content than granulated and was originally produced for the manufacture of mineral waters. However, it has found use in sugar confectionery for specific purposes, e.g. wet crystallisation.

1.4.1.2 *Granulated*. A white sugar which is sold industrially and domestically and which constitutes a very high proportion of total production.

1.4.1.3 *Industrial granulated*. This sugar has a very slight off-white colour and is used where a white sugar is unnecessary, e.g. in the manufacture of toffee, fudge and chocolate.

1.4.1.4 *Cubes*. These are usually produced nowadays by moistening granulated sugar with about 1% water, pressing into cubes and drying.

1.4.1.5 *Nibs*. These are agglomerates of granulated sugar crystals, made by dampening the sugar, thoroughly drying, and breaking up the resulting hard mass. The product is sieved to various sizes.

1.4.2 *Caster*

A white sugar, of small crystal size, for domestic and industrial use. It can be either boiled in the vacuum pans or milled from granulated and therefore has the same composition as granulated.

1.4.3   Icing

Icing is produced by milling granulated sugar, the best qualities being double-milled. Often an insoluble anticaking agent is added.

1.4.4   Liquid sugars

There are advantages and disadvantages in using liquid sugars, for example ease of handling and being already dissolved against the extra water to transport and to evaporate. When the total solids are under 75%, precautions must be taken to avoid microbial spoilage.

Liquid sugars come in many forms. Mineral water or granulated sugar can be dissolved in distilled water to produce the highest quality. For most purposes in the confectionery industry, the decolorised liquor from the refining process is supplied, instead of evaporating it to produce granulated sugar. Relatively impure mother liquors (i.e. those which contain too much colour, ash etc. to produce white sugar) can be sold as such, when these small amounts of impurities are not of prime importance and show savings in cost. Still lower grade syrups can be used to provide colour and flavour. All or part of the sucrose may be inverted and the total solids may be between 66 and 84%.

1.4.5   Brown sugars

There are basically two types. The first is, in effect, raw sugars produced by the sugar factories. These can have a good flavour but some may suffer from variation in quality, particularly regarding hygiene and foreign matter. The second type is produced in sugar refineries. Originally they were 'boiled' sugars; that is, 'impure' sugar solutions were evaporated until brown sugars of various qualities were produced. However the process is very slow and nowadays brown sugars are produced by combining mixtures of 'impure' syrups with white sugar of the appropriate crystal size. This process also gives more uniform products.

1.4.6   Molasses

A one million tonnes a year cane refinery will produce 600–800 tonnes of molasses per week, from which no more sugar can be extracted. Some is used for human consumption, but the bulk goes to cattle food and to the fermentation industries, e.g. alcohol and citric acid. Treacle is clarified molasses and can be mixed with higher purity syrups to mellow the taste. Within limits, its composition can be altered (e.g. in terms of total solids and ratio of sucrose to invert sugars) to simplify product formulation.

1.4.7 Microcrystalline sugars

Sugar syrup is evaporated to around 95% solids and then subjected to intense shear. The sugar crystallises instantly as very fine crystals (5–20 μm), the dried, milled and sieved final products being agglomerates of these crystals. Sugars produced in this way have special properties—for example, whites dissolve very rapidly and browns are free-flowing.

1.5 Composition of sugars

For details of the methods of analysis of sugars, the reader is referred to the standard textbooks of food analysis, to the methods contained in EEC directives and to the ICUMSA (International Commission for Uniform Methods of Sugar Analysis) published methods.

1.5.1 White sugars

Refined white sugar is probably the purest food known, containing over 99.95% sucrose, on a dry basis. The composition varies a little between refiners, but Table 1.1 gives an indication of the values which may be expected. Pure sucrose has been included to demonstrate the ultimate of the sugar refiners' art.

The composition of the ash varies a little from source to source and between cane and beet sugar but, in practical terms, is of no real significance. However, an imperfectly refined sugar which happened to have a high percentage of phosphate in its ash could have an undesirable buffering effect when inverting with cream of tartar. Colour is measured in International Units (IU). Other methods of colour measurement (e.g. Lovibond) are inapplicable due to the low level of colour, but can be used in darker solutions.

Table 1.1 Composition of white sugars

	Pure sucrose	Mineral water	Granulated	Industrial granulated
Maximum impurity limits				
Invert (%)	0.002	0.010	0.015	0.20
Ash (%)	0.002	0.005	0.013	0.13
Colour (IU)	8	8	17	220
SO_2 (ppm)	1	1	15	15
Average moistures (%)	0.010	0.012	0.020	0.070
Average organic non-sugars (%)	0.001	0.004	0.012	0.065

Table 1.2　Composition of brown sugars

	Raw demerara	Refinery brown sugars		
		Light	Medium	Dark
Total sugars (%)	99.3	95.8	95.0	94.2
Non-sugars (%)	0.5	2.0	2.5	3.5
Water (%)	0.2	2.2	2.5	2.3
Colour (IU)	2900	3000	7000	21 000

1.5.2　Brown sugars

Table 1.2 shows a typical composition of a raw demerara sugar and three types of refinery brown sugars. The non-sugars from the original cane are responsible for the flavour. Stickiness is a property associated with brown sugars and, by and large, the higher the molasses content (i.e. invert sugar, water and non-sugars) the more sticky is the sugar. Prolonged storage in a low relative humidity leads to slow evaporation of the water and results in the sugar becoming very hard. Both these attributes lead to difficulty in handling. There are two alternatives—to use a liquid sugar in which the required amount of brown sugar has been predissolved or to use microcrystalline brown sugars, which are free-flowing.

1.5.3　Liquid sugars

As is demonstrated in Table 1.3, the range of liquid sugars available is extensive. No. 3 is an example of decolorised liquor from the refinery main stream before evaporation in the vacuum pans. It is pure enough to be used for most confectionery purposes. No. 4 is less pure and would be suitable where colour, etc. is not of prime importance. No. 5 is an example of several types of golden syrup which are available. In order to prevent crystallisation at the high solids content the optimum ratio of sucrose to invert sugar (approximately 2 to 3) is used. No. 6 is one of many types of invert sugar available, which range in colour from 30 to 3000 and in solids from 67 to 82%. Commercial invert syrups are never fully inverted: up to 3% of sucrose remains

Table 1.3　Typical liquid sugars

	Dissolved mineral water sugar	Dissolved granulated sugar	No. 3	No. 4	No. 5	No. 6
Invert (%)	0.02	0.03	0.2	0.7	46	77
Ash (%)	0.005	0.015	0.12	0.3	1.2	0.4
Colour (IU)	10	17	50	200	1000	35
Solids (%)	67	67	67	67	83	80

Table 1.4 Example of treacles

	No. 1	No. 2	No. 3
Sucrose (%)	30.5–33.5	29–33	35.5–39.5
Invert (%)	31–35	27–31	16.5–20.5
Ash (%)	6–8	8.5–10.5	10.5–13
Colour (IU)	90 000–120 000	125 000–170 000	180 000–220 000
Total solids (%)	81–82	80–81	79.5–80.5
Organic non-sugars (%)	6.5–8.5	8.5–11.0	12.5–15

uninverted. Further, when the solids content is over 75%, the dextrose part of the invert sugar is likely to crystallise and the mass solidifies.

Then, there is a wide range of blended syrups available which, if required, can be tailor-made to a confectioner's requirements. There are sugar/invert, sugar/glucose and sugar/invert/glucose mixes in various proportions and of various total solids. In addition, refinery syrups of varying flavour levels can be added, imparting a natural flavour to the end product.

1.5.4 *Treacle and molasses*

Beet molasses is rarely used in confectionery, due to its unpleasant flavour. The flavour of cane molasses is very strong and is often mellowed by adding higher grade refinery syrups. When this is done, the products are usually called 'treacle'. Table 1.4 shows three examples of treacles, no. 1 being of higher quality than no. 2, which in turn is better than no. 3. Starting with the original molasses, adjustments can be made to the sucrose, invert, water and molasses content.

1.6 Bulk storage of sugar products

1.6.1 *Dry sugar*

Sugar is this form is normally stored in vertical cylindrical silos which can be internal or external and are made from a variety of materials. The most common in use in mild steel with a white epoxy lining. External silos require insulating, and whether inside or out the stored sugar must be protected from chilling. Such temperature differentials will manifest themselves in an enemy known as 'moisture migration', which results in sugar adhering to the silo wall with resulting discharge problems. Similarly, dry caking will result from the sugar being stored in humidity conditions which are too dry. The tolerance is wide but should be between 60 and 75% relative humidity (RH) at around 25°C. However, chilling and hence the avoidance of draughts is of paramount importance.

It is a statutory requirement that all sugar silos must be protected against explosion risks.

Pipelines from the silos should be as straight as possible with few bends, and no bend should have a radius less than 1 m.

Obstruction such as divertors, magnets, etc. should be avoided. It is important that the system is properly designed and adequate in volume to convey sugar without damage to the crystal. This is particularly important when the sugar is measured by volume.

Dry sugar in the right conditions is easy to handle and will keep indefinitely. Fine sugars and icing do not lend themselves to bulk handling and require special treatment.

1.6.2 Liquid sugars

These are around 67% solids and are best stored at ambient. They are easily handled using stainless-steel positive displacement pumps and are stored in unheated vertical cylindrical tanks made of stainless steel, but there has been an increasing use of glass reinforced plastic/polypropylene tanks for economic reasons. The whole essence of success is in the proper implementation of a sterilisation and hygiene procedure, in which tanks and intake pipes are sterilised before each delivery.

Low-pressure steam is recommended for the prescribed time and temperature elevation, e.g. 90°C for 30 min. Steam leaves little risk of contamination. Clean-in-place systems and sterilants can, of course, be used but must be protected against mistakes. Chloride-based sterilants are not recommended in the presence of stainless steel and tanks should not be 'pickled'. Tank hygiene should have the protection of proper microbiological sugar tank vents and be protected against overfill or accidental vacuum. Level glasses, sample cocks and valves other than butterfly pattern are not recommended on hygiene grounds.

Liquid sugar tanks can be external but in such an event should be insulated and weather-proofed. This should include exposed pipework. If this is not done, cold weather may make the material difficult to pump and may induce the sugar to crystallise.

1.6.3 Syrups and treacles

Here the viscosities and densities are much higher, and as a result these materials are stored at an elevated temperature to maintain them in a reasonably easy-to-handle state. Normal delivery temperature is 50°C and should be maintained around this level. This is achieved by using zoned electric blankets and trace heating, which should always have adequate emergency thermostatic control, or water jacketing. Steam jackets, coils or elements within the material are not recommended.

Localised overheating must be avoided, as some of these materials have exothermic properties which can be triggered where heat is introduced to reheat cool material. In other respects the same remarks apply as for liquid sugars. Again, in the right conditions all these materials are easy to handle, therefore it is of importance that potential suppliers of equipment are made aware of the particular characteristics of the individual materials. This information is readily available from most sugar suppliers.

1.7 Properties of sugar and sugar solutions

1.7.1 *Inversion*

Sucrose, which is a disaccharide, can be broken down into a mixture of two monosaccharides, known as dextrose (glucose) and laevulose (fructose), which are together known as invert sugar. Initially, 342 parts of sucrose combine with 18 parts of water to produce 180 parts of dextrose and 180 of laevulose. However, laevulose tends to break down and the ratio in the end is not always 1:1. Inversion is promoted by the actions of acid, heat and mineral matter, separately or in combination. It can also be accomplished by using the enzyme invertase. This is the way in which sucrose is metabolised in the body. Acidity has the most pronounced effect and can invert sugar solutions at room temperature. For example, a 65% sucrose syrup held at 20°C for 3 months produces 10% inversion at pH 3.2 and only 0.1% at pH 5.5.

The reaction is greatly speeded up by heat. However, at pH 5–5.5 and above very little inversion should take place, unless the temperature is high (say over 270°F). Even then, it should be limited to a few per cent unless the boiling time is greatly extended. However, if the pH is below 4 during boiling, and in particular below 3.5, it is possible to invert 50% of the sugar.

Mineral matter can also induce inversion. For example, salt should not be added at the beginning of boiling when making butterscotch on a gas stove.

1.7.2 *Boiling point*

The boiling point of a sugar solution is a fixed figure for a particular concentration and advantage is taken of this in making confectionery. There are several points which should be borne in mind:

(1) There is some lack of agreement between various workers, particularly at high concentration. Table 1.5 shows approximate figures.

(2) Glucose boils at a lower temperature than sucrose, whereas invert boils at a higher temperature.

(3) Temperature rises slowly at lower concentrations and therefore temperature is not a very accurate guide to concentration at lower boiling points.

(4) The boiling point can be reduced by boiling under vacuum, when

Table 1.5   Approximate boiling points of sugar solutions

°F	Sucrose (%)	Glucose (%)	Invert sugar (%)
214	40	42	
215	50	52	
217	60	62	
222	70	73	
227	75	81	
232	80	85	77
241	85	89	82
252	90	93	87
285	95	98	93

reductions of 25–40°F may be obtained. Vacuum boiling is normally used only for high boilings, to reduce colour and invert production.

(5) Boiling point is affected by altitude. For approximately every 500 feet rise in altitude the boiling point of water drops by 1°F.

(6) With some very viscous materials it is not easy to boil consistently to a given temperature. One alternative is to boil to a given consistency. The following examples show the approximate temperatures reached:

Feather	230°F
Soft (or small) ball	240°F
Hard (or large) ball	250°F
Light crack	265°F
Hard crack	290°F

1.7.3   Densimetry

Specific gravity (SG) is a ratio or relative density and is the ratio of the weight of a given volume of liquid divided by the weight of the same volume of water, whereas density is weight per unit volume (i.e. g/ml or lb/cubic foot).

Degrees Brix (or Balling) is the percentage of sucrose by weight, not volume. It is important not to confuse weight/weight (w/w) with weight/volume (w/v). For example, 50 g of sugar dissolved in 50 g water is 50% w/w, whereas 50 g sugar dissolved in water and *made up* to 100 ml is 50% w/v; 50% w/v is about 42% w/w. Fifty grams of sugar dissolved in 100 ml is 33.3% w/w.

The Baume (or Beaume) scale is widely used in the industry and the relationship with specific gravity is

$$\text{Baumé} = M - \frac{M}{S}$$

where M is a modulus (a conventional number) and S is specific gravity.

$$M = 144.3 \text{ in the UK}$$
$$M = 145 \text{ in the USA and in parts of Europe.}$$

Tables are available showing the relationship between Baumé (°Be), Brix (°Bx) and specific gravity (SG) Readings are greatly influenced by temperature (there is the possibility of a 10% error between 20 and 80°C), and it is therefore important to know the temperature or, preferably, to cool the syrup to 20°C before measurement. Tables exist showing the change of SG etc. with temperature. As a rough guide, there is about 4°Be difference between readings taken hot and cold, and care is necessary when interpreting a recipe which states, for example, 'boil to 30°Be'.

The SG of glucose and of invert syrups is slightly different from sucrose, and appropriate tables are available when accuracy is required.

1.7.4   Refractive index

The refractive index (RI) of a substance is the ratio of the velocity of light in a vacuum to its velocity in the substance. Light is 'bent' when passing from one substance to another, and advantage is taken of this to construct an instrument to determine sugar concentration. RI varies with temperature and a hot syrup on a cold refractometer will give a hazy line. RI also varies with the type of sugar and accurate tables are available for each sugar. Refractometers are calibrated in refractive index and in per cent sucrose by weight, and so would read low for invert and high for glucose. Empirical corrections can be devised, but for control purposes it is convenient to boil to 'X' reading. Refractometers are much more accurate than thermometers and should be used whenever possible.

1.7.5   Solubility

Sugar is readily soluble in water, and at room temperature one part of water will dissolve two parts of sugar (67%). The solubility rises to 83% at 100°C. However, as sugar is dissolved in water, the *rate of dissolution* decreases as the sugar concentration increases and if, for example, an attempt is made to prepare a saturated solution by stirring at room temperature the last few per cent of sugar will dissolve very slowly. The remedy, of course, is to use heat.

Sugar solutions can exhibit the phenomenon of supersaturation, that is a solution can be prepared which contains more sugar than the saturation level. For example, by heating and allowing to cool undisturbed to room temperature, a 74% solution may be prepared for wet crystallisation. Such solutions, not surprisingly, are unstable, and vibration and/or the ingress of solid particles (which act as nuclei) result in rapid crystallisation of the excess sugar.

When sugar is present in a solution, together with invert sugar and/or glucose syrup, a higher total concentration of the mixed sugars can be achieved than may be obtained with the individual sugars alone. In sugar/invert sugar mixtures, above the range 76–78% total sugars there is the likelihood of dextrose crystallising. However, stable solutions at much higher concentrations can be achieved when using regular glucose.

1.8   Conclusion

It has been possible, in one chapter, to present only a short introduction to the industry's basic ingredient, since sugar is a very widely studied material. Several societies and journals are devoted exclusively to its study and countless books written about it. An attempt has been made to highlight those aspects of most use to the confectioner but, for more extensive coverage, the reader is referred to the bibliography.

2   Alternative bulk sweeteners

T. PEPPER

A variety of alternatives to sugar is available to the confectioner, and these sugar substitutes can be used to replace sugar for either technological or health reasons. Until recently they have found few applications in the confectionery industry, principally because early attempts to utilise them were unsuccessful and the resultant products were considered inferior to sucrose-based standards. Applications know-how has now been improved and the range of commercially available sugar substitutes has been expanded. Consequently it is now possible to produce much higher quality products, since the limitations of individual sweeteners can be overcome by the use of blends. This approach parallels conventional procedures, which rarely utilise sucrose as the sole sweetener.

This chapter discusses selected sugar substitutes with particular reference to confectionery technology. It also reviews the major applications of sugar substitutes and gives consideration to any modifications to standard procedures that may be required with their use.

Alternative bulk sweeteners can broadly be divided into two categories:

(1) Sugars.
(2) Sugar alcohols.

Alternative sugars are generally used to replace a proportion of the sucrose in confectionery products in order to modify the sweetness and/or textural properties. Sugar alcohols (also known as polyols) are generally used to replace all of the conventional carbohydrates in the manufacture of non-cariogenic, diabetic or dietetic confections. There are, however, exceptions in each case.

A related product is polydextrose. This is a reduced-calorie bulking agent which has no intrinsic sweetness but which is used together with bulk or intense sweeteners to replace sugar in confectionery products. Various alternative bulk sweeteners are discussed below and their physical properties are compared in Table 2.1.

Table 2.1 Physical properties of bulk sweeteners

	Relative sweetness	Solubility at 20°C (% w/w)	Viscosity at 25°C (60% DS) (mPas)	Water activity at 25°C (60% DS)	Boiling point at 90% DS (°C)	Heat of solution (cal/g)	Molecular weight	Melting point (°C)	Specific rotation at 20°C (°)
Sucrose	1.0	66.7	50	0.88	120	−4.3	342	160–186	+66.5
42 DE glucose syrup	0.3	Non-crystal	116	0.90	119	NA	460	NA	+140
Glucose	0.7	47.2	23	0.83	127	−25.2*	180	83*	+52.7
Fructose	1.8	78.9	25	0.83	130	−12.0	180	102–105	−91.0
Lactose	0.25	16.0	Crystallises	Crystallises	‡	−10.3*	342	202*	+52.5
Sorbitol	0.6	68.7	25	0.83	130	−28.0†	182	99–102†	−1.7
Xylitol	1.0	62.8	19	0.82	132	−36.6	152	92–96	0
Maltitol crystalline	0.8	62.3	50	0.88	124	−18.9	344	147	+106.5
Maltitol syrup	0.6	Non-crystal	58	0.90	122	NA	416	NA	+115–120
Isomalt	0.45	24.5	Crystallises	Crystallises	124	−9.4	344	145–150	+91.5
Lactitol	0.35	56.5*	63	0.88	125	−12.5*	344	94–98*	+13.5–15.0
Mannitol	0.6	14.5	Crystallises	Crystallises	‡	−28.9	182	165–168	0
Polydextrose	0	80.0	160	0.91	118	‡	162–5000	130	0

*Data for monohydrate.
†Data for γ-form.
‡Data not available.

2.1 Alternative sugars

2.1.1 *Glucose*

The monosaccharide glucose occurs widely in nature where it is found, together with fructose, in most fruits and in honey. It is also commonly known as dextrose, particularly in the confectionery industry where the word glucose is often an abbreviation for glucose syrup. Another synonym is grape sugar.

Industrially, glucose is usually manufactured from starch by enzymatic hydrolysis. Alternatively, it may be produced from sucrose by hydrolysis (inversion) to its constituents glucose plus fructose, followed by separation. Glucose is commercially available in either monohydrate or anhydrous form. The monohydrate form, containing about 9% water, is most commonly used in the confectionery industry, although anhydrous glucose is preferred for chocolate manufacture.

Glucose has a lower sweetness, lower solubility and lower viscosity than sucrose. It is however a better humectant and provides better preservative properties owing to its lower water activity. It also has a noticeable cooling effect arising from its negative heat of solution.

Since it is a reducing sugar, glucose is more reactive than sucrose. Glucose solutions have a greater tendency to browning on boiling (particularly between pH 5 and 6) and participate more readily in the Maillard reaction with proteins.

The principal confectionery applications of glucose are in compressed tablets (where it is used for its high-energy image) and in fondants and cream pastes, where its cooling effect is considered appealing.

Glucose fondant is slow to crystallise and does not grain using a conventional beating process. Instead, it is prepared by seeding the boiled syrup with 5–10% fondant or finely powdered glucose. Crystallisation takes up to 1 day. This unusual manufacturing procedure makes glucose fondant very convenient for shell work, since it is deposited in the fluid state. However, the fondant has a slightly waxy mouthfeel.

In other products glucose is used to modify the texture. Replacement of 5–15% of the sucrose with glucose will have the effect of lowering the overall crystal size and/or tenderising the confection. It will also increase the tendency to crystallisation during manufacture or storage.

2.1.2 *Fructose*

Fructose, also known as laevulose or fruit sugar, is another monosaccharide found in fruits and in honey. Fructose may be manufactured from sucrose by isolation from invert sugar, or from starch by isolation from high-fructose glucose syrup.

Fructose is the sweetest of all sugars, being nearly twice as sweet as sucrose in the crystalline form. Fructose solutions are typically 20–50% sweeter than sucrose solutions of the same concentration, the actual sweetness value depending on the anomeric state of the fructose at the time of tasting. Crystalline fructose exists as the β-D-pyranose anomer, which is the sweetest form. When it is dissolved in water, rapid mutarotation occurs, resulting in the formation of the less sweet furanose forms. The equilibrium between the pyranose and furanose forms is governed by temperature. At high temperatures mutarotation occurs to a greater extent and so the perceived sweetness is reduced. Other factors influencing sweetness are the concentration and pH of the solution.

Fructose is very soluble in water, having a solubility of 79% to 20°C. Fructose solutions are low in viscosity (comparable to glucose) and are very resistant to crystallisation. Fructose can therefore be used in liquid fillings to increase the dissolved solids and thereby minimise dissolution of the shell. Fructose is slightly soluble in alcohol and this enables the solids to be increased in liqueur fillings, once again helping to extend shelf life.

Fructose is considerably more hygroscopic and has better humectant properties than either sucrose or glucose. It is also more reactive, being a ketose rather than an aldose sugar. Hence fructose has an even greater tendency to browning than glucose.

Fructose is metabolised in the liver independently of insulin and may consequently be tolerated by non-insulin-dependent diabetics, provided its caloric content is taken into account. Recent studies have shown that fructose may also have a beneficial effect for diabetics, since it helps to improve glycaemic control [1]. Fructose is currently used in diabetic marzipan, jellies, cereal bars and chews as well as in diabetic chocolates and pralines. However, it is difficult to incorporate in high boilings due to its hygroscopicity and propensity for browning.

A relatively new application for fructose is in compressed tablets intended for sportsmen, where its ability to provide a sustained energy source is considered advantageous.

In conventional confectionery products, fructose may be used to increase the sweetness, inhibit crystallisation, improve moisture retention, promote caramelisation or to enhance fruit flavours. Low levels of fructose can usually be incorporated with little modification to the original recipe. Higher replacement levels (over 5%) may require an adjustment to the ratio of sucrose to glucose syrup solids if a crystal phase is required in the confection.

2.1.3   Lactose

Lactose, also known as milk sugar, is a disaccharide molecule comprising glucose and galactose. It occurs naturally in milk where it constitutes 40% of the dry substance. The main commercial source is whey, from which it is extracted by either crystallisation or precipitation. Lactose is usually crystallised as the α-monohydrate, which melts at 202°C, although some β-

lactose anhydride (melting point 252°C) is also produced for special applications.

Lactose has a relatively poor solubility (16% at 20°C) and is considerably less sweet than sugar (relative sweetness 0.1–0.3). These properties restrict its suitability for confectionery manufacture.

The main application for lactose is as a binder/diluent in pharmaceutical tablets. In the confectionery industry, lactose may be used either to reduce sweetness or for reasons of economy, since it is cheaper than sugar. Lactose has been recommended for use in fondant where reduced sweetness is particularly advantageous. It is also said to improve whiteness [2]. In other applications the incorporation of lactose is limited by its low solubility.

Maximum sucrose replacement levels of 5–35% have been suggested for various confectionery applications [3]. In non-grained confections, the lactose content should not exceed 10%.

2.2   Sugar alcohols

2.2.1   *Sorbitol*

2.2.1.1   *Occurrence and manufacture.* Sorbitol is a monosaccharide sugar alcohol which occurs in a variety of fruits, berries and seaweeds. Industrially it is manufactured by catalytic hydrogenation of glucose derived from either starch or sucrose by hydrolysis.

Sorbitol is commercially available as either a crystalline powder or a syrup. Crystalline sorbitol is a polymorphic substance which can exist in a number of different forms. Four different crystalline structures and one amorphous form have been identified and characterised, the γ-form (melting point 99°C) being the most stable [4]. Liquid sorbitol is produced in two forms:

(1) Pure sorbitol syrup (70% w/w).
(2) Non-crystallising sorbitol syrup (70% w/w) containing about 50% sorbitol and 20% other polyols.

The non-crystallising solution is more commonly used.

2.2.1.2   *Physicochemical properties.* Sorbitol is a fairly hygroscopic product. It is less sweet than sucrose, having a relative sweetness of 0.6, and (like glucose) produces a distinct cooling effect when consumed in the crystalline form, due to its negative heat of solution.

Sorbitol is very soluble (69% at 20°C) and supersaturated solutions may easily be prepared. However, in comparison with sucrose, higher boiling temperatures are required to achieve any given level of solids. Sorbitol solutions are lower in viscosity than sucrose solutions of the same concentration. Water activity is also lower; thus sorbitol solutions have a greater preservative effect.

Sorbitol has a good humectant capacity and may be used to retard moisture loss in soft confections. Chemically it is very stable, having no free carbonyl group. It is resistant to browning, does not participate in the Maillard reaction and does not decompose in either acid or alkaline environments. However, sorbitol does have the ability to form complexes with metal ions [5] and this can help retard the development of rancidity in fats, especially where nuts are used.

2.2.1.3 *Metabolic properties.* Sorbitol is absorbed slowly from the gastro-intestinal tract, and is metabolised independently of insulin. Accordingly, sorbitol is a useful sweetener in the diabetic diet. However, due to its slow absorption rate, sorbitol can induce osmotic diarrhoea if consumed in large amounts [6].

2.2.1.4 *Dental properties.* The sugar alcohols are characterised by their resistance to fermentation by the oral bacteria. *In-vitro* experiments have shown that acid production from sorbitol is significantly less than from sucrose [7]. Consequently the decrease in oral pH is minimal and demineralisation of the dental enamel does not occur. Clinical studies have confirmed that sorbitol is virtually non-cariogenic [8, 9]. Frequent consumption may result in adaptation, leading to an increased number of sorbitol-fermenting micro-organisms, although this is considered to be of minor importance in persons having a normal salivary function [10].

2.2.1.5 *Confectionery applications.* Sorbitol is primarily used in the manufacture of diabetic and sugar-free (i.e. non-cariogenic) confections. The most important applications include chewing gum, compressed mints, high boilings, gums, pastilles and chocolate. Sorbitol performs well in compressed mints owing both to its refreshing cooling effect and to its inherent compressibility which enables the production of dense, hard tablets having a smooth texture and mouthfeel. Sorbitol tablets may be formed by direct compression with no need for prior wet granulation.

In chewing gum, sorbitol is typically used together with maltitol syrup, which provides the liquid phase, and saccharin or aspartame which are needed to boost the sweetness. A proportion of mannitol may also be included in order to inhibit crystallisation. If desired, chewing gum dragées may be hard-coated with sorbitol. Suitable procedures have been described in the literature [11].

Sorbitol cannot be used to manufacture high boilings by conventional means, due to its low viscosity. It is, however, possible to prepare deposited high boilings. In this process the boiled mass is seeded with 1–3% powdered sorbitol which promotes crystallisation and hence brings about a setting effect. The crystallinity is rather difficult to stabilise, and if it is not well controlled a cloudy surface appearance can develop on storage. The incorporation of up to

10% mannitol will help in this respect, however it will also increase the setting time.

Gum arabic-based pastilles can be made with sorbitol by conventional procedures. Softer textured gelatin jellies may require the inclusion of other polyols (e.g. xylitol or maltitol syrup) in order to prevent crystallisation on storage.

In addition to its applications in dietetic confections, sorbitol is used in conventional confectionery products as a humectant or a plasticising agent. The addition of 5–10% sorbitol to grained products such as fondant or fudge helps control sucrose crystal size and reduces the tendency for tailing during depositing. It also increases the solids content in the syrup phase, thus lowering its equilibrium relative humidity (ERH). This in turn improves microbiological stability and retards drying out.

In filled high boilings 1–2% sorbitol can be added to plasticise the candy shell for improved machinability. In the liquid filling sorbitol can be used to increase the solids, retard crystallisation and lower the viscosity.

2.2.2 Xylitol

2.2.2.1 *Occurrence and manufacture.* Xylitol is a five-carbon sugar alcohol which occurs in a variety of fruits and vegetables. Commercially it is manufactured from the hemicellulose xylan, which is found in all woody plants. The traditional raw material is birch wood. Other possibilities include corn cobs, almond shells and sugar cane bagasse. The manufacturing procedure involves hydrolysis of the xylan to xylose, followed by catalytic hydrogenation to yield xylitol.

2.2.2.2 *Physicochemical properties.* Xylitol is the sweetest of the sugar alcohols, having exactly the same sweetness as sucrose in most applications. It has good solubility in water (63% at 20°C) and in closed containers any degree of supersaturation is possible. The energy required to dissolve 1 g of xylitol is 36.6 cal, the highest value known for either sugars or sugar alcohols. Thus xylitol produces the greatest cooling effect.

Xylitol solutions are lower in both viscosity and water activity than equivalent concentrations of other polyols, but do not have particularly good humectant properties. Owing to the low molecular weight of xylitol, higher boiling temperatures are required in order to attain any given dry substance value.

One of the unusual properties of xylitol is its ability to form metastable melts. Molten xylitol is a clear, colourless liquid with a honey-like viscosity at room temperature. In sealed containers xylitol will remain in the molten state indefinitely. However, crystallisation occurs immediately if triggered by seeding or agitation [12]. These unique crystallisation properties may be exploited to develop novel methods of confectionery manufacture [13].

Another feature of xylitol is its excellent stability.

It is thermally stable and can be heated to over 200°C without browning or decomposition.

It is chemically stable reacting neither with proteins via the Maillard reaction nor with any other food components during normal food processing operations.

It is microbiologically stable, resisting fermentation by many food spoilage organisms [14].

2.2.2.3 *Metabolic properties.* Like sorbitol, xylitol is absorbed slowly from the digestive tract by a passive diffusion process. Therefore if large amounts are consumed, a considerable portion may reach the lower gut causing laxation. Two metabolic pathways are available for the utilisation of xylitol.

(1) Direct metabolism of absorbed xylitol (mainly in the liver).

(2) Indirect metabolism of unabsorbed xylitol via fermentation by the intestinal flora.

Neither process is mediated by insulin, enabling xylitol to be tolerated by non-insulin-dependent diabetics [15].

2.2.2.4 *Dental properties.* The most notable property of xylitol is its proven contribution to the prevention of tooth decay. The dental profession has concluded that xylitol is a completely non-cariogenic substance [16]. In addition, numerous clinical studies (reviewed by Bär [17]) have shown that xylitol also has a beneficial effect, since it inhibits the development of new cavities. Reductions of up to 80% have been reported. This cariostatic property is unique to xylitol and has not been demonstrated for any other sugar alcohol.

The mechanism by which xylitol exerts its observed effects is not yet fully understood. A number of factors are thought to contribute including:

(1) Xylitol is not fermented at all by the oral bacteria [7].

(2) Xylitol reduces the quantity and adhesivity of plaque [18].

(3) Xylitol encourages the development of a less cariogenic flora by selecting specifically against *Streptococcus mutans* [19,20].

(4) Xylitol inhibits demineralisation and encourages remineralisation [21].

2.2.2.5 *Applications in confectionery.* Xylitol is currently used in a variety of sugar-free and diabetic confectionery products. By far the leading application is chewing gum, where xylitol performs particularly well due to its high sweetness and refreshing cooling effect. It is generally necessary to modify standard formulations in order to increase cohesiveness and plasticity.

Additionally, care must be taken to maintain the kneading temperature below 55°C, in order to prevent local overheating, which could melt the xylitol.

Xylitol can be used in the hard panning of chewing dragées or of other confectionery centres. Conventional equipment is employed, however the temperatures of the engrossing syrup and drying air are both lower than with sugar-panned goods. Xylitol can also be used for soft panning, in combination with maltitol syrup, which provides the liquid phase.

Xylitol can act as the sole sweetener in recrystallised hard candies; alternatively it can be combined with other polyols in the manufacture of clear high boilings by conventional processes. Owing to its low viscosity the proportion of xylitol should not exceed 15–20%. Higher quantities will result in a tendency to stickiness and cold flow in the final product.

Xylitol has successfully been incorporated in jellies and pastilles based on gum arabic, gelatin or pectin. Crystallisation of xylitol is prevented by means of sorbitol or maltitol syrup, therefore the cooling effect is not experienced. No manufacturing difficulties are encountered. However it may be necessary to increase the dry substance and/or level of gelling agent in order to compensate for xylitol's lower bodying effect.

Fondant is another application for which xylitol is well suited. Here it is used together with sorbitol or maltitol syrup, which form the syrup phase. Xylitol fondant has a good texture, a very white appearance and a pronounced cooling effect that combines well with both mint and fruit flavours.

The cooling effect of xylitol is also experienced in compressed tablets. The compressibility of xylitol is poorer than that of sorbitol, but can be significantly improved by granulation. Tablet hardness is also lower, but can be increased by mixing with sorbitol [22].

Toffees and fudge can be manufactured with xylitol in combination with maltitol syrup, isomalt or polydextrose, which are needed to provide body and texture. The typical caramel colour and flavour will not develop due to the absence of a reducing carbonyl group. However, the addition of natural or artificial colours at the end of the boil is a satisfactory alternative.

Xylitol can also be incorporated in many other types of confection, including marzipan, chocolate and pralines.

2.2.3 Maltitol and maltitol syrup

2.2.3.1 *Occurrence and manufacture.* Maltitol is a disaccharide sugar alcohol comprising glucose and sorbitol. It is found naturally in chicory, roasted malt and the bark of certain trees. Industrially it can be manufactured by hydrogenation of maltose derived from starch by enzymatic hydrolysis, however pure crystalline maltitol is not yet widely available.

Maltitol syrups containing 50–90% maltitol are manufactured by hydrogenation of the corresponding high-maltose glucose syrups. The carbohydrate spectrum within the syrup can be tailored to suit specific applications by selection of an appropriate enzyme system and control of the

Table 2.2   Composition of commercial maltitol syrups

Manufacturer	Trade name	Sorbitol (%)	Maltitol (%)	Higher polyols (%)
Lonza	Hystar® 4075	13	23	64
Lonza	Hystar® 3375	14	18	68
Lonza	Hystar® HM-75	13	50	37
Roquette	Lycasin®	Max 8	50–55	37–45
Cerestar	Maltidex™ 200	Max 8	Min 52	30–45
Lonza	Hystar® 5875	7	60	33
Xyrofin	Finmalt™ L	Max 8	62–70	22–37
Roquette	Maltisorb®	Max 8	72–78	20 (approx.)
Cerestar	Maltidex™ 100	Max 2.5	Min 72	20–30
Melida	Malbit® Liquid	2.5–3.5	73–77	16–25
Melida	Malbit® Crystalline	1–3	86–90	7–13

hydrolysis conditions. The carbohydrate compositions of several commercial syrups are shown in Table 2.2. Syrups containing 50–55% maltitol are currently the most widely used, however there is a tendency to move towards higher maltitol contents.

Maltitol syrup is normally supplied at 75% dry substance. A crystalline form is also available from one manufacturer.

2.2.3.2   *Physicochemical properties.* The technological properties of maltitol syrups are largely determined by their carbohydrate composition. In general, sweetness is determined by the maltitol content; hygroscopicity and humectancy are determined by the sorbitol content; and viscosity is determined by the proportion of higher polyols.

Crystalline maltitol has a relative sweetness of 0.8, a melting point of 147°C and a solubility of 63% at 20°C. The negative heat of solution is low, thus maltitol does not give rise to a cooling effect when dissolved in the mouth.

A typical maltitol syrup containing 50–55% maltitol has a relative sweetness of 0.6 on a dry substance basis. It is resistant to crystallisation, even at low temperatures or high concentrations, and inhibits crystallisation of other polyols.

Maltitol syrups are slightly higher in viscosity than sucrose solutions of the same concentration, and considerably more viscous than solutions of the monosaccharide sugar alcohols. They boil at slightly higher temperatures than equivalent solutions of sucrose and, in common with other sugar alcohols, they are resistant to both caramelisation and Maillard browning.

2.2.3.3   *Metabolic properties.* The main pathway for the utilisation of maltitol and maltitol syrups involves digestion by the intestinal enzymes and subsequent absorption of the liberated glucose and sorbitol. Unabsorbed sorbitol and undigested maltitol or higher polyols are subject to microbial fermentation in the lower gut. Due to its incomplete absorption from the intestine, the consumption of large quantities of maltitol can have a laxative effect. For the same reason, it is believed that maltitol has a reduced caloric value.

The suitability of maltitol for the diabetic diet is still the subject of controversy, since almost half of the ingested dose appears as glucose in the blood, and consequently has an insulin demand. However, owing to the relatively slow liberation of glucose, the glycaemic response to maltitol consumption is modest, and the insulin response is significantly lower than would be obtained with glucose [23]. Thus maltitol appears to occupy an intermediate position being tolerated better than sucrose or glucose, but worse than fructose or sorbitol.

2.2.3.4 *Dental properties.* Maltitol is resistant to fermentation by most of the oral bacteria [24] and is considered to be virtually non-cariogenic. The higher molecular weight components of maltitol syrup can be slowly hydrolysed liberating reducing groups, which are then available for fermentation. Additionally, some fermentation of the free sorbitol is possible (see 2.2.1.4). Acid production is however significantly lower than from sucrose.

Unlike xylitol and (to a lesser extent) sorbitol, maltitol syrup has not yet been the subject of many clinical studies. Nevertheless, the available data lead to the conclusion that maltitol syrup is a low-cariogenic sugar substitute [25, 26], although the cariogenic potential may be increased in syrups containing a large proportion of high molecular weight components.

2.2.3.5 *Applications in confectionery.* Maltitol syrups have been used in a wide variety of applications either alone or in combination with other polyols. Their function in sugarless chewing gum has already been discussed (2.2.1.5). Another important application is in high boilings, which can be manufactured simply by adding acid, colour and flavour to a boiled maltitol syrup. Here it is necessary to reduce the moisture content below 1% (preferably below 0.5%) in order to minimize stickiness and cold flow. This entails boiling under vacuum to at least 160°C. Maltitol high boilings are very hygroscopic and must be wrapped immediately in moisture-proof packaging. Shelf life can be significantly improved by incorporating 4–7% mannitol [27]. Gum arabic may also be included in order to reduce cold flow; alternatively, the incorporation of polydextrose achieves the same effect [28].

Caramels and chews can be prepared from maltitol syrup. However, it may be necessary to boil to a lower residual moisture content and subsequently cool to a lower temperature, in order to compensate for the lower viscosity of the mass. Additionally, it is necessary to increase the quantity of fat compared with standard products in order to overcome the greater degree of stickness.

Gums, jellies and pastilles based on gum arabic and/or gelatin may be successfully made with maltitol syrup. Maltitol syrup is also used to prevent the crystallisation of other polyols in hard and soft confections.

In addition to its applications in sugar-free confections, maltitol syrup has been recommended as a humectant in conventional confectionery products. Total or partial replacement of conventional glucose syrup by maltitol syrup has been shown to reduce the rate of moisture loss from soft confections [29].

2.2.4   Isomalt

2.2.4.1   *Occurrence and manufacture.* Isomalt is an equimolar mixture of two disaccharide alcohols: L-D-glucopyranosyl-1,6-D-sorbitol (GPS) and L-D-glucopyranosyl-1,1-D-mannitol (GPM). It is not a naturally occurring product but is manufactured from sugar in a two-stage procedure:
  (1) Enzymatic conversion of sucrose to isomaltulose.
  (2) Catalytic hydrogenation of isomaltulose.
In aqueous systems GPS forms anhydrous crystals and GPM crystallises with two molecules of water. Consequently isomalt contains about 5% bound water.

2.2.4.2   *Physicochemical properties.* Isomalt is a non-hygroscopic product which melts at 145–150°C. It has a fairly low relative sweetness (0.45–0.6) and must usually be blended with other (sweeter) polyols or with intense sweeteners. It also has a low negative heat of solution and therefore does not impart a cooling effect when consumed in the crystalline form.

Isomalt has a very low solubility (24.5% at 20°C) which limits its use in confectionery applications. Solutions of isomalt have slightly higher viscosities than equivalent sugar syrups, and boil at slightly higher temperatures.

Isomalt is extremely stable chemically due to the absence of a reducing function. It is, nevertheless, possible to hydrolyse the disaccharide bonds in extreme conditions. For example, boiling for more than 1 h at pH 2 results in about 10% hydrolysis [30]. This is likely to represent the most severe conditions encountered during food processing operations.

2.2.4.3   *Metabolic properties.* Hydrolysis of isomalt by intestinal disaccharidase enzymes results in the liberation of glucose, sorbitol and mannitol. Owing to the very low rate of hydrolysis, only about one-third of the ingested dose is absorbed from the intestine. The remainder (in the form of intact isomalt and its hydrolysis products) is transported to the lower gut, where it is fermented by the bacterial flora.

Due to the slow and incomplete absorption of isomalt, large doses may have a laxative effect. Incomplete absorption is also thought to contribute to a reduced caloric value. Isomalt is considered to be suitable for diabetics since blood glucose and insulin response is significantly lower than that experienced with sucrose or glucose.

2.2.4.4 *Dental properties.* Isomalt can be fermented by oral bacteria, although acid production is considerably lower than from sucrose [31]. Animal studies have indicated that isomalt is significantly less cariogenic than sucrose but significantly more cariogenic than xylitol [32]. Clinical studies in humans have not yet been reported.

2.2.4.5 *Applications.* Isomalt can be used in a variety of sugar-free confectionery products including high boilings, compressed tablets, marzipan, chews, liquorice and chocolate.

Stable high boilings can be prepared from isomalt alone despite its low solubility. This could be due to the fact that isomalt is itself a mixture of two different polyols, each of which may inhibit crystallisation of the other. The resultant product is much less hygroscopic than conventional sucrose/glucose syrup standards, however the sweetness is insufficient. Intense sweeteners can be added, if desired, at the end of the boil. Alternatively the inclusion of about 15% xylitol will improve sweetness.

Compressed tablets also benefit from the low hygroscopicity of isomalt. A wet granulation stage is required in order to improve the compressibility.

In other applications isomalt is best used in combination with other polyols, which are needed to inhibit crystallisation as well as to increase the sweetness.

2.2.5 *Lactitol*

2.2.5.1 *Occurrence and manufacture.* Lactitol is a disaccharide sugar alcohol comprising galactose and sorbitol. It does not occur naturally, but is manufactured by catalytic hydrogenation of lactose. Lactitol can be crystallised in either the monohydrate (melting point 120°C) or dihydrate (melting point 75°C) form. Both forms are commercially available.

2.2.5.2 *Physicochemical properties.* Lactitol is a non-hygroscopic product with a moderately sweet taste (relative sweetness 0.3–0.4). It has a low negative heat of solution and thus does not impart a cooling effect when dissolved.

Lactitol has reasonably good solubility in water (54.5% at 20°C) and solutions are similar in terms of viscosity and water activity to equivalent sucrose solutions, however boiling point elevation is slightly higher.

Lactitol has greater chemical stability than lactose due to the absence of a reducing carbonyl group. Thus, like the other polyols, it does not react with proteins in the Maillard reaction. However, hydrolytic decomposition to its constituents galactose and sorbitol occurs during storage at low pH and high temperature. For example, 15% decomposition was detected in lactitol solutions stored for 2 months at pH 3.0 and 60°C [33]. At higher temperatures (180–240°C) lactitol is partly converted into anhydro derivatives (lactitan), sorbitol and lower polyols.

2.2.5.3 *Metabolic properties.* Neither intestinal hydrolysis of lactitol nor absorption of intact lactitol occurs to any significant extent [34, 35]. Therefore, virtually the entire ingested dose passes to the large intestine where microbial fermentation takes place. The major end products of the fermentation are volatile fatty acids, which are subsequently absorbed and further metabolised via established metabolic pathways.

Owing to its extremely poor digestibility and negligible absorption from the intestine, lactitol is believed to have a reduced caloric value. It also has a certain laxative effect.

Lactitol does not provoke significant rises in blood glucose or insulin levels and is therefore a suitable sweetener for diabetic products [33].

2.2.5.4 *Dental properties.* Lactitol may be fermented slowly by oral bacteria. However, acid production and subsequent demineralisation of dental enamel are considerably less than from sucrose or sorbitol [36]. Animal experiments have demonstrated that lactitol is virtually non-cariogenic [37]. Equivalent data in humans have not yet been reported.

2.2.5.5 *Applications in confectionery.* Lactitol can be used in a variety of applications including chocolate, chewing gum, high boilings, jellies and pastilles.

High boilings can be prepared from lactitol alone, which forms a fairly stable glassy structure. The viscosity of the boiled mass is high enough to enable traditional kneading and forming procedures to be used. Furthermore, the very low hygroscopicity of lactitol ensures that stickiness is not a problem during either manufacture or storage.

Surface crystallisation can develop on storage, although this will be prevented by incorporating other polyols, e.g. maltitol syrup. Additionally, intense sweeteners are usually needed to boost the sweetness.

Other confectionery products rely on the use of lactitol/polyol combinations. The ratio depends on the nature of the polyol used and whether or not the confection is intended to have a grained texture.

2.2.6 *Mannitol*

2.2.6.1 *Occurrence and manufacture.* Mannitol is a monosaccharide sugar alcohol found widely in nature. It is the only sugar alcohol occurring in high enough concentrations to permit extraction from natural sources on a commercial scale. Originally mannitol was extracted from manna, a sweet exudate of the flowering ash; it is also possible to obtain mannitol from seaweeds as a by-product of alginate production [38]. However, mannitol is most commonly manufactured by hydrogenation of fructose using either invert sugar or high-fructose glucose syrup as the raw material. Mannitol is then isolated from the resultant mixture of sorbitol and mannitol by fractional crystallisation.

2.2.6.2 *Physicochemical properties.* Mannitol is a non-hygroscopic crystalline product with a melting point of 165–168°C. It has a comparable relative sweetness to sorbitol (0.55–0.65), but a much lower solubility (14.5% at 20°C), which restricts its use in confectionery products. Despite its negative heat of solution, mannitol does not impart a particularly noticeable cooling effect when consumed in the crystalline form. This is due to its low rate of dissolution.

Since it has the same molecular weight as sorbitol, mannitol has a very similar effect on viscosity, water activity and boiling point elevation. Resistance to browning is another characteristic property which mannitol shares with the other polyols.

2.2.6.3 *Metabolic properties.* Mannitol is absorbed slowly and incompletely from the small intestine. Part of the absorbed portion is metabolised via the glycolytic pathway; the remainder is excreted unchanged in the urine [39]. The unabsorbed portion passes to the large intestine where it is subject to bacterial fermentation.

Mannitol is considered acceptable for use in the diabetic diet. However, owing to both its low laxative threshold and its technological limitations, it is less frequently used than sorbitol or fructose.

2.2.6.4 *Dental properties.* Like sorbitol, mannitol is fermented much more slowly than sucrose, and has been shown to reduce the development of new caries when used as a partial replacement for sucrose [40]. Mannitol is consequently considered to be essentially non-cariogenic, although it has been speculated that adaptation may eventually occur [41].

2.2.6.5 *Applications in confectionery.* Owing to its poor solubility, mannitol has found few applications in confectionery products. Furthermore, it rarely constitutes the sole sweetener. Instead, it generally forms a comparatively small proportion of the sweetener blend, being used to modify the textural properties or keeping qualities of the confection.

The most important applications for mannitol are chewing gum and compressed tablets. In chewing gum, mannitol functions as an anticrystalliser, inhibiting the crystallisation of sorbitol. It is also used as a dusting agent to prevent sticking of the sheets during lamination.

Mannitol is often employed as an excipient in compressed pharmaceutical tablets. In confectionery tablets it is sometimes used to improve the mouthfeel of sorbitol.

Mannitol may be incorporated in sugar-free high boilings, chews or toffees in order to reduce stickiness and hygroscopicity. Diabetic chocolate has also been prepared from mannitol.

2.2.7 *Comparison of sugar alcohols*

To a greater or lesser extent, the sugar alcohols all possess the following characteristics which differentiate them from conventional sugars:

Lower cariogenicity.
Lower insulin demand.
Lower caloric value.
Higher chemical stability.
Higher thermal stability.
Higher microbiological stability.
Laxative effects at high doses.

The polyols differ from one another in terms of sweetness intensity, sweetness profile, cooling effect, hygroscopicity, solubility, humectancy, viscosity and water activity. These and other properties are compared in Table 2.1.

In general, the monosaccharide alcohols (except mannitol) tend to be fairly hygroscopic products. They have a significant negative heat of solution that provides a noticeable cooling effect in grained confections. (NB: no cooling effect is experienced in ungrained confections.) In some circumstances they may also generate a characteristic burning aftertaste which arises from their high osmotic pressure, although this effect is masked by higher molecular weight components or in acidic environments.

Due to their low molecular weight, the monosaccharide alcohols have rather low viscosities. Consequently they are easy to handle and pump and have good flavour-release properties. However, they provide less body than sucrose. The lower viscosity does not usually present a practical problem, since structure is provided by the crystal phase in grained confections and by the gelling agent in gums and jellies. In a few applications (notably high boilings, chews, caramels) the lower viscosity increases the tendency for cold flow and it is therefore necessary to restrict the proportion of monosaccharide polyols or to incorporate hydrocolloid thickening agents. In most applications it is necessary to reduce the moisture content compared with standard formulations.

The disaccharide alcohols tend to be non-hygroscopic products which do not provide a cooling effect. They have higher viscosities and water activities, and lower boiling point elevations than the monosaccharide alcohols. In these respects, they bear a greater resemblance to sucrose.

Maltitol syrup does not appear to fall in to either category since it exhibits characteristics of all its constituent molecules. In particular it is noted for its hygroscopicity.

With the exception of xylitol, all of the polyols are less sweet than sugar, and it is necessary to incorporate intense sweeteners in order to match standard confectionery products. If intense sweeteners cannot be used (either for legislative or for marketing reasons) the incorporation of xylitol helps to boost the sweetness to an acceptable level.

With the exception of maltitol syrup, none of the polyols is sufficiently soluble to resist crystallisation at the high concentrations typical of confectionery products. Mannitol is particularly prone to graining. On the other hand, isomalt does not crystallise as readily as might be expected on the basis of its solubility. For example, in high boilings, crystallisation appears to be totally inhibited providing the moisture content is very low. This property is a function of the high viscosity in the boiling, which reduces the mobility of the molecules. In systems having a lower viscosity (e.g. gelatine jellies) graining soon occurs if the proportion of isomalt is too high.

The tendency to crystallisation is a property shared with sugar, and is easily resolved by using the polyols in combination. The use of combinations also enables the confectioner to overcome the limitations of individual sweeteners by optimising the physical properties according to the requirements of the end product. This may entail either trying to match standard confections as closely as possible or capitalising on the properties that differentiate polyols from sugars in order to develop entirely new tastes or textures.

2.3 Polydextrose

2.3.1 Occurrence and manufacture

Polydextrose is a randomly bonded condensation polymer of glucose, containing minor amounts of bound sorbitol and citric acid. Residues of unpolymerised glucose and sorbitol are also present as impurities. It does not occur in nature, but is synthesised from a mixture of glucose and sorbitol together with a small amount of citric acid which acts as a catalyst.

Polydextrose is commercially available in three forms:

(1) Type A, an acidic powder (pH 2.5–3.5).
(2) Type K, a partially neutralised powder (pH 5–6).
(3) Type N, a partially neutralised aqueous solution at 70% dry substance (pH 5–6).

2.3.2 Physicochemical properties

Polydextrose is a fairly hygroscopic, amorphous powder that forms a clear melt above 130°C. It can be somewhat difficult to dissolve, necessitating high-speed, high-shear mixing equipment if concentrated solutions are required. Dispersion properties are improved if polydextrose is dry-blended with other soluble components of the mix (e.g. sugars or polyols) prior to dissolution.

Polydextrose forms highly concentrated solutions (80%) which are resistant to crystallisation. Polydextrose solutions are clear to yellow in colour, with a non-sweet, slightly acidic taste. They are higher in viscosity than equivalent sucrose solutions and also have higher water activities.

Polydextrose solutions are prone to browning when heated above 130°C, due to the formation of hydroxymethylfurfural and laevoglucosan. The browned solutions are obviously unsuitable for the manufacture of light-coloured confections. They also have a distinct burnt flavour. The partially neutralised forms of polydextrose (types K and N) may be used in low-boiled confections, but are even more prone to browning than the acidic form (type A) when boiled to high temperatures.

2.3.3   Metabolic properties

Polydextrose is a very indigestible substance. Not more than 1% of the ingested dose is absorbed from the small intestine, and even this is not metabolised. Approximately half of the unabsorbed polydextrose is fermented in the lower gut by the colonic micro-organisms. The remaining 50% is eliminated in the faeces.

Due to its minimal absorption from the gastrointestinal tract and its high resistance to microbial degradation in the colon, polydextrose has a reduced caloric value [42]. In the United States, the FDA has formally endorsed a claim of 1 kcal/g. This value is also generally accepted in other countries.

Since polydextrose is not metabolised via the glycolytic pathway, it does not provoke significant rises in blood glucose or insulin levels. It is therefore considered an acceptable component of diabetic foods [43].

2.3.4   Dental properties

In common with polyols, polydextrose resists fermentation by the oral bacteria. Under *in-vivo* conditions, polydextrose is hypoacidogenic probably due to contamination by traces of residual glucose. Animal studies have confirmed that polydextrose is much less cariogenic than starch or sucrose [44].

2.3.5   Applications in confectionery

Polydextrose can be used in the manufacture of high boilings since it forms a stable glass structure. However, during boiling, the mass develops an orange colour and burnt flavour. Furthermore, it has an extremely high viscosity which makes incorporation of colours, flavours and intense sweeteners very difficult. The addition of maltitol syrup has the effect of diluting the polydextrose, making the undesired colour and flavour less noticeable. It also reduces the viscosity, thus improving handling properties. The incorporation of xylitol is even more efficient in this respect, enabling heat-sensitive flavours to be added to the boiled mass at a lower temperature.

Owing to its high viscosity and resistance to crystallisation, polydextrose may be used to inhibit the crystallisation of polyols or to provide body and resistance to cold flow. In this context it has been successfully combined with xylitol in reduced-calorie chews; with sorbitol or xylitol in gelatine jellies; and with isomalt in fondant. Colour development is less pronounced in these applications owing to the lower processing temperatures involved. Pectin jellies are more difficult to formulate, due to the acidity and buffering capacity of the polydextrose, which interferes with the setting of the pectin.

In addition to its application in sugar-free products, polydextrose is used in combination with fructose for diabetic lines, or with sucrose in standard reduced-calorie lines. In the latter case, polydextrose must be buffered in order to minimize sucrose inversion. Suitable applications include caramel, marshmallow, nougat, starch jellies and high boilings.

2.4 Legislation and labelling

In most countries the sugar alcohols and polydextrose are classified as food additives rather than food ingredients. This means that a petition for approval must be submitted in each case before application in food is permitted.

At the time of writing, approvals for sorbitol, xylitol, mannitol and maltitol syrup are fairly widespread. Approvals for lactitol, isomalt, polydextrose and pure maltitol are more limited. The sugar alcohols should be labelled by their chemical name on any product ingredient list. If a nutritional claim is made for the product, it is usually also compulsory to make a declaration of the nutritional composition. This must include the percentages of carbohydrate, protein and fat and the caloric value per 100 g.

Whilst polydextrose is generally acknowledged to provide 1 kcal/g, there is currently no consensus regarding the most appropriate caloric value for sugar alcohols. In a few countries, reduced-calorie claims (2 kcal/g) have been approved for lactitol, maltitol and isomalt. In other countries, these claims have been rejected. However, due to the growing body of evidence demonstrating that sugar alcohols are only partially metabolised, it is becoming increasingly accepted that they provide fewer calories than conventional carbohydrates. Due to the lack of comparative studies and the diversity of methods used for determination, it is difficult to assign relative caloric values for different polyols. The literature does, however, indicate a fairly narrow range between 2 and 3 kcal/g. Consequently, in a recent Proposal for a Council Directive [45], a caloric value of 2.4 kcal/g has been suggested for all polyols.

2.5 Concluding comments

Sugar can be relied upon to give a consistent performance at a relatively cheap price, and it is extremely unlikely that it will ever lose its position as the number one sweetener for confectionery products.

Sugar alcohols occasionally find applications in conventional confections, however they are more often used in the manufacture of dietetic lines for which health-related claims are often made. Typical label claims might include the phrases 'sugar-free', 'does not promote tooth decay', 'suitable for diabetics', 'reduced calorie' or 'lite'.

The market for foods which are perceived as being healthier is growing steadily. Consequently, speciality confections are likely to increase in importance provided they taste as good as, or better than sucrose standards. The use of sugar alcohols in appropriate combinations can assist in meeting this challenge.

References

1. E.J. McAteer, G. O'Reilly and D.R. Hadden, *Diabetic Medicine* **4** (1987) 62.
2. Anon, *Conf. Mf. Mktg* **21** (1984) 13.
3. Anon, in *The Alm Guide to Lactose Properties and Uses*, Association of Lactose Manufacturers, The Hague (1988).
4. J.W. Du Ross, *Pharmaceutical Technology* **9** (1984) 42.
5. H. Cross, T. Pepper, M.W. Kearsley and G.G. Birch, *Stärke* **37** (1985) S132.
6. H. Förster and H. Mehnert, *Akt. Ernährung* **5** (1979) 245.
7. W.M. Edgar and M.W.J. Dodds, *Int. Dent. J.* **35** (1985) 18.
8. I.J. Möller and S. Poulsen, *Community Dent. Oral Epidemiol.* **1** (1973) 58.
9. R.L. Glass. *Caries Res.* **17** (1983) 365.
10. D. Birkhed, S. Edwardsson, S. Kalfas and G. Svensäter, *Swed. Dent. J.* **8** (1984) 147.
11. D.A. Whitmore, *Food Chemistry* **16** (1985) 209.
12. F.A. Voirol, in *Carbohydrate Sweeteners in Foods and Nutrition*, eds. P. Koivistoinen and L. Hyvönen, Academic Press (1980).
13. Suomen Sokeri Oy, British Patent 158 35 73 (1981).
14. K.K. Mäkinen and E. Söderling, *J. Food Sci.* **46** (1981) 950.
15. W. Hassinger, G. Sauer, U. Cordes, J. Beyer and K.H. Baessler, *Diabetologia* **2** (1981) 37.
16. I. Mandel, in *Dental Dialogue*, Proceedings of a Symposium at the University of Michigan, January 28, 1988. Sponsored by Xyrofin.
17. A. Bär, *World Rev. Nutr. Diet.* **55** (1988) 1.
18. J. Verran and D.B. Drucker, *Arch. Oral Biol.* **27** (1982) 693.
19. J. Banoczy, M. Orsos, K. Pienihäkinen and A. Scheinin, *Acta Odont. Scand.* **43** (1985) 367.
20. S. Assev and G. Rölla, *Acta Pathol. Microbiol. Scand., B. Microbiol. Immunol.* **92** (1984) 89.
21. M.T. Smits and J. Arends, *Caries Res.* **19** (1985) 528.
22. Nabisco Lifesavers Inc., British Patent 1,526,020 (1978).
23. M.W. Kearsley, G.G. Birch and R.H.P. Lian-Loh, *Stärke* **34** (1982) 279.
24. S. Edwardsson, D. Birkhed and B. Mejare, *Acta Odont. Scand.* **35** (1977) 257.
25. G. Frostell, *Dtsch Zahnärztl. Z.* **32** Suppl. 1 (1977) 571.
26. K.K. Mäkinen and P. Isokangas, *Progress in Food and Nutrition Science* **12** (1988) 73.
27. A. Rapaille, *Stärke* **40** (1988) 356.
28. H. Kastin, U.S. Patent 4,528,206 (1985).
29. C. Kramer, Paper presented at the annual meeting of the AACT, Calloway Gardens, Georgia (1987).

30. P. Sträter, in *Alternative Sweeteners*, eds. L. O' Brien Nabors and R.C. Gelardi, Marcel Dekker Inc., New York (1986) Chapter 11.
31. E.J. Karle and F. Gehring, *Dtsch Zahnärztl. Z.* **33** (1978) 189.
32. J.S. Van der Hoeven, *Caries Res.* **14** (1980) 61.
33. C.H. Den Uyl, in *Developments in Sweeteners—3*, ed. T.H. Grenby, Elsevier Applied Science, Amsterdam (1987) Chapter 3.
34. U. Nilsson and M. Jaegerstad, *Br. J. Nutr.* (1987).
35. D.H. Patil, G.K. Grimble and D.B.A. Silk, *Gut* **26** (1985) A1114.
36. T.H. Grenby and A. Phillips, *Caries Res.* **21** (1987) 170.
37. J.S. Van der Hoeven, *Caries Res.* **20** (1986) 441.
38. P.J. Sicard, in *Nutritive Sweeteners*, eds. G.G. Birch and K.J. Parker, Applied Science Publishers (1982) Chapter 8.
39. F.L. Iber and S.M. Nasrallah, *Amer. J. Med. Sci.* **258** (1969) 80.
40. O. Larje and R.H. Larson, *Arch. Oral Biol.* **15** (1970) 805.
41. G. Frostell, *Acta. Odont. Scand.* **22** (1964) 457.
42. S.K. Figdor and J.R. Bianchine, *J. Agric. Food Chem.* **31** (1983) 389.
43. W. Bachmann, M. Haslbeck and H. Mehnert, *Akt. Endokr. Stoffw.* **3** (1982) 124.
44. H.R. Muhlemann, *Swiss Dent.* **2** (1980) 29.
45. *Official Journal on the European Communities* No. C282/8, Nov. 5 (1988).

3 Glucose syrups and starch hydrolysates

D. HOWLING and E.B. JACKSON

3.1 Introduction

Glucose syrups or corn syrups have long been used as key ingredients in the confectionery industry, and their properties have been presented many times (e.g. Ref.1). The objective of this current review is to bring that knowledge up to date, as many interesting developments in this area are being made for the food industry in general and the confectionery industry in particular.

Glucose syrups are defined by the EEC and *Codex Alimentarius* as follows:

EEC

Glucose syrup is a refined, concentrated aqueous solution of D (+)-glucose, maltose and other polymers of D-glucose obtained by the controlled partial hydrolysis of edible starch.

Codex

Glucose syrup is a purified concentrated aqueous solution of nutritive saccharides obtained from starch.

Thus the origin of glucose syrups is starch. In Europe maize starch is the most common source of starch though potato and wheat starch are also used.

Whatever the source of the starch it comprises two distinct fractions: amylose, in which the anhydroglucopyranose units are linked exclusively in the 1–4 positions, giving a linear molecule, and amylopectin, which is branched due to the presence of 1–6 links. The molecular weight and ratio of these two fractions determine the rheological properties of the starches but have only a limited effect on the hydrolysis of starch. High-amylopectin starches yield better clarity in very low-DE (dextrose equivalent) maltodextrins, but otherwise the glucose properties are similar.

Today major advances are being made by the use of enzymes and this is discussed in section 3.2, but first let us consider the technology available before the use of enzymes, which so far as glucose syrups are concerned, is 30 years ago. Then starch was hydrolysed by the use of mineral acids, usually in batch converters, though more recently by continuous processes. In either case

Table 3.1 Sugar composition of acid-converted glucose syrups

Glucose syrup	Dextrose equivalent			
	30	34–36	42–43	55
Dextrose	10	13.5	19	31
Maltose	9	11.5	14	18
Maltotriose	10	10	12	13
Maltotetraose	8	9	10	10
Maltopentaose	7	8	8	7
Maltohexaose	6	6	7	5
Maltoheptaose	5	5.5	5	4
Higher sugars	45	36.5	25	12

starch was mixed with mineral acid. Sulphuric acid was used for some time, but the problems with insoluble sulphates led to the use of hydrochloric acid. This placed constraints on the materials of construction, but the use of high grades of stainless steel led to commercial processes.

The use of mineral acid had major disadvantages in certain areas, and this really centred on the fact that the hydrolysis was random in its activity. This meant that intermediate DE products of high quality could be made and were reproducible in carbohydrate distribution provided constant conditions of temperature, acid dose, concentration and time were used. However, no control over the relative quantities of say glucose, maltose, etc. could be exerted.

However, for mild conditions, the chain length of the linear fractions of starch could not be guaranteed to be sufficiently reduced to give a clear non-retrograding solution. In this case the oligosaccharide fractions which have by chance not been sufficiently attacked reassociate, forming insoluble crystallites which cause haze. If higher doses of acid or more stringent conditions are used, actual ring fission of the glucopyranose residues takes place and colour precursors, e.g. hydroxymethyl furfural (HMF), and bitter compounds are formed.

To put this into quantitative figures, syrups below 30 DE and above 55 DE of the quality required by the food and confectionery industry could not be adequately produced. In between these limits glucose of good quality could be made and still is today (see Table 3.1).

3.2 Enzymes in glucose syrup production

How then have enzymes improved the range of glucose syrups available to the confectioner?

Table 3.2 Sugar composition of acid/enzyme syrups

Type	High maltose		High conversion (Amyloglucosidase)	
DE	42	48	63	70
Dextrose	6	9	37	43
Maltose	45	52	32	30
Maltotriose	12	15	11	7
Maltotetraose	3	2	4	5
Maltopentaose	2	2	4	3
Maltohexaose	2	2	3	2
Higher sugars	30	18	9	10

3.2.1 Specificity

First of all enzymes give specificity. Provided that the glucose manufacturer could produce a soluble non-retrograding starch substrate at 60°C, he could avail himself of amylolytic activity to produce starch hydrolysates of controlled/tailored sugar distribution. The need to use mineral acid was not avoided because this was used to provide the non-retrograding substrate and a series of acid/enzyme syrups was created (see Table 3.2).

This specificity gave the possibility of making sweeter, more highly converted, syrups of good colour and taste (63 DE) widely used in marshmallows, preserves and beer fermentation. High-maltose syrups in which the use of maltogenic enzyme of largely vegetable origin, e.g. wheat, barley and soya, could be used to enhance the content of maltose. The hydrolysates found applications in confectionery and brewing.

Finally the specific use of α-amylases allowed soluble, non-retrograding, low-DE glucose syrups or maltodextrins to be produced. These products found use in the production of vending powders, baby foods and coffee whiteners.

3.2.2 Total enzyme conversion

In the mid-1970s the ability to degrade starch itself wholly by enzyme action became possible. This came about with the advent of microbial α-amylases capable of amylolytic action above the gelatinisation temperature of starch, i.e. above 70°C. These calcium metalloproteins reinforced by the addition of calcium ions enabled starch slurries to be gelatinised directly and converted to low-DE intermediates which were non-retrograding at less than 10-DE, and as such enabled the initial progress of the use of enzymes to be extended further. Hence even lower DE maltodextrins could be made which did not retrograde. They provide a range of powdered products which are invaluable and widely used in food and confectionery (see Table 3.3).

Total enzyme conversion using thermostable α-amylases and maltogenic enzymes (fungal α-amylases, vegetable β-amylases) allowed maltose syrups of

Table 3.3 Saccharide spectra of spray-dried maltodextrins and glucose powders

	DE							
	8–10	11–14	15–17	18–20	20–23	26–30	33–35	36–38
DP_1	0.3	0.5	1.0	1.0	1.5	1.5	1.5	1.5
DP_2	3.0	3.5	5.0	6.5	7.0	13.0	27.0	35.0
DP_3	4.5	6.0	10.0	11.0	11.0	21.5	21.0	21.0
DP_4	3.7	5.0	7.0	7.4	7.1	12.4	10.4	10.6
DP_5	3.5	4.9	6.2	6.3	7.6	8.6	3.4	2.1
DP_6	6.4	9.7	11.8	12.6	15.5	6.4	2.9	1.3
DP_7 ⎱	9.0	10.7	11.0	11.4	13.5	⎰ 3.0	2.2	1.3
DP_8 ⎰						⎱ 1.7	1.2	1.4
DP_9	2.6	3.0	2.1	2.1	1.4	1.6	1.1	2.7
DP_{10+}	67.0	56.7	45.9	41.7	35.4	30.3	29.3	23.1

Table 3.4 Sugar composition of enzyme-converted glucose syrups

	DE		
Glucose syrup	42	53	65
Dextrose	2.5	2.0	34.0
Maltose	56.0	75.0	47.0
Maltotriose	16.0	14.0	3.0
Maltotetraose	0.7	0.5	2.0
Maltopentaose	0.4	0.4	1.5
Maltohexaose	0.7	0.6	1.0
Higher sugars	23.7	7.4	11.5

higher maltose levels (approximately 55%) to be produced (see Table 3.4). These have led to significant improvements in confectionery, particularly in high-boiled products, where better control of the rheology of the sugar mass has resulted in the ability to use higher sugar replacement levels and thus to obtain better texture, better shelf life, low colour formation and other properties.

The maltose story continues because of the use of starch debranching enzymes, e.g. pullulanase, has enabled higher levels of maltose, e.g. 75%, to be produced. These products have been widely used in the brewing industry and as substrates for the production of crystalline maltose and maltitol.

3.2.3 Hydrogenerated starch hydrolysates

Hydrogenerated starch hydrolysates from sorbitol to maltitol and hydrogenerated glucose syrups are used increasingly in the so-called 'sugar-free' confectionery, and sorbitol is also used in diabetic products.

Sweeter products in the 60–70 DE range produced by enzyme routes have controlled sugar compositions, allowing their use in proprietary medicines, beer and processed foods, as well as in the confectionery industry.

The use of all enzyme hydrolysis has allowed starch hydrolysates of high dextrose (glucose) content to be made (>97%). This has allowed the achievement of higher yields in glucose/dextrose production whether anhydrous or monohydrate, and the manufacture of hydrolysates of specific use in the fermentation industry. Dextrose can be used to produce confectionery tablets with a smooth cooling sensation on the palate.

3.2.4 Fructose

The most significant advance brought about in the starch industry by enzymes involves the actual isomerisation of the monomeric unit whereby fructose can

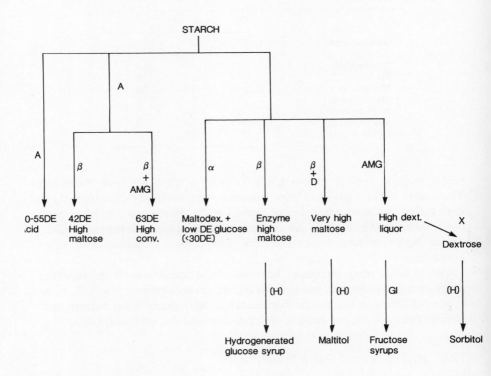

Figure 3.1 Starch products for the confectionery industry excluding blended products. Key: A, acid conversion; α, α-amylase; β, β-amylase; AMG, amyloglucosidase; (H), hydrogeneration; X, crystallisation; GI, glucose isomerase; D, debranching enzyme.

be produced from starch. With the discovery of an enzyme, an isomerase, which could isomerise glucose to a 42% fructose-containing equilibrium mixture having a sweetness level equivalent to sucrose, a new generation of products was born. These had obvious potential in the soft drinks area, and today many products in the USA contain high-fructose corn syrup (HFCS). In Europe the product is not so widely used due to the imposition of a production quota by the EEC.

Further chromatographic separation has allowed higher levels of fructose to be realised, and syrups containing 55% fructose are now used in soft drinks in the USA. 90% fructose syrups have been produced in this way and have subsequently been crystallised to allow crystalline fructose to be produced. This material has been used in diabetic products in certain European countries where it is permitted for that use and in dietetic products. The rationale here is that the high sweetness of fructose, up to 1.8 times the sweetness of sucrose, allows less to be used in a product to achieve the same sweetness.

The use of fructose-containing syrups as blends is finding applications in the confectionery industry in areas where in the past invert sugar has perhaps been used before, but with a greater versatility in the fructose levels and sweetness values.

So far we have considered the method of converting the starch into the hydrolysates which are required to produce the basic chemical composition of the glucose syrups. These are summarised in Figure 3.1. There are however other aspects of the manufacture of glucose syrup which have important implications for the user.

3.3 Refined glucose syrups

3.3.1 *Refining glucose syrups*

After the conversion of the starch by either acid or enzyme conversion, a detailed process of purification or refining takes place followed by evaporation in order to produce the water white viscous liquid which is so familiar to all confectioners. Initially the conversion takes place at 30–40% concentration, and the sugar solution has to be clarified to remove the protein and lipid fractions which have been liberated from the starch granule during conversion. In a maize-derived syrup this lipid/protein fraction or 'mud' as it is called comprises 0.8% of the solids. In wheat this will be slightly higher, whilst if potato is the base starch the fat/protein content will be very low. The phosphate level of potato is the major impurity at this stage. Mud is removed either by rotary vacuum filtration or by centrifugation followed by in-place filtration, and the material passing this filter is clear and ready for further processing. The pH of this stage is critical, and the process works best at the isoelectric pH of the protein—usually in the region of 4.5.

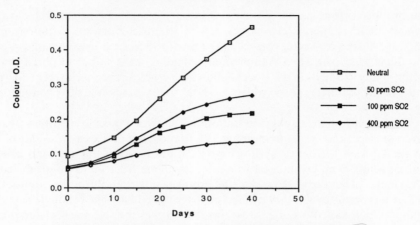

Figure 3.2   Heat colour stability of resin-refined glucose syrups at 60°C.

The final stage of refining is the area where the trace organic impurities, furan derivatives, protein hydrolysates, etc. are removed. Traditionally this was done by using activated carbon. The carbon was either granular, in towers or columns which could be regenerated by heating in furnaces, or powdered, used only once in filter beds. The advantage of powdered carbon is that there is less contamination between different grades of glucose produced sequentially and the blend of carbons chemically or steam activated could be chosen to give the optimum colour removal and heat colour stability for a particular type of glucose.

Here however there are now new developments which give much superior colour removal and colour stability. This involves the use of ion-exchange resins to effect the refining. This is based on the fact that the colour-forming bodies, protein hydrolysates, etc., are basically ionic in nature and can be removed very efficiently on these resins. The improved colour performance is shown in Figure 3.2 in data produced in the laboratory of Cerestar (UK) Ltd.

3.3.2   Resin-refined glucose syrups

Resin-refined glucose syrups allow one of two benefits to be exploited by the confectioner. Either he can get better colour stability at the same SO_2 level or he can obtain his traditional colour stability with a reduced SO_2 level in his product. It is unlikely however that all SO_2 can be removed, as its effect as an antibrowning anti-Maillard agent is a diminishing benefit, with the first 50 ppm having the major effect, as can be seen in Figure 3.3.

Another consideration has to be borne in mind when dealing with these new, improved, refined glucose syrups, and that is that they are totally demineralised because the resins take out not only the charged organic molecules but also the inorganic ions. Once again this brings benefits to the

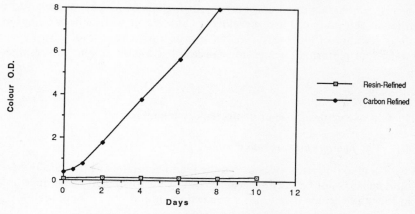

Figure 3.3 Heat colour stability of glucose syrups at 60°C.

confectioner, but he should understand the properties of the resin-refined syrups if he is to obtain the benefits without any problems in his production.

The first benefit is the reduction of ash. The level of ash in an acid-converted glucose syrup carbon-refined is 0.6% and in an enzyme–enzyme high-maltose carbon-refined syrup 0.25%, but either acid or enzyme–enzyme syrups resin-refined have ash levels of 0.025%. This reduced ash gives better flavour (less salt) and better clarity. There are few calcium ions to cause insolubility, together with the removal of sulphate and phosphate ions which also can cause haze. Chloride ions, which cause corrosion if not handled in plant suitably constructed for chloride ions (lined vessels of high-quality stainless steel) are also significantly reduced.

The removal of ionic materials also has implications for the pH levels and buffering power of the glucose. The effect of the glucose on the pH of the candy system is much reduced, since the buffering power is significantly reduced. This is again basically an advantage, as colour formation/inversion caused by the pH of the system is not affected at all by the glucose added. Where acid is added care must be taken in the formulation to ensure lower pH values are not obtained. The use of buffered acids is a simple way of avoiding this phenomenon.

Inorganic ions are sometimes used beneficially by the confectioner who, for example, has used the presence of calcium ions in glucose to aid with the setting of low-methoxyl pectin systems. Other applications call for control of other ions, e.g. magnesium.

In demineralised syrups these ions are to all intents and purposes absent. However, confectioner is able to add back exactly the ions he requires and does not have to rely on compensating for the somewhat variable ion levels of existing carbon-refined glucose syrups.

Thus it can be seen that the dramatic advances in glucose syrup composition which the introduction of enzymes has brought, and which were referred to earlier in this chapter, have heralded a new era in which the refining and colour stability of glucose syrups have been raised to a level where a new standard of performance and consistency is available to the confectionery industry.

3.4 Glucose syrups in sugar confectionery manufacture

3.4.1 *The fundamentals of sugar confectionery*

Why is a glucose syrup necessary in the manufacture of sugar confectionery? Could sucrose not be used by itself? To find the answer to these questions, consider the various properties a confection should have. These are:

(1) The confection must not undergo fermentation, mould growth or other microbiological spoilage during a long storage life.

(2) The confection must not undergo any change in its physical properties during this storage.

(3) It must have the desirable physical properties normally associated with the particular confection, e.g. it must not be too hard to eat comfortably, its texture and solubility must be pleasing to the palate and, not least, it must be flavoured correctly and be sweet-tasting.

(4) It must be pleasing to the eye. This factor is determined by the art and skill of the confectioner.

3.4.1.1 *The confection must not undergo any form of microbiological spoilage.* Whilst there is no completely clear-cut line, experience indicates that if the solids content is below 75% w/w certain moulds and yeasts will grow in carbohydrate solutions and spoilage will result. If, on the other hand, the solids content is above 75% w/w, then this is unlikely to occur. It must be remembered here that when considering sugar confectionery we are not dealing with a material kept under *commercially sterile* conditions, as with canned foods for instance, but with a product which must keep under normal, non-sterile conditions. The confection must be self-preserving in its own right since every source of infection cannot be kept away from it.

Now the saturation solubility of sucrose in water at 20°C is only 67.1% w/w. Thus sucrose alone cannot give us a product with a solids content sufficiently high to prevent microbiological spoilage. What can be done to alter this, and to permit us to prepare a solution stable against crystallisation with a solids content of 75% w/w or over at normal temperatures, i.e. 20°C? The answer is to have present in the solution with sucrose a sugar other than sucrose, a process known as 'doctoring'.

3.4.1.2 *The confection must not undergo any changes in its physical properties.* The main change in physical properties to be considered is the appearance of undesired crystals, which is called 'graining'. This crystal formation in sugar confections which should be free of any crystals is normally due to the formation in the confection of crystals of *sucrose* during storage. Such crystals spoil the appearance of the product and, in addition, cause an unpleasant roughness on the tongue.

In the case of high-boiled sweets, it is obviously impossible (using the traditional proportions of sucrose and glucose syrup) to obtain a product of 97% w/w solids content which is not supersaturated with respect to sucrose. However, it is well known that in practice using, for instance, 1.5 parts of sucrose to 1 part of 43°Be glucose syrup a high-boiled sweet can be prepared which can be stored for several years without any 'graining' taking place.

This is possible because high-boiled sweets are an example of what physicists call 'the glassy state'. Although they appear solid, they are in fact supercooled, non-crystalline liquids, liquids which are so far below their melting or softening point that they have assumed solid properties without crystallising. As such, they can be considered as liquids of enormously high viscosity, and high viscosity interferes very considerably with the process of crystal formation.

Consider what happens when a crystal forms. First of all, there must be a 'nucleus', that is a completely submicroscopic crystal to act as a starting point for the crystal to form. These 'nuclei' are formed spontaneously if the supersaturation is sufficient, but the higher the viscosity the slower the rate at which they form. The molecules of the substance crystallising have to 'hit' and 'stick' to the nucleus, being brought to it by the continuous, very rapid movement of the molecules in all liquids and solutions. But this movement is very severely limited in a solid or in a liquid of extremely high viscosity.

It is thus the extremely high viscosity and what one can call the pseudo-solid state of high-boiled sweets which in fact inhibits 'graining', i.e. the crystallisation of sucrose, during storage. However, even if the supersaturation *is* high, 'graining' can still take place, and this will happen if the 'doctoring' is too low.

Of course, when the boiling has been poured on the slab, and whilst it is being manipulated, its temperature is quite high, and quite clearly it is a very thick liquid and not a solid at all. Its viscosity in these stages, whilst high, is not nearly so high as when the final sweets have cooled to room temperature and solidified. In fact, during the cooling period on the slab and the later manipulation an insufficiently 'doctored' boiling will most definitely 'grain'.

The stability of a confection and in particular a high-boiled sweet is therefore due to the sugars present being in a glassy state. This state is metastable, and once crystallisation is started 'graining' is progressive. A change in the choice of raw material and the ratio of sugars in the recipe can affect the stability and the rate of 'graining'.

When confections are held in a humid atmosphere they will immediately begin to absorb water. This is present as a film of water around the surface of the product, which rapidly dilutes non-crystalline mixture of carbohydrates. Crystallisation then commences, promoted by the lowered viscosity of the syrup film.

The solubility of carbohydrates increases as the temperature rises. Thus the higher temperatures experienced during a boiling process at atmospheric pressure mean that the supersaturation with respect to sucrose is less than at the lower temperatures experienced during a vacuum boiling process. This explains why a higher proportion of 'doctor' must be used with a vacuum boiling process than is used with an atmospheric pressure process. If this higher proportion of 'doctor' is not used in a vacuum process, then 'graining' during processing is always a danger.

In the case of toffees, the solids content (eliminating the fat from our calculations) is usually about 90% w/w. Therefore, the situation here is rather different from that in the case of high-boiled sweets, where the solids content is of the order of 97–98% w/w. This lower solids content in toffees means that the viscosity of the sugary mass is very much lower. Thus toffees lack the antigraining effects of the very high viscosity of high-boiled sweets, and must be more highly 'doctored'. For this reason, a ratio of sucrose to 'doctor sugar solids' of 1.24/1, or even in some cases 1/1, is used.

However, in spite of this heavy 'doctoring', toffees usually do have an appreciably shorter storage life before 'graining' sets in than is the case with high-boiled sweets.

3.4.1.3 *The confection must have the correct physical form.* High-boiled sweets, toffees and marshmallows are examples where graining is detrimental to the appearance of the sugar confection. There are however certain confection which must have some 'grain' for them to have their traditional form, i.e. fudges and 'fondant'.

In the manufacture of 'fondant' a greatly underdoctored mixture is boiled to a comparatively low temperature, cooled and then beaten to start off the crystallisation of sucrose; the degree of doctoring, the temperature and the mechanical action ensure that a multitude of very fine sucrose crystals are formed. It is on the success of the production of a very large number of very small sucrose crystals that the smoothness of the fondant depends.

Fondant is of course a confection in its own right, but it is also used to promote crystallisation in fudges. The principle of the manufacture of a fudge is that a boiling is cooled to a temperature found by experiment to give the correct degree of supersaturation, and then very fine sucrose crystals in the form of fondant are added to 'start off' the crystallisation process. Obviously, here, details of manufacture and also the correct degree of 'doctoring' are matters of great importance. 'Pulled' sweets are another example of mechanical action being used to produce very fine sucrose crystals. In this case in much smaller number than in the case of fondant. Here the amount of doctor is, of course, much higher than in the case of fondant, and also the viscosity is much higher owing to the much higher solids content, both factors combining to reduce the number of sucrose crystals formed.

3.4.1.4 *The confection must be pleasing to the eye and the palate.* This really involves the art of the sugar confectioner. However, one aspect of taste which a glucose syrup can influence is sweetness, and this can be controlled to a degree by the type of syrup selected.

Since all the sugars produced by the hydrolysis of starch are reducing sugars, a measure of the total reducing power is also a measure of the total degree of hydrolysis of the starch. Thus the dextrose equivalent (DE), defined as the total reducing power of the glucose syrup expressed on a dry solids basis as dextrose, is a measure of the degree of hydrolysis.

Thus as the DE increases the mean molecular weight decreases, the quantity of lower sugars, dextrose and maltose increases and the physical properties of the glucose syrup are influenced, as can be seen in Table 3.5. The major factors that are of interest to the confectioner are expressed in Table 3.6

Table 3.5 Technological properties and functional uses of glucose syrups

Property of functional use	Type of syrup	
	Lower DE	Higher DE
Bodying agent	←———	
Browning reaction		———→
Cohesiveness	←———	
Colour stabilisation		———→
Crystallisation control	←——————————→	
Emulsion stabiliser	←———	
Fermentability		———→
Flavour enhancement		———→
Flavour transfer medium		———→
Foam stabiliser	←———	
Freezing point depression		———→
Humectancy	←——————————→	
Hygroscopicity		———→
Increased vapour pressure	←———	
Nutritive value	←——————————→	
Osmotic pressure		———→
Preservation		———→
Prevention of coarse ice crystals	←———	
Prevention of sucrose crystallisation	←———	
Sheen producer	←——————————→	
Solubilising effect	←——————————→	
Sweetness		———→
Thickening agent	←———	
Viscosity	←———	

Table 3.6 Functional property of glucose syrup in sugar confectionery

Type:	Low DE	High maltose	High maltose	Standard	Intermediate	High DE	High DE
Conversion:	Acid 36/14/12	Acid/Enzyme 42/6/56	Enzyme/Enzyme 42/2/56	Acid 42/17/13	Acid/Enzyme 55/31/18	Acid/Enzyme 63/37/32	Enzyme/Enzyme 68/40/44

Hygroscopicity

Browning reaction

Crystallisation control

Sweetness

Viscosity

Cohesiveness

Prevention of graining

Bodying of graining

Nutritive agent

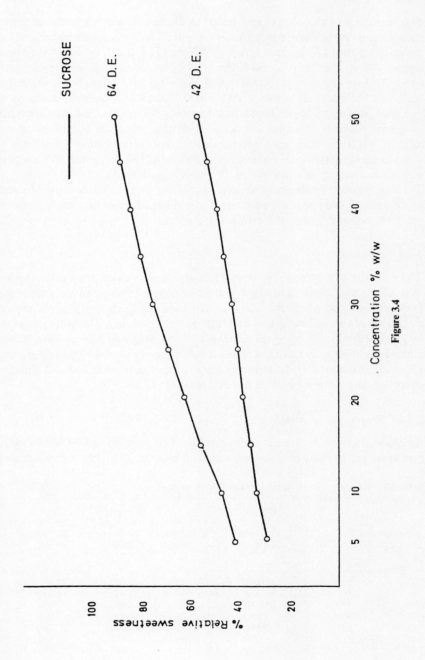

Figure 3.4

3.4.2 Sweetness

The sweetness of glucose syrup if tested in dilute solution is somewhat lower than sucrose at the same concentration. Figure 3.4 shows figures produced for aqueous solutions of glucose syrup by Nieman [2]. It can be seen from these figures how the relative sweetness of glucose syrup increases with concentration and how it increases with dextrose equivalent. Sucrose on this scale has the nominal value of 100. These figures for aqueous solutions of glucose syrup alone do not show the interesting synergistic effect which occurs in glucose/sucrose mixtures. As a result of this effect the sweetness of the mixture is greater than the sweetness calculated from Nieman's figures.

An example of this is that a mixture of 50% of 42 DE syrup and 50% sucrose can have a sweetness in excess of 75% at 50% solids.

These figures of sweetness should only serve as a guide because the real perception of sweetness depends upon a number of other factors, e.g. rate of solution, concentration of food on the palate, etc.

3.4.3 Viscosity

The viscosity of glucose syrup is very important in confectionery manufacture as it affects the handling of sugar masses in process, release of air, depositing performance and shelf life. In this last case high viscosity gives slower migration of sucrose molecules and thus inhibits graining. The body imparted by glucose syrup in gums gives resistance to cold flow and deformation during cutting, wrapping and storage. Thus it can be seen that, by choosing glucose syrup of a different DE, different viscosity values can be obtained and different effects on the confectionery product obtained (Table 3.7).

3.4.4 Prevention of graining

All glucose syrups exercise some control over sucrose crystallisation in high-boiled sweets. In these confections, which are essentially highly supersaturated

Table 3.7 Viscosity (cp) of acid-converted glucose syrups

Temperature		Glucose syrups			
		43 Baumé 32 DE	43 Baumé 42 DE	43 Baumé 52 DE	43 Baumé 62 DE
°F	°C				
70	21.1	140 000	100 000	45 000	24 000
80	26.7	85 000	50 000	18 000	14 000
100	37.8	23 000	12 500	7600	5100
120	48.9	7700	4250	2650	1800
140	60.0	2900	1700	1050	710
160	71.1	1250	740	475	330
180	82.2	620	370	240	170

Table 3.8

Percentage of solids present		Solids content of solutions just saturated with sucrose at 20°C (% w/w)
Sucrose	Invert sugar	
100	0	67.1
78.6	21.4	70.0
67.6	32.4	72.0
57.6	42.4	74.0
48.8	51.2	76.0

Table 3.9

Percentage of solids present		Solids content of solutions saturated with dextrose at 20°C (% w/w)
Sucrose	Invert sugar	
47.5	52.5	76.1
40.0	60.0	73.6
30.0	70.0	73.6
20.0	80.0	67.7

solutions of sucrose, the latter will always tend to recrystallise both at the production stage and during storage. Unless this tendency is prevented by the addition of an inhibitor (or doctor as it is called, e.g. glucose syrup), recrystallisation will continue, resulting in graining. Because of the extremely low moisture content in high-boiled sweets and the resulting high viscosity, graining may take place quite slowly under ideal storage conditions.

However, once initiated either by the picking up of moisture or by the seeding of the confection with non-dissolved sucrose graining may take place very rapidly. The grain-inhibiting effect of glucose syrup is twofold. First, the increased viscosity in the glass of the high-boiled sweet prevents migration of sucrose molecules and nucleation, as described above. The second important property is the control of crystallisation by increased sucrose solubility.

If sucrose and invert are present together in solution, a concentration can be reached whereby the sucrose content is only just prevented from crystallising. Table 3.8 shows the solids content of the solutions which are just saturated with sucrose. From this it can be seen that sucrose itself is saturated at 67% solids, and in a 50/50 mixture with invert sugar it becomes saturated with respect to dextrose at 76% solids (see Table 3.9). However, in the presence of glucose syrup much higher solids can be obtained before saturation is achieved (Table 3.10). This is important not only in high-boiled sweets but in products where microbiological stability is required, e.g. marshmallow, and where the control of graining is important, as in fondants and fudge formulations.

Table 3.10

Percentage of solids present		Solids content of solutions just saturated with sucrose at 20°C (%w/w)
Sucrose	42 DE glucose Syrup solids	
100	0	67.1
78.6	21.4	70.0
67.6	32.4	72.0
57.6	42.4	74.0
48.8	51.2	76.0
40.9	59.1	78.0
34.1	65.9	80.0
28.4	71.6	82.0
23.7	76.3	84.0

3.4.5 *Hygroscopicity*

The relationship between a food product and its environment is important to the shelf life of that product and hence of great importance to its overall economy. The controlling factor is the equilibrium relative humidity (ERH) of the product. If the ERH is low the product will attract moisture and become sticky, and is in some cases liable to microbiological spoilage. On the other hand, if the ERH of the product is high, it will tend to lose moisture and become dry. This again is deleterious to the product.

The ERH at a given temperature is a function of the concentration of solids dissolved in the aqueous phase. If more molecules are dissolved in the aqueous phase the ERH is decreased.

Equilibrium relative humidity of a sugar confection can be quite accurately calculated by the use of the Money–Born equation [3]:

$$\text{Equilibrium relative humidity} = 100 \times N_0/(N_0 + 1.5\ N)$$

where N is the number of gram-molecules of the various carbohydrates present,

and N_0 is the number of gram-molecules of water present.

The number of gram-molecules is obtained by dividing the weight of the substance present by its molecular weight, and the molecular weights we have to use are:

Sucrose	342.3
Invert sugar	180.2
Dextrose	180.2
40 DE glucose syrup solids	340
63 DE glucose syrup solids	260
Water	18.02

The molecular weights (which are obviously average molecular weights) for

Table 3.11

Type case	Doctor	Equilibrium relative humidity (%)
Marshmallow	Invert	73.3
	40 DE glucose syrup	80.0
	63 DE glucose syrup	77.5
Toffee	Invert	49.2
	40 DE glucose syrup	58.4
	63 DE glucose syrup	54.9
High-boiled sweet	Invert	23.0
	40 DE glucose syrup	28.0
	63 DE glucose syrup	26.0

the two glucose syrups are obtained by calculation elevations of these two products.

Consider three cases representing the conditions obtaining in a product: one such as a marshmallow, taken as being 24% water, 48.8% sucrose and 51.2% 'doctor' solids; one representing the conditions in the sugar portion of a toffee, which is taken as containing 10% water, 45% sucrose and 45% 'doctor' solids; and one representing a high-boiled sweet, which is taken as containing 3% water, 63% sucrose and 34% 'doctor' solids. The results of applying the Money–Born equation to these cases are shown in Table 3.11. It will be seen that in all cases when invert sugar is used as a 'doctor', the relative vapour pressure of the confection is lower than when 40 DE glucose syrup is used. This means that sugar confections doctored with 40 DE glucose syrup will be less liable to pick up moisture from the atmosphere than when invert is used, a very important point in the relatively moist atmospheric conditions which apply in Europe and many other parts of the world.

If a slightly more moisture-retaining 'doctor' than 40 DE glucose syrup is wanted, then 63 DE glucose syrup will be suitable. Dextrose has the same effect or equilibrium relative humidity as invert sugar as its molecular weight is the same.

There is another important factor to be taken into consideration here: a high-boiled sweet containing 34% of invert sugar would be impossibly hygroscopic, the difference between 34% invert sugar (impossible) and 34% 40 DE glucose syrup solids (perfectly satisfactory) being too great to be explained solely by the difference between 23% and 28% ERH. The factor which comes in here, in all probability, is the ability of 40 DE glucose syrup to 'skin' the skin which forms on the top of this material when it is exposed to the air. In a high-boiled sweet the 40 DE glucose syrup component has probably imparted a 'skin' of this nature to the outer surface of the sweet, which greatly hinders the penetration of moisture *into* the sweet. The lower the moisture content of the sweet, the greater this 'protective skin' action. This could partly explain why high-boiled sweets for export to tropical countries should have as low a moisture content as possible, the difference between 3% moisture and 2% being highly significant in this connection.

The range of acid-converted glucose syrups has a wide range of properties to choose from, and glucose syrups of this kind are widely used in the confectionery industry.

3.4.6   Acid/enzyme glucose syrups

There are limitations to acid conversion, in that below 30 DE, because of the random nature of the acid attack, one cannot guarantee that all of the starch molecules have been sufficiently hydrolysed to prevent retrogradation, and hence cloudy 'starch-positive' glucose syrups could be produced. Similarly, at levels above 55 DE the stringent conditions that are necessary give rise to high colours, off flavours, etc. These restrictions have been overcome by the use of enzymes after an initial mild acid conversion to solubilise the starch. More specific enzymic hydrolysis allows high-quality glucose syrup of even wider DE range to be produced with even more comprehensive properties. Not only does the use of enzymes allow wider DE values to be obtained, it allows control of sugar compositions to be exercised. An example of this is high-maltose syrups in which low dextrose contents and high maltose contents are produced.

Acid/enzyme syrups have therefore extended the range of properties available such that high viscosity, higher sweetness and lower browning products can be produced, and these syrups are widely used.

By substituting the acid conversion step by enzyme liquefaction using high-temperature stable α-amylase products followed by β-amylase treatment, an all-enzyme hydrolysis is possible, giving greater control and producing syrups of lower dextrose, higher maltose and lower viscosity.

3.4.7   Viscosity and 42 DE high-maltose syrups

Comparisons of syrup viscosity and candy viscosity are shown in Figures 3.5 and 3.6. This reduced viscosity of the syrup and the candy mass at a given DE has a number of advantages for the confectioner in pumping, depositing, control of fondant viscosity and air retention. Glucose viscosity is affected by the amount of higher molecular weight material which has not been converted to the lower sugars, dextrose and maltose. In Table 3.12 is shown an example of two syrups with similar DE dextrose and maltose levels which have widely differing viscosities due to the difference in the percentage of higher sugars (oligosaccharides).

The syrup with 3% more oligosaccharide of a molecular weight greater than 25 000 daltons has a 50% higher viscosity. The control of the quantities of higher sugars in glucose syrups is very important to the rheology of the glucose syrup in its application. By the use of low-viscosity syrups, higher sucrose

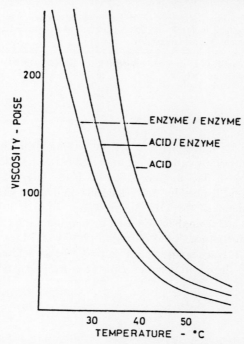

Figure 3.5 Viscosity–temperature relationships for glucose syrups made using different conversion methods.

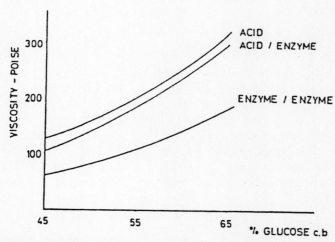

Figure 3.6 Candy viscosity as a function of glucose concentration (commercial basis, c.b.) at a given total sugar solids.

Table 3.12 Viscosity of 42 DE high-maltose syrups as a function of the high molecular (> 25 000) content as determined by gel permeation chromatography

Percentage of molecules > 25 000 mol. wt	Viscosity 80% DS 40°C (poise)
1.87	65
4.85	98

replacement can be made without serious tailing problems in depositing, handling problems of the candy mass, and with better release of entrapped air and easier mixing of flavours, colours, etc. These later developments have brought with them the need for more accurate analysis of glucose syrups than simple measurement of the DE. Sugar composition is all-important. The technique that is increasingly being used by manufacturers and confectioners alike is high-performance liquid chromatography (HPLC).

A typical HPLC trace is shown in Figure 3.7 for an acid-converted glucose syrup. Figure 3.8 shows an enzyme–enzyme-converted glucose syrup.

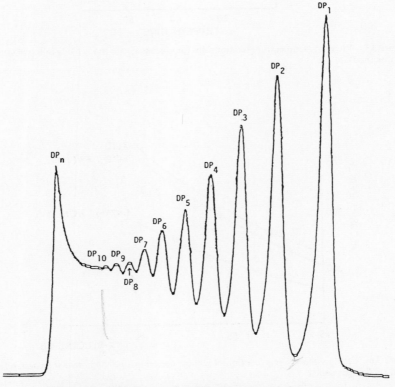

Figure 3.7   HPLC trace of 42-DE acid-converted glucose syrup.

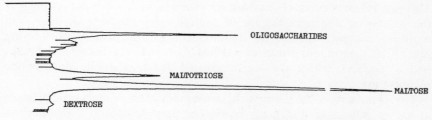

Figure 3.8 HPLC trace of 42-DE enzyme–enzyme high-maltose syrup.

3.4.8 *Enzyme/enzyme high-maltose glucose syrups*

In practical terms the major limitation of increasing the usage level of glucose syrups in confectionery has been that of reaching a satisfactory balance of higher sugars levels (which are limited by viscosity or textural parameters) and dextrose levels (which are limited by shelf life considerations and colour formation). The former range of glucose syrups could move in one direction but not both. Now, with the advent of modern enzyme technology, it is possible to control carefully the sugar spectrum to get the best balance of properties. An example of this is shown in Table 3.13 which compares a high-boiled sweet manufacture with three different glucose syrups and various sucrose–glucose syrup ratios. The overall balance is maintained using enzyme–enzyme glucose syrup at a 100 sucrose to 180 glucose syrup ratio.

The formation of enzyme–enzyme high-maltose glucose syrup by reducing both higher sugars and dextrose levels allows significant changes in glucose/sucrose formulations to be made while preserving the following characteristics:

Low processing viscosity.

Low dextrose, and so low hygroscopicity and good shelf life.

Low colour formation obtained by low dextrose and demineralisation.

Good textural properties.

Better heat conductivity.

Table 3.13

	Glucose syrup type		
	DE 42 Acid-converted	DE 42 Acid/enzyme	DE 42 Enzyme/enzyme
Dextrose	15	6.0	3.5
Maltose	12	39.0	55.0
Polysaccharide	73	55.0	41.5
Sucrose/glucose syrup	100/80	100/100	100/180
Total reducing sugars (including 2% process inversion)	17.6	19.4	25.2
Monoreducing	6.9	3.7	2.8
Disaccharide/sucrose + maltose	63.3	70.6	71.4
Higher sugars (%)	27.9	24.1	24.1

This new range of products enables, for example, high solids depositing and the processing and manufacture of confectionery products at their final moisture content, without the requirement for the use of post-drying operations. Continuous processes and flow lines can be created without breaks and bottlenecks, which are usually created due to a drying stage in the manufacture.

The manufacturer can improve the consistency of his products and produce at higher efficiencies and lower costs. The ingredients and their selection sometimes require considerable change from normal when changing an existing product line to continuous production. The overall objective in formulation change is to maintain the best of the qualities of the existing product so that it can be eaten without the consumer noticing any obvious changes. The wide variety of properties, constantly being improved by modern technology, ensures that its use is limited only by the ingenuity of the confectioner.

References

1. D. Howling, in *Sugar: Science and Technology*, eds. G.G. Birch and K.J. Parker, Applied Science Publishers, London (1979) 259.
2. Nieman, *Ned. Chem Ind* **2** (1960) 257.
3. Money and Born, *J. Sci. Food Agric.* **2** (1951) 180.

Further reading

H.E. Horn, *Corn sweeteners: functional properties. Cereal Food World*, **26** (1990) 219.
D. Howling, *et al.*, in *Glucose Syrups: Science and Technology*, eds. S.Z. Dziedzic and M.W. Kearsley, Elsevier Applied Science Publishers, London and New York (1984).
R. Lees and B. Jackson, *Sugar Confectionery and Chocolate Manufacture*. Leonard Hill Books, Glasgow (1973).
H.M. Pancoast and W.R. Junk, *Handbook of Sugars* 2nd edn, Avi-Publishing Company Inc.

4 Gelling and whipping agents

A. RIX

Gelling and whipping agents are used to provide a wide range of textures in the sugar confectionery industry. The gums and jellies are an increasingly popular range of products. Each of the gelling or whipping agents contributes its own particular characteristics which can be used to manipulate the final texture of the finished product.

The purpose of this chapter is to give a brief introduction to some of the more commonly used gelling and whipping agents. For a more in-depth understanding of these ingredients further references have been listed at the end of the chapter.

4.1 Agar agar E406

Agar agar is a dried hydrophilic, colloidal polysaccharide from red seaweeds and related marine species. It is available as white to pale yellow agglutinated strips or in flake or powder form. It may have a slightly characteristic odour and mucilaginous flavour. It is soluble in boiling water and insoluble in cold water and most organic solvents. It has a molecular weight of over 20 000

Agar is extracted from a wide range of seaweed varieties which grow in many areas of the world. The main suppliers are Japan, New Zealand, Denmark, Australia, South Africa and Spain. The gel strength varies according to the source, and checks should be carried out on each delivery to determine gel strength. It is produced by hot-water extraction and purified by using either successive freezing and thawing or by concentration under vacuum. Bleach is often added during the process to produce a lighter coloured final product.

Normally agar is dissolved in 30–50 times its weight of water, usually premixed with about 10 times its weight of sugar to prevent lumping. Very high viscosities are achieved with concentration up to 10%.

In normal production the agar is dissolved in boiling water before addition to the remainder of the batch so that the hydration is not retarded by the higher soluble solids content. Since a large amount of water is required to make a good solution, agar is not recommended for continuous production techniques. Open steam-heated pan is still regarded as the best method for the manufacture of agar jellies.

Agar is unaffected by heat at neutral pH but rapidly degenerates in acid conditions, therefore with agar confections the batch is usually dropped to around 60°C before the addition of any acid. The optimum gel strength is achieved about pH 8–9. At solids contents 76–78%, the gel strength is good, but it reduces as the solids go over 80%.

Agar provides good gel strength. It forms a firm gel at concentrations as low as 1% and is usually used in confectionery at the level of 1–1.5% of the sugar–glucose–agar recipe.

It is used for the characteristic hysteresis of its melting temperature. It melts at a temperature in excess of 85°C but does not set until the temperature drops to 30–40°C.

Jellies made with agar tend to have a short texture, and other ingredients are often added to improve the eating quality, e.g. jams and fruit pulps.

Locust bean gum has been shown to have a synergistic effect on gel strength, whereas both alginates and starches reduce gel strength.

Agar jellies take considerably longer to set in moulding starch than pectin jellies.

Agar is not absorbed by the body during digestion and can therefore be used in low-calorie confections.

Agar does not carry flavour well, and as a result of this and its sensitivity to acid and particular types of texture it is being replaced by pectins or modified starches.

4.2 Alginate E401

Alginates were first isolated by Stamford by alkaline extraction from brown algae, a process used for iodine production. Commercial extraction is from seaweeds such as *Laminaria digitata*, *Ascophyllum nodosum* and *Fucus serratus*. Each of the seaweeds provides a differing proportion of the main attribute of alginate.

Calcium alginate has the formula $[(C_6H_7O_6)_2Ca]_n$ with a molecular weight 32 000–250 000. It is a white to yellow granular powder, colloidal, insoluble in water, acids and organic solvents. It is soluble in alkaline solutions of substances which combine with the calcium.

The extraction of alginate is based on two properties:

(1) Alkaline alginates are soluble in water.
(2) Alginic acid and its callcium derivatives have very limited stability in water.

Initially the seaweeds are macerated with dilute mineral acid so that the

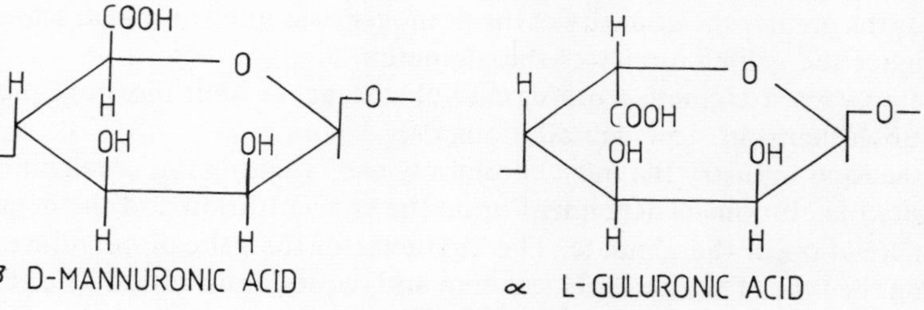

Figure 4.1.

alginate is converted to alginic acid while undesirable components such as mannitol and mineral salts are removed.

The product of this process is then ground in the presence of alkali, which neutralises the alginic acid and converts it to the soluble alginate of the salt used. All the insoluble materials, celluloses and proteins, are removed by standard filtration, flotation and settling techniques.

The addition of mineral acid to the alginate solution causes precipitation of alginic acid. This precipitate is then washed and dried. The alginic acid is neutralised with different alkaline bases according to the type of alginates required. The final product is then dried-milled and sieved to the desired particle size.

Alginates are comprised of mannuronic and guluronic acids (see Figure 4.1). These can link to form homogeneous segments in which guluronic acid binds to guluronic acid and mannuronic acid binds to mannuronic acid, or alternating segments of guluronic to mannuronic acid binding. Only guluronic segments can adopt the form of a buckled ribbon with a structure similar to that of pectin with its galacturonic segments. In the presence of calcium ions the homogeneous guluronic acid segments ccan associate to form an 'egg box' type aggregate (see Figure 4.2).

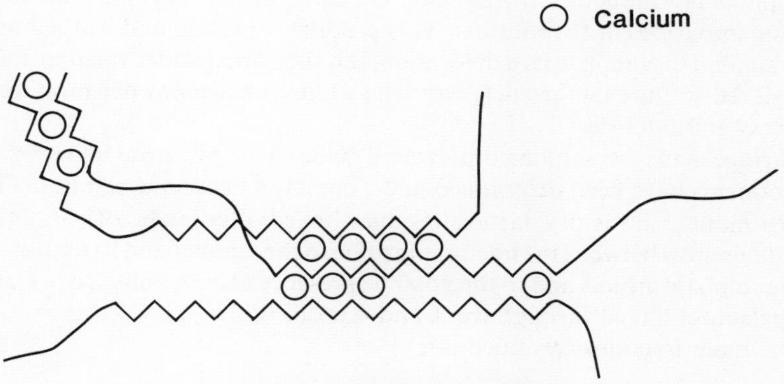

Figure 4.2 Egg box-type bonding.

Thus the greater the quantity of the homogeneous guluronic acid segments, the higher the gelling ability of the alginates.

The powdered alginate requires careful storage, to limit moisture pick-up and subsequent but slow degradation.

In the food industry the most commonly used gelating ion is calcium. The viscosity of solutions is dependent upon the concentration and the degree of polymerisation of the alginate. The character of the gel can be adjusted by varying the type of alginate, pH, calcium and sequesterant ratios. The gels are resistant to dehydration and do not melt on reheating, when the strength induced by calcium is greater than that induced by thermal agitation. In this way it behaves identically to highly demethoxylated pectin.

4.3   Carrageenans

The name carrageenan is derived from the county of Carraghen on the south coast of Ireland, where Irish moss was used in foods and medicines more than 600 years ago. Red seaweeds were used because of their unique property in gelling milk when they were heated together.

Commercial production of carrageenan evolved in France from the lichen collected along the French coastal areas. The lichen, a blend of *Chondrus crispus* and *Gigartina stellata*, is still harvested along the shores of Normandy and Brittany.

The lichen remains the major source of carrageenan production. However, other seaweed sources can be used to obtain products of the desired property or combination of properties suited to the customer's application.

After washing, seaweeds are extracted with hot water. During the process seaweeds are crushed in alkaline solution to maximise the extraction. The hot extract solution is filtered through diatomaceous earth and is poured through a pressure filter to produce a clear carrageenan solution. The carrageenan is precipitated by the addition of alcohol. The carrageenan coagulates into fibres, leaving impurities in the solution. This product is pressed and washed again with alcohol to complete its dehydration. It is then dried under vacuum, milled and sieved to the exact particle size. The white to beige powder produced is tasteless and odourless.

Carrageenans are sulphated polymers made up of galactose units. Several components have been determined and a common backbone can be defined.

The main chain is D-galactose residues linked alternately α-(1-3), β-(1-4). The differences between the fractions are due to the number and to the position of the sulphate groups and to the possible presence of a 3,6 anhydro bridge on the galactose linked through the 1 and 4 positions.

The main fractions identified are:

Iota (ι) carrageenan.
Kappa (κ) carrageenan.

Lambda (λ) carrageenan.

Mu (μ) carrageenan.

Nu (ν) carrageenan.

The proportion of the different fractions varies with the species of the seaweeds, the habitat and the time of harvesting.

The gelling carrageenans are the kappa and iota fractions. These are not found as pure macromolecules. There is always a small part of the ι in the κ fraction and vice versa. Other components can also be found in the macromolecules, particularly μ and ν carrageenans.

The gelation of κ and ι carrageenans is induced by the association of chains through double helices. In native carrageenans there are 'kinks' caused by the presence of κ and ι fractions. This makes the regular sequences too small to create stable linkages, and only weak gels can be produced.

To improve the gelling properties, carrageenans are extracted in an alkaline system. This process catalyses an elimination of the 6 sulphate groups present in μ and ν carrageenan units. This induces the 3, 6 anhydro-galactose formation of μ and ν carrageenans. The chains become more regular and the gel strength is greatly increased.

In seaweeds there is an enzyme present which carries out this conversion naturally. μ and ν carrageenans can therefore be considered precursors of the κ and ι fractions.

4.4 Gelatin

Gelatin does not exist naturally but is produced by the partial hydrolysis of collagen in the raw material substrate. Collagen is a structural component in animal tissues, present in skin, bone and connective tissue. The raw materials are sourced from slaughterhouses, meat-packing plants or tanneries. The products from tanneries have already been salted or limed for preservation.

Collagen is made up of films and fibrils. Industrial modification of collagen to produce gelatin is by stepwise destruction of the organised structure to obtain the soluble derivative gelatin.

These are two categories of gelatin.

(1) Type A: produced by the acid processing of collagen from skins and ossein.

(2) Type B: produced by the alkaline processing of collagen from ossein and hides.

Ossein is the raw material derived from bones which have been degreased. The material is treated with hydrochloric acid to decalcify the bones, leaving a flexible product which is washed to remove acid residues.

The extraction of gelatin from the raw material is initiated by either liming or acidulation, which disrupts the molecular linkages within the collagen.

Gelatin is then extracted by hot-water hydrolysis. This is carried out as a batch operation. Several extracts are produced with a concentration of 5–10% gelatin. This liquor is then filtered and subsequently concentrated in vacuum concentrators. The colour and clarity of the finished product will vary depending on the extraction run and whether bleach has been used during processing. With each extraction run the product becomes progressively darker. The resulting solution is sterilised by heating to 145°C. This solution is cooled and the resulting gel is minced and dried. The dried product is then ground and sieved to produce the desired particle size. It is only at this stage that analytical tests will characterise the particular gelatin. It is as a result of these tests that the final product is packed from a blend of batches to be sent to the customer.

A typical analysis of a gelatin would be:

Moisture   14%
Protein   84%
Ash   2%

Gelatin picks up water in a moist atmosphere and should be stored in a cool, dry store. At above 16% moisture mould growth is possible. Gelatin solutions from an ideal medium for bacterial growth. Hygienic procedures must be implemented when using this product in solution and equipment must be throughly cleaned.

The customer should always ensure that a certificate of microbiological quality accompanies deliveries or arrange for appropriate tests to be carried out on the received product. The microbiological quality of the product is important not only for the maintenance of good manufacturing practice and product safety, but also for the functionality of the product.

The gel strength of the finished product may be expressed in a number of ways. Those in common use in the UK are grams Bloom, Boucher units, FIRA degrees and jelly strength. Most of the test instruments measure the force

Table 4.1 Relationship between a solution of 100 Bloom strength gelatin and equivalent jelly strength of other Bloom grades. Valves are concentration (%) of gelatin required to give a similar jelly strength

Bloom strength of gelatin (%)							
60	80	*100*	140	160	200	225	260
7.7	6.7	*6.0*	5.1	4.8	4.3	4.0	3.7
10.3	8.9	*8.0*	6.8	6.3	5.7	5.3	5.0
12.9	11.2	*10.0*	8.4	7.9	7.1	6.7	6.2
15.5	13.4	*12.0*	10.1	9.5	8.5	8.0	7.4
18.1	15.7	*14.0*	11.8	11.1	9.9	9.3	8.7

From R. Lees and B. Jackson *Sugar Confectionery and Chocolate Manufacture*, Leonard Hill Books, Glasgow (1973).

Table 4.2 Relationship between Bloom strength of various gelatins held in solution having equivalent jelly strength

Bloom strength of gelatin (%)	Gelatin needed to produce equivalent jelly strength (%)				
	60 Bloom	100 Bloom	160 Bloom	200 Bloom	260 Bloom
60	10.0	12.9	14.9	18.3	20.7
80	8.6	11.2	14.2	15.8	18.0
100	7.8	10.0	12.6	14.1	16.1
120	7.1	9.1	11.5	12.9	14.7
140	6.6	8.4	10.7	12.0	13.6
160	6.1	7.9	10.0	11.2	12.8
180	—	7.5	9.4	10.5	12.0
200	—	7.1	8.9	10.0	11.4
220	—	6.8	8.5	9.5	10.9
240	—	6.5	8.1	9.1	10.4
260	—	6.2	7.8	8.7	10.0

From R. Lees and B. Jackson, *Sugar Confectionery and Chocolate Manufacture*, Leonard Hill Books, Glasgow (1973).

needed to produce a fixed deformation, or the deformation caused by a fixed force. The most commonly used measurement is Bloom (see Tables 4.1 and 4.2).

Commercial gelatins are generally obtained from 60 to 260 Bloom, though strengths up to 400 are available.

The viscosity of a sample of gelatin has only a minimal effect on the viscosity of the final products. The main considerations are the quantity of gelatin added and the total solids of the mix.

The pH has a highly significant effect on the gel produced. Gelatin has a large protein component made up of a variety of amino acids (Table 4.3). At a specific pH a protein will have an equal number of positive and negative charges on the molecule. This unique pH is known as the isoelectric point. These values for gelatins are in the ranges shown:

	pH Range
Alkaline process	4.8–5.1
Acid process	
— Ossein	6.5–8.5
Skins	7.5–9.5

It is therefore highly desirable to do checks on the gelatin at the intended final pH of the product.

The isoelectric point is important when mixing gelatin with other colloids, because of the danger of mutual precipitation if the colloids are carrying opposite charges. This can happen if two different types of gelatin are mixed. It is at the isoelectric point that there is maximum turbidity and foaming. In solutions containing high sugar concentrations, precipitation does not seem to be a practical problem.

Table 4.3 Amino acids obtained after hydrolysis of 100 g of gelatin

Alanine	8.0–11.0 g
* Arginine	8.0– 9.0 g
Aspartic acid	6.0– 7.0 g
Cysteine	—
Cystine	Traces
Glutamic	11.0–12.0 g
Glycine	26.0–31.0 g
* Histidine	0.7– 1.0 g
Hydroxylysine	0.8– 1.2 g
Hydroxyproline	13.0–15.0 g
* Isoleucine	1.4– 2.0 g
* Leucine	3.0– 3.5 g
* Lysine	4.0– 5.0 g
* Methionine	0.7– 1.0 g
Phenylalanine	2.0– 3.0 g
Proline	15.0–10.0 g
Serine	2.9– 4.2 g
* Threonine	2.2– 2.4 g
* Tryptophan	—
Tyrosine	0.2– 1.0 g
* Valine	2.6– 3.4 g

* Those listed as 'essential' amino acids in human nutrition.
Adapted from ref. 23.

Excessive heat progressively reduces gel strength, and solutions should not be heated above 80°C. Gelatin solutions are often added after the main cooking operation is complete, but before any acid addition.

In the final gum or jelly product ossein gelatin produces a harder, more brittle, gel than the more rubbery texture produced using skin gelatin.

4.5 Gellan gum

Gellan gum is the extracellar polysaccharide obtained by the aerobic fermentation of *Pseudomonas elodea*. The substrate consists of a carbohydrate, such as glucose, with a nitrogen source and inorganic salts. Aeration, temperature and pH are strictly controlled through the fermentation. On completion of fermentation, propan-2-ol is added to precipitate the gellan gum in its high-acetyl form. The low-acetyl form is generated by treating the broth with hot alkali before the alcohol addition. Filtration of the low-acetyl gum produces a high clarity of gellan gum.

Gellan is composed of rhamnose, glucose and glucuronic acid in the ratio of 1:2:1.

High- and low-acetyl gums have very different properties. High-acetyl gellan gum dissolves in deionised water to give viscous solutions, and in the presence of salts forms thermoreversible gels which are somewhat elastic and are similar to xanthan and locust bean gums. Low-acetyl gellan gum gels by cooling hot solutions of the gum in the presence of cations such as sodium, potassium, calcium and magnesium. Gellan gum is similar to carrageenan in being able to gel with monovalent or divalent ions.

Gel strength is dependent on ion and gum concentration. The divalent ions calcium and magnesium provide maximum gel strength at concentrations approximately 1/25 of those required for the monovalent ions, sodium and potassium.

Low-acetyl gellan will not gel in the presence of sugar at a concentration above 50%. This problem can be reduced by using glucose syrups to replace sugar, but high levels of glucose will also inhibit gel formation.

Low-acetyl gums are stable between pH 3.5 and 8. Changes in pH do not alter the setting points of the gels but do appear to have an effect on melting temperatures. Low-acetyl gellan gum gels show greater hysteresis than agar gels. Setting points are usually around 30–40°C with melting points around 100°C.

Gellan is often used in conjunction with other colloids.

Gellan can be used in starch jellies, pectin jellies, fillings and marshmallows.

4.6 Acacia gum—gum arabic E414

This is a natural gum exuded from the acacia tree which shows significant increase in development immediately following the rainy season. The vagaries of the climate in growing areas have caused wild fluctuations in price in recent years, resulting in manufacturers' search for alternatives.

It is very soluble in water to give an easy-flowing solution, but is insoluble in alcohol.

The kibbled gum can be dissolved in cold water in proportions of between 80 parts of gum and 100 parts of water minimum, to a maximum of 50 parts of gum and 50 parts of water. At 25°C gum arabic can be dissolved in water to produce solutions up to 50%. Solutions of this concentration are very viscous with the inherent difficulty in handling viscous materials.

The mixture is gently heated to dissolve the gum arabic. It is imperative that the mix is not allowed to boil. Excessive heat will degrade gum arabic, reducing the viscosity of the finished product from the theoretically achievable value. When the gum is completely dissolved the extraneous matter is removed by sieving through filter cloths or by centrifugal cleaning equipment. All sources of gum arabic are likely to be contaminated by vegetable debris from the trees and sand from the collecting environment. In some cases sugar solution may be added to the gum, prior to cleaning, to assist in the cleaning operation.

The viscosity of the final solution is inversely proportional to the temperature and is affected by pH. Gum arabic solution shows a maximum viscosity around pH6 with rapid fall-off above and below pH9 and 4 respectively.

Gum arabic was used originally because of its ability to inhibit strongly graining of sugar confectionery.

4.7 Pectin

Pectic substances are matrix components in the cell walls of higher plants. The compounds are insoluble in aqueous solution and are referred to as protopectins.

Pectin consists mainly of the partly methylated esters of polygalacturonic acid and their ammonium, sodium, potassium or calcium salts. The molecular weight is between 20 000 and 100 000.

Pectin is obtained by aqueous extraction of edible materials such as citrus fruits and pressed sugar beet pulp. Powdered pectin is a white to light grey or brown, odourless powder with a mucilaginous taste. It forms a colloidal, opalescent solution in water and is insoluble in alcohol.

The protopectin is hydrolysed using acid in hot aqueous solution. The aqueous extract contains soluble products such as neutral polysaccharides, gums and others.

The insoluble material is separated by pressing and filtration. The pectin is separated from the extract by precipitation in alcohol. The precipitate is purified by further washing procedures, progressing from alcohol/water mixtures to pure alcohol.

The fibrous product obtained is pressed, then dried under vacuum before being ground and sieved. This process produces high-methoxy (HM) pectins. Acid or alkaline demethylation of the pectin extract will form low-methoxy (LM) pectins.

LM pectins are defined as having a degree of methoxylation of less than 50% i.e. less than 50% of the functional groups on the molecule are methoxylated.

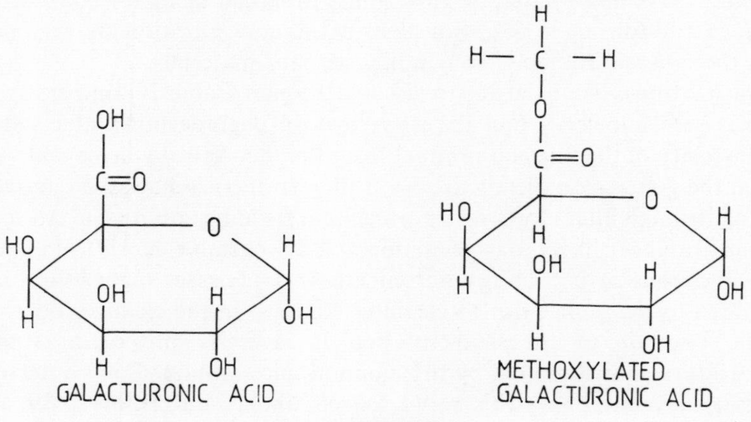

GALACTURONIC ACID

METHOXYLATED GALACTURONIC ACID

Figure 4.3.

The major components of pectin are polysaccharides, composed largely of D-galacturonic acid units linked through 1–4 glycosidic bonds (see Figure 4.3).

In amide pectins a proportion of the —COOH groups are converted to —$CONH_2$. The degree of methoxylation or amidation is referred to as %DM or %DA respectively.

The grade strength of a pectin is defined as the number of grams of sugar with which one gram of pectin will produce a gel of standard firmness, when tested under standard conditions of acidity and soluble solids content. Hence when buying pectin it is essential to know the test method used, the most commonly used being the American SAG. The standard strength for pectin in confectionery is 150 grade.

4.7.1 High-methoxy pectin

High-methoxy (HM) pectin will gel in the presence of sugar contents in excess of 55% and at the appropriate pH.

Since HM pectin is a partly methoxylated polygalacturonic acid, on each unit there is either an acid or methoxyl group. The methoxyl group is hydrophobic and unchanged, however the acid group will be either in a hydrated form or in the unchanged neutralised form. The DM of the pectin is very important in controlling the mechanism of the gelation of HM pectins. Generally, the higher the DM, the easier the gel forms, the higher the setting temperature and the shorter the setting time. Thus a pectin of 75% DM is called an extra-rapid set and that of 60% a slow-set pectin.

As pectin is a weak acid, the degree of dissociation is dependent upon the pH of the system. In the case of a 65% DM approximately half of the acidic groups will be dissociated at around pH 3.5. As the pH drops, fewer pectin acid groups will be dissociated. Clearly the actual number of charges as a result of dissociation will depend not only on pH but also on the DM, which controls the absolute number of acidic groups available, e.g. to achieve approximately 12% charged acid groups, the pH will have to be about 3.5 for a 75% DM pectin and about 3.0 for a pectin of 60% DM.

The pH of the pectin solution is critical during heating. Above pH 4.5 slow-set pectins will undergo excessive thermal degradation, and below pH 3.2 in the presence of sugar the pectin may pre-gel.

During cooking the product mixture is normally buffered to maintain the pH within controlled limits. Pectins can be purchased pre-buffered or the manufacturers can add citrates, tartrates, etc. to act as the buffering agent.

4.7.2 Low-methoxy pectin

There are two types of low-methoxy (LM) pectins.

(1) Conventional, with a DM of between 25 and 50%. These are prepared by the acid hydrolysis of HM pectins.

(2) Aminated LM pectin. These normally have a degree of amination (DA) of between 12 and 25%. Most countries legally limit DA to a maximum of 25%. Aminated LM pectins are prepared by treating HM pectins in aqueous alcoholic ammonia.

LM pectins gel in the presence of polyvalent ions, in less sweet and higher pH conditions than HM pectins. In practice LM pectins are gelled using calcium ions (see Figure 4.2), which may be added as soluble calcium salts or may be present naturally in other ingredients such as milk. Since LM pectins are gelled in this manner, the high sugar concentrations essential for the gelation of HM pectins are not required.

The variation in pH of the product has less effect than with HM pectins. Gels can be produced in the pH range 2.6–6.8. The LM pectin gels are more elastic and softer than those produced with HM pectins.

Unlike HM pectins, LM and particularly amide LM pectins can be produced so that they remelt at just above the settling temperature and will reform on cooling. This has particular advantage in the re-use of scrap materials.

4.8 Sources of starch

The most common sources of starch are tapioca, wheat, potato, sago, maize (corn) and rice (see Table 4.4). For confectionery use in the UK and Europe the main sources are maize and potato.

While the other cereal starches are used in confection in different parts of the world, maize starch is the most commonly used and will be used as the primary model for this section. Starch is used widely, alone and in conjunction with other gelling agents, to produce a wide range of jelly and gum products.

The kernel comprises four main components: starch, gluten, fibre and germ. The wet-milling process is designed to separate these fractions.

Table 4.4 Properties of common starches

	Maize	Wheat	Potato	Sago
Type of gel				
(a) Clarity	Opaque	Opaque	Clear	Moderately clear
(b) Texture	Short	Short	Very cohesive	Soft
Stability to retrogration	Poor	Poor	Fair	Fair
Freeze–thaw stability	Poor	Poor	Poor	Poor
Resistance to shear	Fair	Fair	Poor	Poor
Size of granules (μm)	5–25	2–10	5–100	20–60
Amylose/amylopectin ratio	26/74	25/75	24/76	27/73
Gelatinisation temperature (°C) (Koffer hot-stage method)	62–67–72	58–61–64	59–63–68	60–66–72

Maize is soaked in the presence of H_2SO_4 for 40–50 h. This softens the kernels before they are transferred to the mills. In the mills the kernel is torn open, freeing the germ, but little other damage is done. After passing through the germ separator the main stream passes to the refining mills for complete grinding to release the remaining kernel components. The fibre is extracted on inclined cylindrical sieves. Centrifuges are used to separate starch and gluten. The protein level is reduced to a very low figure by treatment in highly efficient hydrocyclones which wash the starch repeatedly with warm water.

The whole wet extraction of maize leads to a lower residual protein level than comparable wheat products. The purified starch suspension is spun in centrifuges to give a moisture content of around 33%. This starch is injected into a hot airstream and passed through a flash drier to provide a finished product of 12–14% moisture content.

Starch is a carbohydrate formed from dextrose monomers. The polymerisation may result in long linear chains (amylose) or branched chains (amylopectin). The particular ratio of these two types depends on the individual variety of the plant source, e.g. the amylose fraction in tapioca is 17% compared to 22% in potato starch and 27% in maize starch. Some specialised varieties of maize are almost entirely of the amylopectin type. Certain types of maize corn are almost entirely amylose-structured starch. (Because of these very large molecular weight polymers, the cooled starches exhibit unusual viscosity characteristics of considerable value in the food industry.) Amylose starches exhibit a characteristic tendency for the polymer chains to adhere parallel to each other in bundles. The presence of large numbers of free hydroxyl groups along the chain exerts a powerful attraction on similar groups in adjacent chains, increasing the binding attraction to form the bundles.

Microscopic examination shows that the starches are made up of tiny granules whose size and shape are characteristic of the plant source. The structure of starch granules can be described in terms of the attractive forces acting between adjacent molecules. In each of the concentric layers of the granule the linear and branched chains are orientated radially. These chains tend to draw together to form micelles. A chain may well be involved in the structure of several adjacent micelles. It is this structure that holds the granule together and makes it insoluble in water and it is this structure that gives rise to the dark cross pattern of a spherocrystal under a polarising microscope, as associated micelles ruin an essentially crystalline lattice. Clearly these attractive forces between molecules can be overcome if sufficient energy is put into the system.

Potato starch has relatively large oval granules with shell-like striations eccentrically arranged around the centre. Rice starch has the smallest grain size. Maize has a similar polygonal structure to rice caused by the compacting pressures experienced during growth.

Granular starch is insoluble in cold water, but if a starch–water mixture is heated beyond a critical temperature the granules suddenly lose their polarisation crosses and begin to swell. As this occurs the starch is said to have gelatinised. Gelatinisation for an individual grain will occur over a temperature range, 64–72°C for maize starch. As the temperature increases the granules swell further until they 'interfere' with each other, producing the characteristic viscosity increase noted when cooking starch. At this stage the individual grains are remarkably elastic. If the cooking process is continued or if high shear is applied to the mix, some of the swollen granules break and so the viscosity decreases. However, sufficient granules survive to give textural body to the mix.

The initial gelatinisation corresponds to the opening of the loose areas between the micelles bundles. Water is able to penetrate the granular structure, causing the swelling. Persistent micelles will hold the granular structure together during the swelling phase. Even prolonged cooking does not completely dissolve the structure. Only extreme conditions such as autoclaving will bring about complete solvation.

Starches which have very few branched chains are gelatinised with great difficulty and can withstand even the most severe conditions without completely dissolving. Starches with high fractions of branched chains swell rapidly and break up with continued cooking. Conventional maize starch is intermediate in behaviour between these two extremes. During cooking maize thickens at first and then thins out slightly as cooking continues to 95°C. When the mix is cooled the viscosity increases quite sharply. Potato starch starts to gelatinise at a lower temperature and reaches a higher viscosity for the same concentration. With continued cooking the viscosity drops much more rapidly than maize and the recovery of viscosity (set-back) on cooling is less.

Waxy maize is a speciality maize which originated in China. The term waxy refers to the waxy appearance of a cleanly cut kernel. To prevent the loss of the waxy characteristic because of crossing, waxy maize has to be grown in isolated areas where cross-pollination is not likely. The starch produced from this maize is almost 100% branched chain. Unlike conventional maize starches, waxy maize pastes are clear, fluid and non-gelling. This non-gelling characteristic can be used to stabilise other starches by reducing their tendency to gel.

4.8.1 Conversion starches

By modifying the molecular structure, processors can produce customised starches for particular purposes. The changes are described as conversion of the starch.

4.8.1.1 Thin-boiling starches. One of the most commonly used grades of starch is the thin-boiling or fluidity starches. These differ from unmodified starches in that firstly the cooked solutions have a lower viscosity and

secondly the products are tailored to give a range of viscosities which are given fluidity numbers to identify them, e.g. 20, 40, 60, 75 and 80. A starch with a fluidity of 80 is less viscous than one with a fluidity of 20.

Thin-boiling starches are prepared by treating a 'starch-milk' with a small quantity of acid. The mix is heated to a temperature below the gelatinisation temperature. When the desired degree of concision has been achieved the mix is neutralised and the starch filtered off and dried.

The acid has hydrolysed some of the bonds resulting in a less linked structure with some reduction in the molecular weight of some of the chains. Although the granule appears unchanged under the microscope, it disintegrates when cooked, giving a reduced viscosity compared to unmodified starches.

4.8.1.2 *Pregelatinised*. The starch is gelatinised and then dried on heated rollers. The dried material swells in water and forms a viscous paste. Pregelatinised starches have many applications, notably for instant food products. Virtually all types of starches can be pregelatinised.

4.8.1.3 *Oxidised starches*. Oxidised starches are prepared in a similar way to thin-boiling starches using hypochlorite instead of acid. The oxidation causes random attacks on the linear molecules so that they are unable to associate into micelles. This stabilises the starch against gelling. Each oxidised starch has its own character, but oxidised starch pastes are more stable than the boiling starches, which are noted not for stability but for the gel strengths.

4.8.1.4 *Starches with special gelatinisation properties*. Speciality starches for particular application can be produced by treating starch to produce a cross-linking between some of the molecules. This change reduces the cohesiveness of the paste and stabilises the viscosity against breakdown on cooking or shearing. If further cross-linking is carried out, the gelation temperature rises whilst the final paste clarity and non-gelling properties are retained.

The gelatinisation high-viscosity peak of amylopectin is reduced by this treatment, and the viscosity of the converted starch increases more gradually during cooking. If the treatment is continued large numbers of the molecules become iron-linked and the cohesive nature of the amylopectins is transformed into softer textured paste properties. These more highly polymerised starches are less prone to variations in viscosity during cooking and smoother texture is retained on ageing. The conversion does not result in the loss of the excellent non-gelling characteristics of standard amylopectin.

4.8.2 *Speciality starches*

In addition to all the starch types discussed above there are now many kinds of highly specialised starches available to the confectionery industry for particular applications.

4.9 Tragacanth E413

This is a gum exudate obtained from *Astragalus* which occurs as white to yellowish pieces of powder which is odourless and has a mucilaginous taste. It swells to give thick pastes in cold water; dispersion is quicker at 50°C. It is soluble in alkaline and aqueous hydrogen peroxide solutions, but is insoluble in alcohol. Tragacanth is often used with gum acacia to improve the texture of lozenges.

4.10 Xanthan gum E415

A polysaccharide gum produced by *Xanthomonas campestris*. It occurs as a cream-coloured powder, soluble in water, insoluble in alcohol. Xanthan gum is a secondary metabolite of *Xanthomonas campestris* produced during the commercial aerobic fermentation of carbohydrates. Fermentation is carried out in a batch process. The pH, degree of aeration, temperature, foaming and agitation are all carefully monitored. Following completion of fermentation the broth is sterilised and the fermenter emptied, cleared and sterilised before the next fermentation. The gum is recovered from the broth by the addition of propan-2-ol. The precipitate obtained is washed and pressed to remove residual alcohol. The product is then dried, ground and sieved to a specific particle size. The ground product is then bleached to produce homogeneous lots. The finished product is packed in well-clad containers, excluding air and moisture.

Xanthan gum is a mixed polysaccharide with a molecular weight of approximately 2.5 million. The monomer units are D-glucose, D-mannose and D-glucuronic acid. The backbone of the molecule is identical to cellulose i.e., β-D-glucose units linked to the 1–4 position. L-D-Mannose, β-D-glucuronic acid and a terminal β-D-mannose form a trisaccharide side chain. There are also acetyl groups associated with the D-mannose units adjacent to the chain and pyruvate groups on the terminal D-mannose units. The pyruvate and acetyl group content varies according to the substrain of the *Xanthomonas campestris* used in the fermentation. The glucuronic acid units and pyruvate groups impart acidic characteristics that are neutralised by sodium, potassium and calcium ions for commercial products.

Xanthan gum is readily dissolved in hot or cold water to produce an opaque solution of relatively high viscosity. This solution exhibits pseudoplastic flour characteristics, i.e. the viscosity of the solution decreases rapidly when shear is applied. As the shear rate decreases there is an immediate return to the high original viscosity. This characteristic makes xanthan an excellent suspending agent at low concentration.

Because the structural rigidity of the gum gives it properties not normally experienced in a typical anionic polysaccharide, addition of salt to a salt-free solution increases the viscosity. Most polysaccharide solutions show decreasing viscosity with temperature, however after an initial decrease xanthan exhibits increasing viscosity in a salt-free solution. The heat and pH stability of xanthan are also remarkably good.

Xanthan forms a thermoreversible cohesive gel system with locust bean gum.

4.11 Whipping agents

Whipping or foaming agents act as surfactants by assisting in the formation and stabilising of air cells within the structure of the products. The agent is responsible for the reduction of the surface tension, helping the deformation of the liquid and facilitating expansion against its surface tension. A continuous cohesive film is formed around the air vacuoles; the film resists localised thinning.

The most versatile whipping and foaming agents used in the confectionery industry are those based on proteins. The differing physical properties of the proteins are responsible for the variation in their performance as form formers and stabilisers. Disordered and flexible proteins have better properties than globular proteins. Availability of the hydrophobic and hydrophilic groups is also important. Proteins which have few hydrophobic groups have a poor foam-forming capacity and the bubble structure is unstable.

Maximum foaming properties occur near the isoelectric point of the protein when the electrostatic repulsion between polypeptide chains decreases. This permits clear packing of the polypeptides at the air/liquid interface.

Increasing temperature will increase denaturation of the polypeptide at the interface. Hydrophilic interaction will be increased, which will increase film thickness and viscosity around the bubbles, leading to increased foam stability. However, if the temperature is too high excess denaturation occurs, leading to destabilisation of the foam.

The requirements of a good whipping agent are:

(1) Solubility in the aqueous liquid phase.
(2) They must concentrate at the liquid–air interface.
(3) They must denature during the manufacturing process and so form a structure with sufficient mechanical strength to support the form.

Whipping agents reduce the density of the finished product and modify the texture considerably. Confection such as marshmallows could not exist without whipping agents.

4.11.1 Egg albumen

Egg albumen crystal is produced by drying liquid egg white in shallow trays, breaking up the sheets and then grinding to finished size.

Egg albumen is now frequently used in a spray-dried form. The spray-dried albumen provides a material free from offensive odours and flavours. These spray-dried products include the 'fluff-dried' albumen, produced by prewhipping the egg to produce a foam which is then dried rapidly.

There is some use for fresh liquid albumen or fresh albumen mixed with sugar.

Whatever form of egg albumen is used, it is essential to carry out checks on the microbiological quality. The product must be stored hygienically and all process and plant areas subjected to a strict cleaning schedule to ensure that there is no contamination of product or personnel.

Egg albumen is the most commonly used whipping agent because of its excellent whipping properties associated with reasonable stability and the characteristic of readily denaturing with temperature. The temperature of coagulation in a sugar solution rises from 65°C in a 40% syrup to 75°C in a 60% syrup.

It possesses the capacity to form uniform foams of good volume and softer eating qualities than those produced with other whipping agents. It will also ensure foam stability in the presence of other components and upon heating. This reflects the unique combination of proteins with differing physical properties that occur in egg white. Ovalbumin constitutes approximately 54% of the protein in egg albumen. There may be as many as 40 different proteins in egg white. Baker and Maxwell have identified 22 protein components.

4.11.2 *Gelatin as a whipping agent*

Gelatin is used as a whipping agent particularly for mallow products. Although it does not produce a mallow as tender as that produced using albumen, it is easy to use and provides a stable product.

The depression of surface tension produced by gelatin is much greater in concentrated sugar syrup than in water, so that tests to evaluate deliveries, based on a water foam test, may be of little value. Equally, a 30–45% sugar solution is needed to maximise the efficiency of the whipping operation.

Gelatin of Bloom strength in the range 180–220 is often used for mallow products and a low-viscosity gelatin produces a greater volume of foam.

Whether the gelatin is prepared for whipping or as a gelling agent, it should first be dispersed in cold water to soak. Gelatin is difficult to disperse in hot syrups. The degree of swelling during soaking is dependent on pH. Gelatin can absorb up to 40 times its own weight of water under specific conditions.

4.11.3 *Milk proteins*

Native proteins are generally water-insoluble, those which are water-soluble tend to be pH-sensitive and precipitate at their isoelectric point. They are also easily denatured by heat, and the methods of extraction usually result in defects in the fundamental characteristic and adverse flavours. Native proteins have high molecular weight and can ciuse allergic responses in sensitive individuals.

4.11.3.1 *Hydrolysed proteins.*
Hydrolysis of proteins yield peptides and amino acids. The three-dimensional skeleton of the protein is disrupted as the peptide bonds are broken. Although acid or alkali hydrolysis is possible, enzymic hydrolysis is preferred when producing water-soluble proteins, as it produces a uniform product from batch to batch.

4.11.3.2 *Modified proteins.*
There are a large number of possible modifications improving surfactant properties, water solubility and stability.

Hyfoama (Quest International) is a widely used milk protein whipping agent that gives good results. The two grades normally used are Hyfoama DSN and Hyfoama 88. Addition rates are 0.3–0.5%, approximately half the level required for egg albumen.

Hyfoama does not require presoaking, is less sensitive to overbeating and develops its full stability in the presence of sugar.

4.11.4 *Soya protein*

Modified soya proteins can be used as whipping agents. The proteins can be extracted from oil-free soya flakes. This extract then needs to be treated enzymically to modify the proteins before it is spray-dried. It is claimed that the product has several advantages.The treated soya protein is compatible in use with egg albumen so that full or partial replacement is possible. The replacement is on a one for one basis.

In manufacturing, the soya product does not require presoaking and should be dissolved by adding 2–3 times its weight of water and stirring to aid dispersion. It provides a faster whip with a lower density than similar formulations based on egg albumen. It is heat-stable, and is not adversely affected by very hot syrups. It is not denatured by high temperatures, which makes the soya extract suitable for aerating continuous production products.

The soya extract will maintain stability when shipped well beyond the time required to achieve maximum volume, as well as exhibiting stability in the presence of fat. In the final product the soya protein foams do not collapse with ageing. The soya problems appear to give a more fluid body than egg albumen-based products.

Further reading

Anon., Fruit chews and nougat without albumen. *Confect. Prod.* **44** (1978) 11.
Anon, New cold water swelling starches offer increased functionality. *Food Eng.* **60** (1988) 4.

D. Blanford, By gum. *Food* **26** (1986) 3.

Bulmers H.P. Ltd., *A Beginner's Guide to Pectin Confectionery.*

Bulmers H.P. Ltd., *Introduction to Pectin.*

I.W. Cottrell and P. Kovacs, *Algin. Food Colloids*, ed. H.D. Graham, (1977) 438–63.

General Foods Corporation (R.A. Williams *et al.*), Pectin compositions (gelling-agent). US Patent 4:268:533 (En). A.X.

K.J. Hannigan, Agar gels—without boiling. *Food Eng.* **54** (1982) 5.

E.J. Hughes, Aerated sugar confectionery products, in *Emulsifiers, Stabilisers and Thickeners in the Food Industry* 1, eds. P.B. Bush *et al.*, Natal Technikon Printers, Durban (1986) 53.

E.B. Jackson and A. Rapaille, *Starches—Their Technological Properties Related to their Use in Gum Confectionery.* FIE European Conference 1988.

N.R. Jones, Uses of gelatin in edible products, in *Science and Technology of Gelatin*, eds. A.G. Ward and A. Courts (1977) 365–94.

P. Kovacs and K.S. Kang, Xanthan gum, in *Food Colloids*, ed. H.D. Graham (1977) 500–21.

A.A. Lawrence, *Natural Gums for Edible Purposes.* Park Ridge, NDC (1976).

P. Leiner & Sons Ltd. (R.J. Croome), Gelatin compositions. US Patent 4:082:857. A.

C.D. May and G. Stainsby, Factors affecting pectin gelatron in *Gums and Stabilisers for the Food Industry 3*, ed. G.O. Philips, Elsevier Applied Science Publishers, London (1986) 515.

R. Meyer, Ultrastructural changes in egg albumen subjected to heating, whipping and freezing with and without functional additives. Thesis, Cornell University, 141 pp. (*Bull. Int. Inst. Refrig.* **56** (1976) 2, Abstr. No. 76–0663).

M.J. Miles, V.J. Morris and M.A. O'Neill, Gellan gum, in *Gums and Stabilisers for the Food Industry 2: Application of Hydrocolloids*, ed. G.O. Phillips, Pergamon Press, Oxford (1984) 485–98.

National Starch and Chemical Corporation (C.W. Chiu), Potato starch product. US Patent 4:228:199 (En). A.X.

National Starch and Chemical Corporation (C.W. Chiu), Tapioc starch. US Patent 4:229:489 (En). A.X.

D.B. Nelson, C.J.B. Smit and R.R. Wiles, Commercially important pectic substances, in *Food Colloids*, ed. H.D. Graham, (1977) 418–37.

San-Ei Chemical Industries Ltd (S. Ohashi and K. Fujiwara), Gelling agent containing low-methoxyl pectin. Japanese patent 28:087:78 (Ja). A.

G.R. Sanderson and R.C. Clark, Gellan gum, a new gelling polysaccharide, in *Gums and Stabilisers for the Food Industry 2: Application of Hydrocolloids*. ed. G.O. Phillips, Pergamon Press, Oxford (1984) 201–10.

Sanofi Bio Industries. *Hydrocolloids.*

L. Saulnier and J.F. Thibault, Extraction and characterisation of pectic substances from pulp of grape berries. *Carbohydr. Polym.* **7** (1987) 329–3.

W.J. Sime, The practical utilisation of alginates in food gelling systems, in *Gums and Stabilisers for the Food Industry 2: Application of Hydrocolloids*. ed. G.O. Phillip, Pergamon Press, Oxford (1984) 177–8.

5 Oils, fats, milk and related products

J.N.S. HANCOCK, R. EARLY and P.D. WHITEHEAD

5.1 Oils and fats: introduction

Fats form a major part of the human diet. They provide energy and nourishment and some of them also play an essential role in the body's metabolism for the production of prostaglandins. As a means of improving the acceptability of other types of food, they have a multitude of uses. They are a major component of many forms of confectionery, and as confectionery production becomes more sophisticated so too must our methods of production and modification of oils and fats.

The main sources of oils and fats are land and marine animals and the fruits and seeds of vegetable matter. The use of land-animal fat in sugar confectionery is restricted to milk fat, and virtually no marine oil is used. Most confectionery today is manufactured from vegetable fats. It is traditional to refer to fats which are liquid at room temperature as oils.

5.2 The chemistry of oils and fats

The main constituents of oils and fats are triglycerides, which are formed by the combination of a glycerol molecule with three fatty acid molecules. In the triglyceride model shown in Figure 5.1, R_1, R_2 and R_3 represent the three

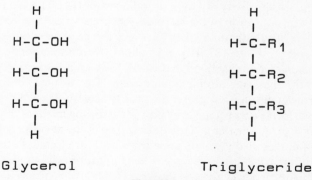

Figure 5.1.

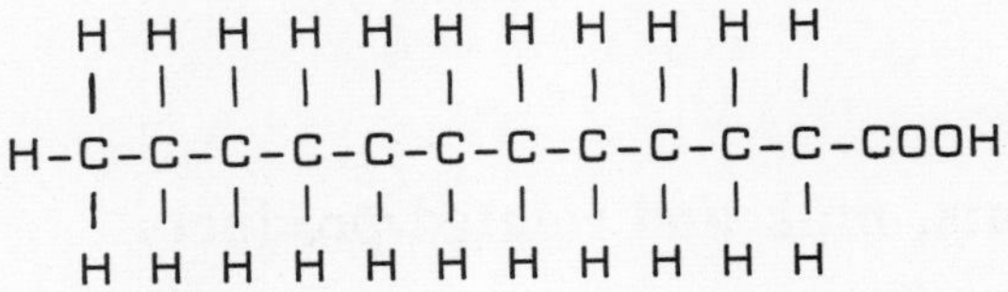

```
     H  H  H  H  H  H  H  H  H  H  H
     |  |  |  |  |  |  |  |  |  |  |
 H - C - C - C - C - C - C - C - C - C - C - C - COOH
     |  |  |  |  |  |  |  |  |  |  |
     H  H  H  H  H  H  H  H  H  H  H
```

A saturated fatty acid

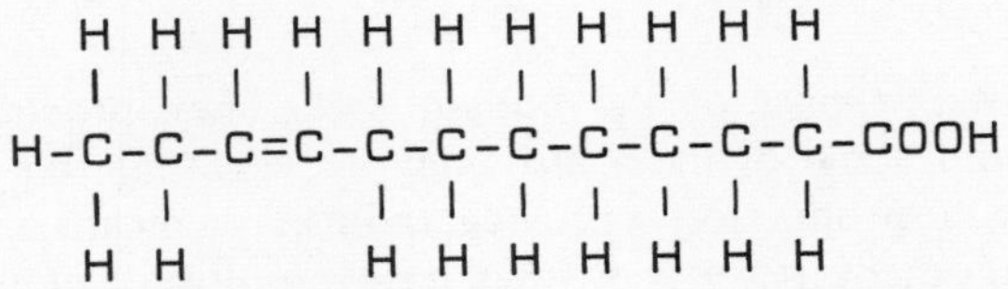

```
     H  H  H  H  H  H  H  H  H  H  H
     |  |  |  |  |  |  |  |  |  |  |
 H - C - C - C = C - C - C - C - C - C - C - C - COOH
     |  |           |  |  |  |  |  |  |
     H  H           H  H  H  H  H  H  H
```

An unsaturated fatty acid

Figure 5.2.

fatty acid molecules. It is the variation in the amounts of each fatty acid and their position within the tryglycerides which determine the differences in chemical and physical properties between oils and fats. For this reason, fatty acids and their properties will be considered before triglycerides themselves.

5.2.1   *Fatty acids*

Fatty acids are essentially straight hydrocarbon chains with a single carboxylic acid group attached to one end (Figure 5.2). These chains may or may not contain any double bonds. When two or more double bonds occur, the fatty acids are said to be polyunsaturated. Similarly, with one double bond they are monounsaturated and with no double bonds they are saturated. A commonly quoted property of a fat is its iodine value (IV). This is a measure of the degree of unsaturation of the fat and there are several standard methods [1–3]. Triglycerides with an IV of 86 have an average of one double bond per chain, and with an IV of 172 they have about two double bonds per chain.

The inclusion of a double bond in the carbon chain allows many structural alternatives for the same atomic composition. This isomerisation plays an important role in the physical properties of fatty acids and fats. A double bond may have two forms according to the positional arrangement of the hydrogen atoms on each side of the bond (Figure 5.3). The *cis* form is the natural form occurring in unmodified fats, but some *trans* acids are found, for example in milk fat and marine oils. The *trans* configuration causes less physical disruption to the carbon chain, and thus *trans* acids are less reactive and have a higher melting point than their *cis* equivalent.

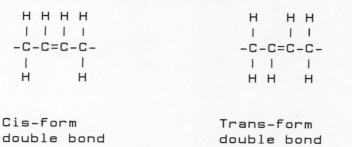

Figure 5.3.

Most natural fatty acids have an even number of carbon atoms in their chain and are systematically named depending on the number of double bonds and the relative position of the double bonds. However, they also have trivial names, which are usually derived from the major source of the acids. They are described by a shorthand system in which the number of carbon atoms follows the letter C, and the number of double bonds is placed after a colon following this number. Thus linoleic acid which has 18 carbon atoms in the chain and two double bonds is written as C18:2. Table 5.1 shows the fatty acid composition of the oils most widely used in confectionery fats, together with the common names of the various acids.

It can be seen that most natural fats contain both saturated and unsaturated fatty acids. For saturated fatty acids, the longer the carbon chain, the higher the melting point. For unsaturated acids, the more double bonds in the chain, the lower the melting point. The melting points of triglycerides are considered later.

An important chemical property of fatty acids is their susceptibility to oxidation or rancidity. During storage, the unsaturated fatty acids in an oil will react with the oxygen in the surrounding atmosphere to form a hydroperoxide. The hydroperoxides are not directly responsible for off-flavours, but they do break down further to give aldehydes and ketones, and it is these substances which cause the rancid odours and flavours. Thus, for a recently processed oil, the quantity of hydroperoxides present is a guide to its degree of oxidation. The peroxide value (PV) is the most commonly used method of measuring this quantity [1–3]. The usual PV specification for a fresh oil is less than 1 milliequivalent per kilogram of oil. This can be mis-leading in an old oil or an oil which has been mistreated, and in this case the anisidine value should be measured. It follows from the above that oils with a greater degree of unsaturation (that is, a higher iodine value) are more prone to oxidative rancidity. The rate of oxidation is increased if pro-oxidants such as small amounts of iron or copper are present. A popular method for measuring the stability or resistance to oxidation of an oil is using the Rancimat apparatus [4].

The oxidation process is a chain reaction, and it accelerates once it has

Table 5.1 Typical fatty acid composition (%) of the major oils used in confectionery

Name of fatty acid	Nomenclature	Milk fat	Cocoa butter	Palm oil	Soyabean oil	Rapeseed oil	Coconut oil	Palm kernel oil	Maize oil
Butyric	C4:0	4							
Caproic	C6:0	3							
Caprylic	C8:0	1					7	3	
Capric	C10:0	3					7	4	
Lauric	C12:0	3					48	48	
Myristic	C14:0	10		1			18	16	
Palmitic	C16:0	26	28	45	11	5	9	9	12
Stearic	C18:0	13	33	5	4	2	3	2	2
Oleic	C18:1	25	35	39	22	59	6	15	32
Linoleic	C18:2	3	3	10	54	21	2	2	51
Linolenic	C18:3	1	1		8	10			1
Arachidic	C20:0								
Gadoleic	C20:1					2			
Behenic	C22:0								
Erucic	C22:1					1			
Lignoceric	C24:0								
Others		8			1				

reached a certain stage. The time before this acceleration occurs is called the introduction period. The Rancimat enables this induction period to be measured. The test is usually carried out at 100 or 120°C to accelerate the oxidation process, giving induction periods of between 2 and 50 h. It is essential to investigate the correlation between the shelf life of a confectionery product and the Rancimat result of the oil used. This is time-consuming but necessary to ensure that the correct induction period is being specified.

Oils should be stored in the dark with minimum exposure to the atmosphere and at the minimum temperature required to keep them fluid, usually about 10 degrees Celsius above the final melting point. A reduction in the rate of development of rancidity can also be achieved by the use of antioxidants such as BHA and BHT. These seem to work by blocking the propagation process and thus extending the induction period. There are antioxidants, e.g. tocopherols and tocotrienols, which occur naturally in oils and fats. These can be present at quite high levels in vegetable fats but are partially removed during refining and modification, which are discussed later.

There is a second type of rancidity which can lead to problems in the manufacture and storage of confectionery. Hydrolytic rancidity is the breaking down of a tryglyceride in the presence of moisture and a catalyst to produce free fatty acids (FFA). The presence of free fatty acids lead to poor flavours. In particular, free lauric acid gives rise to the characteristic 'soapy' flavour which has a very low taste threshold. Enzymes often act as catalysts for hydrolysis and care should be taken to ensure they are absent when using coconut or palm kernel oils.

5.2.2 Triglycerides

As previously mentioned, it is the amount of each fatty acid and their distribution within an oil that determines its properties. The amount of any particular fatty acid in an oil can be found quite easily using the technique of gas–liquid chromatography. It is on this basis that oils are classified into laurics (coconut, palm kernel), palm oil, soft oils (soyabean, rapeseed, sunflower, etc.) and vegetable butters. The distribution of the fatty acids amongst the triglycerides of a fat is more difficult and requires special analytical techniques [5].

If a triglyceride has three fatty acids which are identical, it is called a simple triglyceride. When they are dissimilar, it is called a mixed triglyceride. A shorthand notation consisting of three letters is commonly used to describe triglycerides. POS, for example, has palmitic acid and stearic acid in the outside or 1,3 positions and oleic acid in the middle or 2 position. Each triglyceride type has its own melting point, the ones with three saturated fats obviously being in the higher range. As natural fats are made up of many triglyceride types, it can be seen that they do not have a single melting point, but gradually become more fluid as the temperature is increased. For this reason, it is usual to describe the melting of a fat by expressing its solid fat content at various temperatures. For confectionery fats, the common temperatures of interest are 20, 30, 35 and 40°C, as these include ambient storage temperatures and palate temperature. The solid fat content (SFC) of fats can be measured quite easily using pulsed nuclear magnetic resonance techniques [6].

The physical structure of a triglyceride molecule in the solid phase resembles that of a 'chair'. This structure can be packed in several ways as shown in Figure 5.4. These different packing modes, together with variations in the tilt angle and chain orientation, lead to several stable structures for most triglycerides. This phenomenon is called polymorphism. X-ray diffraction has

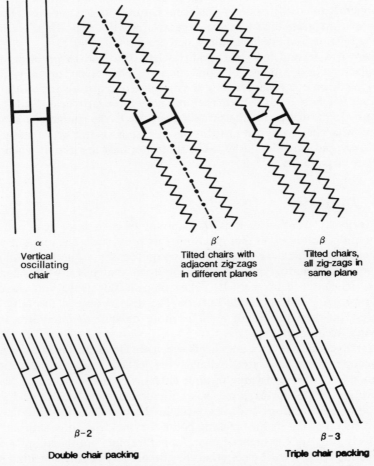

| α | β′ | β |
| Vertical oscillating chair | Tilted chairs with adjacent zig-zags in different planes | Tilted chairs, all zig-zags in same plane |

β-2

β-3

Double chair packing   Triple chair packing

Figure 5.4 Schematic diagrams comparing the polymorphic forms of triglycerides. (From ref. 7.)

been used to identify three main crystallisation patterns. These have been named the alpha (α), beta prime (β'), and beta (β). The α-form is formed by shock cooling and is unstable and becomes transformed into the β'-form in a short time. The most stable form is usually the β-form. The time of transition from β' to β can vary from days to months depending on the type of triglyceride, its processing and storage conditions. This β' to β change is the cause of fat bloom in chocolate and other products. A fat with a preponderance of one triglyceride or closely similar triglycerides tends to be β-stable. If a fat has a broad range of fatty acids present, it tends to be β'-stable. The fact that nature produces such a wide variety of fatty materials allows the oils and fats technologist a wide choice of materials for his particular purpose. The processes used to manufacture oils on a large scale will now be described.

5.3 The production of oils and fats

The production of oils for use as ingredients in foods or for use as a cooking medium was an ancient craft. Today it is a sophisticated, highly technical

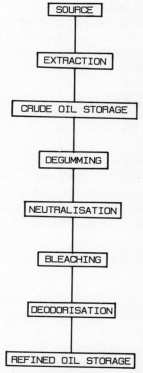

Figure 5.5 The usual processing stages for a refined vegetable oil.

process. It should be considered as a branch of chemical engineering, although this is not the image the food industry likes to project. The unit processes used in production are usually minor variations on a common theme. The sequence is shown in Figure 5.5, and a brief description of each stage is given below.

5.3.1 Extraction

There are two main methods of extracting vegetable oils and fats from the fruits and seeds of plants. These are (1) physically via mechanical expelling, and (2) chemically using solvent extraction techniques; or a combination of both methods may be used. Before either of these stages, the seeds are cleaned to remove dirt, stones and foreign materials. This can be a dusty process, and care should be taken to control the dust as this may contain bacteria. This is particularly important when handling cocoa beans. It is also usual to reduce the size of large seeds to aid the oil-removal process.

In the physical method, the seeds are squeezed in a fluted screw press, where the cell walls are broken and the oil released. This can be done using warm or cold seeds. Although higher yields and greater control can be achieved using warm seeds, there is an increasing market for cold-pressed oils, which are seen as more nutritious by some market sectors.

Solvent extraction involves the recirculation of a solvent (usually light paraffinic petroleum fractions) through a bed of seeds which have been flaked to increase their surface area. Various designs of equipment are used, but in all cases careful control of the solvent is required. Following extraction, the solvent must be removed from the oil-rich solution and from the resulting solid material or meal. It is usual to combine the mechanical and solvent processes as pressing becomes inefficient when the oil content drops below about 10%. This also economises on the more expensive solvent processes which are employed. Solvent-extracted oil can be more difficult to process, as it usually contains more non-fat components, which have to be removed. The material which results from the extraction processes is called crude oil. Crude oils contain many non-oil materials, are highly coloured and have strong flavours and smells. Refining is the term given to the combined processes of converting the crude oil into the clear bright and bland material required by the confectioner.

5.3.2 Degumming

The crude oils contain a class of substances called 'gums', which are the phospholipids and colloidal proteinaceous material from the cell walls of the plant. If they are not removed, they can settle out later during processing and storage and can cause problems during subsequent modification stages. They can also produce high refining losses. However, after a simple and inexpensive treatment, the gums which are removed can be sold as commercial lecithins.

Soyabean oil typically contains 3% phospholipids. About 1% of water is intimately mixed with the oil. The mixture is heated to about 90°C and held for about 15 min, during which time the phosphatides absorb water and become insoluble in the oil. These can now be removed using centrifugal separation. Some of the phosphatides in the oil will have become stabilised and are not hydratable. The addition of a small amount of phosphoric or citric acid (about 0.5%) will enable these to be removed, although the mechanism is not yet fully understood. After the degumming process, the phosphorus content of the oil should be below 10 ppm. This process also has the advantage of removing metal ions, thus improving the stability of the finished oil.

5.3.3 Neutralisation

Following degumming, the material is neutralised to remove the free fatty acids, which are present at levels between 0.5 and 6% in most crude oils. This involves the addition of a slight excess of dilute alkali, usually sodium hydroxide at about 25°C to the oil. This converts the free fatty acids into soaps, which are oil-insoluble (Figure 5.6).

After heating the mixture to about 90°C to break the emulsion, the soaps are removed by centrifuging. The neutral oil is further water-washed to remove the final traces of soap to less than 50 ppm. Some pigments are also removed by the neutralisation stage.

5.3.4 Bleaching

The purpose of the bleaching stage is to remove the majority of the colouring pigments that are present in the oil. This is achieved by mixing between 1 and 2% of bleaching earth with the oil. Bleaching earth is a naturally occurring montmorillonite clay which has been acid-washed to increase the surface area and alter the pore size. The mixture is maintained at 110°C for about 45 min. During this time, the pigments are adsorbed onto the surface of the earth, which is then removed by mechanical filtration. In modern plants, efficient leaf filters are used in tandem to maintain continuity. The colour of oils is usually measured using a comparison with standard colours or slides, e.g. the Lovibond system [8]. Measurement of the colour at this stage is not always useful, as some may be removed during deodorisation. Some trace metals are

$$RCOOH \quad + \quad NaOH \quad \longrightarrow \quad RCOONa \quad + \quad H_2O$$

| Fatty acid | Caustic soda | Sodium salt | Water |

Figure 5.6.

also removed during this bleaching process. It is important that the colours are removed if the oil is to be used in products in which the colour, or lack of colour, is an important parameter, e.g. salad cream.

5.3.5 *Deodorisation*

Deodorisation is the final stage of purification of an oil or fat. Its main purpose is to remove the impurities and byproducts which cause flavours and odours in the finished oil. It is these products, such as aldehydes, ketones, alcohols and hydrocarbons, etc., which cause the typical 'smell' of an oil refinery. The process is essentially one of steam distillation under vacuum. The temperature at which it takes place depends on the type of oil being processed and varies between 200 and 270°C but can be as low as 150°C for cocoa butter processing. The vessel is under a vacuum of about 1–6 mmHg during the process, which ensures that further oxidation does not take place. The bubbling of steam through the body of the material ensures a good concentration gradient between the liquid and the gas and leads to rapid removal of the volatile components. Most free fatty acids are removed at higher temperatures than the odiferous compounds, so the FFA content is a good measure of deodorised oil quality. The thermal treatment during deodorisation also tends to bleach the oil, as any carotenoid pigments are broken down and removed. Most modern deodorisers are of the continuous or semicontinuous design. Great care is taken on the recovery of energy and the hot oil is usually used to heat the incoming oil. The cooling of the finished product is also a requirement before it is again exposed to oxygen. Citric acid is usually added to this finished product as a final stage in scavenging any free metal ions which might act as pro-oxidants.

In some oils, particularly in palm oil refining, the neutralisation stage is omitted and the first stage of the deodoriser is used to deacidify the oil. This method is called 'physical' refining and reduces the losses in the overall processing of the oil.

The deodorised oil is then ready for use by food manufacturers or for packing for direct sale to the consumer. It should be clear and bright and have very little taste or smell. The functionality, i.e. the physical properties, is the most important attribute of an oil or fat. Consequently there has been much effort put into modifying the properties to suit the needs of the manufacturers.

5.4 Modification

The major modification methods range from simple blending operations to the complicated process of biomodification. This latter area is still in its infancy and has some major obstacles to overcome. It will require large financial investments, and these may not be made until the legal status of the modified oils is determined. However, there is little doubt that its use will increase as the mechanisms involved become clearer.

5.4.1 Blending

The simplest form of modification of oils and fats is blending. This might be done with fats of similar properties such as soya and rape, or with fats of

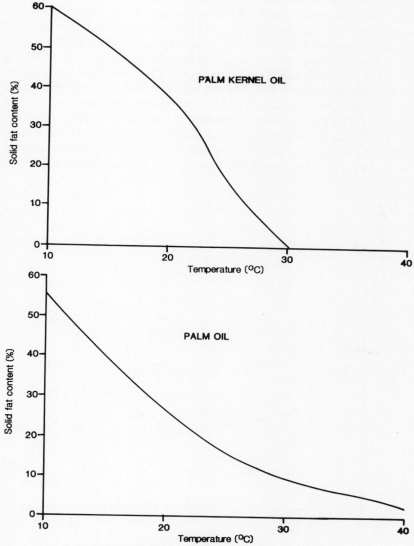

Figure 5.7   The melting profiles of palm kernel oil and palm oil.

different properties. This can produce some interesting effects. Let us consider the blending of palm kernel oil and palm oil. Palm kernel oil is a lauric fat with medium-length fatty acid chains and a short melting range. Palm oil has longer chain fatty acids and a higher slip melting point and longer melting range. Their melting curves are shown in the usual fashion in Figure 5.7. The fact that these fats have large molecular size differences means that they are incompatible, and the long range order exhibited by solids is frequently interrupted in the mixture of triglycerides present. This leads to the blend being softer than one would expect from the sum of the components. This softening effect is called a eutectic. A neat way of demonstrating the effect is to construct an isosolid diagram as described by Rossell [9] and Timms [10].

From the solid fat contents of various blends, the temperatures at which the blends have particular solids are extrapolated. These temperatures are then plotted against the composition of the blends to produce an isosolid diagram. The result of this transformation for the palm kernel/palm oil mixture is shown in Figure 5.8. This may be viewed in the same way as a contour map. The closer together the lines, the steeper the melting rate, and conversely, the wider apart the lines, the longer and flatter the melting profile. If no eutectic effect is present, then the lines would be straight and simply join the relevant

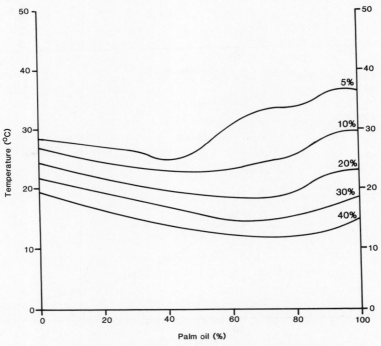

Figure 5.8 The isosolid diagram for blends of palm kernel oil and palm oil.

temperatures at each of the vertical axes, i.e. the component fats. A drop towards the baseline indicates a softening of the mixture. Thus considering the 5% isosolid line, this being roughly equivalent to the slip melting point, it can be seen that there is a gradual reduction as the harder palm oil is added until a 50/50 blend is reached. At this stage there is a rapid increase in hardness to the 70/30 blend, where it flattens before rising to the 100% figure. In using such a mixture, care must be taken not to use blends which change solids profile rapidly with a slight change in composition. Such a blend would be very sensitive to slight changes in proportions or in the addition of rework. However, in other areas, the eutectic effect of blending can usefully be employed to soften harder fats and reduce their melting range.

5.4.2 Hydrogenation

Hydrogenation is currently the most widely used modification process. It has a history going back to the early days of margarine manufacture. It is essentially the addition of hydrogen to the double bonds of fatty acids in the presence of a catalyst, usually nickel. This reduction in the degree of unsaturation of the oil means that liquid oils are converted to semisolid, plastic fats. The hydrogenation reaction is usually carried out as a batch process, although continuous hydrogenation equipment is available. In this equipment, gaseous hydrogen, liquid oil and the solid catalyst are brought together. The rate of hydrogenation depends on the nature of the oil, the activity and concentration of the catalyst, and the temperature, pressure and degree of agitation maintained in the vessel. The reactions which occur during hydrogenation are complex and take place simultaneously.

As well as the stepwise transformation of linolenic to linoleic to oleic to stearic acid, there is isomerism of *cis* to *trans* form. The positional movement of double bonds along the fatty acid chain also occurs. *Trans* acid formation usually occurs to a greater or lesser degree. The detection of *trans* acids generally indicates that hydrogenation has been used to produce a fat, although it should be noted that up to about 2% *trans* acids can be produced during refining. The net rates at which the various hydrogenation products are produced can be used to describe the performance of a particular catalyst. The ratios of these rates are called the selectivity of the catalyst. A detailed description of the theory and practice of hydrogenation is given by Patterson [11].

The skill of the refiner is to select a catalyst and process parameters which produce a hydrogenated product with the desired composition and character. For example, the use of a catalyst which has been deliberately poisoned with sulphur, together with a low hydrogen pressure and a high temperature, will achieve the production of the *trans* isomers of the oil. Thus, a harder fat with a shorter melting range can be produced. This is useful for producing hardened lauric-type properties from soya oil or rapeseed oil, thus making them suitable as toffee fats. The melting range of fats can also be shortened by the use of further modification techniques.

5.4.3   Fractionation

During fractionation, an oil is split into its higher melting components, the stearin, and its lower melting components, the olein. This can take place naturally over a long period of time, as originally occurred during the 'winterisation' process, or it can be achieved using several processes involving crystallisation and separation.

In the simplest process, dry fractionation, the oil is cooled at a carefully controlled rate to induce crystallisation, and the crystals filtered off on a continuous-belt filter such as that designed by Tirtiaux [12]. This process is used widely to produce palm olein and palm stearin from palm oil. The olein is a very good frying oil, while the stearin is used to give plasticity to margarines without using *trans* fats. Fractionation is also applied to butter oil in many European countries. Other methods of fractionation include solvent fractionation and detergent fractionation processes. These methods are more capital-intensive but give improved yields, reduced processing times and increased purity. They are particularly beneficial for triglycerides of long-chain fatty acids, which are higher in solids at the temperature of fractionation. The production of high-quality cocoa butter equivalents requires sharp melting fractions of exotic oils, and these are best produced using solvent fractionation.

Winterisation is a form of dry fractionation in which a small quantity of solid fat is removed from a large amount of liquid oil. Here again, mechanical filtration systems are usually employed. This process is applied to liquid oils which may cloud during storage at cool temperatures to improve consumer acceptance. In the USA, large quantities of partially hardened soyabean oil are winterised in this way.

5.4.4   Interesterification

Interesterification involves heating the fat at about 100°C in a vacuum with a catalyst such as sodium methoxide. It results in a random arrangement of fatty acids among the triglycerides. This 'randomisation' produces a fat with different physical properties. This can be shown by considering the isosolid diagram of the previous example of blends of palm kernel oil and palm oil. The results for the interesterified blends are shown in Figure 5.9. It can be seen that the isotherms follow similar curves but are spread more widely in the 70–100% palm oil region. This extended range means that the fat has a flatter melting profile and is in its plastic region for a greater temperature range. This is useful for producing spreads and shortenings. By changing the distribution of the fatty acids on the triglycerides, the natural polymorphic form of the crystals

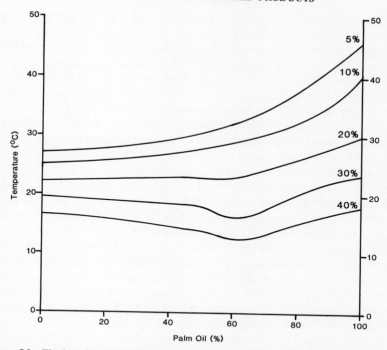

Figure 5.9 The isosolid diagram for interesterified blends of palm kernel oil and palm oil.

can be changed. Thus a β'-forming fat can be produced, which has smaller crystal size and greater liquid oil-holding properties. Again this can be useful in manufacturing spreads. Sometimes a steeper melting curve is obtained, for example when interesterification is applied to a blend of palm kernel oil with a hard fat such as palm stearin. Such fats are used to manufacture chocolate-flavoured coatings for confectionery countlines.

It is common for all these fat modification processes to be used consecutively to produce a fat of the desired properties. If the product is replacing a high-priced one then it is likely that it can carry the higher processing costs within the price structure.

5.5 Selection of fats for confectionery uses

The most important features when considering the use of a fat are listed below:

(1) Textural performance during 'eat'.
(2) Flavour during 'eat'.
(3) Shelf-life of product.
(4) Functionality during manufacture.
(5) Price.

The textural performance during eat is probably the most important aspect as it will play an important part in the consumer's decision to repurchase the product. Most fats are used in modern versions of classic applications where the textural performance depends on the amount of solid fat present at various temperatures. A cream, for example, should melt rapidly in the mouth giving a liquid texture during mastication. Thus, a short melting range is required, which is fully melted well below body temperature (37°C). These properties are well displayed by palm kernel oil, the classic creaming fat. On the other hand, toffee fats require some plasticity to provide chewiness and this is achieved by having a longer melting range which will end slightly above body temperature. This was originally provided by using butter. However, to reduce the price of the product, it was common to blend in some hardened palm kernel oil.

For most confectionery fats, the solids at 5°C intervals between 20 and 40°C should be examined. A range for the solids values at these temperatures should be agreed between the customer and the supplier. The use of pulsed nuclear magnetic resonance (NMR) techniques as described previously has become the industry standard for acceptance testing. These SFCs provide much more information than a simple slip melting point, which is also time-consuming and less reliable. A further major consideration is the crystallisation stability of the fat. The change from one polymorph of a fat to another results in textural changes which can be considerable.

Most fats are required to be bland in flavour when used in confectionery, as the flavour arises from the other ingredients. However, some fats have a residual flavour even after they have been well-refined. This can be an advantage or a drawback depending on the use. Again a tasting method and degree of flavour should be agreed and incorporated into the product specification. It is one of the simplest and quickest tests to do, and all fats should be tasted on arrival at the user site.

Most products are manufactured with a particular shelf life in mind. This may be as short as 3 months for some cake-like products or up to a year in the case of toffees. Here again, the type of fat and degree of saturation of the fatty acids must be considered. Highly unsaturated fatty acids are prone to oxidative rancidity. Lauric-type fats give rise to soapy-type flavours during hydrolytic rancidity. Some fats, e.g. palm, contain large amounts of natural antioxidants such as tocopherols. The addition of other ingredients which contain natural antioxidants can improve the stability of the whole system. However, as previously stated, careful correlation of these results with the results of long-term keeping tests must be carried out. Also, the presence in the oil of pro-oxidants such as copper and iron must be kept to a minimum and target levels and maxima should be included in the specification. To ensure that manufacturing and packing speeds can be maintained during production, the sensitivity of the processing stages to slight changes in solids profile or rate of crystallisation should be monitored. It is usually possible to define a certain set of conditions which must be met for successful processing. These may only be empirical but, even so, if discussed with the fat manufacturer in the early stages of product development, they should enable the most suitable fat to be provided.

Finally, and sometimes most importantly, the price of the fat blend in a recipe must be considered. There are three main market areas for confectionery fats (apart from the cocoa market), viz. laurics, soft oils and palm oil. It should be the aim of all product development departments to have a library of recipes for each product. Each recipe should use a fat or fat blend from each of the market sectors. This will allow the purchasing department to have the full flexibility to take advantage of price movements within the markets. Unfortunately, the steepness of the melting profile of palm kernel oil cannot be economically reproduced in rapeseed oil. Thus, the functional quality of a product will be a compromise between the perfect 'eat' and market forces. Here, other interpersonal skills are required by the confectioner.

5.6 Milk and related products: introduction

For countless generations milk has played an important, and possibly incomparable, part in the human diet. It has served as a liquid food and has been fermented both accidentally and intentionally to make products such as yoghurt and cheese. In recent years however, developments in dairy science and technology have enabled the production of a wide range of ingredients for the food manufacturer, by the processing of milk and the separation and modification of milk components.

Whilst much development work has sought to tailor functional ingredients for use, for example, by the bakery, meat and ready meals sectors of the industry, the requirements of the confectionery industry are by comparison no less important. In fact, it would be no overstatement to say that the confectionery industry constitutes one of the key markets for milk and milk-based ingredients.

By understanding the chemistry and functional properties of milk's various components, and by seeking to understand the functional needs of confectionery products, the dairy technologist works in partnership with the confectioner to develop ingredients which are nutritious, beneficial in their performance and cost-effective.

Also, it is important to consider that, while consumer awareness of additives and food ingredients has increased, in some instances an adverse perception has resulted. Milk ingredients are however perceived to be natural, and are held in high esteem by both manufacturer and consumer.

Thus milk and milk-based ingredients offer the confectioner considerable and diverse opportunities; and it is worth reflecting that some products, for example milk chocolate, toffee and caramel, would either not exist or pale by comparison without the inclusion of milk. This part of the chapter therefore seeks to impart to the reader some understanding of the chemistry and functional properties of milk, and also an appreciation of the use of various milk-based ingredients in sugar confectionery.

5.7 The composition of milk and functional properties of its major components

The nutritive value of milk and its various functional properties are intrinsically linked to the many components contained in this complex fluid.

For the food manufacturer the major components of milk, being milk fat, proteins and the milk sugar, lactose, are probably of greatest importance since most of the functional properties reside with these constituents. However, this is not to say that minor components such as calcium and phosphate are not functionally important. The typical composition of (whole) cow's milk is given in Table 5.2.

5.7.1 The milk fat

Whole milk is essentially an oil-in-water emulsion in which the milk fat forms a globular dispersion, stabilised by the so-called fat globule membrane. The membrane is composed, principally, of protein and phospholipids, and its function is to prevent the fat globules from flocculation and coalescence, and to protect the fat from enzyme action. The membrane does however contain various reactive substances and enzymes which influence deteriorative reactions such as lipolysis and autoxidation in milk products which contain membrane material. The total area of membrane is significant, being approximately $80 \, m^2/l$ [13].

The milk fat is comprised of numerous different lipids, of which 95–96% are triglycerides of fatty acids, the remainder being significantly diglycerides, monoglycerides, cholesterol, free fatty acids, phospholipids and cerebrosides.

Table 5.2 The composition of whole milk (principal components)

	Grams per 100 g
Water	87.8
Fat	3.9
Protein	3.6
Casein	2.7
Whey proteins	0.9
Lactose	4.6
Calcium (mg)	115
Vitamin A (μg)	53
Vitamin B_2 (mg)	0.17
Vitamin D (μg)	0.03

Although the melting points of the milk fat triglycerides range from -40 to $72°C$, the final melting point is $37°C$, since the higher melting triglycerides dissolve in the liquid fat.

Milk fat produced during the summer months is softer than that of winter production due to an increase in short-chain fatty acids, caused by different feed materials. Summer milk fat is also yellower than winter fat as a result of increased levels of the pigment β-carotene.

For many confectionery uses the wide-ranging melting profile of milk fat represents few problems. However, if harder or softer milk fats are required, these can be achieved by the process of fractionation. Dry fractionation is most commonly used, in which the triglycerides in liquid butter oil are crystallised at different temperatures and separated with a vacuum filter, with both the flavour and colour concentrating in the soft fractions whilst the hard fractions become paler and blander.

Of the many functional properties of milk fat (Table 5.3), possibly the most important is the unique flavour, which is widely exploited in the manufacture of products with richness and connotations of quality, which cannot be achieved with other fats. The principal components of milk fat which are responsible for flavour are:

(1) γ- and δ-hydroxyacids.
(2) β-ketoacids.
(3) Lower fatty acids up to C12.
(4) Some unsaturated acids.

The hydroxyacid triglycerides rearrange spontaneously to give the highly flavoursome γ- and δ-lactones [14]. This occurs slowly at low temperature, even at $-10°C$, whilst at $180°C$ complete conversion occurs within 2 h.

The β-ketoacid triglycerides are converted to methyl ketones, whose flavour is reminiscent of blue vein cheese, by heat and water, although the conditions required are more severe than for lactone formation.

The lower fatty acids which can give a strong undesirable flavour are released by heat, or commonly lipolysis. At levels of 100 ppm or greater the presence of C4, 6, 8, 10 and 12 acids would denote lipolytic rancidity, whilst at lower levels they contribute to the desirable flavour of butter.

Table 5.3 The functional properties of milk fat

- Air incorporation
- Antistaling: through mosisture dispersion and retention
- Creaming
- Flavour
- Flavour carrier
- Gloss
- Heat transfer medium
- Layering
- Shortening

The unsaturated fatty acids in butter are, importantly, arachidonic (20:4), linoleic (18:2) and oleic (18:1) and their isomers. They are present in significant quantities, and their oxidation, initiated by OH radical from copper and ascorbic acid or by enzymic activity, can yield desirable flavours or, if in excess, characteristic off-flavours. Thus, premixes containing milk fat should not be stored in copper vessels for any length of time before cooking.

5.7.2   The milk proteins

Of all the components of milk, the proteins exhibit the most diverse functionality and have the greatest potential for use as food ingredients. The major milk protein (75–85% of the total protein) is casein, which exists in micellar form, of macromolecular size. The micelle is composed of various caseins, α-casein, α_s-casein, β-casein, κ-casein and γ-casein, bonded with Ca^{2+} to form calcium caseinate, which is further stabilised with calcium phosphate, magnesium and citrate ions.

The isoelectric point of casein is 4.6, and the simplest definition of casein is 'that protein which is precipitated from skimmed milk at 20°C by acidification to pH 4.6' (the normal pH of fresh skimmed milk being 6.8, for comparison). The supernatant which occurs when casein is precipitated contains several proteins, collectively called the whey proteins. Chemically the caseins can be readily differentiated from the whey proteins since each casein polypeptide contains at least one ester-bound phosphate group and the whey proteins contain none. However, for the food manufacturer the functional distinction between the two groups of proteins is more important.

The whey proteins (approximately 18% of the total protein) are mostly globular proteins which, unlike casein, are easily heat-denatured. The major whey proteins are α-lactalbumin and β-lactoglobulin, whilst the minor proteins are bovine serum albumin, a major component of blood serum; immunoglobulins, antibodies synthesised in response to antigens foreign to the cow; lactoferrin and transferrin, iron-binding proteins; and the proteose–peptone fractions, believed to be derived from the fat globule membrane and β-casein.

Table 5.4 illustrates the functional properties of casein and the whey proteins, which influence the choice of ingredient for a particular application.

Various methods, such as ultrafiltration and ion-exchange chromatography, now exist for the separation from milk, modification and fractionation of milk proteins. Thus the range of milk protein ingredients available to the industry includes acid casein, rennet casein, caseinates, casein–whey protein co-precipitates, whey protein isolates and whey protein fractions. Additionally, by careful control of the temperature and holding time used in the preheat treatment of skimmed milk, prior to evaporation and spray drying, the degree of whey protein denaturation in skimmed milk powder can be controlled. Thus powders conforming to the American Dried Milk Institute

Table 5.4 The functional properties of casein and whey proteins

Function	Milk proteins	
	Casein	Whey proteins
Heat denturation	0	+ + +
Heat gellation	0	+ + +
Emulsifying capacity	+ + +	+ +
Emulsion stability (hot)	+ + +	+ +
Emulsion stability (cold)	+ + +	+ + +
Foam stability	+ +	+ +
Viscosity	+ + +	+
Sensitivity to low pH	+ + +	+
Sensitivity to Ca^{2+}	+ + +	+

Key:
High   + + +   Low   +
Moderate   + +   None   0

Table 5.5 ADMI classification of skimmed milk powder and preheat conditions for powder production

ADMI category	Undenatured whey protein per g powder	Temperature/holding time
Low heat	> 6.0 mg	72–75°C/15–30 s
Medium heat	1.51–5.99 mg	85-105°C/1–2 min
High heat	< 1.50 mg	120-135°C/2–3 min

(ADMI) classification of skimmed milk powder can be manufactured, as shown in Table 5.5.

The benefits of milk proteins in sugar confectionery are manifold. It is particularly their role in forming and stabilising emulsions, stabilising foams and influencing viscosity through thickening and gelling which makes these proteins so valuable.

5.7.3 Lactose

In nature, lactose is found only in milk. It is a distinctive sugar, being less sweet than sucrose (Table 5.6) and it has unique physicochemical properties. Lactose is a disaccharide which yields D-glucose and D-galactose on hydrolysis and can be designated as 4-O-β-D-galactopyranosyl-D-glucopyranose. It occurs in either of two crystalline forms, or as a non-crystalline amorphous glass.

Of the crystalline forms, α-lactose monohydrate ($C_{12}H_{22}O_{11} \cdot H_2O$) is crystallised from supersaturated solutions at temperatures below 93.5°C, and this is the form of the ordinary commercial lactose most commonly used by the food industry.

The other crystalline form, β-lactose anhydride, is crystallised from supersaturated solutions at temperatures above 93.5°C. Amorphous lactose

Table 5.6 The relative sweetening powers of concentrations (%) of lactose and other sugars

Lactose	Sucrose	Dextrose	Fructose
1.90	0.5	0.89	0.42
3.46	1.0	1.84	0.76
6.54	2.0	3.57	1.66
15.74	5.0	8.25	4.19
25.92	10.0	13.86	8.62
34.60	15.0	20.00	12.97

Table 5.7 The functional properties of lactose

- Low sweetening power (27–39% of sucrose)
- Humectant
- Browning (Maillard reaction and caramelisation)
- Flavour development (Maillard reaction and caramelisation)
- Flavour absorption
- Suppresses sucrose crystallisation
- Free-flow agent
- Increases dispersability of some foods
- Enhances emulsifying and creaming properties of shortenings

occurs when a lactose solution is rapidly dried, the product containing an equilibrium mixture of α- and β- lactose. α-Lactose monohydrate, which has a number of interesting functional properties (Table 5.7), is non-hygroscopic and is commonly used as an anticaking agent and flow agent. In contrast, amorphous lactose is hygroscopic and is therefore beneficial in pan coating; for example, the material to be coated, e.g. jellies, can be surface-moistened with syrup and panned in lactose powder to build a coat and seal the product. The lactose absorbs the troublesome moisture, holding it as water of crystallisation and giving the product a dry touch [15].

Probably one of the most important reasons for the use of milk or milk-based ingredients in sugar confectionery is colour and flavour development.

Lactose is a reducing sugar and reacts principally with the lysine residues of the milk proteins to give the brown pigmentation and characteristic flavour associated with cooked milk. The reaction, known as the Maillard reaction, is irreversible and occurs at a significant rate at temperatures in excess of 110°C.

At 180°C or higher, direct caramelisation of lactose will also yield colour and flavour, and both reactions are of importance to the confectioner, particularly in the manufacture of toffee and caramel.

5.8 The application of milk and milk-based ingredients

5.8.1 Sweetened condensed milks

Milk in its natural form is of limited use to the confectioner because of its high moisture content and consequent short shelf life. For example, a caramel recipe incorporating fresh milk would require extended boil times to remove the water, and this would lead to excessive colour generation, increased energy costs and the risk of inversion of sucrose in the recipe.

A solution could be to concentrate the milk solids by evaporation prior to use, but there are limits to which the solids can be increased before unmanageable viscosities, age gellation and the potential for lactose crystallisation occur. Typically, full cream milk can be concentrated to 45% solids and skimmed milk to 40% solids before these difficulties are encountered. However, at these concentrations the milk is still susceptible to microbiological spoilage and hence has a short shelf life of only several days. Also, the amount of moisture remaining makes it an unsuitable ingredient for use in caramel-type boilings.

By adding sucrose to milk prior to evaporation, much higher solids are achievable, and a sugar content of 62.5% or greater in the aqueous phase increases the osmotic pressure of the product, thus preventing most forms of microbiological spoilage. A shelf life of 12 weeks is typical provided storage conditions are cool and dry, and this product, well-known as sweetened condensed milk, has for many years been the most popular source of milk solids for the sugar confectionery industry.

In the manufacture of sweetened condensed milks, sucrose is dissolved in standardised milk (milk with a regulated fat content) and the mixture is pasteurised to destroy spoilage organisms and enzymes. The heat treatment will also influence the final viscosity of the product, which will be in the range of 20–50 poise.

Following pasteurisation the mix is concentrated to approximately 73% solids, to achieve the required sugar-in-water ratio, and may be homogenised as a further means of viscosity control.

At high solids the lactose becomes supersaturated, and if allowed to crystallise freely will produce large crystals which give the product a sandy texture. Microcrystalline lactose is therefore added to the concentrate to act as a seed, controlling the size of lactose crystals to below 30 μm.

Sweetened condensed skimmed milk, sweetened condensed semiskimmed milk and sweetened condensed whole milk are all used by the confectionery industry, typically in caramel, toffee and fudge manufacture, where they represent 10–30% of the premix weight. Compositions of the concentrates are given in Table 5.8.

The Maillard browning and caramelisation of the sugars in sweetened condensed milks during boiling is of obvious importance for colour and flavour development. However, the milk proteins in sweetened condensed milks contribute significantly to the emulsification of fats and give body, texture and mouthfeel to the final product.

Thus, the level of milk solids in a caramel is vital to the quality of the finished product; for example, low levels of milk in a cheap recipe can produce a product which is opaque, susceptible to hot flow during processing and cold

Table 5.8 The composition of milk-based concentrates

	Sweetened condensed skimmed milk	Half-cream sweetened condensed milk	Sweetened condensed milk	Novamel	Novatec	SDCO4
Fat	1% max	4% min	8% min	0.75%	0.75%	0.75%
Protein	10.7%	9.0%	8.1%	10.0%	8.0%	10.0%
Lactose	14.7%	13.3%	11.6%	6.0%	12.0%	13.0%
Glucose	—	—	—	11.0%	22.0%	23.0%
Galactose	—	—	—	11.0%	22.0%	23.0%
Sucrose	45.0%	45.0%	44.8%	30.0%	—	—
Ash	2.3%	2.1%	1.8%	2.0%	6.0%	3.0%
Total solids	73.0%	73.0%	74.0%	71.0%	71.0%	73.0%

flow during storage, and can result in stickiness, softness, inferior flavour and a poor-quality chew.

Additionally, if poor-quality sweetened condensed milk with large lactose crystals is used, there is little chance of the crystals redissolving during boiling, and they will therefore appear as coarse crystals in the caramel, subsequently causing premature graining of the product during storage.

In the manufacture of fudges, milk solids are important in producing the characteristic colour and flavour of fudge and controlling the texture and shelf life. Insufficient milk solids can cause the product to flow after manufacture and become unacceptably sticky.

5.8.2 Hydrolysed whey syrups

Whey, the byproduct of cheese manufacture, is a yellow/green opaque solution containing lactose, proteins, minerals and some lactic acid; the total solids content is typically 6.4%, of which 75% is lactose.

Whey is particularly prone to spoilage, as a consequence of its low solids and contamination with cheese starter organisms. It is therefore necessary to concentrate and spray dry whey in order to preserve its nutritional and functional value. Simple concentration of whey in order to increase the osmotic pressure and thus reduce the potential for spoilage is ineffective, as the low solubility of lactose ensures that lactose crystallisation occurs before the required concentration is achieved.

An alternative to spray drying is therefore to hydrolyse the lactose in whey to yield glucose and galactose, which are both more soluble and also sweeter than lactose. The increase in the solubility of the sugars in whey enables concentration to 72% total solids without the threat of crystallisation, and giving a shelf life of up to 12 weeks.

There are two basic methods of hydrolysing whey. One involves reacting free enzyme with the whey for a predetermined length of time, followed by heat treatment to destroy the enzyme. The alternative, and commercially more attractive, method is to immobilise the enzyme onto a suitable inert carrier. Corning Glass developed a procedure for the immobilisation of β-galactosidase onto silica beads during the early 1970s, and a continuous hydrolysis plant based upon this technology is now in operation in the UK.

Fresh-chilled cheddar cheese whey is pasteurised and fed into hydrolysis columns containing the immobilised enzyme. The degree of hydrolysis is controlled by the flow rate and the temperature within the columns; and following hydrolysis, the whey is demineralised by passing through ion-exchange media. At this stage the solids content of the lactose-hydrolysed whey is similar to the incoming whey and is therefore highly susceptible to microbiological spoilage. The whey is therefore heat-treated again before being fed to the evaporator for concentration, in a carefully controlled process to prevent denaturation of the whey proteins and consequent loss of functionality.

A range of hydrolysed whey syrups, collectively known as sweet dairy concentrates, can be manufactured with this process, and Table 5.8 illustrates the different compositions.

The syrups are of particular benefit to the confectionery industry as partial or total replacements for milk solids, as the ideal reactants for the Maillard reaction are present, i.e. the reducing sugars, glucose, galactose and lactose, and the whey proteins.

Up to 100% of sweetened condensed milk can be replaced by sweet dairy concentrates in enrobed fudges and caramels, and they are also ideal for deposited soft caramel in chocolate shells, since the caramel will be less viscous, allowing a lower depositing temperature, enabling burn-through of the shells to be avoided [15].

In recipes which are sensitive to mineral content, the partly demineralised SDCO4 can be used, whilst in caramels and fudges where more body or stand-up is required Novamel is one suitable replacement for sweetened condensed milk, since it contains a similar casein and sucrose content to sweetened condensed milk, and therefore provides similar functional properties. However, some process and recipe changes may be required when substituting Novamel for milk solids, as the increase in monosaccharides causes an elevation of the boiling point during processing, with an increase of between 1 and 2°C of the final boil temperature in order to maintain the required final moisture content.

There are however several advantages to be gained by using Novamel:

(1) Sweetened condensed milk is seeded with lactose to control the growth of large crystals, but Novamel and sweet dairy concentrates do not require lactose seeding because the remaining lactose is unsaturated within the syrup, and will not therefore crystallise.

(2) The flavour is similar to that produced by sweetened condensed milk; however, in some formulations, a distinctly buttery note is produced.

(3) The casein in Novamel is completely soluble, therefore caramel made with it is exceptionally smooth in texture.

(4) Resistance to cold flow is often better than caramel manufactured with sweetened condensed milks, provided attention is paid to premixing the ingredients correctly prior to boiling.

(5) Novamel is not as vulnerable to seasonal variations in milk composition and supply as sweetened condensed milk.

(6) In a two-phase system, for example caramel wafers, there is a tendency for moisture to migrate from the caramel to the wafer, because the equilibrium relative humidity (ERH) of the wafer is lower than that of the caramel. This leads to a drying out and hardening of the caramel and a softening of the wafer. Novamel however reduces the tendency for moisture migration by two mechanisms. Firstly, a greater degree of water binding is achieved by the added casein than by native micellar casein in sweetened condensed milk. Secondly, the colligative properties of the monosaccharides—glucose and galactose—marginally reduce the ERH of the caramel.

5.8.3 Milk powders

The use of sweetened condensed milks and/or sweet dairy concentrates may not always be possible if the requisite handling and processing plant is not available. Additionally, confectionery manufacture in tropical and subtropical climates can, because of high ambient storage temperatures, significantly reduce the effective shelf life of milk concentrates such that an alternative is essential.

Skimmed milk powder (SMP) and to a lesser extent whole milk powder (WMP) are therefore logical and effective alternatives, since their low moisture contents, e.g. $< 3.7\%$ for skimmed milk powder, ensure a long shelf life.

The milk powders are manufactured by evaporating whole milk standardised and homogenised to give 26% fat in the final powder, or skimmed milk with virtually all of the fat removed by centrifugal separation, to yield a concentrate of typically 48–55% solids, which is suitable for spray drying. Evaporation removes some 85–90% of the water in milk and is, of course, more cost-effective than spray drying. Additionally, the drying of a relatively high solids concentrate assists the manufacture of a high-bulk density powder, which has obvious handling benefits. Following evaporation, spray drying removes virtually all of the remaining water from the atomised concentrate droplets, yielding free-flowing, dustless powders with low water activity and, consequently, extended shelf life.

In confectionery manufacture, skimmed milk powder, for example, can be recombined with butteroil and sucrose to make sweetened condensed milks identical to those manufactured by traditional methods. The SMP is dissolved in water at 45–55°C, a temperature critical to the effective rehydration of the milk proteins, and butteroil is metered into the milk followed by the addition of sucrose, which is completely dissolved by raising the temperature of the mix to 75°C. This also serves as a pasteurisation, and subsequent homogenisation can be used to control viscosity if required.

The recombined sweetened condensed milk can be used directly in the manufacture of toffee, caramels, fudge, etc.

5.8.4 Milk fats

Cream, which is manufactured by the centrifugal separation of whole milk, yielding the byproduct of skimmed milk, can be used in the production of high-quality confections. However, pasteurised cream has a relatively short shelf life even at refrigeration temperatures. An obvious alternative is of course butter, which also contains less water for subsequent removal.

Butter is manufactured by churning cream at typically 40% fat and 5–10°C, depending on the seasonal influence on milk fat hardness. At the low temperatures most of the triglycerides are crystallised, and the churning action causes the milk fat globule membrane to rupture, thus allowing the milk fat to coalesce, forming butter. The butter is washed to remove traces of buttermilk, which contains non-fat milk solids, some milk fat and the membrane material which gives buttermilk its characteristic flavour.

For retail consumption, 1.8% salt is often added to butter for preservative effect and taste. However, for confectionery manufacture, unsalted butter will be preferred.

Butter is used widely in the production of toffees, caramels, fudge and butterscotch as a result of the characteristic flavours which are developed during cooking. As with cream, butter requires particular storage conditions, e.g. refrigeration, and also hygienic handling systems.

However, the benefits of milk fat in a more convenient form can be gained by using butteroil, which is manufactured from either cream or butter. During production, for example from butter, the raw material is completely liquefied by heating to 85°C and holding for approximately 4 min. The non-fat milk solids are removed by centrifugal separation and the fat stream is reheated to 85°C, before passing through a second separator in which remaining solids are washed out with water. Water residues are removed in a vacuum dryer and the resulting butteroil is cooled before filling into 190-kg drums or bulk transporters. The container head-space is flushed with nitrogen to remove air and consequent oxidation problems.

A variant of butteroil which is of particular benefit to the confectioner is flavour-enhanced butteroil. Precooking during the early stages of manufacture accelerates the formation of flavour components such as lactones and ketones, which enhance the quality of the final product.

5.8.5　Hydrolysed milk proteins

Many confections are based on stable foams which are formed by the aeration of materials such as egg albumen, hydrolysed vegetable proteins or importantly, hydrolysed casein. Few native proteins will fulfil the requirements of a good whipping agent, that is:

　　Soluble in water.
　　Soluble in concentrated sugar.
　　Soluble over a wide pH range.
　　Excellent foam formation.
　　Excellent foam stability.
　　Resistance to overbeating.
　　Tasteless in application.
　　Permitted ingredient.
　　Cost-effective.

Thus the modification of proteins is necessary, and this has been achieved by either alkaline or enzymic hydrolysis.

The alkaline hydrolysis of casein, to form a whipping agent, has been practised for some decades now, having been a means of substituting egg white during war-time shortages in the 1940s.

In recent years, developments have concentrated on enzymic hydrolysis and improved control over the range of protein fragments which result. This is important to optimise the foam-forming and foam-stabilising properties, since the former is improved with an increase in short-chain polypeptides, whilst the reverse is true of the latter.

In sugar confectionery, milk-based whipping agents are of particular benefit through their ability to whip in concentrated sugar solutions, without overwhipping. They are consequently used in meringues, marshmallows, nougat, fruit chews and fondant fillings.

5.9　Concluding comments

Although it has not been possible here to present a full account of the nature of milk and its benefits to the sugar confectioner, it should be at least appreciated now that milk is indeed a complex substance with many and diverse uses.

Whilst the traditional applications for milk are well established, increasing demands for innovation may well result in novel uses for milk and the use of non-traditional milk ingredients in the future.

Whatever the future holds though, the importance of milk to the confectionery industry cannot be underestimated, and it is certainly true that some products would cease to exist without the use of milk.

References

1. American Oil Chemists' Society, 508 South Sixth Street, Champaign, Ill. 61820, USA.
2. BS 684. BSI, Milton Keynes MK14 6LE, England, UK.
3. *IUPAC Standard Methods of the Analysis of Oils, Fats and Derivatives*, 7th edn, Blackwell Scientific Publications, Oxford (1987).
4. A.G. Metrohm, CH-9100 Herisou, Switzerland.
5. Carter Lithchfield. *Analysis of Triglycerides*, Academic Press, New York (1973).
6. D. Waddington, in *Fats and Oils: Chemistry and Technology*, eds. R.J. Hamilton and A. Bhati, Applied Science Publishers (1980).
7. R.E. Timms. *Prog. Lipid Res.* **23** (1984) 1.
8. The Tintometer Limited, Salisbury SP1 1JY, England, UK.
9. J.B. Rossell. *Chem. Ind.* 1st Sept (1973) 832.
10. R.E. Timms. *Chem. Ind.* 7th April (1979) 257.
11. H.B.W. Patterson, *Hydrogenation of Fats and Oils,* Applied Science Publishers (1983).
12. Fractionnement Tirtiaux S.A., B-6220 Fleurus, Belgium.
13. P. Walstra and R. Jennings, in *Dairy Chemistry and Physics.* John Wiley & Sons, New York (1984).
14. G. Urbach, The flavour of milk fat, in *The Proceedings of the Milk Fat Symposium*, Australian Society of Dairy Technology (1979).
15. R. Early, Dairy sugars as food ingredients, in *Food Technology International, Europe (1988)*, Sterling Publications, London.

6 Colour and flavour

B. BEACHAM, P.B. RAYNER and C.J. KNEWSTUBB

6.1 Introduction

Colourings and flavourings are *not* added to confectionery to mislead consumers about the quality and nutritional value of the products. They are *not* added solely to retain appearance and flavour for a long shelf life, or to create the impression that expensive ingredients are present at much higher levels, or indeed to suggest that an ingredient is present when it does not exist. However, critics have dubbed colourings and flavourings and flavour enhancers as cosmetic additives that render foods high in sugar and fat, and low in fibre, more palatable and attractive than they are in reality. The critics claim that this leads to poor nutrition, dental problems and diet-related diseases.

A good flavouring makes one's mouth water: the most important physiological function of flavour. Together with impressions of taste, smell, texture and colour, feelings of pleasurable anticipation are evoked, thus promoting the flow of saliva and assisting digestion. Food must be palatable and presented in sufficient variety in order to achieve a nutritionally adequate diet. Colourings and flavourings are essential constituents of human food. Many confectionery products would not exist without flavourings, for example chewing gum, gums and pastilles, and the traditional fruit drop assortment of five flavours would not be possible without flavourings and colourings.

A large number of raw materials are used in the confectionery industry and, together with the nature of the processes and the diversity of the products, present a challenge to the colour and flavour industries.

6.2 Some factors influencing choice

An intimate knowledge of the properties of flavourings and colourings is essential in order to arrive at the ideal choice and thus avoid some of the common pitfalls. Factors to be considered must include:

Effect of confectionery components interacting with the flavour and colour components.

Effect of processing conditions.

Consumer acceptability.

Legislation.

Shelf life of product.

Cost.

Intended product label claims.

Each of these factors could occupy a chapter, and therefore to augment this short analysis further reading at the end of this chapter is suggested.

6.3   Colours for the sugar confectioner

Colour permeates virtually every aspect of our lives—from enriching the world around us to enhancing the visual appearance of the food we eat. It plays a very important role in sugar confectionery since many of the ingredients have little colour in their own right. Since consumers live in a world full of colour and enjoy eating foods coloured by nature, they expect manufactured foods to have similar colours. It is also a fact that colour is extremely important in the perception of flavour. If the colour and flavour of a food are not correctly associated the taster is more likely to identify the food by its colour rather than its flavour.

Luckily the sugar confectioner has a wide choice of colour additives available to produce the desired shades appropriate to the flavours used. When deciding upon a suitable colour the following must be considered:

What colours are permitted by national legislation for a particular confection?

Should the colour be synthetic, natural or a synthesised nature-identical colour? The definition of some colours can differ between countries.

What colours will be compatible with the ingredients, process conditions, packaging, shelf life desired and each other in blends?

In all these decisions it is advisable to seek the assistance of specialist colour manufacturers who can offer guidance from their accumulated experience.

Annatto has two major pigments, bixin (oil-soluble) and norbixin (water-soluble); both give bright orange solutions. Norbixin will dissolve in soft water to colour neutral pH products, but special forms are needed for hard water or acidic conditions. Both pigments are heat-stable but susceptible to oxidation and sulphur dioxide. However, they can be used in most types of confectionery in stabilised forms.

Lutein is an oil-soluble yellow pigment with good heat, light and sulphur dioxide stability. When prepared in water-dispersible form it can be used in most types of confectionery. A common use is as body colour for marzipan, where it gives an egg-yellow shade.

Crocin is a water-soluble bright-yellow pigment which is heat- and relatively light-stable. It is sensitive to sulphur dioxide, which will reduce its colour strength. It can be used in fondant, jellies and high-boiled sweets.

Paprika is an orange/red oil-soluble extract with a characteristic sweet spicy flavour. Due to its flavour it is seldom used in confectionery, but it is heat- and pH-stable.

Apocarotenal is an oil-soluble colour imparting pale orange to orange red shades. Water-dispersible forms are available, making it applicable for most confectionery products. It is stable to light and heat.

Canthaxanthin is an oil-soluble colour which gives an orange to bright-red colour in its water-dispersible form. It is stable to heat and light and can be applied to most confectionery types.

6.4 Natural colours

Natural colours are basically those that occur in nature and use can be made of coloured ingredients such as cocoa powder, toasted carob flour, liquorice and fruit extracts. However, a few of the numerous natural pigments are commercially extracted for use as colour additives and some are synthesised as pure pigments. Table 6.1 lists some of the major naturally occurring food colours. A wide spectrum of colour can be achieved in confectionery using natural colours.

Carotenoids occur very widely in nature and are responsible for many of the striking yellow, orange and red shades of edible fruits, vegetables, flowers, fungi and some animals, fish and birds. The most common encountered carotenoids are fucoxanthin, lutein, violaxanthin, β-carotene, lycopene and apo carotenoids. The majority of carotenoids are oil-soluble, but water-dispersible forms are available. Crocin and norbixin are unusual in that they are truly water-soluble. Carotenoids range in shade from pale yellow through orange to red. They are prone to oxidation but can be protected with antioxidants such as ascorbic acid and tocopherols. They are generally stable to heat and are very intense pigments, frequently being used at levels below 10 ppm of pure pigment. Major commercial carotenoid colours are:

Beta-carotene—this gives a lemon yellow to orange colour depending upon concentration. It is stable to pH change, sulphur dioxide, heat and light, and can therefore be used in most confectionery. Various water-dispersible forms are available. It is advisable when using the carotenoid colours to add these with the flavour at the end of the cooking process to minimise degradation. In general this applies to all natural colours.

Anthocyanins—these are the large water-soluble group of natural pigments

Table 6.1 Common food grade dyes (most are also available as lakes)

Colour	CI 1971 no.	EEC no.	USA FD & C no.	Aqueous solubility (%)	Stability guide				
					Sulphur dioxide	Alkali	Conf. acids	Heat	Light
Reds									
Allura Red	16035	—	Red 40	9	F	P	F	G	VG
Ponceau 4R	16255	E124	NP	8	F	P	G	G	F
Carmoisine	14720	E122	NP	4	G	F	VG	G	G
Amaranth	16185	E123	NP	7	F	F	G	VG	G
Erythrosine BS	45430	E127	RED 3	2	VG	F	P	VG	F
Red 2G	18050	128	NP	4	G	VG	G	G	VG
Orange and Yellows									
Tartrazine	19140	E102	Yellow 5	10	VG	G	VG	VG	G
Yellow 2G	18965	107	NP	8	F	VG	VG	VG	VG
Sunset Yellow FCF	15985	E110	Yellow 6	10	F	G	VG	VG	G
Quinoline Yellow	47005	E104	NP	3	G	F	G	VG	VG
Greens									
Green S (Brilliant Green BS)	44090	E142	NP	2	G	F	G	VG	P
Fast Green FCF	42053	—	Green 3	20	G	P	P	F	F
Blues									
Indigo Carmine	73015	E132	Blue 2	1	P	P	F	P	P
Patent Blue V	42051	E131	NP	4	F	F	P	G	VG
Brilliant Blue FCF	42090	133	Blue 1	20	VG	VG	VG	VG	G
Browns									
Brown FK	—	154	NP	20	P	G	F	F	G
Chocolate Brown FB	—	—	NP	15	G	VG	VG	VG	G
Chocolate Brown HT	20285	155	NP	20	F	G	G	VG	G
Black									
Black PN	28440	E151	NP	7	P	G	F	P	VG

NP, not permitted in the USA
Aqueous stability is given as a guide based on average-strength soluble dyes; purer samples are often more soluble.
Stabilities: P, poor; F, fair; G, good; VG, very good.

responsible for the strawberry red to blue colours of most fruits, flowers, leaves and some vegetables. Commercially most anthocyanin is extracted from black grape skins. Anthocyanins are natural indicators exhibiting red shades in acidic conditions but purple to blue in neutral and alkaline solutions. They are stable to heat and light but show different degrees of stability to sulphur dioxide, pH change and oxygen. They can be used in wide range of confectionery, but hazing can occur in gelatine jellies unless special forms are selected. In marzipan they give a dull purple colour when incorporated as body colour, but if applied as surface colour in an acidified solution they are red.

Beetroot extract—this is not heat- or light-stable so its use is restricted. It is most stable in the pH range 3.5–5.0, where it gives pink to bright-red shades. It can be used to colour fondant or marzipan centres where the chocolate coating or packaging will protect it from the light.

Chlorophyll—this is the generally accepted name for the green pigment present in any organism capable of photosynthesis. The natural extract is olive green and contains levels of lutein and other carotenoids. It has limited stability to heat and light and is more stable in neutral or alkaline conditions. Special forms are available for use in confectionery including high-boiled sweets.

Copper chlorophyll—this is derived from the natural extract and is a bluer green shade. It has good light and heat stability making it generally applicable, however it can precipitate in acidic systems.

Caramels—these are formed when carbohydrates are heated. In confectionery processing this occurs naturally when cooking sugar at high temperatures in caramels, toffee and fudge. Various caramel colour additives are available from pure caramelised sugar to high-strength caramels produced by heating specific carbohydrates with accelerators such as ammonia. Caramel colour can be used in all types of confectionery.

Carmine or cochineal—this is a very heat- and light-stable colour giving pink to bright-red shades. The colour is soluble in alkali but will precipitate if the pH of the confection is below 3. It can be used in a wide range of confectionery.

Turmeric and its pigment *curcumin*—these are a bright-yellow colour with normally poor light stability, however they are stabilised in high-boiled sweets so can be used in this application.

Riboflavin, lactoflavin or vitamin B$_2$—this is an intensely bitter-tasting orange/yellow colour with poor water stability but good acid stability. Its derivative *riboflavin 5'-phosphate* is more water-soluble and not so bitter-tasting. These are both normally synthesised colours and are usually only used for sugar-panned sweets.

6.5   Synthetic colours

Synthetic colours offer a wide spectrum of colours, and most can be blended together to achieve intermediate colours and shades. A guide to their stabilities is given in Table 6.2. Colour manufacturers offer the colours in a wide range of prepared blends together with advice on their usage. Colours are available as soluble powders, prepared solutions, easily dissolved granules, pastes, gelatin sticks or solidified blocks of colour in edible fat for fat-based confectionery. The simplest and least expensive form is the soluble powdered dye. These can be dissolved in distilled or deionised water (prepare paste with a little cold water then make to required volume or weight with hot or cold water). Some colours will react with hard tap water to form hazes. It is preferable to filter colour solutions and only prepare enough for 24 h use since they are susceptible to mould growth. For stock solutions, permitted preservatives can be added, or where solubility permits the solution can be prepared with glycerine and/or propylene glycol or isopropylalcohol.

For products requiring an opaque colour such as sugar-panned goods, chewing and bubble gum, compound fat-based confectionery, fondant, toffee and chews, a lake colour can be used. Lake colours are insoluble pigments prepared by precipitation of water-soluble colours with an aluminium salt or sometimes calcium or magnesium salts onto a substrate of aluminium hydroxide (alumina). Lake colours are manufactured to various strengths between 10 and 40% dye content.

The tinctorial strengths of lakes are not proportional to dye content. Lake colours are used as a dispersion and therefore the particle size must be small enough to achieve an economical and speck-free usage.

Lake colours are insoluble in the pH range 3.5–9.0. They have improved light stability over the equivalent soluble dye; they do not migrate as readily as soluble dyes and can therefore be used where two colours are in close contact in striped confectionery or cased confectionery such as a seaside rock; they can be used in fat-based confectionery containing no water.

6.6   What are flavourings?

Flavourings are complex mixtures of flavouring substances which may include a solvent or carrier, and any one flavouring may contain a large number of individual substances. They can be divided into three broad categories: natural, nature-identical and artificial.

6.6.1   Natural flavouring substances

These can be naturally occurring plant materials such as herbs and spices, or can be obtained from natural sources by microbiological or physical

Table 6.2 Some natural, nature-identical and chemically modified food colours for confectionery

Colour	Major pigments	CI 1971 no.	EEC no.	Principal sources
Carotenoids yellow to red				
β-Carotene*	β-Carotene	75130	E160a	Carrots, alfalfa, maize, *dunnaliella* algae
Annatto	Bixin, norbixin	75120	E160b	*Bix orellana* seeds
Lutein	Lutein	75100	E161b	Tagetes or Aztec marigold, alfalfa, egg yolk, orange peel
Crocin	Crocin		E160c	Saffron crocus, *Gardenia jasminoides* fruit
Paprika	Capsanthin and capsorubin		E160e	Sweet red pepper (*Capsicum annum*)
β-Apo-8′ carotenal†		40820	E161g	Citrus peel
Canthaxanthin†		40850		Edible fungi
Miscellaneous Yellow				
Turmeric	Curcumin	75300	E100	Turmeric root (*Curcoma longa*)
Riboflavin† (vitamin **B2**)			E101	Milk yeast
Riboflavin 5′-phosphate†			101a	Derivative of riboflavin
Reds				
Anthocyanins	Anthocyanins		E163	Black grape skins, blackcurrants, elderberry, red cabbage, hibiscus, cranberry, purple corn, whortleberry
Beetroot extract	Betanin, vulgaxanthin		E162	Beetroot (*Beta vulgaris*)
Cochineal	Carmine and carminic acid	75470	E120	Extract of cochineal insect
Greens				
Chlorophyll	Chlorophyll and chlorophyllins	75810	E140	Green leaves, grass, alfalfa, nettles
Copper chlorophyll‡	Copper chlorophyllin	75810	E141	Derived from above
Browns				
Caramel	Melanoidins		E150	Food grade carbohydrates with accelerators used in process, e.g. ammonia
Blacks				
Vegetables carbon black	Carbon		E153	Carbonised vegetable matter
Whites				
Titanium dioxide			E171	Naturally occurring mineral

Gold (E175), silver (E174) and aluminium (E173) can be used for surface coloration.

*Available in pure synthesised form or natural extract.   †Normally used in synthesised pure form.   ‡Chemically modified natural colour extract.

procedures such as extraction distillation and concentration, e.g. orange oils, vanilla extract from vanilla pods.

6.6.2 Nature-identical flavouring substances

These are obtained by synthesis or isolated through chemical processes from a natural aromatic raw material and are chemically identical to a substance present in natural products intended for human consumption, either processed or not.

6.6.3 Artificial flavouring substances

These are also chemically synthesised, but so far have not been found to exist in nature, e.g. ethyl vanillin (similar in character to vanillin but approximately $2\frac{1}{2}$ times stronger in impact).

6.7 Natural, nature-identical or artificial? Advantages and disadvantages

6.7.1 Natural flavourings

Advantages

Some natural flavourings contain flavour precursors which when processed can add desirable characteristics to the finished product.

Natural flavourings may offer marketing advantages in the form of label claims as long as the word 'natural' is considered to be superior to the word synthetic or artificial.

Disadvantages

Most natural flavours are low in flavour impact, and therefore high dosages are needed. This is costly and technologically not acceptable in the manufacture of certain products where a low residual moisture in the final product is essential for shelf life considerations, e.g. boiled sweets, or where heat-stable flavours are required. Some natural flavours can be concentrated, but even with maximum concentration the dosage necessary remains too high to give the required impact. Concentrating can alter the flavour character.

6.7.1.1 *Flavour variation.* Most natural flavourings vary in flavour character depending on the variety of fruit, herb or spice. The degree of ripeness at harvesting can add to this variation. Add changes in processing, and it is obvious that a uniform product is difficult. Biochemical reactions can continue in natural flavours, sometimes giving off notes.

6.7.1.2 *Wastage facter*. For 1000 kg of mashed strawberries it is only possible to obtain 80 kg of strawberry juice. Nine hundred and twenty kilograms of natural food is destroyed or used as cattle feed. Can such wastage be afforded?

6.7.1.3 *Safety and nutritional value*. Natural flavourings are neither safer nor more nutritious than synthetic flavourings. Their present assumed superiority is not based on scientific evidence. It is a pity that some of our major retailers are not prepared to re-educate the consumers in scientific realities. But it is clear of course that this would be a difficult endeavour, especially in view of the complexity of the term 'natural' and in view of the consumers' increasing concerns about ecological problems.

6.7.2   *Nature-identical and artificial (synthetic) flavourings*

Advantages

No problems with supply position.

The flavour strength is such that flavouring costs are much cheaper than the equivalent natural product necessary to produce a similar flavour effect.

No flavour variation, and the flavourings are more heat-stable. There is no wastage of natural food.

Nature-identical materials are not new and unknown chemicals. They are the materials present in our food which has been consumed on a regular basis. Some artificial flavouring substances can show cost savings over some of the nature-identical substances with similar flavour characteristics.

Disadvantages

Synthectic flavourings may not be acceptable for many export markets due to certain components, including the carrier solvents.

6.7.3   *Conclusion*

There is no doubt that synthetic flavouring substances are essential to augment or in some applications to replace natural flavouring substances, but the consumer should be free to judge the end product on taste sensation alone without the constraints of having to consider whether the composition is natural, nature-identical or artificial.

Flavourings for sugar confectionery are invariably mixtures of natural and synthetic substances, but it should be remembered that, in the UK, if a natural flavouring contains *any* nature-identical components then the flavouring is nature-identical and if it contains *any* artificial components it is artificial.

Table 6.3

Product	Dosage for 100 kg ready-to-eat product (g/100 kg)
Boiled sweets	100
Fondant centres	50
Fat-based centres	200–250
Pectin or sugar Jellies	60–100
Gelatin jellies	150
Caramels	200
Chewing gum	800–1000

6.8 Flavour strength: dosage levels

This can be expressed in g/100 kg of end product or as a percentage. Most flavour houses standardize in a strength of 1:1000 or 100 g/100 kg of product (1000 ppm). A relation exists between the normal dosage in various confectionery products (Table 6.3).

These are general starting recommendations, but they need to be modified in the light of processing conditions and product composition and will depend as well on regional and national preferences of taste.

In order to achieve a standard flavour strength and ensure solubility of the flavouring substances, approved solvents in food are used, and the choice of solvent is of paramount importance. Many flavourings contain over 50% of carrier solvent and so, as a major ingredient, it has specific effects on the ingredients of sugar confectionery materials.

6.9 Functions of carrier solvents and powders

These render the flavouring substances soluble in the confectionery product. Vanilla extract is soluble in aqueous systems because it contains water and ethyl alcohol as solvents. Butter flavours with vegetable oils as carrier render them soluble in fat.

They also act as diluents for strong aqueous flavours, or essential oils enable the flavour to be dispersed uniformly throughout the product. They enable a mixture of heterogeneous flavouring substances to be homogeneous by careful selection of a mixture of solvents.

Powder carriers are substances which do not act as solvents but as diluents or for encapsulating in spray drying of liquid flavours. The particle size of powdered carriers should be such that a homogeneous mixture is assured.

6.9.1   *Ideal properties of carrier solvents*

There is no universal no. 1 solvent: the choice must meet the requirements.

The flavouring substances must be protected by the solvents in withstanding processing hazards such as high temperatures, oxygen and moisture.

Ethyl alcohol and isopropyl alcohol are very volatile, and therefore these solvents would not be practical in high-temperature processes, as vaporization of these and some of the flavouring volatiles might result.

Monopropylene glycol and glycerin are hygroscopic and could cause some high-boiled sweets to pick up moisture and become sticky. This property might be beneficial in marshmallows in retaining moisture.

6.10   Factors affecting stability of flavouring compounds

6.10.1   *Degradation*

6.10.1.1.   *By heat.* Continuous automated processing usually means that the flavouring has to be injected into the cooked sugar mixtures. Even distribution of the flavouring is essential, and the temperatures can reach 160°C, and for longer periods of time at temperatures in the region of 140°C. Vacuum cooking can also lead to flavour loss. Open-pan cooking is likely to result in greater losses of volatiles than closed systems. It has already been mentioned that the choice of carrier solvent is very important, and whereas ethyl alcohol boils at 78°C, and isopropyl alcohol at 82°C, there are approved food solvents with higher boiling points which would protect the loss of volatiles in the manufacture of boiled sweets, i.e. monopropylene glycol 185°C, triacetin 260°C and diacetin 280°C.

6.10.1.2   *By light or oxygen.* Citrus oils may be oxidised, leading to rancid off-flavours. Care is required in selecting flavourings for products containing a lot of air, e.g. nougats and marshmallows.

6.10.2   *Chemical reactions between the flavouring components*

Flavouring compounds can consist of over 50 different chemical substances representing a number of reactive groups, and therefore it should be expected that chemical reactions take place between the components, or indeed between the flavouring components and the confectionery components.

Fortunately it is possible in essence to avoid these reactions through an adequate compository technique. Thus, drastic modifications of the flavouring character are very rarely observed. Of course migration of hydrophilic substances into the aqueous phase, and hydrophobic substances into the fat phase, can take place. Also, the flavouring of chewing gum should be treated with care, owing to the hardening or softening of the gum base with certain flavourings.

6.10.3 *Microbiological stability*

Nature-identical and artificial flavourings do not pose a problem. The components are more less sterile, and the majority have been distilled (heat treatment) and are free from moisture, and also contain solvents such as ethyl alcohol and monopropylene glycol at levels exceeding 40%.

Natural flavourings must be protected in order to ensure that they are free from micro-organisms which may cause contamination of the final product. Heating to 120°C for more than 20 min would kill most of the micro-organisms, but would also affect the flavour profile. Chemical preservation has been criticised by the antiadditive lobby, but fruit juices and citrus oils are often stabilised at source. Airtight low-temperature storage, and the use of added sugar to fruit juices to above 65° Brix increases the osmotic pressure and inhibits the growth of micro-organisms.

6.11 Packaging, storage, handling and dispensing

Containers for flavourings should be chemical-resistant. They should prevent the loss of flavour aroma and the ingress of moisture and air. The containers should be odourless and tasteless, durable and economical. Glass is completely free from odour and taste, and small-volume samples are usually packed in glass. Glass is also chemical-resistant to flavouring substances, and, to protect them from light, tinted glass is usually the choice. However large volumes are rarely packed in glass due to its weight and fragile nature. There is the danger that pieces of glass could end up in the final confection.

Lacquer-lined drums are ideal containers, being lighter and tougher than glass, but the inner lacquer should be checked for efficiency of lacquering and care should be taken not to damage this lacquer by careless handling or transportation. Unlined drums are not ideal as trace amounts of certain metals, particularly iron, can cause colour changes with certain essential oils such as clove and thyme, and with acidic flavourings containing a range of substances such as maltol, ethyl maltol, vanillin and ethyl vanillin. Checks for metals should also be carried out on some of the raw materials, particularly the carrier solvents, which may be present in large amounts.

Low-density polyethylene is not ideal, as it is affected by some solvents, resulting in softening and deformation of the containers. Permeability is also a problem. High-density polyethylene is less permeable, and is not affected by carrier solvents.

Aluminium bottles are used for flavourings that are compatible with the aluminium. They are particularly useful in avoiding high transportation costs where weight is the governing factor. Powders are usually packed in moistureproof bags contained in cardboard boxes, fibreboard kegs or metal containers.

There is no universal packaging material for all flavourings. The choice is dependent on a number of factors including storate conditions.

Flavourings containing high levels of fruit juice gradually lose their fresh colour due to oxidation of the naturally occurring pigments.

Citrus oils should be stored ideally at between 4 and 8°C in efficiently sealed containers in order to ensure a shelf life of approximately 6 months. Deterioration is caused by oxidation, and therefore the size of the containers should be kept to a minimum compatible with consumption to avoid a large head space in the containers. The majority of other flavourings stored under cool conditions will generally have a shelf life of at least 12 months.

If flavourings are stored at too cold a temperature, there is a possibility of precipitation of flavour components or wax. Wax may be filtered out, but if flavouring components were filtered off the flavour would be changed. Such products would have to be carefully warmed with stirring until the precipitate is redissolved into solution.

6.12   Handling of flavouring components: safety precautions

Flavourings are concentrated food ingredients, and should not be consumed as such. There are no harmless substances, but there are harmless ways of using these substances.

Most confectionery companies measure or weigh flavourings and colourings into batch quantities in a dispensing room, and therefore it is extremely important that they are handled safely.

Avoid breathing the vapour. These materials are safe when properly used, but inhalation of high concentrations of vapour may cause drowsiness, headaches and giddiness. Severe exposure may lead to unconsciousness. Always use in a room which is well ventilated, but avoid draughts. Avoid contact with the skin and eyes. These substances may irritate the skin. Substances in the eyes will be irritating. Avoid naked flames. Some of the materials are flammable, and all are combustible, and of course do not take internally. Ensure that any vessel containing materials, if not used immediately, is covered. Transfer to proper storage containers as soon as possible. Protect the eyes with safety glasses or face shield. Use chemical-resistant gloves. In case of fire, never use water jet. Use carbon dioxide, dry chemical or foam extingishers. Contain spillages by the use of earth or spilsorb. Do not empty into drains.

Suppliers of flavourings and colourings will supply you with a health and safety data sheet for every substance or compound supplied, and if the container has a hazard sign or warning symbol then reference should be made to the sheet to ascertain the particular hazard.

6.13 Legislation and labelling

For all legislation, there must be a need. It must be fair to all parties, and it should be capable of being enforced, and should be enforced.

Food flavourings and colourings must comply with the Food Act 1984. It is an offence to add anything to food that may render it injurious to health. It is also an offence to make misleading statements on product labels or in advertisements, and therefore it is essential that the flavouring or colouring is honestly described. This is usually covered by a comprehensive specification listing all the possible declarable components. In 1989 the EC Council has adopted a framework directive for Community legislation on flavourings used for food. The directive specifies definitions for different types of flavourings. It also outlines labelling provisions, defines maximum levels for contaminants and provides for establishing directives on individual flavouring categories based on the information provided on the inventories. No decision has been made on whether the categories will be regulated by positive, negative or mixed lists. This directive applies to labelling of flavourings and not to food products.

The Food Labelling Regulations 1984 contain several clauses connected to the composition of flavourings, particularly the 'wholly or mainly' clause, which lays down the criteria for depicting a picture of a fruit on a product label.

It is possible for the same flavour compound to be natural in Italy, nature-identical in Germany and the UK, but artificial in France. In the United States if ethyl acetate is prepared from natural ethyl alcohol and natural acetic acid, the flavouring would be classified as natural in the States, but would be nature-identical in the UK. It is obvious that advice should be sought from the supplier for each intended export market.

6.14 Concluding comments

Having worked in the confectionery industry for 22 years before joining Givaudan and the world of flavouring substances, I can speak from experience in recommending the following course of action:

DO NOT evaluate flavourings solely by odour on a smelling strip, or tasting in sugar syrup. Whenever possible evaluate in product, albeit on a small-scale pilot plant, accepting that modifications may be required when translated up to production batch quantities. The quantity and stability of the colouring materials should be similarly assessed.

DO consult your suppliers of flavourings and colourings and discuss:

Product composition.
Processing conditions—temperature and time, open or closed systems, etc.
Shelf life required.
Legislation.
Possible label claims.

The close cooperation between user and supplier will ensure that the present high standard of onfectionery products will continue.

Further reading

Council Directive 88/388/EEC, Framework directive for community legislation on flavourings used in food.
J.N. Counsell, in *Natural Colours for Food and Other Uses*, ed. J.N. Counsell, Applied Science Publishers, London (1981).
J.N. Counsell, in *Developments in Food Colours 1*, ed. J. Walford, Applied Science Publishers, London (1980).
H. Dietrich, Silesia Confiserie Manual No. 3, vol. 2, eds. A. Meiners, K. Kreiken & H. Jorke. Silesia-Essenzenfabrik Ger-hard (Hanke K.G., Abt. Fochbuchere).
J.D. Dziezak, Applications of food colorants, Food Technology, April 1987.
B.A. Gubler, H. Gremli, C. Verde, and J. Wild, Some aspects of interaction between food and flavour components, *Proceedings of the Fourth International Congress on Food Science and Technology*, vol. 1 (1974) 456–62.
HMSO 1984 No. 1305, *The Food Labelling Regulations 1984*, HMSO London.
G.G. Jeffries, C.J. Knewstubb and J. Coulson, in *Developments in Food Colours 1*, ed. J. Walford, Applied Science Publishers, London (1980).
H. Klaui, in *Natural Colours for Food and Other Uses*, ed. J.N. Counsell, Applied Science Publishers, London (1981).
C.J. Knewstubb and B.S. Henry, in *Food Technology International Europe 1980*, Sterling Publications Ltd.
R. Lees and B. Jackson, *Sugar Confectionery and Chocolate Manufacture*, Leonard Hill, Glasgow (1973).
Roche Carotenoids and Confectionery Applications Sheets, F. Hoffmann La Roche & Co. Ltd.
Technical data sheets from: Williams (Hounslow) Ltd., D F Anstead Ltd., Colorcon Ltd., Overseal Foods Ltd. Givaudan Ltd (Dubendorf).
R.H.J. Watson, in *Natural Colours for Food and Other Uses*, ed. J.N. Counsell, Applied Science Publishers, London (1981).

7 General technical aspects of industrial sugar confectionery manufacture

R. LEES

7.1 Introduction

The successful manufacture of sugar confectionery products is dependent on a limited but key group of physical and chemical changes which influence recipe composition and methods of production. The effects are sometimes complementary, but they sometimes compete in the way they contribute to the development of desirable qualities in sugar confections, and in particular good shelf life, fine eating qualities and desirable flavouring. These inter-relating factors can be classified under six broad headings:

Compositional effects.
Change of composition.
Change of state.
Environmental behaviour.
Evaporation.
Sweetness or acidity.

Processes used for the manufacture of sweetmeats rely on some if not all these factors to develop product quality, and the changes have a profound influence on the choice of processing techniques. These factors contribute to the production handling characteristics, which can in turn affect such aspects as the viscosity of the product and its versatility during shaping and wrapping. Well-tested manufacturing procedures have been subjected to significant improvement in recent years, and there has been a concurrent modification of commonly used ingredients to enhance desirable marketing and manufacturing features. However it is the underlying properties of the ingredients and the well-tried production techniques which continue to dictate the way that the prepared material is to be treated and sold.

Change has been largely a matter of reconfiguring existing processes with consequential improvement in plant engineering, leading to improved heat transfer, increased efficiency in mixing and improvements in the introduction of and dependence on integral software incorporated into modern mass production plant. Change has resulted not from any fundamental discovery affecting the underlying scientific principles of confectionery manufacture but rather new ingredients have been developed which enhance the properties of materials needed in a recipe for a sugar confection. This chapter discusses those properties which influence the production and storage of sweetmeats and documents recent information which has made an impact on the knowledge about products or the way they are manufactured.

7.2   Compositional effects

The composition of recipes for the manufacture of sugar confections is based on the use of carbohydrates (sugars), fats, thickeners and stabilisers, and proteins.

7.2.1   *Sugars*

The three basic carbohydrate sources are sucrose (cane or beet sugar), glucose and other speciality syrups produced by the selective hydrolysis of starch, and invert sugar prepared from the breakdown of sucrose. Together these three groups of sugars provide the bulk sweetening material for the different confectionery products.

7.2.1.1   *Sucrose.* The major component used in manufacture is cane or beet sugar, and this ingredient is very nearly pure sucrose. Most cane or beet sugar contains traces of mineral salts found when ashing the product. Sucrose, a disaccharide, can be split to form two simpler monosaccharides, usually known as dextrose (α-D-glucose) and laevulose (β-D-fructose). These sugars are also known under the alternative names of glucose and fructose, and all four names tend to be used interchangeably within the sweet industry.

The minor traces of salts present in commercial sugars provide an inhibiting effect on the breakdown of sucrose to the simpler sugars present in invert sugar. This type of hydrolysis is desirable for certain types of confectionery products such as cream centres, and is induced by the delibrate addition of fruit acids or more preferentially by enzymes.

Vink [1] reported that traces of dextran were found in sugar extracted from cane but not from beet. This trace impurity was considered to give rise to viscosity effects during the manufacture of confectionery products, influencing both plasticity and elasticity. The presence of dextran in cane sugar is considered by Vink to explain the distortion effects sometimes encountered during the manufacture of count lines.

7.2.1.2   *Transformed sugar.* A free-flowing variety of sucrose is available known as transformed sugar. It is composed of microcrystalline agglomerations of sucrose whose surface area differs from the conventional product. This change produces a large absorptive capacity whilst still remaining stable under normal environmental conditions.

7.2.1.3 *Glucose syrup*. Glucose syrup is a mixture of various carbohydrates held in water and is manufactured by utilising the breakdown of starch when treated by acids or enzymes under controlled conditions. The hydrolysis process is followed by a series of purification stages to achieve the necessary quality desired for a food-grade ingredient. The source of the starch, choice of process conditions, selection of enzyme and methods used to purify the product can influence composition and particularly the speed and extent to which hydrolysis takes place during the reaction process. The syrup, when produced from corn starch, is sometimes called corn syrup in older American publications. Typical compositions for glucose syrups used in the sweet industry are given in Table 7.1.

7.2.1.4 *Speciality starch syrups*. Many speciality starch syrups are available, and one of the most interesting is *high-fructose starch syrup* (HFGS or HFCS). This is produced by a further tranche of treatments on conventional glucose syrups using enzymes such as α-amylase, glucoamylase and glucose isomerase. Around two-fifths of the sugars present in the syrup are fructose, the sweetest of all the common sugars. The level of fructose can be increased by introducing further stages into the processing sequence, but this can only be achieved at a high cost. The resultant syrups are similar in their properties to those found when using invert sugar syrup. Confections made with products containing a high level of fructose require a lower boiling temperature but require a raised temperature for depositing. This is due to the lowered viscosity of the final mass. A further range of syrups has been developed by the selective hydrogenation of the base syrup in the presence of a suitable catalyst. The resulting products are sweeter and have a reduced tendency to crystallise.

Table 7.1 Principal sugar constituents present in commercial glucose syrup used in the manufacture of sugar confectionery. DE rating and composition (%)

	Acid conversion			Enzyme conversion	
	Low-DE	Regular-DE	High-DE	High-DE	High-maltose
DE value	34	42	52	62	43
Monosaccharides (dextrose)	12	19	32	36	7
Disaccharides (maltose)	11	15	14	31	46
Trisaccharides	10	13	10	13	11
Tetrasaccharides	8	9	6	3	4
Higher sugars	59	44	20	17	32

Note: Under US Federal terminology the higher sugars are described as higher oligosaccharides.

A second class of speciality syrups is *high maltose syrups*, in which maltose can be present at levels of up to 60%. These syrups are prepared by the use of selective amylases and contain a mixture of α- and β-maltose. The resulting product is less sweet than sucrose and is used where this property is considered a desirable attribute. Powdered *isomaltitol* is also high in maltose and is produced by the enzymic conversion of sucrose.

7.2.1.5 *Invert sugar*. The other primary sugar used in manufacture is invert sugar. This is not a pure sugar but a mixture of dextrose and fructose formed when sucrose is broken down into two simpler sugars—dextrose and fructose. Water is an essential feature of the reaction and becomes incorporated into the breakdown products. The reaction is stimulated by the presence of an acid or by the use of an enzyme.

7.2.1.6 *Polydextrose*. Another new ingredient available to the confectioner is polydextrose, which has a low-calorie content. It is a polymer of dextrose with sorbitol and an acid. The ingredient is hygroscopic in character and has a viscosity which is greater than sucrose. Its value is that it can be processed into confections with similar properties to boiled sweets. The material is acidic in nature and must be buffered to inhibit the development of invert sugar in mixed recipes. The use of polydextrose has been described by Liebrand & Smiles [2].

7.2.1.7 *Sorbitol, xylitol and mannitol*. These are commercially available for use in recipes for sweet products. These are not sugars in the conventional sense but polyhydric alcohols, more usually known as sugar alcohols. These materials are promoted for their role in inhibiting changes during storage or as a low-calorie replacement for sucrose or for their value in minimising tooth decay when compared to conventional sugars. Bacteria found in the mouth are less likely to attack products made from these materials and do not form the acidic compounds which break down and then dissolve the enamel which protects human teeth. Solubility varies considerably between the three types of materials.

7.2.1.8 *Lactose hydrolysates*. The careful choice of processing conditions for the selective hydrolysis of *lactose*, a sugar present in milk products and for this process obtained from whey, produces lactose hydrolysates. These hydrolysates are high in two simpler sugars, namely *galactose* and *dextrose*. A typical enzyme used to achieve hydrolysis is β-galactoside. The resulting product has a lesser tendency to crystallise when compared to lactose and an increased contribution to sweetness in the confection. The hydrolysed whey syrups now available have good water retention properties, behaving in a similar way to invert sugar syrup.

Lactitol, also on offer to the confectioner, is produced by the hydrogenation of lactose and is distinctly hygroscopic in its behaviour.

Another product produced from lactose by the action of alkalis is *lactulose*. This appears to have similar humectant properties to sorbitol, although considerably more hygroscopic in nature.

7.2.1.9 *Intense sweeteners.*

The use of intense sweeteners such as saccharin, aspartame and acesulphame potassium (acesulphame K) has found little adoption in the sweet industry. This is because most confectionery products require a high-mass viscosity to assist in processing and to gain consumer acceptance for their texture. Sweetness levels are rarely identified as a problem when taste trials are carried out on recipes which use traditional ingredients. Recently a new class of ingredient has been described by Jenner *et al.* [3]. The so-called *sucralose* is a chlorinated sucrose which is intensely sweet and has value in the manufacture of low-calorie products.

The use of the newer sugars in the manufacture of sugar confections has been reviewed by Dobson & Pepper [4].

7.2.1.10 *Sugar nomenclature.*

The structural formulae for common sugars and related compounds found in the sugar confectionery industry are listed in Table 7.2.

Rules for the structural nomenclature of most organic substances have been developed by expert groups under the aegis of International Union of Pure Applied Chemistry (IUPAC). The international rules for sugars were published as tentative rules for nomenclature by the IUPAC Commission on the Nomenclature of Organic Chemistry (CNOC) and the IUPAC–IUB Commission on Biochemical Nomenclature. Guidance on these rules was published in 1971 [5].

'Aldose' or 'ketose' is used in a generic sense in nomenclature of carbohydrates to denote the reducing or potentially reducing group of a monosaccharide. The concept of reducing groups in certain carbohydrate materials is particularly important both in structural terms and to the sweet industry. Their classification into reducing or non-reducing sugars indicates whether the carbohydrate has a free aldehydic or ketonic carbonyl group, and this is related to the oxidation properties possessed by the material.

Reducing sugars can be readily determined by analysis, and their level can be readily related to both product and ingredient quality and the likely behaviour on use. The analytical procedures rely on the breakdown of complex copper salts by sugars with reducing properties but not by those which are non-reducing in character. Modern techniques rely on the identification and quantification by the use of high-pressure liquid chromatography or enzymic conversion coupled on occasion with optical polarimetry. Sucrose is non-reducing in its properties whilst invert sugar

Table 7.2 Structural formulae for the common carbohydrate and related material used in the manufacture of sugar confectionery

Common name	Chemical name of pure material	Structural formulae
Sucrose (cane or beet sugar, saccharose)	β-D-fructofuranosyl α-D-glucopyranoside	
Dextrose (glucose, grape sugar, corn sugar)	α-D-glucopyranose	
Fructose (laevulose, fruit sugar)	β-D-fructofuranose	
Galactose (cerebose)	α-D-galactopyranoside	
Lactose (milk sugar)	4-O-β-D-galactopyranosyl-α-D-glucopyranose	
Lactitol	4-O-β-D-galactopyranosyl-D-glucitol	
Maltose	4-O-α-D-glucopyranosyl-D-glucopyranose	
Sorbitol	D-glucitol	

Table 7.2 *Continued*

Common name	Chemical name of pure material	Structural formulae
Mannitol		
Xylitol		
Maltol	3-hydroxy-2-methyl-4-pyrone	
Starch (amylum)		

Note: The systematic names given are based on the trivial names glucose, galactose, etc. rather than the IUPAC names for the sugars of glucohexose, galactohexose, etc.

mixture (or more precisely its constituent sugars) have reducing properties. D- and L- prefixes are used in the chemical description of sugars and denote configurational relationship.

(+) and (−) symbols also appear and indicate the optical properties of the sugars. The suffix relates to the ability of a sugar in solution to alter the optical rotation of polarised light and again forms the basis of an analytical test procedure. Thus the optical rotation ($d_{20°C}$) for pure sugar is + 66.5° and when inverted is − 20.0°.

7.2.2 Fats

Three other broad classes of base ingredients are used in the industry as well as sugars. The first of these is confectionery fats, which can be tailored chemically to suit the type of product being manufactured. One of the commonest fats in use in the manufacture of sweets is hydrogenated palm kernel oil and is relatively simple in chemical structural terms. Most sugar confectionery fats are non-lauric in origin. Their brittleness, hardness and flavour carryover are related to their extraction and treatment, and in particular to the type or types of fatty acids that are present and whether the fat is saturated or unsaturated. Fats are used to improve texture and to lubricate the product to achieve better chewing characteristics.

Keeney & Bruin [6] used scanning electron microscopy and compression testing to examine the role of fat in sugar confectionery and specifically in caramels. This work showed that the sugar phase was the supporting medium for the product and below a critical moisture level structural strength depended on the protein content of the product. The number and size of the fat globules were found to be important in their contribution to the mechanical properties of the sweet. Fat dispersion appeared to be dependent on the degree of agitation. Numerous fat inclusions were found on the surface of the test confections and their size was related to the presence of milk protein.

7.2.3   Thickeners and stabilisers

The third class of ingredients used in the manufacture of sugar confections is gelling agents, and this class can be extended to include thickeners and stabilisers. The ingredient range includes gelatin, agar agar, pectin, starch and gums. Most can be modified chemically or extracted preferentially to obtain materials with specific properties. Some of these products are extremely complicated in structural terms and can be complex mixtures. *Gelatin* for example contains proline, arginine and hydroxyproline. *Pectin* contains a high number of galacturonic acid units in the form of methyl esters. The degree of esterification controls the rate and quality of the gel produced using the pectin. Thus rapid-set pectins are likely to have esterification levels of 75% whilst slow-set pectins are only 50% esterified. The use of these materials improves resistance to water attack from atmospheric deposition and resistance to graining by inhibiting crystallisation.

7.2.4   Proteins

The final class of base materials in the production of sweetmeats is proteins, such as those found in milk and used in the manufacture of caramels. The presence of proteins in a recipe can give rise to one of the major chemical reactions which takes place during the production of sugar confectionery and chocolate and has a profound influence on the quality of the product. Caramels have a considerable resistance to *deformation* once formed, and this strength is derived from the choice of ingredients used in the recipe. This *body strength* is necessary to prevent the deformation of the piece, as most sugar confections containing milk solids are relatively high in water content. Flow or deformation can still occur, particularly at the ends of each cut piece of confection, and the extent is traceable to the type and scale of reaction which takes place during manufacture. The effect is due to the internal structure of the product, which can be visualised as a product with sectional layers sliding under shear forces. The shear properties are due to the viscosity effects contributed by the reaction between milk protein and reducing sugars and to the level of fat present in the confection.

Shear forces are applied whilst the product passes through the forming rollers, during cutting and whilst the warm confection is being wrapped. *Recovery*, known as the elastic response or shear elasticity, is nearly complete for other natural products such as rubber, but confections which contain milk have a very slow response time. This slow recovery leads to problems during production as the sweet shrinks during cutting and whilst it is held on store, allowing the wrapper to become loose, particularly at its ends. Some loose wrappers may separate from the product, but a more troublesome fault is the ingress of air through the faulty wrapping. The oxygen contained in the air affects the exposed surface of the confection causing the fat to develop *rancidity*. A secondary effect is the condensation of water from the air under adverse environmental conditions leading to sugar leaching and graining.

The scale of the problem of deformation can be traced to the inter-relationship of the milk protein and the level of reducing sugars in a recipe and the conditions experienced during processing which promote a reaction to take place. Generally it has been found that the greater the mechanical working of a confection containing milk protein during production then the greater is the effect of shear forces on the sweetmeat.

The molecular weight of macromolecules such as proteins is extremely high, being greater than 17 000 for milk protein and over 40 000 for those found in egg albumen.

Viscosity of the product also has a significant role in gaining acceptability for the product amongst purchasers. Textural responses by consumers are influenced greatly by the viscosity of the confection during chewing, and this property is significantly affected by even minor changes in water content.

7.3 Change of composition

There are three primary chemical reactions taking place during the manufacture of sugar confections and a number of secondary reactions depending on composition.

7.3.1 *Caramelisation*

Cane or beet sugar (sucrose) deteriorates in heated conditions to form coloured breakdown products in the process known as caramelisation. This also takes place when minor traces of acidic impurities are present together with traces of fructose (laevulose). The resultant product is 5-hydroxyl methyl furfural which develops *browning* in a sugar syrup.

7.3.2 *Inversion*

The second important reaction is the breakdown of sucrose into its two simpler sugars, as described in Section 7.2.1.5. This process is known to the confectioner as inversion. The reaction can be induced deliberately as a means of developing desirable characteristics in a sweetmeat. An example is where significant quantities of invert sugar are required in a syrup phase to produce a flowing eating texture. Invert sugar is also produced by design where it is added to a recipe or developed during cooking as a whole or part replacement for glucose syrup. Finally the reaction can occur accidentally by the presence of trace acidic materials inducing breakdown during processing.

Invert sugar is a mixture of two simpler sugars dextrose and fructose. One hundred grams of sucrose will yield 105 g of invert sugar when treated in the presence of water, and the resultant mixture will contain 52.5 g of glucose and 52.5 g of fructose. It is believed that the early products from the action of invertase, an enzyme commonly used to convert sucrose into invert sugar, are not a 50:50 mixture. An intermediate stage takes place in which a form of fructose predominates in a two-thirds to one-third ratio. According to Blanchard and Albon [7] this stage is quickly overcome and the expected equal-part mixture of the two sugars is formed.

Invertase is used in sugar confectionery products such as the centre of

Table 7.3 Typical reducing sugar contents found in sugar confectionery products

Typical range for reducing sugar content (%)	Type of products
3.0–4.9	Paste work
5.0–9.9	Cream paste
	Fudge
10.0–14.9	Butter confections
	Chewing gum
	Gelatine jellies
	Pectin jellies
15.0–19.9	Caramels and toffees
	Hard creams
	High-boiled sweets
	Turkish delight
20.0–25.0	Butterscotch (traditional)
	Marshmallow
	Soft creams

Developed from information given by Lees [8].

coated creams to soften these types of sweets whilst they are held on store and before their sale to consumers.

The presence of high levels of invert sugar can result in problems due to the hygroscopic nature of the comparatively high levels of fructose produced by inversion, which will attract water from the atmosphere under adverse environmental conditions. An indicator of the hygroscopic character is given by the level of reducing sugars in a confection as reported by an analyst. Typically the reducing sugar content reported for a confection is a combination of those parts of the components of glucose syrup which have reducing properties, lactose, any added dextrose, invert sugar solids and any other sugar component with similar properties. Reducing sugar contents for a range of confectionery products are given in Table 7.3.

The rate of hydrolysis by an acid on sucrose during inversion is more than one thousand times the rate experienced with other disaccharide materials such as lactose or maltose, although these substances contain similar chemical linkages. Although only one form of fructose is produced during the breakdown process, two crystalline forms of glucose with different optical properties are produced.

7.3.3   Maillard reaction

The third chemical reaction encountered during the manufacture of sweetmeats is the Maillard reaction. This takes place between the amino groups present in amino acids, proteins and peptides and the so-called 'glycosidic' hydroxyl groups (reducing groups) in sugars. The reaction products are brown condensation pigments known as melanoidins, which contribute flavour, colour and texture. The reaction was first described by Maillard in 1912 [9] and was later more fully reported by the same researcher in 1916 [10]. The process is not fully understood, although it is suspected that there are a number of steps in the reaction before the final products are formed.

The Maillard reaction occurs during the roasting of cacao and when milk protein is held under heat in the presence of reducing sugars. The latter conditions apply in the manufacture of caramels, toffee and fudge. The reaction stimulates the development of flavour, the creation of a desirable texture and produces an improvement in handling properties.

Hydrolysed whey syrups have a greater ability to undergo the Maillard reaction, improving colour and flavour. However, lactitol does not take in this reaction due to the structural changes which take place on hydrogenating lactose.

Scheiber [11] has suggested that in the manufacture of products where the Maillard reaction is not a desirable feature enzymic treatment can be used to reduce the degree of browning, but only at the expense of the removal of glucose. The same author has also suggested that enzymic methods are used for the removal of oxygen to prevent rancidity of products on prolonged storage.

7.3.4 *Secondary reactions*

Other chemical reactions occurring during sweet manufacture involve the breakdown of protein in gelling agents and in whipping agents such as egg albumen. These usually occur under the presence of heat and are accelerated under acid conditions.

7.4 Change of state

7.4.1 *Crystallisation*

The main effect which involves a change of state during the production of sugar confectionery is the move from ingredients held in a highly saturated syrup to their presence in the confection in crystalline form. Pure sucrose crystals are members of the monoclinic system of *crystal classification* and are probably present in sphenoidal symmetry [12]. The type of sucrose crystal present in a confection is not in the pure shape of a spherulitic crystal but is slightly malformed. This is because other ingredients present, such as other sugars and gelling agents, cause distortion in the crystalline form of sucrose.

Sucrose can be dissolved in water and will reach *saturation level* at a concentration of 66.6%. However it is possible to continue the process, dissolving more sucrose in water to create a *supersaturated solution*. These solutions of the sugar in water, which are of higher concentration than can be achieved at their stable saturation point, will grain or crystallise under appropriate circumstances. A supersaturated solution of sucrose formed at a raised temperature may or may not deposit sucrose crystals on cooling. The syrup passes through a series of zones classified by Oswald [13] as labile, false grain, metastable and stable. The values for each of these zones are calculated by relating the weight of material present in 100 g of water at a fixed temperature against the values found under the same conditions at saturation. Crystallisation does not occur in the stable zone no matter how the solution is treated. This zone represents the saturation concentration of 66.6% for sucrose in water at 20°C with an S value of 1.0. Crystallisation does not occur naturally in the metastable zone unless influenced by an outside effect—vibration, stirring, presence of seed crystals. This effect occurs particularly in the false grain zone. Crystallisation invariably occurs in the labile zone. The figures for the zone boundaries for pure sucrose are under 1.0, 1.0, 1.25 and 1.35 respectively.

Higher concentrations of sucrose in supersaturated syrups in the metastable zone will not crystallise unless disturbed by outside influences such as the presence of undissolved fragments of sugar dust or agitation. Solutions with a concentration level for sucrose of 87% or above ($S = 3.3$) are also difficult to crystallise, particularly where traces of less crystallisable sugars such as fructose, invert sugar mixture etc. are present. Crystallisation in sweet manufacture is usually induced by adding *seed crystals* contained in a syrup phase such as fondant or by the use of intense agitation to stimulate the development of crystal nuclei as was used traditionally in the method of tempering chocolate. This procedure used intense agitation to induce the cocoa butter to crystallise in the correct stable form.

The *rate of crystallisation* in a seeded product is dependent on the temperature at the point of addition, the ratio of seed crystals to total syrup phase, the amount of sucrose present in solution above saturation level, the degree of agitation, the number of crystal nuclei present in the dosing seed and the viscosity of the mix. High-viscosity conditions inhibit the speed of crystallisation. Crystallisation in unseeded products is dependent on the rate of formation of the crystal nuclei and the subsequent speed of growth on these nuclei.

Work by Van Hook and Brodeur [14] indicates there is an initial induction period before crystallisation takes place, which is then followed by a growth stage. Crystallisation is accompanied by a distinct and detectable rise in temperature caused by the release of the latent heat of crystallisation.

Although it is difficult to imagine from their visual appearance, large macromolecules such as proteins are crystalline in structure. The crystalline nature of these materials is being revealed using X-ray diffraction analysis, which supplies images of the molecules from the patterns obtained when X-rays are scattered by crystals. The way that atoms are present in the repeating units and the arrangement of these units makes up the crystal, and this partly determines the properties of the relevant macromolecules. The importance of this structural information to the confectioner is that biochemical techniques can be chosen to produce proteins or enzymes with greater resistance to heat or to the pH of solution, thereby improving their performance under processing conditions. To complicate matters further, proteins can exist in different polymorphic forms and this can create difficulties in development of specially tailored materials.

7.4.2 *Polymorphism*

Polymorphism is the ability of a material to exist in two or more crystal forms. Cocoa butter, for example, can exist in at least four forms, of which only one is considered stable for the production of chocolate confectionery.

This second major change of state is particularly associated with the manufacture of a high-boiled sweet. In this product mixtures of sugars are held in solution with water contents as low as 2%. Theoretically, the less water that is left in a confection then the greater should be the tendency for the syrup to crystallise. This is not the case, because in these low water content products, sucrose no longer is held in crystallisable form. It is present as a glass or, put more precisely, in an *amorphous state* [15]. This amorphous form should be as stable as other amorphous materials such as common window glass. This latter material is closely related to a boiled sweet in structural behaviour. A sugar boiling will remain stable provided sufficient water is removed during manufacture and the product has been protectively packed to prevent the ingress of water. Unfortunately, sugar confections tend to pick up moisture from the atmosphere and this water is deposited on the surface of the sweet. The deposited water leaches sugar from the confection. Water in the syrup will evaporate as the external temperature conditions change and the syrup crystallises. The crystal grain which occurs induces a layer-by-layer change of state in the main body of the confection moving from the stable amorphous state to the crystalline state. A method for calculating the conversion of amorphous sucrose into crystalline sucrose has been suggested by researchers Makower & Dye [16]. Keeney & De Bruin [6] found that sugar nucleation in caramels developed at the fat globule–sugar syrup interface.

7.4.3 Starch

Starch also undergoes a change of state during the gelatinisation process used to produce a starch jelly. The starch molecule is composed of amylose and amylopectin fractions. In the process of starch gelatinisation, heat must be applied to non-modified, non-cold water-soluble varieties to cause the starch to swell in water. The energy which results from heating induces a change within the amorphous areas of the starch granule, stimulating hydrogen bonding to occur between the starch molecules and water molecules. Water then ingresses into the starch granules, causing swelling and putting further stress on the structure of the material. At a particular temperature range which is dependent on the source of the material and its treatment during extraction and purification, the original structure becomes totally disrupted, losing its original crystalline identity.

The temperature at which this process takes place is usually referred to as the *gelatinisation point*, although as indicated it is a range rather than a single point. Visible signs are the change from an opalescent solution to a relatively clear mix which, if sufficient concentration of starch of the right type has been used, sets or gels on cooling.

The presence of sugars inhibits the process of gelatinisation. Prolonged heating will also destroy the gel by causing disruption of the structure, resulting in leaching from the swollen granules into the liquid fraction, affecting the gel-forming capability.

7.4.4 Enzymic changes

As described previously the major biochemical process used in the manufacture of sugar confectionery is the use of invertase. This enzyme can be considered as promoting and then accelerating a reaction but does not become incorporated into the new molecule.

Enzymic changes are found widely in nature, although their use in the food industry under the broad description of biochemical reactions attracts adverse comment from food purists.

Invertase is used in the manufacture of creams which are to be covered with a chocolate or other form of coating and the centre allowed to liquefy to satisfy consumer preference. The use of alternatives such as fruit acids to stimulate inversion is inefficient and the process cannot be controlled to provide the same high level of quality of manufactured confection. The enzyme is both heat-sensitive and affected by use in low-pH conditions. For practicable purposes, invertase solutions should be added at temperatures lower than 65°C (149°F).

The term invert, widely used in the confectionery industry, is confusing in stereochemical terms as it has a different meaning in configurational nomenclature, implying the transposition of two substituents.

The most significant uses of biochemical processing in the manufacture of sweets are concerned not with the product but with the production of basic ingredients. Specific amylases and glucose isomerase are used to convert starch into speciality glucose syrups. Elsewhere *Aspergillus niger* is used on appropriate sugars to manufacture citric acid in a more economical way than can be achieved by extraction from natural sources. Enzymic methods are also employed in the production of speciality gums which have enhanced thickening, stabilising and setting properties.

7.5 Environmental behaviour

Sugar confections will either pick up or lose moisture to the atmosphere depending on the external conditions to which they are being subjected. It is possible to calculate or determine a value which relates storage behaviour to the external environmental conditions, and in particular to the relative humidity of the air. This value is known as the *equilibrium relative humidity* (*ERH*). The ERH is influenced by the composition of the syrup phase, particularly its water content, which may be present as bound water or free water. It is the free water that influences the storage behaviour of the product. A syrup phase may be liquid in a mixed-phase product such as fondant or appear as an apparent solid in boiled sweets. Total water content is irrelevant as a measure of behaviour when bound water is present but is a guide to the efficiency of manufacture. Each component present in a confection has an effect on the release of water to the surrounding atmosphere. The presence of dissolved solid matter affects the relative vapour pressure of the mini-atmosphere surrounding the sweet. The *water activity* (a_w) of a product is of greater significance than a knowledge of its moisture content when considering likely storage behaviour. This value takes account of the chemical make-up of the individual components present in a recipe ingredient and in particular the presence of hydrophilic groups (having a strong affinity for water) and hydrophobic groupings (lacking an affinity for water) in their structure. The derived figure can then be related to the water activity in the surrounding atmosphere. Modifications to the recipe for the confection will vary the value derived for water activity.

The *equilibrium relative vapour pressure (ERVP)* of the product when measured under a fixed constant pressure and temperature or calculated from a knowledge of the recipe is directly relatable to the equilibrium relative humidity (ERH). This latter value relates the equilibrium vapour pressure of the confection to the vapour pressure for water when measured under the same conditions. Water activity (a_w) is the ERH value divided by 100.

Further guidance for the confectioner is provided by the *moisture sorption isotherm (MSI)* of a product, which can be plotted by relating the moisture content calculated on a dry solids basis to water activity. This curve can be used to predict product behaviour under different cooking conditions.

Methods for the determination of moisture contents have been reviewed by Kaarmas [17]. The methods for calculating ERH have been described by Lees & Jackson [18] using the procedures developed by Grover [19] and Norrish & Stuart [20]. Richardson [21] has also reviewed these procedures and the work of Money & Born [22]. The same author usefully relates water activity and equilibrium relative humidity to the microbiological deterioration of sugar confectionery by moulds and bacteria. The influence of water activity on the behaviour of food products and their control has been considered by Rockland & Nishi [23].

Table 7.4 Molecular weights of carbohydrate and related materials used in the manufacture of sugar confectionery

Product	Molecular weight
Sucrose	342
Lactose	342
Regular glucose syrup solids	ca 330
Maltose	342
Maltotriose	504
Maltotetraose	667
Maltulose	342
Invert sugar solids	180
Fructose	180
Dextrose	180
Galactose	180
Sorbitol	182
Lactitol	344
Lactulose	342
Mannitol	182
Xylitol	152
Polydextrose	Over 1000

Table 7.5 Range of ERH values found in sugar confectionery products

Type of confectionery	Equilibrium relative humidity (%)
High-boiled sweets	20–30
Caramels	42–52
Fudge	58–70
Starch gums	60–65
Liquorice paste	60–65
Turkish delight	65–70
Jellies	65–70
Marzipan	70–75
Fondant creams	75–82
Milk chocolate	75–85
Plain chocolate	80–85

From Lees [24].

As indicated earlier, ERH is in inverse proportion to the components in solution when expressed as a *molecular concentration* in the syrup phase. Generally, the lower the molecular weight the greater the tendency for the product to attract moisture from the air. However it is the structural make-up of the various recipe components which are important in controlling storage behaviour. The molecular weights for a range of components found in confectionery recipes are given in Table 7.4.

An increase in the molecular concentration in the various phases will lower the ERH value. This effect is particularly noticeable in products where surface drying or skinning occurs, giving added protection on storage, or where wet crystallisation is used to form a protective coat on a soft-structured confectionery product. Typical ERH values of a wide range of sugar confectionery products are given in Table 7.5.

Various *humectants* can be used to minimise the rate of moisture change whilst a product is being held on store. These include sorbitol, glycerol and various grades of speciality glucose syrups. It is the area of reducing or preventing water loss whilst on store that has prompted the introduction of new ingredients. These materials are designed to improve the stability of confections during the sometimes lengthy period of storage before sale to the consumer.

7.6 Evaporation

Most of the production processes used in the manufacture of sugar confections rely on the efficient and effective removal of water to produce a product with good keeping properties and a satisfactory texture. Mixtures of sucrose (pure cane or beet sugar) in water will form a saturated solution at a constant value

Table 7.6   Concentration of sucrose in water at saturation

Temperature (°C)	Sucrose in 100 g of solution
10	65.32
15	65.92
20	66.60
25	67.35
30	68.18
40	70.01
50	72.04
60	74.20
70	76.45
80	78.74
90	81.00

From Fuente [25].

Table 7.7   Solubility of sugars and related materials used in the manufacture of sweets

Sugar	Concentration in water at 20°C (%)
Sucrose	66.6
Dextrose	47.3
Fructose	78.7
Lactose	18.0
Mannitol	54.9
Sorbitol	70.1
Xylitol	63.0

provided that the external environmental conditions remain the same. The relationship between sucrose concentration and the temperature of solution is given in Table 7.6.

Solubility values for other sugars in water determined at 20°C are given for comparison in Table 7.7.

Solutions of sucrose at the same concentration level in water will boil at the same temperature provided that the external environmental conditions remain constant. The relationship of boiling temperature to concentration is shown in Table 7.8. Mixtures of glucose syrup in water and invert sugar syrup in water behave similarly, having the same boiling temperature at the same concentration provided operating conditions are held constant. However they boil at different temperatures to each other and to solutions of sucrose at the same concentration. This difference is illustrated by the figures contained in Table 7.9. The use of this type of data to calculate theoretical boiling temperatures when developing recipes for sugar confectionery has been described by Lees & Jackson [18]. Reducing the air pressure, for example by

Table 7.8 Boiling point of sucrose solutions at varying concentrations

Sucrose concentration (%)	Temperature at boiling (°C)
40	101.4
50	102.0
60	103.0
70	105.5
80	111.0
90	122.0

Table 7.9 Boiling points of solutions of glucose syrup and invert sugar in water

Concentration of sugar (%)		
Glucose syrup solids	Invert sugar	Boiling temperature (°C)
81.0	72.0	105.5
85.6	76.8	111.1
89.3	81.6	116.1
92.7	87.3	122.2
97.8	93.1	130.0

creating a vacuum in the boiling vessel, will lower the boiling point of all types of sugar syrups but to differing extents.

The presence of non-sucrose ingredients in a confectionery recipe affects both the amount of sucrose that can be dissolved in water and the total concentration of dissolved solids in water. Invert sugar, the breakdown products of sucrose formed when treated with an acid or enzyme, and glucose syrup, produced by treating starch with an acid or an enzyme, increase the total solution concentration but depress sucrose concentration (Table 7.9).

Minor changes in the residual water content of a sugar confection will have a significant influence on consumer acceptability and are due to the differences in eating quality arising from variations in texture. These textural changes in a sugar confection can be the result of three competing effects:

(1) Changes in water content.
(2) Changes in concentration of solid matter held in the syrup phase.
(3) Compositional changes.

The effect of composition and changing the concentration has been discussed earlier in this chapter. Variations in water content are directly attributable to the degree of evaporation of the confection during processing, and this is fixed by the composition of the recipe and the use of a predetermined boiling temperature. In single-phase confections such as a

Table 7.10 Typical water contents for a range of sugar confectionery

Product	Type	Class	Water content (%)
Boiled sweets	Single-phase	S	1.5–3.5
Jellies	Single-phase	S	20.0–22.0
Tablets	Multiphase	C/L	0.6–1.4
Chocolate	Multiphase	C/S	1.0–2.0
Rock	Multiphase	G/S	4.0–6.0
Nougat	Multiphase	S/C/G	5.0–7.0
Caramels	Multiphase	S/C	5.5–7.0
Cream paste	Multiphase	S/C	5.5–6.5
Marshmallow	Multiphase	G/S/C	12.0–18.0
Fondant/creams	Multiphase	S/C	12.0–13.0

KEY
G   gaseous phase present in a significant amount, usually as air;
S   syrup or liquid phase present in a significant amount, usually as a solution of the soluble ingredients in water but could be present as liquid fat;
C   crystal or solid phase usually present as a crystallised sugar or fat but could be an insoluble component.

high-boiled sweet, the level of water determines the hardness of the product. However the choice of ingredients can have an important effect on the consumer perception of the product. The use of low-DE glucose syrups with high levels of the higher oligosaccharides gives a hard product with chewy rather than good crack characteristics. In a two-phase confection such as fondant, where a crystal phase coexists with a syrup phase, variations in both boiling temperature and composition have significant effects on the texture of the product. A range of typical water contents for sugar confections is given in Table 7.10.

7.7 Sweetness and taste

Sweetness is one of the four basic *taste sensations* experienced when eating foods. These four primary sensations are sweet, sour, salty and bitter. Each taste sensation makes a specific contribution to the flavour of the confection. There are additional effects not directly related to oral perception including cooling, numbing, drying, salivation, tooth coating, mouth coating and irritation, and these are contributed by the choice of ingredients [26]. Most sugar alcohols contribute a cooling effect on the tongue.

The overall *flavour sensation* when eating a sweet is a combination of two factors. The first is taste, which is the sensation developed by the lingual organs, the organs of the tongue. Secondly there is a smell sensation which is detected by the olfactory organs in the nose. The various sensations experienced when consuming food are brought together within the brain to produce a final overall flavour recognition and satisfaction level experienced by the consumer.

Table 7.11 Relative sweetness of various carbohydrates

Type of carbohydrate	Relative sweetness
Fructose syrup	102
Sucrose	100
Xylitol	90
Maltitol	68
Glucose	60
High-DE glucose syrup	58
Maltose	43
Regular glucose syrup	38
Lactose	26

Based on data published by Kearsley *et al.* [28].

The effect of using different sweetening ingredients on the overall taste is difficult to measure as the sensation experienced by the consumer is influenced by the level of acidulent used in the product and specifically the pH value derived from the type of food acid and the texture of the confection. The procedure for measuring sweetness has varied considerably amongst researchers, and the results reported show differences in the listings for the strength of the taste sensation. A useful review has been given by Hyvonen [27].

The *ratings for sweetness* which have been reported vary according to the type of sugar, the temperature of solution for testing or, if presented as a crystal, the crystalline form and size in which the product is presented. This variation has some implication for the confectioner and explains why comments from consumers vary on the different levels of sweetness detected when eating crystallised products containing or encased with a fine coating of different crystal sizes. Practical experience indicates that the ratings given by Kearsley [28] and partly reproduced in Table 7.11 are relatable to the sensations experienced when eating sweets.

The varying sweetness of confectionery ingredients appears to be related to the stereochemistry of the structural units in the sugar. The evidence for this theory has been reviewed by Hallenberger [29].

Acidity is the second of the natural taste stimulations experienced when eating confectionery. Citric acid, lactic acid, malic acid and tartaric acid are all found in nature and used for creating an acid sensation in sweets. Most are produced synthetically due to the high cost and difficulty in extracting the natural material. The level of usage and their behaviour in solution is important in creating the desired level of effect on the palate. Their effect on the taste sensation is related to the pH value of the acid when it is dissolved in water. Their use in the food industry has secondary benefits of preservation and resistance to micro-organisms, but these subsidiary properties are of minor value to the sugar confectionery industry. Taste characteristics for the different acids are listed in Table 7.12.

Table 7.12   Taste characteristics of the food acids available for use in the production of sugar confectionery

Food acid	E number	Characteristic
Acetic	E260	Strong, pungent
Citric	E330	Clean, high-quality, easily dissipated
Fumaric	E297	Strong, slow to clear
Lactic	E270	Mild, slow to clear
Malic	E296	Strong
Tartaric	E334	Sharp

The *E numbers* given in the Table 7.12 relate to permitted additives which have been approved under legislation enacted by the European Community and, under appropriate conditions, have appeared on pack listings from 1 July 1986. A full discussion on food additives and their role will be found in the work of Jones & Flowerdew [30], Food Policy Research Centre of the School of Biochemical Research, University of Bradford [31], European Communities Commission [32] and in various Food Additives and Contaminants Committee Reports of the Ministry of Agriculture, Fisheries and Food (HMSO).

It is usual to add *buffered acids* such as buffered citric acid and buffered lactic acid as the primary acidulant in a recipe to inhibit the reactive effects of acid flavouring materials on sugars. The buffer salts are usually sodium citrate (E331) or sodium lactate (E325). Calcium salts of citric acid (E333) and potassium salts (E332) are used for a similar purpose in the manufacture of jellies and to assist in the development of the gel.

The use of flavourings is necessary in sugar confectionery manufacturing to enhance those features lost during processing and to create taste sensations to achieve acceptance by the consumer. Some products contain large amounts of natural materials such as cocoa, coffee and milk products and may or may not contain artificial flavourings. Other natural flavours found in sweet manufacture include extracts, crystallates or distillates of plant products such as vanilla or the essential oils of peppermint, spearmint, lemon and orange. The remaining class of flavourings is tailored to the needs of producers to withstand the high temperatures involved in processing or the need to remain stable for long periods of time whilst exposed to air. Flavour assessment in the industry varies from correlation of a product to a known and desired quality of flavouring to selection of a flavour by an expert taste panel and its correlation to the tastes preferred by consumers.

References

1. W.V.W. Vink, *Proc. 42nd PMCA Conference* (1988), 136.
2. J. Liebrand and R. Smiles, *Manuf. Conf.* **62**, no.11 (1981).

3. M.R. Jenner, L. Bagley and C.R. Heather, *Food Tech. Int.* (1989) 273, Sterling Publications Ltd.
4. A.G. Dobson and T. Pepper, in *Food Chemistry*, Elsevier Applied Science Publishers (1986).
5. IUPAC CNOC and IUPAC IUB CBN, *Eur. J. Biochem.* **21** (1971), 455.
6. P.G. Keeney and E.J. Bruin, *Proc. 26th PMCA Conf.* (1976).
7. P.H. Blanchard and N. Albon, *Arch. Biochem. Biophys.* **29** (1950) 290.
8. R. Lees, *Faults, Causes and Remedies in Sugar Confectionery Manufacture*, Specialised Publications Ltd (1981).
9. L.C. Maillard, *Compt. Rend.* **154** (1912), 66.
10. L.C. Maillard, *Ann. Chim.*, **9** (1916), 258.
11. W. Scheiber, *Z. Lebensmittel* **6** (1980), 252.
12. R. Lees, *Factors Affecting Crystallisation in Boiled Sweets, Fondants and other Confectionery*, STS 42, FIRA, Leatherhead (1965).
13. W. Oswald, *Z. Phys. Chem.*, **22** (1897), 289.
14. A. van Hook and E.A. Brodeur Jr., *Int. Sug. J.*, **55** (1953), 332.
15. J. Kelleher, *BFMIRA* STS 41, FIRA, Leatherhead (1903).
16. B. Makower and W.B. Dye, *J. Agric. Food Chem.*, **4** (1956), 72.
17. E. Kaarmas, *Food Tech.*, April (1980), 52.
18. R. Lees and E.B. Jackson, *Sugar Confectionery and Chocolate Manufacture*, Leonard Hill Books/Blackie, Glasgow (1973).
19. D.W. Grover, *J. Soc. Chem. Ind.*, **66** (1947), 201.
20. R. Norrish and R. Stuart, *Conf. Prod.*, **30** (1964), 769, 771, 808.
21. T. Richardson, *US NCA/AACT Seminar* (1988).
22. R.W. Money and R. Born, *J. Sci. Food Agric.*, **2** (1951), 180.
23. L.B. Rockland and S.K. Nishi, *Food Tech.*, April (1980), 42.
24. R. Lees, *Second Seminario Latinamerico de Chocolates y Golosinas*, Argentina (1988).
25. C.D.F. Fuente, *Int. Sug. J.*, **60** (1960) 126.
26. M.J. Hudson, *IFST Proc., London*, **19**, no. 3 (1986), 134.
27. L. Hyvonen, *Varying Relative Sweetness*, University of Helsinki, EKT Series No. 546 (1980).
28. M.W. Kearsley *et al.*, *Starke* **32**, no. 7 (1980) 244.
29. R.S. Hallenberger, *Advanced Sugar Chemistry*, Ellis Horwood Ltd, Chichester (1980).
30. N.R. Jones and D.W. Flowerdew, *Food Additives: Description, Function and UK Legislation*, FIRA, Leatherhead (1982).
31. University of Bradford School of Biomedical Research, *Food Additives in Perspective* (1986).
32. European Communities Commission, *Food Additives and the Consumer*, Luxembourg (1980).

8 Boiled sweets

I. FABRY

8.1 Definition

Boiled sweets are, by legal definition, high-cooked, coloured and flavoured sugar masses which are formed into candies of desired shape and size. However this definition is too simplistic, because it does not take into consideration the multiplicity of ingredients other than carbohydrates which are used to produce hard candies with particular organoleptical properties like 'butterscotch', 'milk candy', 'peanut brittle', 'malt-flavoured candy' and 'honey-flavoured candy'. Furthermore, this definition does not take into account the various special technological treatments which can be applied to modify the texture and the appearance of the cooked sugar mass, with a view to producing a wide variety of specialities likes 'honeycomb', 'striped candies', 'satin candies', 'rocks', 'mintoe'.

Technically the term 'boiled sweet' is applied to mixtures of sucrose and glucose syrup which are cooked to such a high temperature that the cooked mass becomes clearly marked by the following characteristics:

(1) Non-crystalline, clear and glassy in appearance, when after the cooking process the cooked mass is not voluntarily opacified by pulling.

(2) An extremely low amount of residual moisture (1–3%) with an equilibrium relative humidity (ERH) below 30%, which can result in a marked tendency to absorb humidity from the atmosphere.

(3) After cooking, the two main components, sucrose and glucose syrup, are accompanied by a variable amount of invert sugar, the result of partial inversion of sucrose which takes place during the cooking process.

Besides white sugar and glucose syrup, which chiefly assure the typical physical glassy texture of boiled sweets, other raw materials must be used to satisfy individual consumer taste and texture, as well as to improve the aesthetic value of the finished products. An infinite number of ingredients can be used for this purpose. Technically they can be classified as follows:

(1) Flavouring agents:
Natural flavours.
Nature-indentical flavours.
Artificial flavours.

Acidulants
  citric acid
  tartaric acid
  malic acid
  lactic acid.
Common salt (sodium chloride).

(2) Colouring agents:
  Natural colours.
  Artificial colours.

(3) Flavouring and colouring agents:
  Brown sugars.
  Cane molasses.
  Caramel syrups.

(4) Raw materials which besides their flavouring and/or colouring properties increase the quality and/or the nutritive value of the finished products:
  Milk and milk products:
    liquid milk
    condensed milk
    dried milk powder
    condensed or dried whey powder
    yoghurt
    butter and butter fat
    cream.
  Honey.
  Liquorice juice.
  Malt extract.
  Nuts.
  Vitamins, etc.

(5) Raw materials which are used to modify the rheological properties of the sugar mass in order to obtain a particular texture, reduce or increase viscosity of the cooked mass, reduce raw materials cost in case of necessity to produce an 'all-sucrose candy', reduce sweetness, reduce stickiness, modify ERH, reduce inversion, increase Maillard reaction, etc. These include:
  Carbohydrates:
    invert sugar
    maltodextrin
    dextrose
    lactose.
  Inversion agents:
    acidulants
    cream of tartar/sodium potassium tartrate.
  Sorbitol.

Fats and emulsifiers.
Neutralising agent:
    sodium bicarbonate
    ammonium carbonate
    sodium citrate.
Buffering agent.

8.2 Classification

The above description shows that the definition 'boiled sweet' comprises a wide range of various products.

A classification is not easy and can be made under different aspects, for instance:

(1) Commercial definition.
(2) Applied forming process.
(3) Structure of finished products.

8.2.1 *Commercial definition*

They are also called 'high boilings', 'high boiling sweets', 'hard candies', 'drops' and are represented by three general types:

8.2.1.1 *Plain hard candy.* This is the generic name for an infinite number of a large variety of candy which, as shown in Figure 8.1, is produced in a wide range of shapes and sizes, flavours and colours as well as textures. They can be classified as follows in four main groups:

(1) Acidified hard candies/fruits drops.
(2) Non-acidified hard candies like peppermint drops, cough drops, etc.
(3) Hard milk caramels.
(4) Hard candies with added-value ingredients such as:
    Honey—honey drops/honeycomb.
    Malt extract—malted hard candy.
    Peanut—peanut brittle.

It is important to note that in most countries, specialities with added-value ingredients must contain a minimum amount of the labelled ingredient, or a minimum amount of one or more of the characteristic components.

8.2.1.2 *Filled boiled sweets.* These are composed of a clear, pulled, striped or grained jacket enclosing a centre which can be liquid, semiliquid, pasty or powdery. The main filling types are:

(1) Simple sugar–glucose syrup filling flavoured with natural, nature-identical or artificial flavour.

Figure 8.1.

(2) Fruit filling which, besides sugar and glucose syrup, contains fruit pulp or jam.

(3) Alcohol filling.

(4) Fat filling based on chocolate, hazelnut or almond paste, peanut butter, etc.

(5) Powdery filling like sherbet filling, liquorice filling.

Some of them, especially those which are grained and soft, are often coated with chocolate by enrobing or panning.

8.2.1.3 *Sugarless boiled sweets.* Clear, pulled or grained sugarless boiled sweets, plain or filled, are characterized by the fact that they are composed of one or a combination of polyhydric alcohols. The following polyols are used:

(1) Sorbitol, mannitol, xylitol—the first-generation polyols.
(2) Maltitol, lactitol, isomaltitol—the second-generation polyols.

As an alternative to polyols, polydextrose can be used. It is a low-calorie filler (1 kcal/g) which is obtained by polycondensation of dextrose in the presence of sorbitol and citric acid.

It is important to note that in most countries their use is subject to legal restriction. In compliance with legal status, sugarless candies can be classified in three main categories:

(1) Hard candies for diabetics.
(2) Tooth-friendly hard candies.
(3) Low-calorie hard candies.

8.2.2 *Applied forming process*

In relation to the applied forming method, boiled sweets can be divided into six main groups:

(1) Drops when using old-fashioned drop rollers.
(2) Candy balls, slices, chips, snippers, etc. using a balling machine.
(3) Plastic candies when using a rotary plastic moulder or a cutting and forming chain.
(4) Deposited hard candies when using a depositing plant.
(5) Rocks, rock slices, candy sticks, etc. when using a cutting machine.
(6) Lollipops when using a drop roller or a mould-depositing system (flat lollipop) or a rotary plastic moulder (ball lollipop) with a stick push-in device.

8.2.2.1 *Drops*. These sweets are made by passing a sheet of presized boiled sugar through two horizontally arranged rollers, with engraved cavities in the shape of one-half of the articles. The sheet of boiled sugar, whose thickness corresponds to the roller gap, is compacted during the passage through the two rollers and adopts the shape of the cavities. The complete article is formed by placing the two halves accurately on the top of each other.

On leaving the rollers, the formed sweets are linked to each other by a very thin film of sugar, and then are passed on to an enclosed cooled conveyor with pulsed air circulation. At the end of the cooling conveyor, the cooled sheet is directed into a perforated drum set at an angle, where the sweets are separated from each other by friction, while the sugar film which held the sweets together at the exit from the rollers is broken up and removed from the drum by falling through the perforation (Figure 8.2).

8.2.2.2 *Balled sweets*. Balled sweets are round or spherical in shape and are made by passing a calibrated rope of sugar through three rollers, shaped according to the desired sweet profile, which, by progressively approaching each other, cut and shape the rope of sugar into a sweet with a so-called rotary shape (Figure 8.3).

The batch of boiled sugar, tempered to the correct plasticity temperature is fed into a batch roller of variable degree of inclination, where four or six conically shaped counter-rotating rollers changing direction every seven or

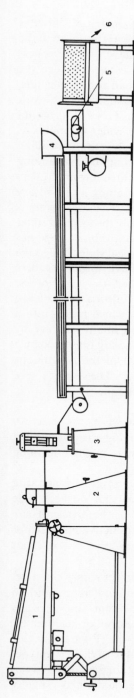

Figure 8.2 Flow chart of drops production on a HEMA–Karl Henkel drop rollers plant. 1, batch roller; 2, presizing rollers for the boiled sugar mass; 3, engraved forming roller; 4, cooling conveyor; 5, drum to separate the sugar film residues; 6, cooled drops.

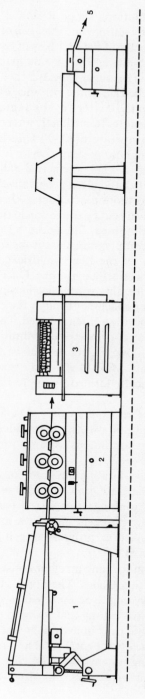

Figure 8.3 Production diagram of balled sweets produced with a classical HEMA balling plant. 1, batch roller; 2, size rollers; 3, balling machine; 4, cooling conveyor which can be connected with a cold table with a to-and-fro movement which keeps the sweet in rotation and thus prevents deformation; 5, cooled balled sweets.

eight revolutions shape it into a cone. The desired diameter of outlet is achieved by setting the outlet gap of the rollers, which in turn is matched to the inlet diameter of the first pair of equalizers in the size rollers. The size rollers fitted with three, four or five pairs of equalizers progressively reduce the diameter of the sugar rope. It is then directed towards the ball-rolling machine, and is picked up at the entrance of it by two pairs of equalizers which work intermittently. It is then cut by a rotary knife into a cylindrical rope of 50, 60 and 70 cm in length. Immediately after cutting, the sugar rope, which still holds its optimal temperature (80–90°C), is fed to a transversal punch in the ball-rolling machine in hold position, where it is passed into the forming rollers standing apart. This is where the actual balling operation starts: three forming rollers are actuated and close progressively towards each other, going into a rotary to-and-fro motion at about 800 revolutions per minute. The sugar rope is progressively cut by squeezing in the area where the cams of the forming roller are superimposed. Influenced by the rotary to-and-fro movement, together with the compression, the cut sugar pieces take on a spherical shape due to the geometry of the free cylindrical space between the three forming rollers pressing against each other. Once the position is reached, the speed of the rotating forming rollers declines progressively and the finished sweets leave the balling machine through the opening of the rollers, which return into a loading position when stopped. The discharged sweets are finally taken up by the cooling conveyor or the vibrating cold table where cooling is assured by a cold air flow. Figure 8.4 shows a production diagram of the continuous 'Startlight Mint-Line' and similar striped candies. The stripes are automatically formed by applying the coextrusion technique.

8.2.2.3 *Plastic hard candy.* Die-formed sweets, also known by the technical term of plastic sweets, are produced by cutting and forming a rope of boiled sugar in continuous rotary-forming die-heads or with a chain-forming machine.

A rotary-forming die-head consists of an eccentrically rotating blade ring and a die-plate ring and carries on its circumference and on each side embossing plungers engraved with the desired shape of the article. These embossing plungers meet in a matrix chamber and are activated by cams which ensure a progressive compression of the cut piece of boiled sugar (Figure 8.5).

A chain-forming machine consists of an upper and a lower rotary chain, set with cutting blades. The upper chains carry on their circumference, and on each side, engraved embossings which are activated by cams and ensure a progressive cutting and forming process. In this chain-forming machine the sugar rope runs in a straight line through the forming die (Figure 8.6).

Practically the total production is at present achieved with these two types of forming systems, since they allow not only for a perfect shaping of the sweets of various structures, but also for the production of an unlimited range of

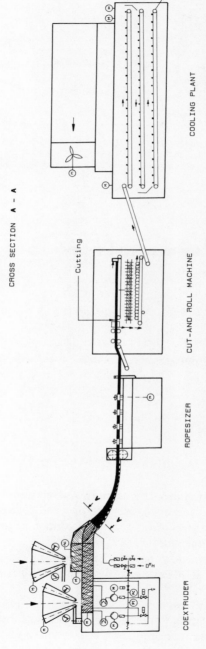

BASIC MASS

STRIPES

CROSS SECTION A – A

COOLING PLANT

Cutting

CUT-AND ROLL MACHINE

ROPESIZER

COEXTRUDER

Figure 8.4 Scartlight Mint-line—System Robert Bosan.

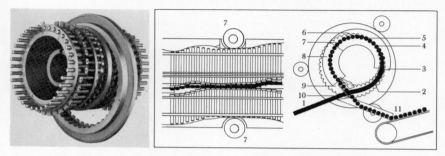

Figure 8.5 Functional diagram of a rotary-forming die-head—System Uniplast. 1, sugar rope feed; 2, sugar rope infeed; 3, preforming; 4, cutting; 5, insertion; 6, pre-embossing; 7, embossing by roller or cam; 8, tension equalization; 9, discharge; 10, sliding section; 11, feed chute to cooling conveyor.

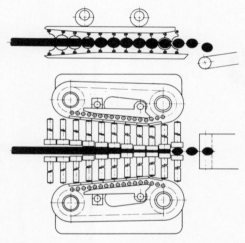

Figure 8.6 Functional diagram of a chain-form die-head—System Strada (Otto Hänsel).

articles in different shapes such as fruits, animals and other so-called 'designed' sweets, which could never be produced on a ball-rolling machine, as well as the whole range of centre-filled sweets that cannot be manufactured on a drop roller or balling machine.

Without going into any technical details, it suffices to say that a die-forming or chain-forming plant consists of five basic machines as shown in Figure 8.7.

8.2.2.4 *Deposited hard candies.* These sweets are of one single colour, with a very smooth surface and practically without entrapped air inclusions. They are made in a continuous process in which a mass of boiled sugar of relatively low viscosity is deposited at high temperature (130–135°C) into Teflon-lined

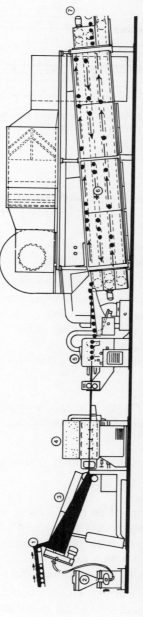

Figure 8.7 Flow chart of a chain-forming plant—System Strada (Otto Hänsel). 1, continuous feeding of tempered high-boiled sugar mass (80–90°C); 2, filling pump; 3, batch roller; 4, size roller; 5, chain-forming die; 6, cooling conveyor; 7, cooled candies.

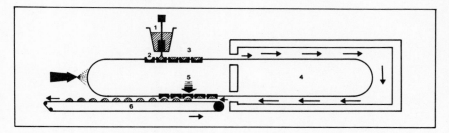

Figure 8.8 Flow diagram of the production of deposited candies—System Baker Perkins. 1, depositing hopper; 2, Teflonised metal moulds; 3, mould circuit; 4, cooling tunnel; 5, ejection station; 6, discharge conveyor.

metal moulds, equipped at the bottom with ejector pins to eject the candies from the moulds, once they have been solidified after passage through a cooling tunnel (Figure 8.8).

To prevent an uncontrolled inversion rate as well as discoloration, the following factors must be observed absolutely:

(1) Only buffered acid can be used, mainly buffered lactic acid.

(2) Sugar mass level in the vacuum chamber where the acid solution is added must be maintained as low as possible.

(3) Sugar mass level in the depositing hopper must be maintained constantly at a level of 8–12 cm.

(4) Deposited candies must be rapidly cooled down from 130/135°C to a temperature below 90°C.

8.2.2.5 *Frame-cut candies.* This technique is reserved for the manufacture of specialities such as 'rocks' and twisted or plain sticks. There are basically two techniques:

(1) Cutting method (Figure 8.9): This method is largely used for sticks made on a system consisting of:

A horizontal batch roller.

A rope sizer-roller, equipped on the discharge side with a cutting head with rotating knife which cuts the formed sugar rope into sticks of 100–150 mm in length with a diameter of 10–12 mm, or into 100–300 mm in length with a diameter of 20–24 mm.

A cooling conveyor taking the sticks into the wrapping section.

(2) Cutting and wrapping method: This method is nowadays widely used for 'rocks', which are sweets of cylindrical shape presenting at their cross-section a picture of fruit, letter or other design made manually, combining elements of transparent and pulled sugar mass of different colours.

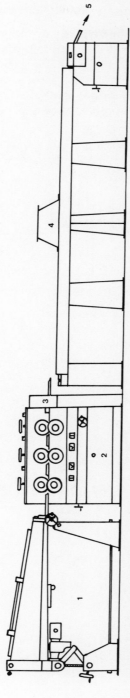

Figure 8.9 Flow diagram of the production of cut candy sticks—System HEMA. 1, batch roller; 2, size rollers; 3, rotating knife; 4, cooling conveyor; 5, cooled candy sticks.

8.2.2.6 *Lollipops.* Basically three types of lollipops can be distinguished:

(1) Flat lollipops (Figure 8.10): The forming techniques can be applied:
   (a) Depositing process by using special moulds.
   (b) Moulding/stamping techniques including the following steps: cutting of a well-tempered sugar rope, free fall of the cut pieces into a mould, and stamping the cut pieces in a rotating disc.
   (c) Moulding/stamping process as shown in Figure 8.11.

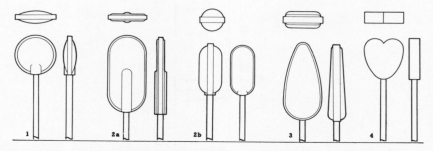

Figure 8.10   1, round, flat lollipop; 2a, elongated, oval, flat lollipop; 2b, flat, spherical lollipop; 3, elliptical, flat lollipop; 4, special flat lollipop shape.

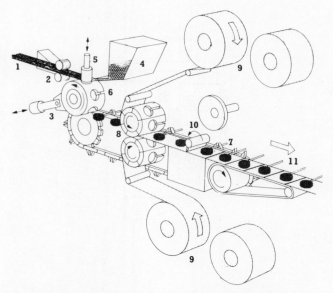

Figure 8.11   Flow diagram of a flat lollipop forming–wrapping machine—System Aquarius ALM 4P/W. 1, sugar rope; 2, sizing feeding rollers; 3, forming plunger; 4, stick feed; 5, cutting and preforming die; 6, forming die-head; 7, chain conveyor with gripper jaws; 8, sealing rollers; 9, wrapping materials reels; 10, rotating cutting knife; 11, transfer to conveyor belt and cooling tunnel.

The rope, continuously fed by the rope sizer, is taken over by a set of sizing and feeding rollers of the forming machine and fed intermittently to the cutting and preforming die. This one pushes the sugar piece into the production moulding, head, which is equipped with six inner moulding dies. The moulding die-head strokes intermittently by 60° anticlockwise with the *stroke movement*. In this position the stick, which comes from the stick-feed (stick-hopper), is pushed into the preformed sugar piece. After another 60° advanced movement, the final forming and the fixed enclosure of the sugar mass around the sticks is assured. Finally the lollipop is ejected by an ejecting movement of the inner dies. At the same time an ejector arm takes over the stick and pushes it into a gripper jaw-transporting chain and feeds it directly to the sandwich-wrapping station.

(2) Ball lollipop: They are mainly produced by applying the 'Rostoplast' forming technique with flap cutters. As shown in Figure 8.12, the filled or unfilled sugar rope is taken over by a set of sizing rollers and fed into the

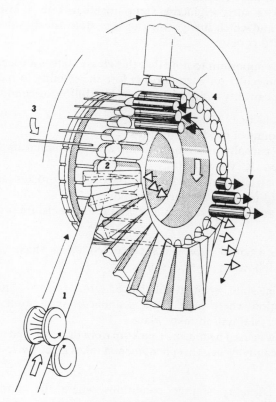

Figure 8.12 1, sugar rope; 2, rope cutting with flap cutters; 3, stick feed; 4, stamping with pressing plungers.

forming die. In the forming die the sugar rope is cut by flaps and then formed by pressing plungers. Flaps and plungers are moved by cams. The sugar pieces in the forming dies receive their sticks from an automatic stick-feeder.

(3) Whistle lollipop: They are produced with a specially designed 'Rosto-plast' forming die-head.

8.2.3   *Structure of finished products*

It has been mentioned that a boiled sweet is characterised by a clear, non-crystalline, glassy structure. But this definition does not take into account the particular physical properties which the candymaker must know and control to assure the quality of the finished product. A more precise definition could be applied:

'A boiled sweet is an amorphous, non-crystalline, supersaturated system obtained from a high-cooked sugar mass which is characterized by a well-balanced ratio of sucrose/glucose syrup together with a low amount of residual water, and which changes into a glassy state directly after forming, as a result of forced cooling'.

However, it is important to note that this glassy state is a pseudosolid state in which the molecules only temporarily lose their ability to move, and that this glassy state can only be maintained when the following conditions are met:

(1) High viscosity.
(2) Low amount of residual moisture.
(3) Complex carbohydrates composition with a minimum amount of higher polysaccharides, i.e. typically 20%.
(4) No uncontrolled inversion during the cooking process and controlled amounts of acid used for flavouring purposes.
(5) Storage at low relative humidity, and use of moisture proof wrapping material.

In other words a boiled sweet is a supercooled liquid which can very easily change to the following physical states:

(1) Crystalline state, when an unbalanced ratio of sucrose/glucose syrup is used, a condition where high shear is applied. As a result 'graining' or uncontrolled crystallisation takes place.
(2) Cold flow caused by moisture pick-up from the atmosphere on the outer surface of the candy. When this phenomenon takes place the following effects can result:

(a) High-humidity storage conditions where the candy constantly absorbs water and dissolves completely.
(b) A thin syrup film where a higher water percentage is formed on the

surface of the candy with the result that the viscosity of this film is much lower than that of the candy. In this supersaturated syrup film, the inhibiting property of high viscosity is much lower and consequently graining will take place. This effect can also occur by moisture penetration from a liquid aqueous filling, through the sugar jacket. As a result the viscosity of the sugar mass decreases from inside to outside and graining takes place progressively.

All these physical effects must be avoided, but in certain cases they can be voluntarily applied to modify the structure and/or the appearance of the finished product. These modifications can be obtained through the accurate adaptation of the formulae and/or the processing conditions. When taking into account these possibilities, boiled sweets can be divided into six general varieties:

(1) Clear boiling sweets: This is the main group. They are characterized by the following quality requirements:
Enhanced clarity resulting from a minimum amount of entrapped micro air bubbles.
Hard and glassy structure.
Bright and uniform colour, no thermal discoloration.
Smooth surface.

(2) Pulled boiled sweets: These are obtained by manual or mechanical pulling as well as by beating. This aeration process is mainly applied for the following reasons:
To obtain a white or pastel-coloured glossy surface as required in the production of the so-called 'satin candy'.
To obtain a crispy structure as expected for certain filled candies, panned centres, etc.
To induce microcrystallisation.
To increase water penetration velocity from an aqueous filling through the sugar jacket of a soft-filled sweet used for panning or a soft-filled candy enrobed with chocolate.
To lower the specific weight.

(3) Combined clear and pulled boiled sweets: This is the 'sweet horn of specialities' which includes all types of striped candies and rocks. Their manufacture needs experience, skill and involves all the art of the sugar confectioner to obtain clear and pulled, highly coloured ropes of sugars:
An attractive outside jacket, such as striped balls, sticks, slices.
An attractive motif which reproduces letters, flowers, fruits, figures: rocks and rock slices.

(4) Grained boiled sweets: This variety includes specialities like 'Edinburgh rock' and 'After dinner mints'. They differ mainly from pulled boiled sweets in having a higher amount of residual moisture and lower percentage of glucose

syrup, to obtain total crystallisation which results in a softer, spongy or crunchy structure.

(5) Sugar-coated boiled sweets: Under this term are classified unwrapped boiled sweets which are covered with a thin layer of recrystallised sugar. This layer is obtained by wetting the ward candies in a rotating dragée pan with a pure sucrose solution (80–82% solids). As soon as all the candies are evenly wetted, warm air is gently blown into the dragée pan. As a result moisture is evaporated and an even, white-sugar film crystallises on the surface of the candies. This process is mainly applied to small candies, which reproduce fruits such as lemon, orange and raspberry. This dry candying process is applied for two main reasons:

(a) To obtain a frosted appearance.

(b) To increase the shelf life of the non-wrapped candies by coating the surface of the candy with a film of crystallised sugar.

(6) Laminated filled boiled sweets: These are peanut butter, hazelnuts or chocolate paste-filled candies characterised by their crunchy texture. This texture is obtained by repeated pulling and folding a filled sugar roll. To ensure the forming process, the multilayered, crunchy roll is enrobed with a thin

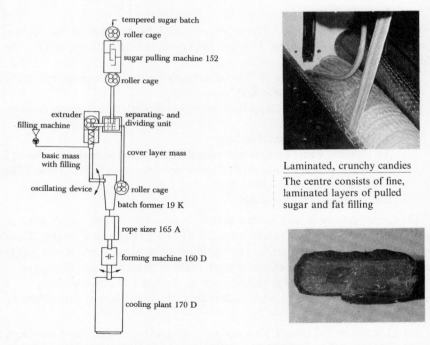

Laminated, crunchy candies

The centre consists of fine, laminated layers of pulled sugar and fat filling

Figure 8.13 Flow diagram of the continous production of laminated, filled candies (crunchy products)—System Robert Bosch.

outside cover. The degree of crunchiness can be increased by using a pulled sugar mass. Today these old fashioned specialities can be produced by automatic methods, as Figure 8.13 shows.

8.3 Ingredients

It is quite erroneous to believe that boiled sweets result from simple basic formulations of sucrose and glucose syrup by applying the average ratios shown in Table 8.1.

It is important to emphasise at this point that the key to ensuring a satisfactory shelf life is an accurate mono-di-polysaccharides balance in conjunction with a low amount of residual water. Variation from following key composition values can lead quickly to graining or moisture pick-up (Table 8.2).

8.3.1 *Water*

Control of the quantity and quality of the water used in the production of boiled sweets is the first step to assure the quality of the finished product. Nevertheless, its influence is often underestimated and only considered as the transient ingredient to dissolve the sugar. In many cases its quality can be the source of inexplicable troubles during the production, for example uncontrolled inversion rate and discoloration during the cooking process (acidic water) or lack of setting by pectin jelly fillings (hard water).

Table 8.1

	Sucrose	Glucose syrup
38–42 DE acid-converted	100	60–80
40–42 DE acid/enzyme-converted	100	80–100
42–44 DE enzyme/enzyme-converted	100	100–180

Table 8.2 Average analytical composition

Residual moisture	max.	3.0%
Invert sugar/inversion rate		
During cooking process	max.	2.0%
After addition of acid	max.	5.0%
Total amount of reducing sugars	max.	23.0%
Total amount of monoreducing sugars	max.	10.0%
Polysaccharides		
To prevent graining	min.	20.0%
To prevent shrinking by stamping process or tailing by depositing process	max.	30.0%

Furthermore, water is also an important technical medium. Reduced output and efficiency of machines can find their source in a hard water.

Finally, the quantity of used water should always be accurately measured and adapted to the applied dissolving method, as well as to the particle size of the sugar. There are two dissolving methods: dissolving under atmospheric pressure and dissolving under increased pressure. By dissolving under atmospheric pressure, the required water ratio varies in relation to the particle size of the sugar, from 33 to 40 parts for 100 parts sugar. By dissolving under pressure the amount of water can be reduced to 10–20 parts. In any case, it is important to note that the quantity of water should be limited to the minimum required amount. The less water used, the faster the cooking process, and the inversion rate is lower, with a longer shelf life.

8.3.2 Sugar

Sugar in crystallised form is mainly used in the production of boiled sweets. Based on the quality criteria of the European Community (EEC) Sugar Market Regulations, two main types of crystallised sugar are used:

(1) Refined sugar, Category 1, with a purity of more than 99.9%.
(2) White sugar, Category 2, with a purity of more than 99.7%.

The detailed quality criteria of both sugar types are summarised in Table 8.3.

As a rule 'white sugar' is normally used. In practice, the purity of Category 2 white sugar is generally near or higher than 99.9%. When a high-quality 'clear hard candy' is expected 'refined sugar' of Category 1 is used.

In practice the following factors are important:

(1) Ash content.
(2) Solubility.
(3) Particle size.
(4) Inversion.

Table 8.3

Quality criteria	Category 1 (refined sugar)	Category 2 (white sugar)
Polarisation (S)		min. 99.7
Invert sugar (%)	max. 0..04	max. 0.04
Moisture (%)	max. 0.06	max. 0.06
Total score according to EEC point score of them for:	max. 8	max. 22
Ash by conductivity	max. 6	max. 15
Colour type	max. 4	max. 9
Colour in solution	max. 3	max. 6

8.3.2.1 *Ash content.* In general the ash content of 'refined sugar' and 'white sugar' is extremely low. However, it is very important to remember that mineral salts have a great influence on the storability of the sugar and that they can be the source of many troubles during the manufacturing process, as well as affecting the quality and shelf life of the finished product. Apart from the increased danger of moisture pick-up during storage, high ash content can be the reason for the following problems:

(1) Higher inversion rate during the cooking process and thereby increased discoloration.

(2) Increased foaming tendency during the cooking process, with reduced output and increased entrapped air bubbles in the cooked mass as a result.

(3) Increased hygroscopicity of the finished product.

(4) When producing old-fashioned 'all-sucrose candy' buffering effect on the 'in-process inversion' with acid or cream of tartar.

In any case, this problem can take place when manufacturing specialities such as 'malted drops' and 'cough drops' with brown sugars or syrups which are used to give additional flavour and colour. Table 8.4 shows the typical analyses of two types of brown sugar [2].

8.3.2.2 *Solubility.* At 20°C a pure sucrose solution can only hold 67% sugar in solution. Consequently it is impossible to produce a pure sucrose hard candy. By cooking under atmospheric pressure a pure sucrose solution starts to be supersaturated and to crystallise at a boiling temperature of 121°C. In consequence crystallisation inhibitors, often called 'doctor solids', which increase the solubility of the carbohydrates mixture, have to be used. However, at a solids content of 97–99% the system sucrose/doctor solids will still be supersaturated with respect to sucrose, but the combination of the 'doctoring effect' and 'high viscosity' can stabilise the candy against graining.

8.3.2.3 *Particle size.* Particle sizes are not legally stipulated, but the trade categories [3] shown in Table 8.5 are generally accepted.

Table 8.4

	Soft brown sugar	
	---	---
	Yellow type	Brown type
Sucrose	91.0%	93.0%
Invert sugar	4.0%	2.0%
Mineral salts	0.8%	1.2%
Nitrogenous impurities	1.2%	1.8%
Moisture	3.0%	2.0%
Colour (EBC)	40	300

Table 8.5

Grain type	Grain size (mm) (for 90% by weight of the sugar)	Bulk density (kg/m³)
Coarse grain	1.2–2.5	900
Medium grain	0.5–1.4	930
Fine grain	0.2–0.75	950
Extra fine grain	0.075–0.30	900
Powder/icing sugar	0.010–0.120	500–700

In boiled sweet manufacture the particle size of sugar must particularly be taken into account when using continuous dissolvers and precookers with a volumetric feeding system as shown in Figure 8.14.

In order to obtain a constant ratio sucrose/glucose syrup the crystal sugar must be characterised by excellent free-flowing properties and a uniform, well-defined particle size, with a minimum of sugar dust. The higher the particle size variation, the more will vary the ratio of sucrose and glucose syrup, especially when the amount of dust is uncontrolled. In this case the proportion of glucose syrup will be increased as a result and the viscosity of the cooked mass will increase significantly. This will affect all the rheological properties of the sugar mass and lead to the following problems:

(1) Irregular distribution of flavours, colours and acids.
(2) Increased amount of entrapped air bubbles and increased cloudiness.

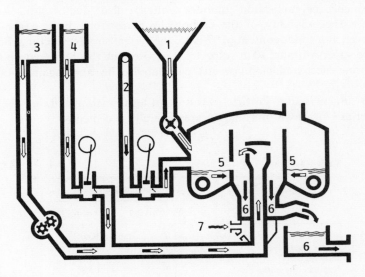

Figure 8.14 Flow diagram of a continuous dissolving and precooking machine with a volumetric feeding system—System Type Solovomat (Hamac–Höller). 1, crystal sugar; 2, water; 3, glucose syrup; 4, other liquid ingredients such as honey, malt extract, dissolved scrap syrup, etc.; 5, sugar solution; 6, precooked sugar/glucose syrup solution; 7, steam.

Furthermore, depending upon the applied forming process, the following problems will arise:

(1) Plastic forming equipment/stamped candies:
   non-uniform plasticity.
   non-uniform size and shape, irregular weight per piece.
   cracked surface.
   increased variation in the amount of filling during the manufacture of filled candies etc.
(2) Depositing equipment/deposited candies:
   Increased tailing problems.
   Irregular weight per piece.

Finally, it is also important to note that the particle size has a great impact on the dissolving speed of the sugar. This has particularly to be taken into account when a continuous dissolving system is used. The dissolving speed depends upon the specific surface of the crystal. The smaller the crystal, the larger its specific surface and the greater its dissolving capability. But in practice, very fine sugar, especially dust, must be avoided due to its tendency to form lumps, with a consequent decrease in the dissolving speed.

The best results in a continuous dissolving system are obtained when using a medium-grain sugar with a spectrum of 0.5–1.4 mm.

8.3.2.4 *Inversion.* The most critical problem in the production of boiled sweets is when uncontrolled inversion take place. This irreversible chemical reaction can cause a considerable discoloration and leads to an extremely hygroscopic product.

Uncontrolled inversion can have many sources. In daily practice principal causes are:

(1) Traces of acid left after the cleaning process.
(2) Abnormally low pH of the prepared sucrose–glucose syrup solution.
(3) Longer cooking time.
(4) Acid is added at too high a temperature and the acidified sugar mass is cooled too slowly.
(5) The level of acidified sugar mass in the depositing hopper is too high.

8.3.3 *Glucose syrup*

Glucose syrup is indispensable as a 'doctoring agent' in boiled sweets to prevent their graining. Additionally, its influence on the forming plasticity (stamped candies) or depositing viscosity as well as on the hygroscopicity of the finished products is another important factor which has to be taken into account.

The amount of glucose syrup needed mainly depends on the following three factors:

8.3.3.1 *Type of glucose syrup.* Worldwide, two types are mainly applied: 'regular acid-converted' and 'acid/enzyme-converted' at about 40 DE. But more and more, in certain countries, so-called 'high-maltose syrups' are used. These are obtained by 'enzyme/enzyme conversion' and are characterised by a low amount of dextrose, a high amount of maltose and a low amount of oligosaccharides and high molecular weight polysaccharides. In comparison to classical glucose syrups, high-maltose syrups offer the following advantages:

(1) Less discoloration during the cooking process.
(2) Cooked sugar mass with lower viscosity, fewer entrapped air bubbles and greater clarity as a result of a lower amount of oligosaccharides and higher molecular weight polysaccharides.
(3) Candies with a decreased tendency to pick up moisture due to the extremely low amount of dextrose.

From these advantages result the possibility of applying a higher ratio of high-maltose syrup than if traditional glucose syrups were used. Table 8.6 gives a comparison of the composition of these three types of glucose syrup as well as the average amount of used glucose syrup and the final composition of the manufactured boiled sweets by 2% residual moisture and 2% inversion rate.

8.3.3.2 *Applied cooking method.* There are four main types of cooker for boiled sweets, namely batch vacuum cookers, continuous coil cookers with discontinuous discharging system, continuous coil cookers with continuous discharging system and thin-film cookers which are mainly used in the

Table 8.6

Characteristics	Type of glucose syrup		
	Acid-converted 40 DE	Acid/enzyme-converted 40 DE	Enzyme/enzyme-converted 43 DE
Composition (%)			
Dextrose	18	7	4
Maltose	14	45	55
Polysaccharides	68	48	41
Average applied ratio sugar/glucose syrup	100/80	100/100	100/180
Amount of total reducing sugars (%)	17.3	19.4	25.7
Monoreducing sugars (%) (dextrose + invert sugar)	6.9	3.7	3.1
Disaccharides (%) (sucrose + maltose)	63.2	70.3	71.2
Polysaccharides (%)	27.9	24.0	23.7
Residual moisture (%)	2.0	2.0	2.0
Total (%)	100	100	100

Table 8.7 Average required ratio of sugar/glucose syrup in relation to the applied cooking method

Cooking method	Inversion rate during cooking process (%)	Glucose syrup type					
		DE 40 acid-converted		DE 40 acid–enzyme converted		DE 43 enzyme–enzyme converted	
		Minimum	Maximum	Minimum	Maximum	Minimum	Maximum
Batch vacuum cooker	1–6	100/40	100/80	100/60	100/100	100/80	100/140
Coil cooker With discontinuous discharging system	0.5–2.5	100/60	100/80	100/80	100/120	100/100	100/180
With continuous discharging system	0.5–2.5	100/70	100/80	100/80	100/120	100/120	100/180
Thin film cooker	0.1–0.3	100/60	100/80	100/80	100/100	100/120	100/180

manufacture of deposited candies. Each of these requires a different ratio of sugar/glucose syrup to assure the best results. The reason for this necessity is related to the variation of cooking time, with as a result different inversion rates, as well as variation in the agitation intensity during the cooking and the discharging process of the cooked sugar mass. Table 8.7 indicates the average ratios which are required in relation to the applied cooking method.

8.3.3.3 *Composition of additional ingredients.* The rheological properties of sugar masses which are flavoured with raw materials such as honey, malt extract, milk, etc. are largely modified. As described below these modifications involve an adjustment of the sugar/glucose syrup ratio.

Honey. Table 8.8 shows that honey must be technically considered as 'invert sugar'. This fact invariably leads to the following problems:

(1) Increased amount of monosaccharides in the finished products and therefore a decreased ERH and an increased tendency to pick up moisture during the manufacturing process and on store.
(2) Highly decreased viscosity with, as a result, an increased danger of graining during the cooking and the kneading process of the sugar mass, especially when high shear takes place.

To achieve a satisfactory contribution against graining and stickiness, a reduced amount of regular glucose syrup of 40–42 DE obtained by acid conversion should be used. In practice, good results are obtained when the following sucrose/glucose syrup ratios are applied to an amount of 5% honey:

Batch vacuum cooker　　100:35
Coil cooker　　　　　　　100:50

Finally, another important point concerning honey boiled sweets is that the boiling point of honey is higher than that of a simple sucrose/glucose syrup

Table 8.8 Average composition of honey

Moisture	17%
Solids	83%
Fructose	38.0%
Dextrose	34.0%
Maltose	7.0%
Sucrose	6.0%
Resins, etc.	5.0%
Undetermined matter	3.0%
Dextrin	2.0%
High sugars	2.0%
Acidity as gluconic aria	1.2%
Ash	0.2%
Nitrogen	0.1%

From ref. [4].

candy. For this reason the cooking temperature must be increased about 1–2 °C and the vacuum time increased to obtain the same solids content.

Malt extract. An average composition for malt extract is:

Moisture	22.0%
Maltose	55.5%
Dextrose	2.0%
Dextrins	15.0%
Proteins	4.5%
Mineral ash	1.0%

The presence of proteins as well as the high amount of dextrins increases considerably the viscosity and the elasticity of the sugar mass. Due to this elasticity, stamped candies show an increased tendency to shrink directly after the stamping process.

To reduce these shrinking phenomena, a reduced amount of glucose syrup must be used, with a preference for a 40–42 DE obtained by acid–enzyme conversion or a 'high-maltose'. In comparison to an acid-converted 40–42 DE, both are characterised by a lower amount of higher molecular weight polysaccharides and thus decreased elasticity.

To a 5% malt extract the following sucrose/glucose syrup ratio can be applied with satisfactory results:

Batch cooker
40-DE acid-converted	100:30
40-DE acid–enzyme converted	100:40
43-DE enzyme–enzyme-converted	100:60

Coil cooker
40-DE acid-converted	100:50
40-DE acid–enzyme-converted	100:60
43-DE enzyme–enzyme converted	100:80

Milk. Mainly full-cream and skimmed, sweetened, condensed milk are used in the manufacture of milk boiled sweets (Table 8.9). When considering their use, various technological factors must be taken into account. Firstly the Maillard reaction, which occurs when proteins and reducing sugars are heated together. This chemical reaction forms complex flavouring and colouring components. The main determining factors for flavour and colour developments are in this case:

(1) The content of amino acids (proteins) and reducing sugars.
(2) The cooking temperature and the cooking time.
(3) pH of the sugar/glucose syrup/milk slurry, optimal in the range of 6.2–7.0.

Table 8.9   Average composition of full-cream and skimmed, sweetened, condensed milk

	Full-cream, sweetened, condensed milk (%)	Skimmed, sweetened, condensed milk (%)
Water	27.00	30.00
Milk fat	8.30	0.30
Milk proteins	8.16	8.81
Lactose	11.86	12.73
Ash	1.98	2.16
Sucrose	42.70	46.00

The higher the content of amino acids and reducing sugars, especially dextrose and invert sugar, as well as the higher the pH and the cooking temperature and the longer the cooking time, the greater the flavour and colour developments.

A second factor that must be considered is that proteins increase the viscosity and the elasticity of the cooked sugar mass. Therefore, as in malted candies, the amount of glucose syrup should be reduced to prevent uncontrolled shrinking phenomena. Again, the best results are obtained with a 40–42 DE acid–enzyme-converted glucose syrup or a high-maltose. But, in comparison to an acid-converted type, a reduced caramel flavour and colour is obtained due to their lower content of dextrose. The following sucrose/glucose syrup ratios can be applied with good results:

Batch cooker
    40–42 DE acid-converted   100:40
    40–42 DE acid–enzyme-converted 100:60
Coil cooker
    40–42 DE acid-converted   100:60
    40–42 DE acid–enzyme-converted 100:80

A third factor which must be considered is that full-cream and skimmed, sweetened, condensed milk are characterised by their high content of sucrose. It is clear that this amount of sucrose must be included in the sucrose/glucose syrup ratio to prevent uncontrolled graining phenomena.

It is also important to consider the lower solubility of lactose as well as the fact that lactose is partly present in the form of microcrystals in condensed, sweetened milk. Both factors can lead to a sandy texture when the dissolving process is not correctly conducted.

Apart from condensed sweetened milk, spray-dried skimmed and whole-milk powder, liquid milk and tailor-made, demineralised, hydrolysed or unhydrolysed whey products can also be used. Every type involves a specific adaptation of the recipe and the processing conditions. When, for example, liquid milk is used, a lower amount of glucose syrup must be applied due to the fact that liquid milk contains approximately 87% water, which leads to an extended cooking time and consequently to an increased inversion rate.

Furthermore small amounts (0.1%) of sodium bicarbonate or ammonium carbonate are used to prevent a quick acidification of the liquid milk. This neutralisation increases the pH of the slurry and simultaneously improves the intensity of the Maillard reaction during the cooking process.

Invert sugar. In some countries invert sugar is used as 'doctor solids' for economical reasons. At this point it is important to emphasise that a suitable 'crystallisation inhibitor' should meet the following requirements:

(1) An ability to increase the solubility of the applied carbohydrates mixture.
(2) Excellent heat stability.
(3) Reduced hygroscopicity.
(4) An ability to increase the viscosity and additionally to improve the plasticity of the cooked sugar mass.
(5) The possibility, depending on economic factors, of reducing or increasing in large proportionss the applied ratio of 'doctor solids'.

Only glucose syrup meets all these requirements. Invert sugar meets only the first one. Boiled sweets based on sugar/invert sugar, all-sucrose candies, are characterised by the fact that they are very hygroscopic and less resistant against graining.

When invert sugar must be used for economical reasons the following methods can be applied:

(1) Direct method—which is based on the use of a predetermined ratio of sucrose/standardised invert sugar, for example:

Batch vacuum cooker   100:20/25
Coil cooker with discontinuous
    discharging system   100:30/35

(2) Indirect method–which is based on the use of a pure sucrose solution which is partly inverted during the dissolving and cooking process by adding controlled small amounts of acid or cream of tartar. This method is quite difficult due to the fact that the inversion rate is subject to large variations. One batch may be inverted to the required amount while the next may be underinverted (quick graining) or overinverted (increased discoloration and hygroscopicity). When cream of tartar is used the following average amounts (per-kg white sugar) can be added:

Batch vacuum cooker   0.3–0.4%
Coil cooker with discontinuous
    discharging system   0.4–0.5%

It is important to note also that in comparison to sucrose/glucose syrup candies the cooking temperature and vacuum time must be increased to obtain a final product with a residual moisture of 1–1.5%.

Table 8.10

(a) Combination of invert sugar and glucose syrup.

	Sucrose	Invert sugar (solids) (%)	Glucose syrup 40–42 DE acid-converted (solids) (%)
Batch vacuum cooker	100	20–15	15–20
Coil cooker with discontinuous discharging system	100	25–20	20–25

(b) Combination of invert sugar and maltodextrin.

	Sucrose	Invert sugar (solids) (%)	Maltodextrin (%)	
			15 DE	20 DE
Batch vacuum cooker	100	15–20	2.5–3.5	4.0–5.0
Coil cooker with discontinuous discharging system	100	20–25	2.5–3.5	4.0–5.0

Better results are obtained when invert sugar is used in combination with a 40–42 DE acid-converted glucose syrup or in combination with maltodextrin. The recipes in Table 8.10 can be applied with satisfactory results. But it is clear that boiled sweets based only on sucrose and glucose syrup will show a better stability against graining and moisture pick-up.

Finally it is also important to underline that flavours, acids and colours must be added precisely to obtain constant results and should be chosen in relation to their heat stability and their inversion rate. Uncontrolled inversion leads irreversibly to unacceptable shelf life.

References

1   H. Hoffmann, W. Mauch, and W. Untze, *Zucker and Zuckerwaren*, Verlag Paul Parey, Berlin (1985).
2   L.G. Hart, *Brown Sugar—Properties and applications in sugar confectionery*, Confectionery Symposium, ZDS Solingen (1979).
3   P. Voss, *Komprimiereigenschaften von Zucker*, Tagung Süsswarenkomprimate, ZDS Solingen (1980).
4   R. Lees, and E.B. Jackson, *Sugar Confectionery and Chocolatee Manufacture*, Leonard Hill, Glasgow (1973).

9 Caramel toffee and fudge

D. STANSELL

9.1 Introduction

Before dealing with the production of toffees, caramels and fudge it is desirable to clarify the nomenclature, which can be quite confusing.

Originally toffees did not contain milk and were high-boiled products containing brown sugar, glucose syrup or invert sugar and fats, usually butter. This type of product was in many ways similar to butterscotch, although not usually boiled to such a low moisture content. It is still used on toffee apples, but in many cases this coating is merely a coloured boiled sugar. These products all have moisture levels below 5%.

The introduction of milk into toffees led to the production of higher moisture products with up to 8 or 9% water content, and for some of these products the name caramel was used. Although various authorities have attempted to differentiate in composition between toffees and caramels, there are many exceptions and the two names can be regarded as synonymous.

Unfortunately the name caramel is also used for the products made by the breakdown of carbohydrate by heat or heat and alkali treatment. These are predominantly used as colouring materials and are not relevant in the present context.

Toffees or caramels can be deliberately made to crystallise or grain and are then known as soft toffees or grained caramels. These products are very similar in eating texture to some fudges but are made by a different process. The name fudge is used for a wide range of products ranging from short crumbly textures to quite plastic masses for which names like Jersey Cream or Italian Creams are sometimes used. In all these products the sugar crystal is developed during the manufacturing process and the structure has stabilised before the product is packed.

9.2 Ingredients

The basic ingredients of toffees and fudge are sugar, glucose syrup, milk protein, fat, salt and water.

9.2.1 *Sugar*

Sugar, apart from providing sweetness, creates a structure in the toffee which helps to prevent cold flow. Being a disaccharide it does not introduce as much chewiness or toughness as glucose syrups due to the absence of high molecular weight sugars, and it is less liable to create stickiness than the monosaccharide sugars such as invert sugar and dextrose. However the most common defect of toffees is crystallisation of sugar or graining during storage, and therefore it cannot be used to excess.

Most authorities seem to agree that the optimum ratio of sugar to non-crystallising sugars in a toffee is 1.1 to 1, and it should be noted that this is the total of sugar and non-crystallising sugars from all sources such as sugar from condensed milk or non-crystallising sugars arising from inversion during processing. Dextrose, of course, does crystallise, but in this context the concentration is too low for crystallisation to occur and non-crystallising sugars may be regarded as all the carbohydrates other than sugar.

At one time various brown sugars were used extensively in toffees for the characteristic flavour they introduced, and although they are still used they are frequently sticky and not suitable for bulk handling. Larger manufacturers these days frequently use granulated sugar with the addition of small quantities of golden syrup, molasses or blended refinery syrups to stimulate the flavour of brown sugars.

Most brown sugars and all the syrups contain a proportion of invert sugar, but, unless some specific requirement such as a need for low viscosity makes it desirable, invert sugar is rarely added to toffee formulations.

9.2.2 *Glucose syrup*

A wide variety of glucose syrups are available for use in toffees, and although their properties vary considerably all have the same effect on sugar solubility. The main effects however are to modify texture and sweetness.

The usual glucose syrup for toffee production is 42-DE acid-converted glucose. Apart from retarding sugar crystallisation, the reducing sugars, dextrose and maltose, take part in the Maillard reaction with milk protein to develop the colour and flavour of toffee. The higher molecular weight sugars in glucose syrups help to give some body and chewiness to the sweet, which may be desirable, but they also introduce some increase of viscosity and toughness. If this should be a problem, very high-maltose syrups with much lower content of high molecular weight sugars can be used and are desirable if high glucose levels are required. This is likely to arise where high temperature conditions during storage give rise to graining problems in the distribution chain.

High-DE glucose syrups can be used to increase sweetness and degree of caramelisation or to reduce viscosity or equilibrium relative humidity (ERH).

Whilst they may find use in toffee used for depositing into chocolate shells or layering on biscuits, they are more likely to be used in fudge than conventional wrapped toffees.

Low-DE glucoses will reduce sweetness and caramelisation, but increase viscosity, chewiness and toughness. They are useful when an increase in chewiness is required. For some purposes the maltodextrins can be used in a similar manner, and since the effect is more pronounced much smaller quantities are required.

Very rarely however will a factory have many varieties of glucose syrup available, and in any case, with premix systems supplying several production lines, premix recipe modification for each product may not be acceptable. In these cases the addition of dextrose or a maltodextrin on a single production line to modify carbohydrate composition may be a more acceptable approach.

9.2.3 *Milk protein*

The normal source of milk protein in toffees is sweetened condensed milk. Fresh milk, apart from creating storage problems, contains far too much water, and the excessive boiling required to evaporate off this water leads to coagulation of the protein and roughening of the texture. This may not be wholly due to the boiling, as under some conditions evaporated milk can give the same effect, and it is possible that the protein is affected by the water activity of the solution.

At one time, the sweetened condensed milk used was whole or full-cream milk. However, due to the EEC policy in relation to dairy products it became uneconomic, and many manufacturers changed to sweetened condensed, skimmed milk, adding the requisite quantity of butter.

It is possible to reconstitute milk powder into sweetened, condensed milk but it is very difficult to eliminate traces of grittiness from undispersed milk particles. Unless suitable homogenising equipment is available, it is doubtful if this operation is worthwhile.

The function of milk protein in toffee is complex. Apart from the reaction with reducing sugars to provide the characteristic flavour and colour, which is apparently specific to milk protein, it also stabilises the emulsion of fat in the sugar phase and possibly binds some of the water.

Whey protein and hydrolysed whey protein are frequently offered as alternatives to whole milk for toffee processing. The whey protein in whole milk has very little effect on caramelisation because of the relatively small quantity present, and this is largely due to casein. Whey proteins however do caramelise and produce a very similar flavour to casein. The main difference lies in the viscosity of the toffee, which is much more fluid. This also results in poor resistance to cold flow, and the toffees can distort badly after wrapping.

Hydrolysed whey is whey containing hydrolysed lactose or dextrose and galactose. These sugars, being monosaccharides and reducing sugars, give more caramelisation than glucose syrup, lower viscosity and, in the writer's opinion, a different flavour from traditional ingredients.

These factors tend to restrict the use of whey, particularly for replacement of milk in established products, but for products which are not established and are, for example, covered in chocolate, where flow is less of a problem, whey proteins represent an alternative option to condensed milk.

9.2.4 *Fat*

Apart from butter, the fats used in toffees are invariably vegetable fats. Years ago hardened palm kernel oil (HPKO) was almost universal, but due to wide price fluctuation it has in many cases been replaced by other fat blends which may contain partially hydrogenated palm, soya, groundnut, rapeseed and other oils.

HPKO is a lauric fat which is characterised by a narrow melting range and brittle texture. The other oils are non-lauric, and although hydrogenated to the same slip point have a wider melting range and are not as brittle as the lauric fats.

Fats for toffees and fudge are desirably almost solid at ambient temperature, and this includes storage of sweets in shops during the summer months. The fat however must melt virtually completely at blood heat, since high melting components tend to form a greasy coating in the mouth which is quite unpleasant. This defines the slip point, which must be about 40°C.

The other requirement is resistance to oxidation, which is normally provided by the degree of hydrogenation required to provide a satisfactory melting point. Oxidative rancidity produces off-flavours of a tallowy nature, and is catalysed by metals, particularly copper and iron. Toffees have been produced in copper pans for many years and oxidative rancidity is not normally a problem. The reason is probably that the emulsification of the fat into the syrup occurs rapidly and contact of the fat globules with the copper is minimal.

Fats can also suffer from lipolytic rancidity, caused by fat-splitting enzymes, frequently derived from other ingredients which have been subject at some stage to mould growth, although the presence of mould may no longer be apparent. With lauric fats, lipolytic rancidity is associated with soapy flavours, and although non-lauric fats give less objectionable taints the same care is required. Whilst some ingredients have from time to time been responsible for lipase infection of products, mould growth in any part of the factory, particularly in obscure corners or inaccessible places, must be guarded against. One very prevalent source used to be the unhygienic practice of using damp cloths to moisten the surface of product or clean working surfaces during processing.

Larger manufacturers will be receiving fats as liquid in tankers and storing in heated tanks. Since hot fats are more readily oxidised, the temperature of storage should be maintained at the minimum required to permit handling.

Solid fats have a longer shelf life, but where stocks are held they should be used in rotation and kept as cool as possible.

Butter is frequently used in toffees, mainly for its flavour. It is sometimes said to be an integral part of toffee flavour, and rancid butter is stated to produce better flavour. Whilst butter may modify the flavour it is not an essential part of the Maillard reaction and many toffees do not contain butter. The use of rancid butter is not a desirable practice since it is an uncontrolled ingredient, but enzyme-modified butter fat is available commercially as a standardised product and fulfils the same purpose. If butter is added to a toffee recipe before emulsification it mixes with the vegetable fat and reduces the overall melting point. If butter is added at the end of the cook, as it frequently is, it is an interesting question as to whether it actually mixes with the emulsified vegetable fat. If it does not this could be a factor in the belief that this method of processing gives a better butter flavour.

9.2.5 *Salt*

Whilst salt is not essential in a toffee, it undoubtedly has a very beneficial effect as a flavour modifier, and toffees tend to be rather insipid without it. Normal levels of usage are about 0.5%.

9.2.6 *Water*

Water is frequently ignored as an ingredient in confectionery, and consequently its use is sometimes not controlled as accurately as it should be. Although it has no effect on colour and flavour, it undoubtedly has a major influence on processing and is certainly a factor in texture. In toffees high water levels are not required, and many manufacturers do not add additional water, relying on that contained in the ingredients.

9.2.7 *Other additivies*

It is possible to produce toffees with no additional emulsifier other than the milk protein, but many manufacturers do use emulsifiers. These are usually soya lecithin or glyceryl monostearate. The purpose of emulsifiers is to stabilise the fat distribution within the sugar mass, because with high-fat-content toffees the manipulation of plastic masses can squeeze out fat, leading to risk of surface oxidation and unsightly appearance. For this reason, and also to maintain a good fat distribution, which lubricates the cutting knives, emulsifiers are more frequently used in cut and wrap processes than deposited toffees.

Other additives which may be used to reduce the tendency of toffee to cold flow are modified starches and gelatin. The modified starches are usually high in amylopectin and are derived from waxy maize varieties. Whilst these additives will reduce cold flow, they will almost certainly increase process viscosity.

9.3 Structure of toffee

Toffee is an emulsion of fat in an aqueous system, but the nature of the aqueous system is complex and not completely understood. It is a mixture of sugars, water and protein which is very resistant to crystallisation. The concept of threshold moisture content in boiled sweets introduced by Lecomber and Branfield related resistance to graining to the glucose solids to water ratio. This can be interpreted as implying a moisture-binding capacity of glucose solids. If this binding capacity is exceeded, graining once initiated will progress to completion. Many toffees have moisture levels just above this threshold value, but it is possible that the milk protein binds water as well, and this has the action of converting the aqueous phase in a toffee into a glass. This would explain why, although many toffees contain odd sugar crystals at ambient temperature, they never grain internally, and graining invariably starts from the surface, presumably due to moisture absorption.

Toffees have a number of textural characteristics. Hardness is a function of moisture content only. Chewiness and toughness on eating are related to molecular weight of the carbohydrates. 'Body' is a function of milk protein quantity and the state of that protein, which appears to be modified by seasonal variation in milk but also by the condensing process. It is also affected by quantity, degree of emulsification and hardness of the fat. Body is a factor in resistance to cold flow. High levels of protein also introduce a degree of elasticity into toffees, which can be a problem in cut and wrap processing.

Protein quantity and state also affect yield stress in a liquid toffee, which alters the flow in depositing processes. Newtonian viscosity however is not so much of a problem.

All these factors interact to affect eating texture. For example, toughness due to sugars can to an extent be offset by high fat contents, and varying ratios of milk protein and high molecular weight carbohydrates can modify the chewiness or toughness. They also allow some degree of tolerance on moisture content, presumably in relation to moisture-binding properties.

9.4 Formulation

Formulation depends to a very large extent on the requirements of the toffee, which may be for wrapping as a sweet, for depositing into chocolate shells, or for layering onto another confectionery product or biscuits. Because the requirements of toffee processing are so diverse, specific recipes would be of little value here, but in general a balanced recipe contains 3 parts of sugar, 5 parts of glucose syrup, 3 parts of sweetened condensed milk and 1.5 parts of fat.

For wrapped toffees, as has been said, the ratio of sugar to non-crystallising sugars should be 1.1:1, but for deposited product milk protein contents above 2% may create problems.

Due to the much lower viscosity developed, whey proteins could be used at higher levels but distortion after wrapping may be unacceptable.

Toffees handled in the plastic state can be much more viscous and higher milk levels, lower DE glucose syrups or modified starches may be used.

For depositing into shells, low viscosities at low temperatures are required and thinning with syrups of low molecular weight sugars may be necessary.

9.5 Processing

9.5.1 Equipment

Whilst originally toffees were made on solid fuel or gas-fired pans, the steam boiling pan has been used for so long that it can be regarded as the origin of modern toffee processing. These pans are fitted with a fairly complex arrangement consisting of a bow-shaped stirrer closely contoured to the pan and fitted with hinged scrapers which are thrown outward by centrifugal force to remove the cooking toffee from every part of the heating surface every revolution (Figure 9.1). Within this bow is a second set of stirring arms which revolve in the opposite direction to the bow.

The reason for this is twofold. The first requirement for good toffee is very efficient emulsification, and since this was originally carried out in the boiling pan a good mixing action was essential. In addition, toffee masses do not conduct heat very well and the toffee would burn on the pan. The scrapers prevent this and the efficient mixing distributes the heat uniformly through the bulk. In spite of this it is probably true to say that no two toffee pans give identical results in terms of finished toffee. The toffee pans are usually fitted with three-speed gear boxes, and the main drive shaft and stirrer assembly can be raised by a worm screw at the end of the cook, to allow the pan to tilt to discharge the toffee.

More modern versions differ mainly in the manner in which the stirrers are removed from the pan.

The emulsification of ingredients is carried out with the stirrers on high speed. Ideally the fats, milk and glucose should be emulsified before the sugar is added. The reason for this is to disperse the fat into an aqueous syrup to prevent it coating the sugar and retarding solution.

When all the ingredients are thoroughly emulsified the stirrers are slowed down and the steam turned on at low pressure, about 60 psi, to bring the mix to the boil. This is done with the pan closed to trap the water vapour and wash any sugar crystal from the pan sides. At this point the pan is opened and the steam raised to full pressure to cook the batch as quickly as possible.

The completion of the cook is usually determined by temperature, but due to the design of many toffee pans it is not possible to insert a thermometer into

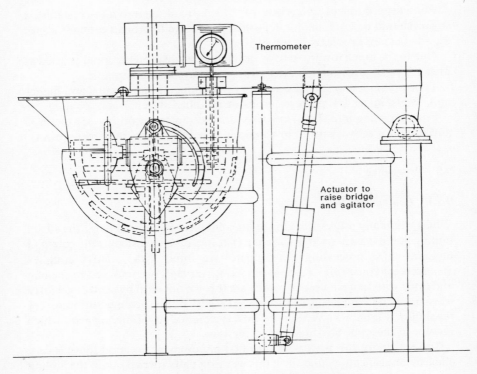

Figure 9.1   Low-type mixer on a tubular frame.

the boiling toffee. In the past a water or crack test was used. A small sample of toffee was taken on a spatula or rod, immersed in cold water and the confectioner judged the degree of cook by its texture. With constant-temperature water and an experienced operator the method was quick and reliable and since at the time thermometers were usually mercury in glass, which was highly undesirable, or vapour pressure or mercury in steel types with slow response, the method was universal. With electronic thermocouple instruments freely available the problem no longer exists, and very few people still use crack testing. It is quite simple to stop the stirrers long enough to take a temperature reading. Hardness differences in toffee are noticeable if temperature varies by $\pm 0.5°C$. However, it should be noted that although boiling temperatures are related to moisture content this is only under specified standard conditions. Different pans can give different moisture contents largely due to small differences in manufacturing tolerances and rates of cooking. It is wise to establish the correct boiling temperature for any pan by a trial boiling from time to time. Alternatively, toffee texture can be assessed by some form of penetrometer after the toffee has stabilised. This normally takes some hours and of course must be carried out at constant temperature. By this means continuous checking on performance can be achieved as a routine, and it is faster than moisture determination using an oven.

Once the toffee has boiled the steam is turned off and the pan vented. Any additions of flavour or butter are made if required, and when thoroughly mixed the toffee is removed from the pan as quickly as possible to prevent further caramelisation. Subsequent processing will be considered later, but these days many alternative toffee-boiling processes are available and should be mentioned first.

With the trend towards continuous processing in the industry various means of continuous toffee cooking were investigated. These followed two lines of development, use of existing high-efficiency cookers and a continuous version of the traditional process. Both systems required a continuous supply of product so premix plants were necessary. Many were developed by confectionery manufacturers for their own use, but the machinery manufacturers also entered the field. All utilised either weighing or metering of ingredients into some form of emulsifying unit. Modern plants use the same principles but are usually microprocessor-controlled. The use of weighing in preference to metering is now almost universal, as it is less affected by product variation such as bulk density or viscosity.

Emulsification of the fat is very important as the globules tend to coalesce during cooking. Not only can this result in fat separation, but changes in the fat globule size affect texture and flow characteristics. It would also appear that changes in the degree of emulsification can occur during storage of premix, but information in this area is lacking.

The caramelisation reaction is time- and temperature-dependent but does not progress at a significant rate below about 112°C. Under batch processing conditions the degree of caramelisation is then affected by the quantity of protein, the quantity and type of reducing sugar and time taken to reach the final boiling temperature.

With a thin-film or scraped-surface cooker the heat transfer rates are high, and evaporation occurs so rapidly that caramelisation has no time to develop. These cookers are fitted with either pressurised preheaters or steam-jacketed holding vessels after the cookers, with variable residence times, so that the degree of colour and flavour development can be controlled.

Coil cookers are also used for lower viscosity products, but all high-efficiency evaporators tend to suffer from the milk protein burning on in some places, and decarbonisation using caustic soda solution is necessary at intervals.

The second approach was a cooker developed specifically for toffee by Tourell in collaboration with Callard & Bowser to simulate the pan operation (Figure 9.2). This employed a preheater unit and two U-shaped troughs arranged in cascade. The first unit or cooker was built up of a number of standard sections to give different capacities, and in theory different steam

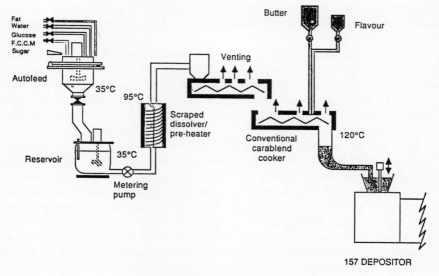

Figure 9.2   Toffee plant.

pressures could be used on each if required. The residence time was controlled by a weir and the cooker contained a complex variable-speed rotor assembly which was machined to close tolerances but not fitted with scrapers. This rotor was designed to give thorough mixing with a degree of back-mixing, and the flow through the cooker was controlled by a metering pump.

The rotor has no central shaft. The stirrer blades are mounted on three equally spaced shafts about halfway between the centre and circumference of the assembly, which in operation prevents build-up of toffee on the stirrer. As this rotor is made in one piece, once the cooker length has been decided it cannot be changed without replacing the rotor.

The second unit was a blender which was identical in construction but smaller than the cooker. This was for flavour and butter addition. This too had a weir to control residence time. All continuous cookers are difficult to control during start-up and close-down periods due to non-standard conditions. With the Tourell cooker, when the feed is stopped the cooker is drained by lowering the weir, but care is needed to maintain the correct temperature.

Recently the plate heat exchanger has been used for confectionery processing, and this can be used for toffee manufacture. The advantages of the plate heat exchanger are compactness and absence of moving parts, apart from the feed pump. In adition to this it is easy to install extra plates and thus vary the capacity. Whilst it can be dismantled for cleaning this is not recommended and probably caustic cleaning at intervals will be required.

Another advantage of the plate heat exchanger is that the dissolving and cooking sections can be parts of the same plate assembly. In the event of lack of caramelisation a holding tube can be inserted between two plates towards the end of the cooking stage, effectively introducing a holding stage for caramelisation to develop.

Many confectionery machinery manufacturers offer toffee-cooking equipment, frequently developed from existing machines developed for other processes.

Premix units vary in degree of complexity and numbers of recipes they can handle but are similar in principle, being based on load cell weighing of ingredient addition and microprocessor control. A frequent problem with these units is inaccessibility and difficulty in checking actual operation. A microprocessor-controlled sequence of weighing, mixing and emulsification is usually available.

Dissolvers can be simple stirred vessels, coil circulation systems or may be pressurised dissolvers to facilitate solution of sugar in low-moisture mixes. High-turbulence scraped-surface heat exchangers are also used.

For the final cooking operation, batch units are still manufactured, but continuous plants are either high-efficiency evaporators with caramelisers or longer residence time cookers. Both types are in common use and various claims are made for the relative benefits available. Neither has really gained the ascendancy, and in many cases selection is based on engineering convenience rather than process characteristics.

Having produced a toffee boil it should not be subjected to excessive mixing as this tends to toughen the texture apart from the risk of introducing grain as the temperature falls. With high-fat toffees an additional risk is fat separation, which can give the toffee an almost fibrous texture.

The next stage in processing is sweet-forming. For many years toffee has been run into trays, cut into slabs, or used as a layer in other confections formed into bars, but now a large quantity is wrapped as individual pieces. Three distinct types of process are used. The slab process, the cut and wrap process, and depositing.

9.5.2 Slab process

For many years slabs were lubricated with mineral oil or high-stability vegetable oils, which frequently contain antioxidants to improve keeping properties. It is likely, however, that mineral oil will be banned from inclusion in foods, and only the vegetable oils permitted.

There is a tendency in any application of release agent to use excess, largely because little thought appears to have been given to means of application. This is undesirable and every effort should be made to keep usage to the minimum.

From the pan or cooker the toffee is transferred to bowls which are either manually poured onto the slab, or may be fitted with a carriage which is lifted on a hoist and runs on the side bars of the slab. Whilst boiled sweets can be pumped, due to the increased risk of graining toffee is rarely pumped.

One of the earlier sweet-forming operations was to level the liquid toffee on the slabs and when cool enough to handle it was cut into sheets, reversed on the slab to even out the cooling and then cut into individual pieces, either in presses or with two-way cutters using circular knives. In many cases slabs have now been replaced by cooling bands or drums. The sweets then go to individual piece-wrapping machines.

9.5.3 *Cut and wrap process*

With the cut and wrap process the operation is slightly different. The cooling process must be uniform but the handling must not be too vigorous. When the toffee has cooled sufficiently in contact with the slab to be lifted it is folded in towards the centre. This may be repeated and eventually the mass becomes firm enough to lift. It should be lifted across the centre so that the surface in contact with the slab folds inwards. It is then laid on the slab again and allowed to spread when the folding is repeated. The purpose of this is to even out the cooling and bring the batch to a uniform temperature of about 110°F (43°C).

It is then placed in a batch roller which rolls the mass into a cone and draws it out into a rope, which goes through a presizer. This is a series of wheels with semicircular grooves machined in the circumference. The wheels are in pairs, and each succeeding pair has a smaller groove and revolves faster. By this means the rope is drawn down to the required size for the wrapping machine. This machine has a final set of wheels which form the rope into the toffee section required, which is usually rectangular. This shaped rope now passes through a rapidly rotating knife which chops the rope into pieces. The pieces are then pushed against wrapping paper which has been cut from a reel by a machine, into the jaws of the transfer wheel where the various stages of folding and twisting the wrap are carried out and the wrapped toffee is ejected down a chute. Other versions fold the paper instead of twisting the ends.

These machines have become progressively faster over the years, and speeds in excess of 1000 sweets per minute are now possible.

Due to the nature of this process the toffee is squeezed and stretched. The squeezing action can express fat from a high-fat toffee, but fat contents of 24% appear to be quite feasible.

The stretching effect is more serious. Although plastic toffee has a degree of elasticity, the colder it becomes the more the elasticity increases. The effect of this is that it can shrink after the pieces have been wrapped and produces distorted ends to the toffees. To alleviate this the toffee should be handled as warm as possible, but in fact it depends on formulation, and operators tend to work by the texture of the rope. In any case it is customary to let the rope slacken and snake before entering the wrapping machine. This allows some shrinkage to occur and reduces the shrinkage after cutting.

With high-fat-content toffees, presizer rolls can be a minor problem. If fat is expressed from the toffee it comes into direct contact with the rolls, which can result in more rapid oxidation. Ideally the rolls should be stainless steel but in the past were frequently plated steel or brass or bronze. In use the plating eventually wears away and the base metal comes into contact with the fat.

Cut and wrap processing is considerably more efficient than separate cutting and wrapping operations.

9.5.4 *Depositing*

The other major means of toffee forming is depositing into silicone rubber moulds. This was largely brought about by the development of the CD depositor, which had no sliding valve mechanism. The combination of using the depositor piston and a ball valve removed many of the potential graining sites for high-boiled products, and no lubrication, which was frequently done with water, was required. However, shearing still occurs and high-sugar formulations are at risk in depositors of this type.

One of the problems associated with depositing toffee lies in the flow characteristics. Since the milk protein can introduce a yield stress factor, the toffee will not flow out in the moulds and achieve a uniform shape. This can result in wrapping difficulties, particularly on high-speed machines.

Toffees will typically have an equilibrium relative humidity of about 45–50%, and twist wrapping is no protection against moisture. This implies that an air-conditioned environment is necessary both during cooling and before final packing, and care must be taken to ensure that the product is not cooled below the dew point.

Deterioration at this stage is not readily apparent, but absorption of traces of moisture will seriously reduce shelf life as crystallisation will rapidly develop on the surface and penetrate the whole sweet.

This in effect produces a grained caramel, but controlled graining is achieved by the introduction of seed crystal during manufacture. The usual seeding medium is fondant, which introduces a large number of sugar crystals of about 10 μm. The quantity required is quite small, less than 1% of the batch, and for cut and wrap toffees or any other form of plastic processing the fondant will be folded in during the cooling operation once the temperature is below 100°C. With deposited toffees the process is more difficult as the temperature is higher than that at which the crystal in fondant will be destroyed. This means that the toffee must be cooled before the fondant is added, and even so larger quantities of fondant will be required. In both cases the toffee will grain after wrapping and slightly warm storage temperatures are required. High temperatures are undesirable because the toffee can easily distort before it grains, and also because the grained toffee will have a much higher vapour pressure than the ungrained toffee. On removal to a colder environment condensation can easily occur within the pack.

9.6 Toffee texture

Toffee textures are sometimes modified by the incorporation of air, which is normally introduced by mixing in a whipped frappé, and toffees are frequently combined with other confectionery products. In these circumstances attention must be paid to the equilibrium relative humidity of the separate components as, if they are different, moisture transfer will occur within the sweet, leading to changes in texture. This also applies to inclusions such as dried fruit or nuts, which should be stoved to prevent moisture being introduced into the toffee and initiating grain.

Reworking toffee products depends to an extent on the type of process involved. Solid rework can be added back either on the slab or into the boiled batch, but it is imperative that no grain has developed on the surface of the rework. It is safer to redissolve the rework to premix solids and feed it back at the premix stage. It has been said that a proportion of rework improves toffee texture, and whilst this may be subjective it certainly improves flow characteristics in depositing processes.

9.7 Fudge

The name fudge covers a wide range of products which are basically toffee formulations but in which sugar crystal has been developed during processing. Normally a fudge will contain more sugar and milk than a toffee, but composition can vary between very wide limits and it is much more important to understand the basic principles involved, since the texture of the finished products is far more dependent on processing than it is on formulation.

The requirements of fudge are that it must be microbiologically stable, it must be firm and it must have a uniform texture. These three requirements virtually define a fudge once the moisture content has been decided. The effect of glucose syrup or invert sugar solids on sugar solubility makes it essential that the concentration of these reducing sugars must be at least 1.5 times, and for safety should be nearer 2.5 times, the moisture content. This will ensure a dissolved solids level of between 75% and 79%.

Most fudges will have moisture contents between 7 and 10%, so the reducing sugars solids must be about 17–25% and the sugar in solution will be about 8.5–12%. This is derived from the work carried out many years ago by Grover on the effect of glucose and invert sugar on the solubility of sucrose.

By this reasoning we can deduce the essentials of our fudge composition. At 7% moisture and 17% glucose syrup solids, about 8.5% sugar will remain in solution. At 10% moisture and 25% glucose syrup solids, about 12% sugar will remain in solution. Thus 32–47% of the fudge composition is defined. The remainder will be sugar crystal fat and milk solids. It is not likely that the fat and milk solids combined will exceed 20%, so the sugar to crystallise out must be of the order of 40%.

Thus the basic fudge recipe becomes:

17–25% reducing sugar solids
45–55% sugar
20% fat and milk solids
7–10% moisture

Comparison with fondant indicates that the solids content in the final fudge to achieve adequate firmness will be of the order of 60%, so the limits can be further reduced. In this case fat, although it melts in the mouth, is regarded as solid phase.

Whatever recipe is used however, much depends on processing. Fudge is a grained product, and some means of graining is required. This can be done by removing part of the cooked batch, cooling it, and working it until it crystallises, when it is added back to the remainder of the hot batch and thoroughly mixed in. Whilst this is feasible it is not usual, and use of fondant to provide seed crystal is almost universal. However, fondant crystal is destroyed in a hot batch, so cooling of the boil to about 105°C is required to ensure adequate crystal being present when the batch is poured.

It is virtually impossible to establish experimentally the amount of seed introduced into fudge, but by making some assumptions which are not strictly justifiable an interesting calculation is possible.

The crystal phase in many fondants is about 60%. This crystal size is often about $10\,\mu m$. Thus 1 g fondant contains 0.6 g crystal. The specific gravity of sugar crystal is 1.58, so the volume of sugar crystal in 1 g fondant is 0.38 ml. $10\,\mu m = 10^{-3}$ cm, therefore the volume of a 10-μm crystal, assuming it to be a cube, is 10^{-9} ml. Therefore the number of crystals in 1 g fondant is $0.38 \times 10^9 = 3.8 \times 10^8$.

Since fudge contains about 40% crystal and the crystal size is of the order of $30\,\mu m$, 1 g fudge contains 0.4 g or 0.25 ml of sugar crystal.

$$1 \text{ sugar crystal} = 27 \times 10^{-9} \text{ ml}.$$

Therefore the number of crystals in 1 g of fudge is 9.2×10^6.

If it is assumed that there is little secondary nucleation and all the seed has grown, this means that 1 g fudge contains

$$\frac{9.2 \times 10^6}{3.8 \times 10^8} = 0.024 \text{ g fondant or } 2.4\% \text{ fondant.}$$

In a cooled fudge batch this is about half the quantity of fondant required, which implies that at about 100°C about half the sugar crystal is dissolved on incorporating the fondant, assuming that no secondary nucleation occurs.

The cooling can be achieved either as part of the processing, when about 5.0% of fondant will be required, or by adding excess fondant and accepting that most of it dissolves. In either case the components of the fondant are part of the overall composition and must be allowed for in the composition of the boiled batch.

Thus the requirements for processing become apparent. The boiled batch is handled exactly as a toffee, and although the batch is going to be crystallised it is imperative that all the sugar is dissolved. At the end of the cook butter may be added if required and either excess fondant added to bring the temperature below 105°C or the batch cooled, usually by passing water through the pan jacket. Although very common practice this is not ideal for many reasons, but the most important is that it can reduce the serviceable life of the pan. Furthermore, raw mains water can enter the steam condensate return lines and have an adverse effect on the factory boilers. The advantage is that any residual product in the pan is redissolved during the processing of subsequent batches.

If fudge is made by cutting sheets of product, the off-cuts can represent about 15% of the output. This can be added back to subsequent cooked batches as a cooling medium. Although the crystal is much coarser than fondant, most of it is dissolved and most of the seed crystal comes from the fondant which is added afterwards.

Having produced a seeded batch at about 100–105°C, it now has to be formed into sweets. The most common method is by pouring onto a slab, cooling, traying off until crystallisation has stabilised and then cutting, but fudge can be deposited into trays or moulds. In all cases the cooling is crucial. Fudge must not be shock-chilled, so cold-water tables must not be too cold. It is desirable that they do not drop below about 20°C. When pouring onto tables it must be remembered that the fudge has to be removed before it is fully stabilised. For this reason it is usually poured onto waxed or siliconised paper so that it can be cut into slabs and transferred to trays for final setting, when it is cut with either revolving knives or guillotines to the required size. The suitability of any paper used to cover slabs should be checked against legislative requirements for food-contact materials.

In general, the slower fudge cools the larger the crystals will be, but if cooling is accelerated it is possible to over-run the crystallisation rate and produce an incompletely grained product virtually the same as a grained caramel. This will require warm storage in trays, and even then may take days to stabilise.

Another problem with cooling fudge is the same problem that arises if fondant creams are overheated before depositing. During cooling they develop pale spots or 'star'. The reason for this is not wholly established, but it is worse with high-sugar-content products and is probably due to a crystal structure forming before the product is adequately cooled. Once this structure has formed further cooling will inevitably lead to contraction of the syrup phase, which will then be inadequate to fill all the gaps between the crystals. Air will be drawn into the surface of the product and pale spots appear.

This is a surface defect and is of little consequence if the fudge is to be covered in chocolate, but it is usually associated with a slightly shorter texture than a correctly cooled batch. In fact the colder a fudge is handled during forming the softer the final texture will be.

Nearly all the problems which arise in handling fudge would appear to be due to uneven cooling. The cooling rate in static air is quite low, and the crystal tends to develop uniformly throughout the product. Any attempt to accelerate the setting process requires very careful assessment of the problems before deciding on the cooling system required.

Another means of making fudge is by extrusion. A cold fudge mass can be fed through an extruder, formed into ribbons and cut to length. The fudge has to be cold so that the fat is virtually solid and is not expressed during extrusion. In some continuous plants an in-line cooler is provided to accelerate crystal growth whilst the fudge is being mixed, and since the mass is being agitated a firm crystal structure cannot build up.

As the fudge is cool, the crystal has already developed, so after extrusion the rigid structure characteristic of cast fudge is never achieved. Extruded fudges are always therefore more plastic than deposited fudge and very frequently are used as centres for chocolate covering.

Another type of bar forming partially cools the fudge mass on a cooled drum or drums and by using a comb arrangement, or slitting knives form the fudge into ribbons which can be cut to length. However, this system is subject to the same restraints as cooling fudge on slabs and requires strict control of the cooling process.

Being a grained product fudge will have a relatively high ERH and will normally dry out in storage. A moistureproof wrap is desirable but it is necessary to ensure that the syrup-phase solids are sufficiently high to prevent mould growth. This implies that fudges intended for longer shelf life will contain less sugar and be softer products than those normally sold as 'home-made' or 'candy' fudges.

Frequently fudge has additional ingredients such as fruit, glacé cherries, nuts and chocolate. For chocolate fudge cocoa mass is often used, and the addition can be made either before or after cooking. Glacé cherries may contain significant quantities of syrup, which must be thoroughly drained before addition to fudge batches, and it is not unusual for cherries to be lightly dusted with icing sugar and stoved before use. Addition of cherries should be left as late as possible, as excessive mixing leads to breakdown of the cherry and colour leaching into the fudge. Nuts do not present problems, but walnuts particularly should be thoroughly checked as they can introduce the risk of infestation.

10 Gums and jellies

E.T. BEST

10.1 Introduction

Hydrocolloid sweets—gums and jellies—now represent about half of the sugar confections sold, and their popularity continues to grow. Examples include hard, soft and foamed gums, laces, tubes and corrugated strips, jujubes, fruit leathers, lemon slices, pastilles, Turkish delight, gummy bears, jelly babies, etc. Gums and jellies are also used in other confections, e.g. reformed fruit pieces [1] or pectin jellies in cereal cluster confectionery [2].

Selection of the hydrocolloid system enables considerable textural modification. The sweets may be shaped by various moulding techniques from fluid liquor, extrusion from semiplastic mass, cutting from preformed slabs, etc. Inclusions such as fruit pieces or liquid centres can be accommodated. Coatings such as sugar sanding, non-pareil, crystallisation, waxing/oiling, soft panning and chocolate are common. In addition, multilayering with, for example, fudge, mallow, nougat or toffee makes this a most diverse range.

This chapter concentrates on the specific batch and continuous operations for the manufacture of these confections, procedures common to other confections not being covered to the same degree. In addition latest manufacturing developments are highlighted. For background information the reader is referred to Lees & Jackson [3].

10.2 Technology and chemistry of the hydrocolloids

Hydrocolloids are the key ingredients of this class of confectionery. They gel and thicken but also stabilise by preventing syneresis, fixing flavours and inhibiting sugar crystallisation, give transparency, brilliance, adhesion and ease foaming for aerated jellies. Preselection of the hydrocolloid (in isolation or combination) should be based upon both the desired characteristics of the finished confection and the functionality requirements of the manufacturing process.

10.2.1 *Agar agar*

This material has different characteristic properties [4] according to the seaweed variety (*Gelidium, Gracilaria, Pterocladia*, etc.) and its geographic origin. It swells in water and exhibits a high gelling power at low (1–2%) concentrations to give a hard-brittle short-breaking jelly of good clarity. The Kobe test can be employed to characterise the strength grade. It is one of the most potent gel-forming agents known. The strength is mainly proportional to the agarose (rather than agaropectin) content, which forms double helices on gelation. Sulphate groups are present in the extract and a high percentage increases the gel elasticity. The presence of the sulphate can cause haze or cloudiness in the gel if hard water is used.

A unique property is its ability to form gels which only set at 32–39°C yet do not melt until 85–90°C (i.e. a high hysteresis). This has advantages in allowing the incorporation of flavours/acids/colours, etc. at cooler temperatures prior to shaping and setting. However in 'Zephyr' candy [5] the slow gelling rate inhibits automation, and furcelleran is displacing agar in this traditional labour-intensive line. The high melting temperature of the gel makes it suitable for products destined for hot climates. Approximately two-thirds of the water in the gel is in a loosely bound form and under certain recipe and storage conditions syneresis may result.

Gel strength is enhanced by sugar and locust bean gum (with a synergistic increase in rupture strength and elasticity) but is diminished by starch. The dextrose equivalent (DE) value of glucose syrup has little effect on break strength, although lower DE values do give more elasticity.

Gum acacia, fruit pulps and extracts tenderise and shorten the texture. Starches and gelatins may be incorporated to modify the eat. A degree of recipe experimentation is desirable because agar phase separation leading to precipitation or textural granularity may result under certain conditions.

The agar/gelatin system is particularly interesting. With 1% agar and 4% gelatin in solution the gel has a modulated agar texture with a melting point around 90°C, yet when the gelatin level in solution is 8% a gelatin-type network forms and the gel weakens and becomes more elastic and the melting point falls to around 40°C.

10.2.2 *Bacterial gums*

Xanthan gum from *Xanthomonas campestris* and gellan gum from the fermentation of *Pseudomonas elodea* (with deacetylation) are now finding application in this type of confection [6, 7].

The extraordinary enzymatic resistance of xanthan is leading to its application in natural fruit jelly bars where its unique pseudoplastic fluid rheology enables almost total viscosity recovery following shear processes. Xanthan gum is synergistic with both locust bean gum and guar gum in respect of viscosity. Thermoreversible gelation with a gel point of around 32°C results from junction zones between the smooth (mannose) regions of the galactomannan and the helical regions of the xanthan. Conformational interference from the 'hairy' locust bean gum sidechains may inhibit gel formation if the gum blend is not heated above 55°C. Xanthan may be employed to reduce the set time of low-sugar starch confections, and also to modify stickiness yet maintain the tenderness. Xanthan is incompatible with high concentrations of gum acacia at low pH but does not have a high propensity to acid hydrolysis. Syneresis can result from the formation of excess junction zones and may be avoided by the introduction of other macromolecules (such as glucose syrup) to induce perturbations in the gel structure. Guar gum can become incompatible with xanthan at very low pH. Xanthan is compatible with starch and pectin.

Gellan is functional at very low concentration (around 0.5%) to give hard-brittle short-textured gels. These gels are more elastic than agar and have shorter textures than pectin. Setting temperature is 40–50°C yet melting temperature is 90–100°C (similar to agar). They require a cation (preferably calcium) for gelation (similar to kappa carragheenan). Approximately 0.5% gellan with 0.1% magnesium chloride gives a gel equivalent to 1.5% agar. Gel strength is proportional to both hydrocolloid concentration and salt concentration.

10.2.3   Gelatin

Food-grade gelatin is made by aqueous extraction from mammalian collagen by lime or acid treatments of ossein or skin, bovine or porcine raw materials. Religious reasons may preclude the use of porcine sources.

Amphoteric nature is exhibited with an isoelectric point (pI) around 4.8–5.1 for limed, 6.5–8.5 for acid ossein and 7.5–9.5 for acid skin. At the pI clarity and surface tension are minimised and viscosity maximised.

The cooler aqueous extractions give higher strength materials than the later hotter extractions. Strength is measured by Bloom value, which is a significant factor in pricing strategy. The higher Bloom grades usually have greater clarity and less colour, flavour, setting time and stickiness. Where a low-Bloom can be employed the larger quantity to achieve the same gel strength may cost the same but give benefits in terms of increased solids yield. Commercial standardised gelatins normally contain a mixture of Bloom values blended to meet other requirements such as viscosity, colour, etc. The material is available in leaf, sheet, granule and powder.

The thermoreversibility of gelatin gels (at around 40°C) gives its main organoleptic feature of a smooth elastic texture which melts agreeably in the mouth. Sugar addition enhances gel rigidity. Reducing sugars can promote Maillard reactions, which may be desirable for caramel jellies or for intensifying the colour of gels made with natural colours. Gel strength is reduced by hydrolysis, which is promoted by temperature, acids, bases, enzymes (e.g. from fresh fruit, especially pineapple) and irradiation. To exemplify, a gel stored for 8 h at 80°C will lose around 25% strength at pH 6, but approximately 75% strength at pH 3. A pH 3 gel at 100°C will degrade at about three times the rate of the same gel at 60°C. Not all acids act the same, even at the same pH. The kinetics of the hydrolysis are non-linear, with most degradation occurring in the early stages.

Guar- and carob-type gums form a cloudy galactomannan precipitate with gelatin. Pectin may be added to gelatin gels to raise the melting point and reduce instances of sweets sticking together. Gelatin reduces the hardness and tackiness of all gum arabic confections and gives extra chewiness to starch systems.

10.2.4   *Gum acacia (gum arabic)*

Gum acacia is a tree exudate, where it forms as 'tears'. Each tree yields between 50 and 100 g per year so this commodity requires a journey of about a 100 km to collect just a few kilograms. This, together with droughts, the encroachment of deserts and the local population using acacia as fodder or firewood, has in recent years caused severe supply shortages and high prices. The material is available in lumps, powdered and as purified, standardised, spray-dried. High winds at the time of maximum exudation can cause sand contamination as well as bark in unpurified materials. Viscosity is affected by the age of the tree, rainfall, age and storage condition of the gum. Quality is to a large extent colour-dependent, with the paler grades preferred although darker grades can be used in dark sweets provided the characteristic astringency is absent.

This material is the traditional and largely irreplaceable hydrocolloid for many long-lasting, chewy, gum sweets and is used at levels from 10–60%. (Wine gums were originally made in Britain's African Colonies from gum acacia and flavoured with wine.) For a high-solids hard gum a greater clarity is obtained than with most other hydrocolloids. Resistance to melt-away, shape stability, good clarity, bland taste and odour with minimal sweetness and pliable texture with low adhesion during consumption are key features. In addition to providing viscosity. body and texture the material is excellent for its fixative properties, giving slow controlled flavour and odour release as the confection is dissolved in the mouth. Being a good film-former it protects flavours from oxidation and retards sugar crystallisation.

As it has practically no nutritional value it can be a basis for diabetic/dietetic products.

Its viscosity reduces greatly with increased temperature, making it suitable for fluid-deposited goods. Viscosity is Newtonian up to 25% concentration and then becomes more pronouncedly viscous with concentration until it becomes pseudoplastic at 40% levels. Maximum viscosity is at pH 6–7.

It is soluble in hot sugar and compatible with proteins, starches and carbohydrates including other plant hydrocolloids under many conditions. Gelatin is frequently added to soften the texture.

10.2.5 *Pectin*

Pectins are mainly obtained from apple or citrus fruit. According to Reidel [8] some apple pectins may have traces of apple flavour and can produce cloudy sweets if the apple starch is not adequately removed. Slight differences can be observed between pectins of different countries. It has been reported [9] that apple pectins can give slightly browner jellies than citrus pectins. Apple pectin can be clearer, sets at a slightly higher temperature and is less viscous than equivalent citrus types.

Pectin gels have a delicate fruit-like short texture and mouthfeel with very good flavour release.

Pectins are characterised by their degree of esterification or methoxylation (DE or DM) and their gel strength (SAG value), which is usually standardised by small additions of sucrose. They may also be buffered or unbuffered, the buffer giving control over gelation speed.

High-methoxy (HM) pectin is normally the choice for fruit jellies and forms a gel when the total solids exceed about 55% and the pH is less than 4. The speed of gelation and the ultimate gel regidity can be controlled not only by temperature but also by type/grade of pectin, degree of esterification, soluble solids, sugar balance, salt content, acidity, etc. Although some care is needed to master the production requirements the material gives fast and controllable gelation.

Low-methoxy (LM) pectin does not require acid and is valuable for flavours such as vanilla, liquorice, peppermint, etc. One can obtain the gel by diffusing calcium ions into the system. At low concentrations LM pectin solutions are thixotropic. Aerated jellies requiring a shorter breaking texture normally employ LM pectin.

Amidated pectins give major slowing of setting and can be used for depositing times in excess of 30 min or depositing temperatures below 60°C (e.g. if alcohol is to be incorporated).

Pectin forms gels at 0.5–4.0% concentration with excellent flavour transfer. Pectin can be depolymerised at high temperatures but does not suffer undue acid hydrolysis. Gelation is very rapid and will form too quickly if the solution is too cold when the acid is added. Low levels of gelatin may be added to pectin gels to reduce their short texture, lowering losses caused by sweet breakage in production.

10.2.6 *Starch*

Corn or maize starch is the most common origin, although sago/tapioca, rice, wheat and potato starches can be employed to modify textures. These types vary in amylose/amylopectin ratio. Amylose contributes little to viscosity at high temperatures but in dilute situations can associate with hydrogen bonding to cause a precipitate. Amylopectin resists retrogradation in cooled cooked solutions but greatly influences viscosity by tangling even at relatively high temperatures. Waxy maize starch has barely any gel strength. Tapioca and potato have a low amount of amylose, giving soft gels when cooked. Starches give greater optical clarity and higher sheen gels than most other hydrocolloids.

Unmodified starches can give unsatisfactory short textures and weak bodies. Food acids can be used with unmodified starches [10] to effect partial depolymerisation during the candy boil, but normally modified starches are used. Traditionally, chemical modification has been employed, but latterly physical processes, particularly those involving pressure and/or shear, have been developed to enable similar benefits without chemical usage.

Acid-thinned starches have their granules weakened as acid preferentially cleaves amylopectin. The granules fragment during swelling giving a marked viscosity reduction. This process reduces hot-paste viscosity to a greater extent than it reduces gel strength, thereby enabling starch usage at higher concentrations, increasing the availability of the amylose for strong gel reassociation. Hot viscosities of around one-fifth those of native starch are possible. They are recommended for their low viscosity in mould-depositing high-solids formulations, and set on cooling to 80–85°C to give tender gels with soft to high strength depending upon dose level and recipe total solids. For slab work slightly faster setting, higher viscosity starches may be used.

Oxidised starches have a proportion of cleaved α-1-4-glycosidic links. These give slower setback compared to acid-thinned starches owing to the bulky carboxyl groups. They are hot water-soluble with medium to low viscosity. They are slow-setting and stable to retrogradation.

Acetylated starches are similar to oxidised in that the bulky acetyl group inhibits retrogradation.

High-amylose starches provide rapid, strong gel setting with short non-sticky textures and may act as partial gelatin replacers. It is possible to get three times the 24-h gel strength with such starches.

Alternatively, the same gel strength as an acid-thinned starch can be achieved at much lower solids concentration. They are unable to be processed in atmospheric kettles as they gelatinise at 140–170°C depending upon type; with the higher temperature cook types giving the strongest gel. They are valuable for reducing drying time and can be employed in the higher moisture formulations needed for starchless moulding and softer gums.

Blends of high-amylose starch and acid-thinned starch can give many of the advantages of both systems. Application in jelly beans is an example where a clear, tender centre is required that is resistant to hardening over time.

Special ultrasetting, high-amylose-type starches are now available without the disadvantage of superatmospheric cooking. These can be used dilute

($< 50\%$ solids liquors) in open-pan boiling or can be jet- or static-cooked (in 75% solids liquors) at 140°C.

Dextrin-based starches can be used as gum acacia alternatives in hard gums, but oxidised and other stabilised types are more effective. Thorough cooking (with, for example, live steam) is essential because undercooking can lead to stickiness, cloudiness and adverse flavours. They have low viscosity, good clarity and if very dextrinised can be cold water-soluble.

10.3   Hydrocolloid pretreatment processes

It is normally advisable to ensure that the hydrocolloid is cleaned, ground, purified, soaked, made soluble or dissolved, buffered or in some way standardised before it is incorporated in the sugar liquors. In particular, to avoid coacervation in mixed hydrocolloid systems it is recommended that solutions of each colloid be prepared separately and blended later [11]. Normally solution is carried out in the absence of sugars because of competition for the water. In the case of the agar/gelatin mixed system, however, it is advisable to use a low-sulphate agar and ensure the presence of both sugar and glucose syrup when blending the two previously prepared solutions.

10.3.1   *Purification*

If crude or impure hydrocolloids (such as lump gum acacia) are being processed they must first be graded, blended and crushed. Large impurities may be removed by sifting, picking, aspiration or density-table separation. A dilute solution of the colloid can then be bleached, sieved, centrifuged, filtered or submitted to froth flotation and sedimentation procedures to remove impurities. If such a solution is likely to stand for more than a few hours it may be necessary to add preservatives such as sodium metabisulphite or acetic acid. Spray-dried purified hydrocolloids can usually be dissolved without pretreatment, although a fine sieve in the line is still advisable to remove any undissolved lumps. According to Anderson & McDougall [12] spray drying of gum acacia can cause autohydrolysis, so dose levels cannot simply be calculated on a solids basis, nevertheless the high moisture content of raw material and the yield losses due to impurities generally make the unpurified colloid less economic in use.

10.3.2   *Soaking*

Large pieces of cold water- soluble colloid equivalent to 16–60 BS mesh can be presoaked to remove the stiffness and produce a 'crumb' or 'flake' which is easily dissolved at a later stage in either water or hot sugar syrup. The hydrocolloid is always added to water, never the other way round. Excess fines in the colloid can cause balling in this process. Fruit juice may substitute for some of the water in this procedure. To prevent the particles sticking together the water should be as cold as practicable [13]. Gelatin swells best when it is distanced from its pI and absorbs up to five times its own weight, although a 1:1 soaking will ensure ease of solution or melting of the crumb at 70°C. Strip agar needs soaking for up to 12 h, powdered agar up to 1 h. Japanese agar needs approximately 32 times its weight of water, New Zealand agar twice that amount as it is about double the strength. When these materials need long standing times, they must be stored under chilled conditions to avoid potential microbiological hazards. Ten organisms per gram may undergo exponential growth to 650 000 in 8 h. Suitable equipment for this operation includes dragée pans with internal blades, ribbon blenders or specially designed tanks with horizontal blades. Soaked 'crumb' may be vacuum-discharged directly to the sugar liquor system.

10.3.3 Dissolving

In direct dissolving of powdered hydrocolloids constant stirring is essential, and the more soluble colloids or finer particle sizes will need maximum agitation although taking less time to dissolve. It is essential to ensure that each grain is an individual entity in the mix to avoid lumping, especially with cold-soluble materials. Ways in which this can be achieved [14] include dispersing in hot glucose syrup (even dry gelatin will not dissolve under atmospheric conditions), dry mixing with sugar (which in addition to acting as a physical separation is a mechanical dispersant during solution formation) or by slowly adding to the liquid with rapid dispersion.

When dissolving it is prudent to err on the dilute side and give adequate time, temperature and agitation to ensure complete solution. Foaming can be a problem because hydrocolloids are good surfactants; a trace of oil or antifoam can help. Temperatures will be kept low to avoid thermal degradation of certain hydrocolloids, but dissolving and storing above 60°C is sensible to minimise bacterial growth.

Xanthan, gellan and guar dissolve in the cold, gelatin at 40°C, locust bean gum needs 85°C. Agars and pectins ideally need boiling for at least 2 min, although dilute pectin solutions (12%) may be dissolved at 60°C. High sugar concentrations, certain cations and hard water inhibit solution; where permitted the use of a sequestering agent helps. Pectins are easier to dissolve if the DM is higher and preferably need a pH above 5 and less than 25% sugar. Buffer salts such as sodium citrate or tartrate can help in pH modulation. Agars need a pH above 8 and a maximum concentration of 3% or else viscosity will be too high. When dissolving starch in an open pan it is best to use approximately eight parts of water per part of starch and to check the clarity to ensure rupturing of the starch granules. A slow boiling should be carried out until the mixture first thins and then starts to thicken. Confectioners say the starch has then been 'cut' and more rapid boiling can follow. High-amylose starches modified for low-temperature cooking should, on the other hand, have a short come-up time to 95°C to prevent lumping. Generally speaking temperature, shear and time all make starch granules more swollen and more susceptible to rupture. Overcooked starch can give undesirable long cohesive textures; undercooked gives thin cloudy sweets. Cross-linked starch is more tolerant to overcooking. Some colloids such as gum acacia need a scraped surface or gentle heat to avoid 'plating out' on the heat-exchange surface.

Various types of dissolving equipment are used in the industry. Simple planetary beaters can suffer from splashing and material losses through sticking to the beater. Foamed masses may be skimmed to remove entrapped air. Bottom-emptying jacketed tanks with stirrers allow the foam to be left behind after a short standing time. Dilute solutions of hydrocolloid may be concentrated using plate evaporators but a deaeration stage is recommended to prevent bubbles reducing the good contact with the heat-exchange surface.

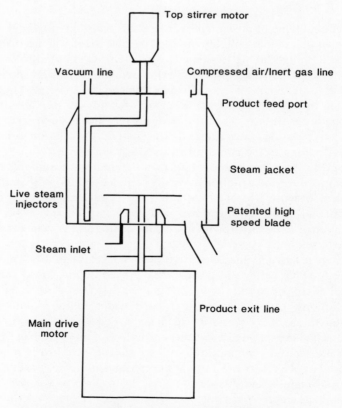

Figure 10.1 'TEMEC'-type hydrocolloid dispersing apparatus.

There are now available very high-speed dispersers in base-emptying scraped-surface jacketed vessels which can prepare very concentrated hydrocolloid solutions directly from the powdered material (Figure 10.1). Some of these are capable of operating with live steam injection, under vacuum, or being pressurised to expel the viscous mass. These latter vessel types can also be used to blend in the sugars if feeding short-residence-time liquor cookers.

When feeding coil, jet or static cookers the hydrocolloids may be simply preslurried, but the retention time/temperature relationship in the subsequent operation must be sufficient to ensure solution.

10.4 Liquor preparation

The main objective in preparing a liquor is to produce a high-solids fluid mass that can be shaped by moulding, slabbing or using dies, etc. (Figure 10.2). It is necessary to achieve a final liquor of at least 75% total soluble solids to preclude mould growth. As sucrose is saturated at 67% at ambient temperature glucose, invert (added or produced in process) or other doctors are used to inhibit crystallisation. Excess or uncontrolled sugar inversion should be avoided during the base liquor preparation to avoid adversely affecting equilibrium relative humidity (ERH) or causing sweating, hygroscopicity, stickiness, excess elasticity, gel weakness or browning by the Maillard reaction if proteinaceous materials are incorporated. When pectin is

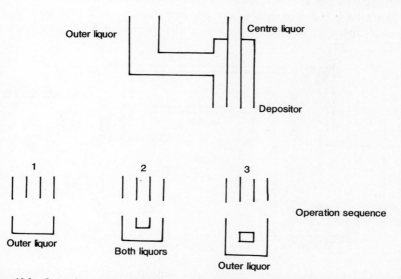

Figure 10.2 Operation of a liquid-filling depositor. The outer liquid could be a high-methoxy pectin and the centre liquid an acidic-flavoured sugar syrup. On reaction a skin will form around the liquid filling.

included in the boil the pH should be below 4.5 to avoid unacceptable pectin hydrolysis, but at this pH a long cook will cause high inversion. If the syrups are prepared separately, higher pHs may be used.

Temperature of the final liquor is critical to setting time (e.g. a pectin liquor at 80°C sets twice as fast as one at 90°C). Viscosity is also affected by temperature, and in depositing systems too low a viscosity will cause splashing at the pump bar and too high will cause tailing. Lower water contents mean that less post-shaping drying will be needed. In addition, higher total solids contents raise the break strength of most hydrocolloids; to get the same gel strength in a lower solids mass one needs higher levels of the more expensive colloid. The type of sugar in the liquor affects the overall gel strength, generally in the order low-DE glucose > high-DE glucose > sucrose > invert > dextrose > fructose. In addition, low-DE glucoses or maltodextrins may be used to raise the sweets' viscosity in the mouth and thereby reduce sensations of stickiness and cohesion.

Common-purpose plants are desirable in mixed confectionery factories, and the same unit operations for liquor preparation may be used for high-sugar boilings, toffees and caramel. This concept was stressed by Van der Schaaf [15] as giving significant savings in maintenance and production flexibility.

Shear rate is significant and generally demaging to the hydrocolloid. Steam-jacketed kettles with slow-sweeping mixers are low in shear. Steam injection dissolvers and plate cookers are medium, and most pumps are medium to high. A long time at low shear will be as damaging as a short time at high shear. Centrifugal pumps are satisfactory for simple vessel transfers and will slip if fed against a back pressure such as caused by a throttle valve or if accidentally fed to a closed or blocked pipe. For gentle positive action against a high

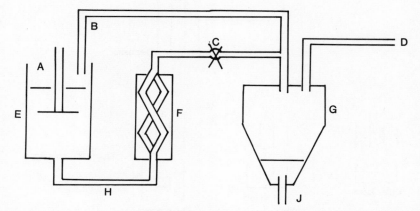

Figure 10.3 Static cooker assembly. A, high-speed stirrer; B, product return; C, back-pressure valve; D, vacuum line; E, feed tank (jacketed); F, twin high-pressure coils in steam chest; G, vacuum separating vessel; H, product feed via positive displacement pump; J, product extract via positive displacement pump.

pressure, as in a static cooker (Figure 10.3), a jacketed, progressing-cavity metering pump is recommended.

10.4.1 Traditional processes

The liquor is prepared from processed sugar syrups (which may contain a heat-stable hydrocolloid) to which separately prepared heat-sensitive colloids (soaked or solution) are added. Some foaming can occur during this operation and the vessel size must allow for this. The blending may be a batch operation using bottom-draining vats or continuous using metering pumps and in-line static mixers. When blending sugar syrup and agar it is necessary to ensure both are warm to prevent cold shock and broken gels resulting.

Sugar syrup preparation is common to other confectionery types and usually follows the use of computerised scales to drive autovibrating feeders for solids (sugar) and metering pumps for liquids (glucose syrup(s)) into a cool-mix slurrying vessel, a hot-mix dissolver, custom-designed reservoir tanks with shear mixing on load cells or other continuous processing systems. Cool-mix ring mains offer the advantage of little inversion compared to the variable inversion rates of hot-syrup ring mains. Plant design should avoid excess bends in pneumatic sugar lines to avoid creation of pulverised sugar which will aid air entrainment. Feed hoppers for dry ingredients should not be subject to rising steam from boiling vessels. The syrups so prepared may be concentrated using plate or film evaporators in the normal way.

Batch operations offer easy cessation in the event of breakdown of subsequent processing equipment.

10.4.2 Continuous cookers

In recent years classical techniques have tended to be superseded by continuous cooking methods, especially those under pressure. This has led to greater uniformity, less intensive labour requirement, higher output and reduced energy expenditure. Short-residence-time cookers (jet or static) allow even heat-sensitive materials such as gelatin to be preblended with the sugar syrups before feeding the cooker. These processes do not involve extensive evaporation of water but cook under more critical conditions of high temperature/high solids. Specially designed grades of hydrocolloid are available for these processes. Pressure dissolving techniques [16, 17] are claimed to produce liquor with the minimum of cooking and they can handle very viscous masses. Dissolving the liquor under pressure needs less water, thereby saving on later evaporation processing.

Jet cookers add some steam to the product (food-grade boiler additives needed) and unless vacuum-assisted flash-off is employed, at best only enable exit solids as high as input solids to be achieved. Nevertheless the action of live steam does give rapid starch cooking with very short residence times. Static cookers use indirect heating through special profile coils, and with this system it is possible to raise the solids by 4–6% on flash-off.

Both jet and static cooking systems control the temperature of cook by back-pressure, and it is possible to adjust the retention time by altering the pipe length to the back-pressure valve or changing product throughout. Careless operation of coil-type cookers or plate evaporators with hydrocolloids can lead to scaling-up or even blockage, but a monitoring of feed pressure should indicate when problems are occurring. On no account should a static cooker be allowed to boil dry.

Vacuum flash-off systems perform four functions, deaeration, pressure release, dehydration and cooling. Cooling of the liquor is important for viscosity reasons in depositing and to enable the addition of other colloids, acids and flavours without denaturation or loss. Deaeration compensates for a little thermal degradation of the hydrocolloid in the cooker because there is no longer a standing down of hot liquor to clear or separate hot liquor debubbling processes. It is desirable to obtain a reservoir in the vacuum separation chamber before starting the vacuum pump to avoid air sucking back into the chamber past the extract pump.

10.4.3 Cooker extruders

A wide range of cooker extruder techniques are available for the preparation of gums and jelly articles [18]. These offer further benefits in processing time and energy. Although extruders can operate around 2500 psi/300°C most gum and jelly applications use less than 1000 psi/150°C. Residence times in the cooker are approximately 30–90 s and moisture contents 15–20%. Low screw speeds (< 300 rpm) are acceptable for most gum and jelly products and reduce equipment wear. The extruder, being a single reactor, can conduct most of the unit operations involved in liquor preparation, thereby reducing capital expenditure, operating costs and processing time.

At high pressures most of the reactions take place near the dry, very viscous state and formulae as well as operating parameters need to be modified for this technique. For example, Vincent [19] suggests gelatin replacement by pectin, although cooker extruders offer the possibility of introducing hydrocolloids at different stages in the liquor preparation. Thermally degradable materials can therefore be added at the last cooled zones of the process where there is just sufficient mixing prior to ejection at the die. Starches cannot only be gelatinised by the continuous mechanical and thermal energy input but also undergo some chemical modification. Emulsifiers may be added as extrusion aids to improve flow, reduce stickiness and improve control over gelatinisation reactions. It is possible to feed dry sugar directly into the barrel as it becomes soluble under the heat and shearing in the traces of water introduced in the glucose syrup. The intense mechanical work is as important as the temperature in decrystallising sugar.

It is possible to apply a vacuum venting zone for degassing/drying the melt of sugar mixes in the cooker extruder. A reverse-pitch screw/paddle configuration, orifice plates or barrel valves should be used prior to this zone to ensure the scrolls are in a starved state. The dangers of product venting up the vacuum port can be obviated by the use of stuffing screws. After this zone it is necessary to ensure a fast transfer of evacuated product back into the body of the extruder and single- or twin-pitch lead screws can accomplish this task. Temperature, pressure and feed rate control are necessary to prevent surging in this area, as a steady surface area/volume ratio is important for controlled evaporation.

Extruders are especially important for the high-fruit liquors such as used in fruit leathers and fruit jelly bars. They avoid lengthy processing and dehydration procedures, minimising thermal degradation and improving natural colour and flavour. Rope-forming at around 90°C allows a plastic hot stage with gel formation just after the die, easing the various shaping procedures. If preparing liquors at finished solids then viscosity becomes crucial. For example a 40% gum arabic liquor at 88% total solids is like molten lava. In this case, for continuous cooking a cooker extruder is necessary.

10.4.4 Minor additions

The last additions to the liquor are normally colour, flavour, acids, fruit juices, humectants and, in the case of aerated jellies, a gas. The most important considerations are the effects of temperature on volatile materials and pH on acid-sensitive hydrocolloids.

With batch processes, before adding the minor ingredients it is sometimes necessary to allow a standing time for air to come out of the liquor. This may be accelerated by centrifugation and skimming, especially if antifoams can be used. The minor additives must then be stirred in gently to avoid further foam generation. Slow-moving planetary-action mixers are suitable.

10.4.4.1 Colours.
These are almost invariably added as solutions and give an indication of the adequacy of this last mixing operation. In addition to legal considerations colours must also be acid-fast, resistant to reducing sugars, stable to operating temperatures and should not separate into basic colours during the gel-setting operation.

10.4.4.2 Flavours.
Adding flavours to warm liquors under atmospheric conditions can lead to loss of volatiles, and in-line mixing is preferable. 'Medicated' flavours (including menthol, herbal) and 'alcohols' such as gin are especially susceptible. If the liquor is destined for stoving then overflavouring is necessary to counteract flavour losses in processing. Because of the low levels and volatility of such additions intimate dispersion is necessary. The choice of flavouring must also take into account stability in the chosen

hydrocolloid system. In agar jellies for example, cherry is said [20] to be more stable than lemon and vastly superior to apple. Flavours are normally lipid-based, and high dose levels can affect foam stability on aerated lines. Rapid setting is advantageous when preparing aerated layers. (Many hydrocolloids can be obtained to standardised degrees of over-run.) Small quantities of salt can sometimes be used to enhance the perception of non-fruit flavours, but care must be taken not to salt out hydrocolloids.

10.4.4.3 *Fruit.* Soft fruit pulps and jams such as strawberry may be extended with apple or apricot pulp to enhance flavour and 'bodying' effect. Fruit juices are preferable for continuous dosing in association with static mixers. The effects on the formulation of 'carry-over' preservatives from fruit such as sulphur dioxide must be taken into consideration.

10.4.4.4 *Humectants.* Glycerine [21] gives a silky sheen to wine gums at around 4%. Humectants also act as an emollient to prevent drying out and becoming rock-hard. Sorbitol and glycerin may also be incorporated to reduce the ERH of the product below 60% and prevent moulds. With ERHs between 60 and 75% the judicious use of acids and preservatives can make the product safe from such spoilage. Excess use of humectants can make the products soft and sticky.

10.4.4.5 *Acids.* The acid is almost invariably the last addition as it has major effects on gel strength and can denature many hydrocolloids if added when the liquor is too hot or will be stood for long times. The acid value of fruit juices, pulps, jams and rework must not be overlooked. Dry acids are sometimes sieved over the surface of the liquor batch, but solutions avoid graining caused by pregelation around each acid crystal. Different acids hydrolyse colloids to different degrees, with fumaric being the most aggressive. Buffer salts can modify the rate of hydrolysis and in some cases combat it.

The taste aspects of buffer salts and different acids can be as important as their functional properties and affect selection. For the same pH reduction stronger acids generally provide less taste. Tartaric is bitter but 25% tarter than citric, which in turn is sharper than malic, which has a smooth taste with a long-lasting tartness. Some acids form insoluble salts with calcium, and recipes high in this cation require lactic acid. The liquid nature of lactic acid enables easy metering without prior solution preparation [22], and with buffering exhibits the lowest sucrose inversion rate of all food acids. Small quantities of acetic acid are sometimes incorporated to inhibit mould growth on jelly surfaces, especially when high fruit contents are present. According to Kinderlerer [23] moulds such as *Chrysosporium inops* or *Chrysosporium xerophilum* may derive essential nutrients from fruit juice in jellies. Hydrochloric acid has been suggested [24] for the acidification of the Russian furcelleran and wine-jelly, fruit-paste candies. Ascorbic acid, as well as enabling vitamin C claims, has been found [25] to reduce the darkening in strawberry and orange fruit jellies, although the hue does move towards the yellow.

Agar liquors must be below 60°C when acids are added (75°C if buffers are present) and degrade below a pH of 5. Pectins gel quickly (30 min) after the acid has been added so continuous addition or small batches with a cycle time of 18–20 min are needed. In the event of production stoppage the pH may be raised to above 4 with sodium bicarbonate to halt the setting mechanism and later reacidified. For these two colloids and gelatin, which suffers acid hydrolysis, the use of metering pumps allied to a colour-, flavour-, acid-dosing system with in-line static mixing elements is recommended.

10.5 Shaping

Depositing (starch or starchless), slabbing (flat or contoured) and extrusion are the principal ways of shaping gums and jellies.

10.5.1 Starch moulding

Although this can be done by hand on a small scale, plants known as moguls are normally used. The latest models contain the following sections. A tray destacker and feeder takes pallets of finished goods and feeds them into the machine. The trays then encounter a starch buck, which has a tray-overturning unit to empty the contents, a depowdering sieve section with a starch-cleaning device, a product-cleaning section which feeds the sweets onto a discharge mechanism, and finally a starch-aerating and tray-filling and levelling operation. The trays are then printed with impressions from a mould board and pass under a heated depositor. Swinging temperature-controlled hoppers (with electronic sensors to detect the movement of the trays) carry the depositor to maintain the position over the impression whilst the depositor bar frees a measured quantity of liquor into each. Continuously moving conveyor chains are a recent feature which reduces jerkiness, avoiding liquor slopping and poor starch-mould shape retention. In addition to synchronised reciprocation in the horizontal plane, the depositor needs lift and suck-back (with, for example, a ball-valve nozzle closure) to break the deposit tails. The deposited trays are then fed into a stacker and palletiser. Optional second deposits for multilayer, centre-filling depositors, top starch sprinklers, multiflavour depositors, faster speeds and facilities for variable dimension trays, palette sizes and stack heights are all available. Automatic guided vehicles can be used with magnetic rails under the floor to transport pallets into and out of drying rooms.

The moulds can be designed to give a variety of shapes (e.g. dummies, bottles, strawberries even teeth [26]) but vertical sides are not desirable.

Traditionally these were made from plaster of Paris but new compounds are now coming to the fore.

The moulding starch itself must be dry ($< 6\%$ moisture), preferably aged and may contain traces of oil to aid in shape definition. Warm starch can be used for agars to prevent thermal shock on deposit and cold starch for gelatins to encourage skinning. Damp starch, dirty starch and starch with tailings not sieved out lead to poor moulding and foreign matter on the sweet surfaces. Starch that is too dry can cause case hardening or crusting. Too little oil or excess new starch prevents the impression being held and leads to dusting problems. Excess oil causes the impressions to crack, leading to seepage and malformed sweets.

Starch trays are traditionally of wooden construction, which copes well with temperature changes, especially if a stoving operation is required. Plastic materials are starting to be used but can go brittle and produce shards if broken.

The dry starch means that this operation should be conducted in a separate room where all precautions are taken to avoid explosion risks, e.g. electrical equipment should be to IP65 standard. The room needs to be spacious, dry, clean and light as many starch trays will have to be moved around.

For very high-viscosity deposits pressurised hoppers and steam jets for tail cutting may be required, although it is more normal to work at less than 5000 cp for moguls. If depositing at high temperature for viscosity considerations, the use of high-maltose glucose in the recipe aids in reducing colour formation. Slow-set types of pectin are desirable, and these should have a DM of approximately 60 to allow deposit before pregelation. The depositing time may be extended by raising the pH or reducing the total solids, but this reduces the final gel strength.

10.5.2 Sugar moulding

It is possible to deposit directly into sugar in a similar fashion to starch depositing. In this case subsequent stove drying is more difficult aand the sugar cannot take up moisture in the same way as starch. Traces of glycerin may be blended with the sugar [27] to facilitate shaping, as this causes the sugar to lose some of its granularity, providing the moisture content is kept around 0.35%.

10.5.3 Starchless moulding

The technique uses either hard moulds of plastic, metal or ceramic which may be Teflon-coated or flexible silicone rubber moulds on a conveyor. The moulds are preformed with the indentation shape of the sweet and the hard moulds have small holes in the base. The moulds are first sprayed with a release agent. The release agent may be sprayed on to the moulds every cycle or only, say, every tenth cycle. Liquor is deposited or pressed into the mould, which then passes through a chilling tunnel. After cooling the moulds are inverted and the sweets ejected onto a plastic-coated delivery band using compressed air or a deformation roller for the flexible moulds. Ejection pin systems are unsuitable for gums and jellies. Adhesion to the belting following demoulding can be a problem unless sufficient release oil is used.

The technique is continuous rather than batch but is not suitable if subsequent drying operations such as stoving in the mould are needed. It is said [28] that the staff involved in starchless moulding can be reduced by as much as 95% compared with a starch-casting operation, especially if off-line tasks such as starch cleaning and drying are taken into account. Mould changes are more difficult than for a mogul, where a simple mould board is employed, but the latest starchless moulders have automatic removal systems permitting circuit changes in approximately 30 min. The excellent regimentation of sweets leaving a starchless moulder means it is possible to produce a range of centres (jelly, fudge, cream, etc.) on the same machine and to feed directly an enrober or crystalliser without the sweets sticking together.

The technique is applicable to quick temperature-setting articles. Pectin jellies at a pH of 3.3–3.6 are capable of demoulding at 50°C after 15 min with the rapid cooling possible in a metal mould. Speciality starches may be required [29] in order to achieve set-up within the 5–20 min retention times on this equipment.

10.5.4 Slabbing

Slabbing is an ideal way of producing multilayered articles because each layer can set before the addition of the next. For this reason it is well suited to pectin and agar. Lemon slices are produced by casting various layers (some aerated) into an oiled, semicylindrical, contoured tray and then cutting into the slices with a wire cutter. Jellies can also be cast into paper-lined trays. For Turkish delight the trays may be liberally dusted with a 50:50 mixture of starch and icing sugar (icing sugar alone will form a crust).

Large table jellies are partially segmented for easy domestic solution. These can be deposited into metal moulds on an oiled cold table and ejected by hand or deposited into oiled plastic moulds and ejected by inserting needles through the jelly and blowing them out with compressed air. The ability of gelatin gels to 'heal' is of importance in this procedure.

Very rigid gels such as agar or pectin can be cast onto oiled, chilled, steel bands or tables and subsequently cut by means of circular knives or strand slitters, laterally or vertically spaced, and led to transverse cutting machines. One can produce square, rectangular, triangular, rhombic or trapezoid shapes in this manner. Teflon supporting rollers in front of the knives prevent product evasion, and the knives are cleaned by scrapers.

10.5.5 Extrusion

Shaping at the cooled extrusion die has the advantage that all the unit operations are done on the one piece of equipment. Shapes such as laces, round or star strings, sticks, sheets, round or star tubes, corrugated ribbons, star-shaped twisted tubes and strings, coextruded centre-filled strings, etc. are possible. Shaping at the die-head does not require subsequent drying operations. The extrudate may be rolled into strips, cooled in tunnels or sliced and guillotined in the normal manner.

10.6 Drying

Drying procedures are primarily applied to starch-deposited goods. There are two main techniques, placing the trays into stoves or standing down and letting the starch absorb the moisture. The normal test for assessing completion of drying is to measure the refractive index of the sweet. For this purpose it is necessary to avoid surface effects by cutting or breaking the sweet open. For hard-stoved goods this is impractical, and in this case the sweets are allowed to cool to room temperature and tested for snap or crack.

10.6.1 Stoving

The pallets have to be moved gently into and out of the stoves to prevent shape disruption. It is not good practice to let the articles set before entering the stove because the back of the sweet will not then pull down smoothly from convex to concave shape but will become wrinkled.

Labelling of the stacks is important to ensure good stock rotation. In some stoves the hot air from the inlets causes darker sweets than those placed near the outlet and positioning by sweet colour may be relevant. If the total quantity of goods in the stove is varied then the moisture removal rates will change. Inconsistent stoving times may result from variable loading practices.

In the stove the factors affecting drying are similar to a washing line. They are the ERH of the sweet, the relative humidity of the air, the temperature and the air speed. Obviously the air itself must be drier than the sweet or else there will be no moisture gradient and no diffusion. Raising the temperature raises the moisture-carrying ability of the air and also accelerates diffusion reactions. Increasing the air speed prevents the sweets sitting in a 'fog' of their own creation, but too high a speed can blow the starch around. Design of the fans and louvring must be such that the air flow is over the sweets and not around the stacks, which is where it will go if that is the line of least resistance. A closed-box system can be used with an in-built dehumidifier fitted with an external drain from the dewpoint condenser. The exhaust heat from the refrigeration unit can then be used to benefit inside the stoving chamber. As well as good air circulation it is necessary to have good insulation and a well-sealed door. In an open-vented stove the make-up air needs drying.

Whereas 1 h drying may be acceptable for a tender gelatin article, up to 10 days may be necessary for a large hard gum. The use of high temperatures and low relative humidities can cause case hardening of the sweets, making it very difficult to achieve an even-textured end product. Thermal degradation of hydrocolloid, sweet darkening and flavour losses also result from excessive temperatures. Too low a temperature causes damp starch. If the stove is held at around 50°C then the starch will be kept dry and off-line starch driers should not be necessary. Synchronous starch drying is therefore one advantage of stoving.

Stoving accelerates the ageing process of starch, and some starch hydrolysis [30] occurs in addition to changes due to thermal and mechnical stress. This aids the starches functionality for moulding purposes. Indeed new starch is ideally blended with old starch at no more than 25% and only after it has been stoved on trays for several days.

Extra stoving may be given to sweets that will be packed loose in large containers (e.g. giant tubes) to minimise deformation.

Stoving procedures enable total solids increases from 70% as liquor up to more than 90%.

10.6.2 *Standing*

Even during standing procedures it is advisable not to shift stacks around excessively or graining may result.

It is possible in unconditioned rooms that the starch can absorb as much moisture from the air as from the sweets. Off-line starch drying is therefore strongly recommended before the starch is relayered into trays. Thermal stresses are less in modern rotary tube driers than the traditional drum or plate-contact driers.

In standing procedures the total solids of the articles are generally raised by up to 3%. Top dusting of starch is recommended to achieve uniform drying on all surfaces.

10.7 Finishing treatments

These processes include washing, destarching, steaming, sanding, crystallisation, oiling and polishing, drying and conditioning. Almost any combination of these processes may be employed depending upon the desired end result. The gum and jelly finishing process may further involve dusting in icing sugar, chocolate or fondant coating, panning and packaging operations; these are not covered.

10.7.1   Washing

Articles with excess release agent from slabbing or starchless moulding operations may need to be washed. This must be followed by drying or conditioned storage to prevent thin films of higher moisture causing microbiological problems with the outside sweet layers if no further processing is proposed. Washing and drying are normally conducted on mesh belts to avoid the sweets sticking together. Steaming can be used as an alternative to washing if the release agent levels are low.

10.7.2   Destarching

Although most of the starch is removed in the mogul operation, the last traces should be taken out if oiling or crystallisation processes are to follow. This can be done with air blasts in pneumatic cleaning systems, winnowing and/or brushing. The latter processes are not suitable for fragile articles, especially agar gels. Certain products will need cooling or time-related hardening before receiving more severe destarching operations.

10.7.3   Steaming

In this procedure the goods are either steamed in baskets or passed through a steam curtain on a mesh conveyor. It is important not to wet the goods unduly. This process gelatinises remnants of moulding starch to achieve bright lustrous exteriors to the pieces. The process is normally a precursor to sanding but can also be used as part of post-polishing finishing where it volatilises most of the oil to give a glazed appearance prior to drying.

10.7.4   Sanding

Having softened the outer skin of the article with steam, the sweets can be sugar-sanded in a sanding drum. A typical device is that in which the sweets are conveyed on a scroll down a centre mesh of a concentric drum. Sugar (usually size-graded) is passed in the reverse direction down an outer scroll with blades to collect and lift the sugar. Multiturbine techniques are also appropriate for dampening and tumbling the product in sugar. After tumbling a second light steaming can be applied to 'heal' the scratches on the surface of the sugar crystals and enhance the finish. The sweets are then dried before being packed.

10.7.5   Crystallisation

This procedure sometimes follows a light sanding operation. The sweets are wetted with a thinning syrup which glazes the final article and a cool drying process completes the crystallisation. A clean frosty bite is achieved on the surface with variable-sized sugar crystals in unseeded systems, whereas a glistening jewel-like structure can be obtained with careful seeding using size-graded sugar. Careful drying procedures are essential to form a hard surface and stop the sweets subsequently sticking together. Too rapid drying can cause very small crystals to form, which gives an unsatisfactory 'candle wax' appearance.

10.7.6 Oiling and polishing

Oiling and polishing serve not only to provide extraglossy appearances but also to prevent gums and jellies sticking together in the packaging and retail distribution operations and to give barrier properties against moisture migrations. It is essential to have the piece as clean as possible before polishing because rough areas will cause light scatter and seriously affect the finished appearance.

A variety of intricate tender shapes such as jelly squiggles with perhaps traces of starch presents polishing problems. Normally Vaseline or a slab oil mixture at levels of around 0.1% is added to the sweets in a dragée pan, care being taken not to load the pan so full that the products at the bottom get crushed. Special oils such as acetylated monoglycerides, mineral oil (subject to local regulations), lard or spermaceti wax have been suggested [31]. In deciding the special combination of oils or waxes the surface area, porosity and piece density must be considered [32]. Commercial and in-house preparations are widely used. Usually the blend of liquid oil/wax is sprayed or slowly ladled onto the tumbling product in several small doses with intermediate setting stages, using cool dry air to achieve uniform coating and provide several buffing periods. Overoiling causes the pieces to stick together and pulls off the coating; overtumbling when hard can cause the polish to scratch, crack or chip. Shellac can be applied post-polishing to give extra gloss.

Another method is to tumble the centres in an oiled canvas drum, and traditionally moleskins were used for this purpose. Multiturbine techniques [33] based on twin contrarotating helical soft-fibred brushes mounted with inverted pitch in double troughs are also appropriate. In the multiturbine technique the exploded rotation process prevents articles sticking together and reduces breakage problems with fragile products.

10.7.7 Drying and conditioning

Gum and jelly articles must be allowed to equilibrate to the packing room humidity before being wrapped to avoid the products sticking together. Sweets have to be gently stirred or vibrated in packaging machine-feed reservoirs, with brush rollers or compressed air being used to back off the excess, and this is a critical area for clogging. Drying and conditioning is especially important if hermetic sealing is undertaken. Moisture-permeable packing more readily allows the product to adjust to ambient conditions without sweating.

Products destined for chocolate enrobing need a good skin otherwise a layer of water vapour may be generated between the jelly and the coating. Additional drying must be undertaken if the products have undergone wet processing stages such as crystallisation or steaming and IR techniques [34] are now coming to the fore in this respect. Typical equipment comprises cassettes of IRT lamps with gold-coated reflector foils and fans for cooling the lamp ends. The degree of heat penetration can be controlled by the wavelengths employed to give surface warming without softening the whole sweet. Good air flows are necessary to remove the humidity so evolved and to cool the outside of the sweet again.

10.8   Rework

In the manufacture of gums and jellies there are several areas where clean materials may be salvaged and recycled, usually to the liquor stage of processing. These operations should never be applied to floor waste or dirty or contaminated materials. Rework operations are a source of potential micro-biological and other quality problems. It is far more economical not to generate such material, but one must be realistic. Care must be taken to identify the source of reworks to ensure that they are returned to the same product and that home trade and export lines do not get blended. Bearing in mind legislation problems, mixed rework may have to be scrapped. It must also be recognised that reworks will frequently contain acids, fruit juices, etc., and prove deleterious to gelling mechanisms.

10.8.1   Skimmings

The foam separated from liquors can be transferred to vats and broken down by submission to jets of live steam. Once the offending air has been released the clear liquors can be drawn off from the bottom of the vats and recycled into the liquor. Due allowance should be made for losses of gel strength in this procedure and maximum incorporation levels calculated. Such reworks are likely to be low in solids content and will not keep.

10.8.2   Starch room waste

This usually results from tray flooding, with sweets joining together across the impressions, splashing, jerking in tray transport and defective moulding. It is preferable to separate these from the production run prior to sweet cleaning. Otherwise the materials will stick together into one huge conglomerate impossible to dissolve. Such materials can be reprocessed into the liquor, bearing in mind the traces of starch which will need adequate cooking.

10.8.3 *Mis-shapes*

These frequently become mixed as gridding and size-grading rollers often operate on sweet assortments. If this material is likely to stick together it can be roughly sugar-sanded in a dragée pan before transport to the rework station. Colour sorting is necessary unless a policy has evolved where all colours can be put into a dark 'tutti-frutti' type sweet. Sorting for small operations can be done by hand, but if volumes are large the various colour-sorting machines[35] may be advantageous. These machines are useful for separating into lights and darks but are rarely 100% efficient in separating individual colours. If such materials have been through stoving or drying procedures they may be difficult to melt down. The use of in-line high-speed dispersators aids in this process. Pectin and similar waste which will not remelt can be treated with suitable enzymes or minced and used to supplement fruit pulps providing the discontinuous texture is acceptable.

10.8.4 *Syrups*

Various syrups and sugars can be collected from different areas of the process. These will usually be coloured and contain traces of acid. If the process can accommodate invert syrup these may be standardised in strength and inversion level. Dark syrups may be accommodated in dark liquors. De-colorisation procedures with carbon black followed by filtration can be valuable. If inversion of sugars is to be limited, reaction of the acids with calcium carbonate can also be undertaken. Filtration may be more efficient if preceded by sedimentation.

10.9 Common faults, causes and cures

10.9.1 *Button backs*

This fault of very convex sweet backs is especially important for tube-packed confections where a degree of nesting or at least close-fitting is needed. Depositing sweets at lower solids will reduce surface tension and initial surface convexity. Stoving will normally pull these backs down providing the starch room is not too cold and undue delays do not occur in transferring sweets to the stove.

10.9.2 *Cloudiness*

This is caused by low-grade or undissolved hydrocolloid, coacervation, salting out, calcium precipitation or air entrapment. Use more water, a longer time or higher temperature for dissolving colloid, a premium hydrocolloid or water softening. Ensure that rework with an incompatible hydrocolloid is not entering the production system. Increase liquor standing time or use vacuum deaeration equipment.

10.9.3 *Crusting*

This is usually caused in deposited goods by damp or overcold moulding starch.

10.9.4 *Crystallisation*

Normally this is sucrose crystallisation, in which case reduce sucrose or increase doctoring by adding reducing sugars, more acid or using more or higher DE glucose syrup. Increasing sweet viscosity by raising total solids or using more colloid may help in gums. For soft jellies do the reverse by reducing the total solids to reduce supersaturation. Occasionally dextrose or lactose crystallisation occurs if excess of these sugars is present. This problem may be met by reducing these materials or stoving longer and/or at a higher temperature to a greater finished total solids.

10.9.5 *Doubles*

In starch moulding this is caused by poor-quality starch, vibrations on drive chain, stacker or in transit of trays of unset sweets. It also occurs in other shaping techniques due to lack of release oil, in sanding or wet crystallisation through lack of tumbling and in polishing or oiling through overloading pans or belts.

10.9.6 *Drying out*

This is usually due to an incorrect recipe with too high an ERH. Often one needs more reducing sugar for sales to colder, drier climates, less for hot climates or summer sales. The use of a higher total solids, more or a higher DE glucose syrup, extra invert syrup, acid inversion or other doctoring techniques will help, but if overdone will cause stickiness. Humectants such as glycerin or sorbitol may be incorporated. Moisture proof wrapping may suffice.

10.9.7 *Foamy backs*

This may be due to insufficient liquor skimming or deaeration. On cast lines, it can be caused by allowing the hopper to run dry, letting air into the depositor. Overvigorous stirring in of minor additions may be responsible.

10.9.8 *Graininess and grainy break*

Undissolved hydrocolloid, sugars added before agar solution has cleared, poorly cooked starch, phase separation of a mixed hydrocolloid system and cutting pregelled liquor (especially pectin) in a depositor may all be responsible. Pregelation may be obviated by reducing total solids, increasing temperature, reducing liquor standing time, modifying acidity or buffering pH.

10.9.9 Mis-shapes

Sweets overbunched whilst soft or insufficiently hardened (may be time- and/or temperature-related) before finishing processes or poor-quality printing of starch is usually responsible.

10.9.10 Mould or yeast growth

This may be due to total solids below 75% or ERH above 0.65. Residual spores may be found in workrooms, rework, depositing starch or brought into workrooms in draughts. Condensation on sweets or microatmospheres in packs, including tightly lidded boxes or bags used for part-processed product, may be responsible, as may addition of unprocessed items after cooking.

10.9.11 Nipped backs and/or tailing

The most likely causes are depositing at too high a viscosity, liquor which is too cold, too high in total solids, too high in hydrocolloid, at incorrect pH or not deposited fast enough (batch too big), the presence of calcium (add sodium hexametaphosphate if allowed) and draughts in depositing room. Tailing can be reduced by increasing suck-back or using a lifting depositor mechanism.

10.9.12 Ringers

This is the presence of a very sharp edge to the sweet back. It is caused by depositing at too low a viscosity or too low solids. In addition to an unpleasant mouthfeel, this fault causes problems in applying coatings such as sugar sanding or wet crystallisation.

10.9.13 Slow gelation

The possible causes include insufficient total solids, insufficient hydrocolloid (some may be undissolved and sieved out), degraded hydrocolloid (check process time and conditions) or incorrect pH.

10.9.14 Stickiness and sweating/syneresis

This can be caused by the ERH being too low, excess reducing sugar, variable acidity, especially of natural fruit juices, pulps, etc., incorrect total solids, undercooking or overcooking, insufficient gelatinisation, coacervation of mixed hydrocolloids, incorrect grade of hydrocolloid, liquefying micro-organisms and excess rework.

10.9.15 *Toughness*

This is usually the result of too high total solids, too low-DE glucose, the wrong grade or too much hydrocolloid.

10.9.16 *Weak set*

Overheated liquor, excess acid, acid added when the liquor is too hot, liquor held too long after acidulation, low-grade, undissolved or insufficient hydrocolloid, under- or overcooking, overinversion, low total solids and excess rework are likely reasons.

10.10 Concluding comments

In common with, but perhaps more than, most other confectionery manufacture, gum and jelly production considerations need to take account of many parameters. These may include, in no particular order: maintenance needs, floor space, the need for modular systems, flexibility in production planning, automation requirements, capacity, raw material, labour and energy costs, hygiene, CIP systems, security of supply, etc.

I have tried to show that this particular class of confection has many advantages with respect to such considerations. The wide diversity of the sweets themselves does not preclude the use of common manufacturing processes and equipment for all scales of production operation. With little additional expenditure the producer can make a very wide range of articles. Common liquor bases can be prepared for subsequent splitting into lines with different colloids, different total solids, textures, shapes, flavours and finishes. This allows advantages of scale as well as variety.

For the future a continuation of the trend towards more sophisticated processing equipment can be expected. Increased development and use of high-speed dispersators, pressure dissolvers, static cookers, cooker extruders, starchless moulders, and even the use of the plastic mould as the final package, are happening today. The future will see such techniques as injection forming, rotary moulding, die stamping, microwave and ultrasonic technologies being applied in completely new ways.

Specialised ingredient developments to match the new engineering technologies and to reduce reliance on the uncontrollable climates, seasons and plant sexual reproduction associated with current agroforestry, marine harvesting, etc. will become commercial. These include greater applications of phytonic research, micropropagation and cell and tissue culturing.

The last few years have seen dramatic developments in this confectionery class, and current research will see even greater changes in the near future. However, I do not believe that the move from craftsman to technocrat will ever take away the sheer artistry so prevalent in gums and jellies.

References

1. B.H. Nappen and P.L. Koval, European Patent Application (1986) EP 0 20439 A2.
2. Anon., *Zucker und Susswarenwirtschaft* **40** (1987) 17.
3. R. Lees and E.B. Jackson, in *Sugar Confectionery and Chocolate Manufacture*, Chapter 12, Leonard Hill Books, Aylesbury (1973).
4. Anon., *Confectionery Production* **53** (1987) 182.
5. Yu.V. Titov, V.A. Panfilov and I. Khlebopekarnaya, *Konditerskaya Promyshlennost* **1** (1986) 35–7.
6. J.K. Baird, P.A. Sandford and I.W. Cottrell, *Biotechnology* **1** (1983) 777.
7. K. Hannigan, *Food Eng.* **55** (1983) 52.
8. H.R. Reidel, *Confectionery Production* **51** (1985) 401, 404.
9. Anon., *Confectionery Production* **49** (1983) 478.
10. R.G. Rohwer and R.E. Klem, in *Starch*, 2nd edn, eds. Whistler, Paschall & BeMiller, Academic Press, New York (1984) 539.
11. Anon., *Confectionery Production* **49** (1983) 428.
12. D.M.W. Anderson and F.J. McDougall, *Food Additives and Contaminants* **4** (1987) 247.
13. Anon., *Confectionery Production* **49** (1983) 331.
14. J. Poppe, *The Manufacturing Confectioner* **53**(3) (1987) 182.
15. H.J. Van der Schaaf, *The Manufacturing Confectioner* **65** (1985) 51.
16. Anon., *Revue des Industries de la Biscuiterie, Biscotterie, Boulangerie, Chocolaterie, Confiserie* **81** (1985) 19.
17. Anon., *Confectionery Manufacture and Marketing* **22**(4) (1985) 24.
18. G. Elsner and W. Wiedmann, *Food Trade Review* **55**(11) (1985) 2.
19. M.W. Vincent, *Confectionery Manufacture and Marketing* **21**(11) (1984) 34.
20. G. Albert, *Susswaren* **29** (1985) 432, 435.
21. H.R. Reidel, *Confectionery Production* **53** (1987) 474.
22. G. Vreeman, *Candy Industry* **151** (1986) 33.
23. J.L. Kinderlerer, *Journal of Applied Bacteriology* **63** (1987) 395.
24. S.N. Stavrov, L.A. Tomak and A.S. Stratichuk, USSR Patent (1986) SU 1 205875 A.
25. L. Freedman and F.J. Francis, *J. Food Sci.* **49** (1984) 1212.
26. W. Troll, German Federal Republic Patent Application (1987) Ref. DE 3619139 A1.
27. N.A. Borozinets and I. Khlebopekarnaya, *Konditerskaya Promyshiennost* **2** (1984) 31.
28. R. Verity, *The Manufacturing Confectioner* **62**(6) (1982) 53.
29. J. Nadison and M. Clay, *Confectionery Production* **52** (1986) 734.
30. E. Wilhelm, G. Tegge and W. Kempf, *CCB International Review for Chocolate, Confectionery and Bakery* **2**(4) (1977) 9.
31. Anon., *Confectionery Production* **49** (1983) 390.
32. D.K. Isganitis, *The Manufacturing Confectioner* **68**(10) (1988) 75.
33. B. Rastoin, French Patent Application (1986) FR 2 575639 A1.
34. M. Lang, *Confectionery Manufacture and Marketing* **20**(3) 11.
35. B.E. Larson and K. Robe, *Food Processing* **45** (1984) 174, 176.

11 Liquorice paste, cream paste and aerated confectionery

E.B. JACKSON

11.1 Liquorice paste: introduction

Liquorice paste, or liquorice or liquorice juice is manufactured for the production of pontefract cakes, count lines, pan centres and as sheets, tubes and rods for liquorice allsorts.

The texture of liquorice paste varies from the relative shortness and softness of pontefract cakes to the brittle hardness of some count lines, but most liquorice lines are smooth and firm and exhibit a chewy toughness; the texture of liquorice is mainly due to the 'nature' of the ingredients and the method of treatment.

The manufacture of liquorice paste (which depends on the gelatinisation of starch) has been developed into a continuous manufacturing process because the high labour costs and long processing times associated with batch production could not be sustained.

The consistency of texture of liquorice paste is maintained by constantly achieving the same degree of starch gelatinisation, and this particular quality is controlled by adhering to the correct ratios of ingredients used, the repeatability and reliability of the process conditions and the constant attainment of the correct moisture content of the finished product.

Any necessary variations in the texture of liquorice paste can be achieved by varying recipe formulations and by varying the degree of starch gelatinisation of the wheat starch within the cooked mass.

A liquorice paste which contains a fully gelatinised starch has a good gloss and is most suited to the production of count lines, e.g. liquorice novelties, whereas a liquorice paste which contains only partly gelatinised starch is short in texture and has a clean bite. Therefore it is necessary to use this partly gelatinised short-eating liquorice to make liquorice allsorts, where the textures of the liquorice paste and the sugar paste need to be similar.

Liquorice paste is manufactured by premixing suitable ingredients to a predetermined moisture content, cooking continuously, extruding, storing and/or cooling and assembling.

11.2   Liquorice paste: ingredients

Liquorice paste is usually manufactured from treacle, wheat flour, liquorice extract and caramel, but many other ingredients can be used, such as sugars, invert sugar syrup, glucose syrup, basic molasses, modified starches, gelatin, colours and flavours such as aniseed oil. Irrespective of the mix of ingredients used, liquorice extract must be present if the product is to be designated 'liquorice', and its necessary inclusion can be confirmed by demonstrating analytically the presence of glycyrrhizin, which is a unique component of liquorice extract.

Over the years, and on a cost basis, a range of satisfactory textures and keeping qualities have been developed for liquorice products by using just wheat flour as the gelling agent, treacle as the bulking and sweetening agent, liquorice extract as a flavour, and caramel as a colouring agent and flavour enhancer.

Development work is necessary to determine the ingredients that are required to produce the necessary organoleptic profile of the final product, bearing in mind that treacle and flour are probably the two cheapest ingredients available for the manufacture of any confectionery.

Two typical liquorice paste recipes used for continuous production could be as shown in Table 11.1 and the final moisture content of the finished product should be in the range of 17.5–18.5%.

Variations in texture can be achieved by varying the flour/treacle ratio, the degree of gelatinisation of the starch in the wheat flour, and the final water content, although liquorice paste containing over 20% moisture is liable to develop mould growth.

In the two recipes quoted in Table 11.1, the caramel component is reduced in the count line liquorice paste, as the sweetness attributable to the allsort sugar paste is not available to counteract the bitterness of the caramel. Therefore, as a generalisation, count line liquorice paste should be sweeter than allsort liquorice paste, and this is achieved either by using a sweeter treacle or by the addition of costly sucrose or invert sugar syrup.

Each ingredient that is used in the manufacture of liquorice paste should be purchased to a specification that has been agreed between the material supplier and the user.

Table 11.1

	Allsort liquorice	Count line liquorice
Treacle (%)	66	63
Wheat flour (%)	30	35
Caramel (%)	3	1
Liquorice extract (%)	1	1

11.2.1   Treacle

Cane molasses is the end product of the refining of cane sugar, when no more sucrose can be extracted economically. The flavour of the molasses is very strong, and can be reduced by the addition of sugar syrups to produce 'treacle'. Treacles can be tailored to a customer's requirements in terms of sucrose, invert sugar, moisture content and flavour. Treacle provides bulk, sweetness, flavour and colour, and it should be noted that the typical flavour of liquorice paste is treacle and not liquorice!

A typical analysis for a treacle to be used for the manufacture of liquorice would be:

Sucrose	$37.5 \pm 2.0\%$
Invert sugars	$18.5 \pm 2.0\%$
pH	5.5 ± 0.5
Refractometric solids at 20°C	$84.0 \pm 0.5\%$
True solids	$81.0 \pm 1.0\%$
Colour	To a preagreed standard
Sulphur dioxide	70 ppm max
Lead	5 ppm max
Arsenic	1 ppm max
Iron	400 ppm max
Sodium	2400 ppm max
Potassium	30 000 ppm max
Calcium	7000 ppm max
Zinc	20 ppm max

This treacle would be a dark-brown viscous liquid with a slightly sharp characteristic flavour and a bitter back-taste; the product would be microbiologically sound and conform to current UK and EEC legislation.

Treacle should be stored in an upright cylindrical tank with an outlet fitted at the centre of a conical base, so that any sedimentation is included in the feedstock to the process. The temperature of the treacle should not exceed 55°C during storage.

11.2.2   Wheat flour

A 'strong' flour, rich in elastic gluten, used to be recommended for the manufacture of liquorice paste, but today flour of a low gluten content is preferred, such as 'soft' untreated biscuit flour of 80% extraction that gives a very satisfactory product when processed through a continuous plant.

Wheat flour is a relatively cheap ingredient and acts both as a bulking and as a gelling agent; it has the property of changing from a thick semifluid cold slurry to a viscous semisolid when gelatinised by heat, and on cooling sets to a firm gel that forms the basis of the manufacture of liquorice paste.

A typical analysis and description of a wheat flour that can be used satisfactorily in the manufacture of liquorice paste would be:

Moisture	14% max
Fat	1.5% max
Protein	8–10% max
Carbohydrate	67–75%
Ash	1.0% max
Fibre	0.5–1.0%
Extraction	78–82%
Viscosity	Less than 500 Brabender units
Particle size	2% max. on a 400-μm sieve
	25% max. on a 250-μm sieve
	85% max. passing a 250-μm sieve

Wheat flour is a greyish white powder that has a characteristic odour and taste; for any given flour the two most important checks would be viscosity, to determine processability, and particle size to confirm mixability into a premix.

11.2.3   Liquorice extract

Liquorice extract or block juice or spray-dried liquorice powder is extracted from the root of the liquorice plant, *Glycyrrhizia glabra*, that is found in a number of countries, including Spain, Turkey and the Middle East. The liquorice root is the only plant known to contain a significant amount of glycyrrhizic acid, and the presence of this unique compound in a confectionery product confirms that liquorice extract is present and allows the product to be called 'liquorice'.

Glycyrrhizin, which is a combination of glycyrrhizic acid, resins, flavanoids and other organic aromatic flavourings, is considered to be the most important component of liquorice extract, in that it determines the quality, flavour and cost of the liquorice extract. Other components present in liquorice extract are starches and gums, sugars, ash and up to 20% water, depending on the type of extract.

The glycyrrhizin content of liquorice extract varies between 10 and 65% according to the raw material source, the extraction methods and the concentration and finishing processes.

Two typical analyses of liquorice extract are given in Table 11.2, together with their differing characteristics.

Liquorice extracts increase sweetness and enhance flavours simultaneously; they have a long-lasting taste profile, in that a prolonged sweet flavour remains after the bitter-sweet taste of the liquorice extract has disappeared.

Spray-dried liquorice extract is a yellowish brown, free-flowing powder with a characteristic mild liquorice aroma, flavour and a bitter-sweet taste.

Table 11.2

	Spray-dried powder	Block juice
Glycyrrhizin (%)	62	33
Reducing sugars (%)	10	10
Sucrose (%)	3	9
Starches and gums (%)	3	23
Ash (%)	10	8
Moisture (%)	5	14
Other extractive matter (%)	2	5
pH	5.3	5.0

Block juice is a block-solid liquorice mass with a strong overpowering liquorice flavour and a bitter-sweet taste.

11.2.4　Caramel

Caramel is used in most liquorice paste products to give the characteristic brown/black colour, and to contribute to the unique flavour.

The caramel used in liquorice paste manufacture is produced by the action of ammonium hydroxide on a carbohydrate material — usually glucose syrup — to give a series of chemical reactions that form an imprecise chemical cocktail; this relatively uncontrolled reaction means there is no definition for caramel, which has led the Food Advisory Committee to recommend that the use of this material be limited to a maximum of 0.2%.

A typical description of a caramel that is suitable for the manufacture of liquorice paste would be:

Appearance	A dark-brown viscous liquid
Taste/odour	A 'characteristic' burnt odour and flavour
Colour	$48\,000 \pm 2000°\text{EBC}$
Viscosity	< 1000 cps at 50°C
Apparent solids	71% wt/wt
pH	5.0 on a 10% wt/vol. solution
Classification	Ammonia caramel (class III)

Caramelisation reactions continue in storage, where the rate is dependent on temperature, resulting in a gradual increase in viscosity and a deterioration in stability. Ideally caramel should be stored at ambient, but to facilitate handling temperatures up to 35°C can be tolerated.

Caramel should be stored in bulk in an upright cylindrical vessel where the outlet is fitted at the centre of a conical base, so that the total mass is fed to the process, i.e. on standing any sedimentation is included in the feedstock.

11.2.5   *Rework*

Liquorice paste is often wrongly considered to be the product which can absorb surplus rework in unlimited quantities, because it is black, is often covered by other products such as cream paste, has a strong flavour in its own right and the method of processing will minimise textural differences. However, the uncontrolled addition of rework often leads to the production of more rework than was originally used.

Rework for use in liquorice paste can include any number of different confectionery products such as gums and jellies, soft pan work, sugar pastes and liquorice allsort off-cuts; these products, which are unsuitable for general sale, can be added to liquorice paste as ingredients in their own right, but it is prudent to prepare a fixed composite that is properly and consistently formulated and suitably prepared (by slurrying, mixing and homogenising to a predetermined water content) and added to the premix as the 'rework ingredient'.

The addition of a properly formulated rework slurry to a liquorice paste premix generally means a reduction in the quantity of treacle used, so that cheap treacle is replaced by more costly rework, with a consequent recipe on cost, whenever rework is added to the mix.

11.3   The manufacture of liquorice paste

Over 25 years ago, most liquorice paste was manufactured by the batch cooking process, where robust open pans were flat-bottomed, steam-jacketed and equipped with heavy-duty stirring gear that continually scraped the mass from the heated surfaces. The capacity of these pans was over 500 kg, and all the ingredients were loaded manually, cooked for between 2 and 4 h depending on the type of product required, and then unloaded, again manually.

The introduction of scraped-surface heat exchanges of the 'Contlerm' and 'Votator' type gave an economic method of continuously producing liquorice paste, thus minimising labour costs and reducing some of the variables associated with batch cooking. Although the quality of batch-cooked liquorice paste was always considered to be superior to that produced by the continuous process, it is not generally accepted that the continuous process produces a liquorice paste of far more consistent and uniform quality when compared to the extreme variables of the batch-produced liquorice paste.

Liquorice paste produced by a scraped-surface heat exchanger can be continuously cooked to the *final* moisture content of 18%, giving a dull, matt, short-eating product which is quite acceptable for covering with a sugar paste, as in liquorice allsorts; this type of liquorice paste would be of an unsuitable appearance for count lines.

To enhance the appearance of count lines, the water content of the cooked mass would be 23–25%, and this figure would be reduced to the required 18% by drying in batches in hot rooms in the final shape, giving a semigloss to the finished product. Steam injection into the hot room at the beginning of the drying cycle would improve the quality of the gloss. A high-gloss liquorice paste can be produced by a scraped-surface heat exchanger at the final moisture content by raising the temperature of cook, but the resultant product would be very shiny, very tough, very rubbery and would not be acceptable in textural terms.

In outline, liquorice paste for allsort production is processed continuously using the unit operations of:

(1) Premixing.
(2) Cooking.
(3) Extruding.
(4) Cooling.
(5) Further processing.

Liquorice paste for count line production would involve:

(1) Premixing.
(2) Cooking.
(3) Extruding.
(4) Storing.
(5) Cooling.
(6) Further processing.

11.3.1 Premixing

All the required ingredients (treacle, wheat flour, liquorice extract, caramel, rework slurry, water) are added to the premix vessel and adjusted to a predetermined water content that is 3% higher than the required final water content of the cooked liquorice paste.

Rolrast premix vessels with a capacity of up to 4 tonnes are steam-jacketed and equipped with heavy-duty stirrers and homogenisers that are capable of mixing very viscous fluids and rework slurries. The premix vessels must always be loaded with ingredients in the same sequence, which will have been designed to give maximum viscosity during the addition of the flour; this high viscosity will enable the flour to be blended into the bulk without the formation of small flour lumps that can give rise to hard pieces of flour after cooking. A typical sequence for loading a premix vessel is:

(1) Add treacle.
(2) Add rework slurry and mix together.
(3) Add half the required quantity of flour.
(4) Mix in and homogenise.
(5) Add caramel and liquorice extract solution.

(6) Add balance of flour and homogenise.
(7) Check water content.
(8) Adjust water content if necessary and recheck.

At no time during the premixing operation should the temperature of the mass be allowed to rise above 65°C, as partial gelatinisation of the wheat starch occurs, causing flow and cooking problems due to the increase in viscosity.

When the premix is at the correct temperature and solids, the whole batch is elevated by pump to a slow-stirred, temperature-controlled buffer tank that gravity-feeds a small fixed-level header tank; this header tank is connected to a positive-displacement metering pump that supplies a constant volume of liquorice premix to the scraped-surface heat exchanger, through heated pipework.

11.3.2   Cooking

The use of a scraped-surface heat exchanger (Figure 11.1) is an economic and efficient method of continuously cooking liquorice paste under closely defined conditions to give a product of consistent quality. Design features of a scraped surface heat exchanger include a central shaft holding a row of floating scraper blades which revolve inside a jacketed heat-transfer cylinder. These blades continuously remove the liquorice paste, which is being held in the narrow space between the central shaft and the internal cylinder wall, and this

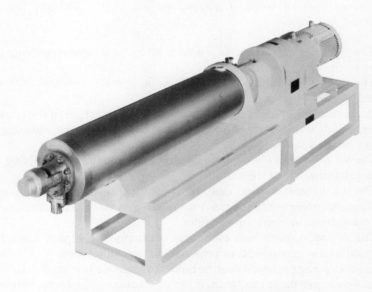

Figure 11.1   Scraped surface heat exchanger.

mechanically induced turbulence enables the equipment to handle highly viscous liquids. The feed pump moves the mass through the system where the speed of flow is dependent on the setting of the pump.

Tubes for scraped-surface heat exchangers used for the manufacture of liquorice paste can be of mild steel, but nickel or other similar metal types are preferred, as these have extra strength and can be chromium-plated to reduce wear. The temperature and back-pressure within the cooking unit is automatically controlled and continuously recorded by instruments in a control panel, which also houses the controls of the metering pumps, the extrusion systems and the conveyor bands.

The liquorice premix is pumped into the barrel of the heat exchanger, where gelatinisation of the starch in the wheat flour takes place; this is effected by heating the mass to a temperature that can vary between 120 and 145°C at flow rates that can vary between 10 and 60 lb per minute depending on the texture of the product required and the size of the plant.

The degree of 'cook' can be varied by adjusting either the temperature and/or the applied back-pressure, which is maintained by a back-pressure valve situated in the pipework leading from the heat exchanger to the extruder.

When the liquorice paste leaves the pressurised cooking system, about 3% moisture is 'flashed off' to the atmosphere, giving a brown, fluffy, sponge-like material at the required moisture content of 18%. This is then degassed in the extruder, i.e. the entrapped steam is condensed within the mass and air is expelled.

The advantages of using a scraped-surface heat exchanger may be summarised as follows:

(1) The liquorice paste can be cooked at its final water content, thus eliminating the need for storing.

(2) The quality of the liquorice paste is far more consistent than that produced by any other process.

(3) Because of the efficient heat transfer and mixing action in the cooking chamber, a high-temperature cooking process can be employed, reducing the cooking time to a few seconds.

(4) The action within the cooking chamber ensures thorough mixing and uniform gelatinisation of the starch.

(5) The cook temperature can be controlled through an automatic controlling/recording system to give a completely stable cooking temperature that is not subject to operator variables.

(6) The scraped-surface heat exchanger is extremely compact, has a high output rate and is economical in terms of space requirements.

(7) Liquorice paste extruders can be linked to sugar paste extruders to make a continuous sugar paste sandwich, if the production of liquorice allsorts is being contemplated.

11.3.3 *Extrusion*

Irrespective of the type of liquorice paste that has been produced by the continuous process, the shaping of the cooked mass is carried out by a heavy-duty extruder that has to be extremely robust to withstand the large pressures that are required for extrusion.

Extrusion can be achieved by using either a large-diameter single-worm extruder, similar to a spaghetti extruder, or a multiworm system, in which the cooked liquorice paste is transferred by rotating worms from the feed hopper of the extruder to the die-plate at the front of the extruder box (Figure 11.2).

The cross-sectional shape of the extruded product often reflects a somewhat blurred replication of the die profile, but if the dies are engineered to take account of the rheology of the viscous liquorice paste then very precise and repeatable cross-sections can be obtained.

Count line liquorice paste is extruded at a non-final water content onto metal trays that run continuously under the die-plate of an extruder, and a knife cuts the product at the end of each trat; the trays are placed in racks that are transported to hot rooms to reduce the moisture content from 25% at extrusion to the required 18%. Drying takes place in a current of hot air at 65°C, and the time required varies between 45 min and 8 h, depending on the dimensions of the pieces being dried.

Figure 11.2 Extruder.

Allsort liquorice paste is extruded at the final water content in the required shape, e.g. a sheet, onto a stainless-steel belt, where the product is cooled continuously to 30°C within a very short time. At this temperature a sheet of sugar paste is applied to both sides of the liquorice paste sheet, to form a sandwich, giving the basis of a liquorice allsort selection when produced in different colours. This layered continuous sheet is further cooled, until it is firm enough to be cut into the familiar liquorice allsort shapes.

Liquorice paste produced by the scraped-surface heat exchanger at the final moisture content can also be extruded as ropes and cut into small cylinders that can be used as part of a liquorice allsort selection; the surface of these units does not have a sufficiently high gloss to be acceptable without additional glazing. Three acceptable methods for glazing extruded liquorice paste ropes are:

(1) Pass through an alginate/liquorice bath, drain and dry in a hot air stream prior to cutting.

(2) Spray or dip into a mixture of zein held in an alcoholic solution of acetylated monoglyceride, and dry before cutting.

(3) Brush on a hot glazing solution of sugars, gum arabic and block liquorice, dry and allow to cool before cutting.

11.4 Cream pastes: introduction

Cream paste belongs to a family of sugar pastes that vary from the brittle hardness of lozenge pastes, through cream pastes, nut pastes and fruit pastes, to the short-eating softness of the fruit noyeaux.

All sugar pastes are prepared by mixing icing sugar with a syrup (a mucilage) that varies according to the type of paste required. For example, a lozenge paste is prepared from icing sugar and a mucilage of gum arabic, glucose syrup and gelatin, whereas a fruit noyau is prepared from icing sugar and a mucilage of sugar, glucose syrup and a soft fruit such as raspberries. To add interest to the texture a little caster sugar is often added to the icing sugar to give a slight grittiness to the product. Cream paste is prepared by mixing icing sugar with a mucilage of glucose syrup, gelatin and fat.

The residual moisture contents of cream paste are used as a means of indicating the acceptability of the product; at 5.5% moisture content, the product is fresh, soft and short-eating, whereas at 3.5% moisture content the product becomes stale, dry and firm. Therefore it is important that the cream paste make-up is consistent and the moisture content constant.

As cream paste consists of solid and liquid phases, in which the liquid phase is saturated with respect to sucrose, it is essential that the maximum crystal formation is obtained as quickly as possible after the completion of mixing, by quick cooling. Quick cooling leads to the formation of small crystals, whereas a slow maturation period gives rise to large crystals, and hence textural problems.

The equilibrium relative humidity (ERH) of cream pastes varies between 65 and 72% depending on the recipe make-up; under normal climate conditions in the UK, cream pastes dry out if left uncovered, but the ERH can be depressed to about 50% by the incorporation of a small quantity of glycerin or sorbitol.

11.5 Cream pastes: ingredients

The main ingredients generally used in the manufacture of cream paste are:

Sucrose, which provides bulk and sweetness.

Glucose syrup, which controls crystallisation, provides binding properties, delays drying out and contributes to bulk.

Invert sugar syrup, which controls crystallisation, acts as a humectant and increases the overall sweetness.

Hard fat, which enables a rigid structure to be formed, lubricates cutters (and teeth) and controls texture.

Gelatin allows the paste to be extruded without breaking and helps to emulsify the fat.

Cornflour cheapens the product, delays drying out and alters the texture.

Coconut flour provides flavour and modifies texture.

11.6 The manufacture of cream paste

Cream paste is manufactured by mixing together icing sugar and a mucilage in a heavy-duty Z-arm mixer, in which a homogeneous mix can be achieved repeatedly; it is essential that the viscosity of the cream paste is constant so that a uniform cross-section can be obtained when extruded through a die-plate.

There are two main processes by which cream paste is made: either with a *non-boiled* mucilage or with a *boiled* mucilage. The method adopted depends on the equipment available and the type of texture required. The current most usual method for the production of cream paste, and the one most suited to a continuous process, is the non-boiled system.

The *non-boiled method* would use the following typical recipe (parts by weight):

Icing sugar	100
Glucose syrup	30
Invert sugar syrup	7
Hard palm kernel oil	7
Gelatin ⎱	1
Hot water ⎰	3

The glucose syrup, invert sugar syrup and the fat are heated together to 200°F, and held until the fat is dissolved. The gelatin solution is then added and mixed in, forming the mucilage. This mucilage is transferred to a Z-arm mixer, and the appropriate colours and flavours added; the icing sugar is fed in continuously as the Z-arms revolve to give a uniform mix of cream paste. The moisture content of this paste can be controlled by varying the amount of water used in the preparation of the gelatin solution.

In a continuous process, the mucilage can be prepared by injecting the liquid fat and the hot gelatin solution into a stream of hot glucose/invert syrup that has been elevated in temperature by passing through a plate heat exchanger prior to being pumped to the Z-arm mixer.

The *boiled method* would use the following typical recipe (parts by weight):

Icing sugar	100
Granulated sugar	15
Glucose syrup	25
Invert sugar syrup	7
Hard palm kernel oil	8
Gelatin }	1
Water }	3

The granulated sugar, glucose syrup and invert sugar syrup are heated in a steam pan and boiled to 230°F. When the boiling has subsided, the fat and the gelatin solution are mixed in; this mucilage is transferred to a Z-arm mixer and the icing sugar added continuously, again to give a uniform mix of cream paste. The moisture content of this paste is controlled by the boiling temperature of the syrup during the preparation of the mucilage.

If cream paste is being manufactured for inclusion in an allsort selection, a textural variation can be achieved by adding 10% desiccated coconut to the mix.

11.7 The extrusion of cream paste

Most cream paste is not used alone, but is layered with other colours of cream paste, or with pectin jelly, or with liquorice paste.

The cream paste is passed through brake rollers and/or extrusion heads to give the required thickness of sheet. The first extrusion is made onto a cold stainless-steel band, and a second layer is added. Other layers can be added to give the required effect, but once layering is complete cooling should be effected as quickly as possible by the use of a cooling tunnel. To avoid the possibility of condensation, the product emerging from the tunnel should be above the dew point, and so be in an ideal condition for cutting using rotary slitters and guillotine cross-cutters.

11.8   Liquorice allsorts

Liquorice allsorts are a traditional mix of liquorice and cream paste confections with some aniseed-flavoured gelatin jellies. The mix is made up of six items which are:

Single sandwich	Two sheets of cream paste separated by a sheet of liquorice. The cream paste is produced in four colours: white, pink, yellow and brown. Both of the cream paste layers are produced in the same colour.
Double sandwich	Three sheets of cream paste separated by two sheets of liquorice. This confection is normally produced in white only.
Liquorice plug	Extruded liquorice rod.
Liquorice roll	Extruded hollow liquorice rod which is filled with white cream paste.
Coconut roll	Cream paste which contains a higher level of coconut flour and which, after colouring yellow or red, is wrapped around the extruded liquorice rod. The roll is usually surface dipped into large coconut shreds. Some 6% by weight of coconut is retained on the rolls.
Non-pareil jelly	A deposited aniseed-flavoured (0.1%) gelatin jelly which has been coated with pink- or blue-coloured non-pareils.

Table 11.3   Dimensions of confections in liquorice allsort selection

Confection	Description	Measurement (inches)	Count/lb
Coconut rolls	Extruded circular liquorice rod covered with cream paste	Uncovered: 3/8 × 3/8 d. Covered: 3/8 × 7/8 d.	75
Plug	Extruded circular liquorice rod	7/8 × 1/2 d.	140
Twist	Twisted extruded liquorice rod	7/8 × 1/2 d.	140
Single sandwich	Paste/liquorice/paste	1/8 layers, 3/4 square	120
Double sandwich	Paste/liquorice/paste/ liquorice/paste layers	1/8 layers, 5/8 square	80

Table 11.4 Mix ratio of liquorice allsorts selection

Confection	Composition	
	Number	Weight (%)
Non-pareil covered jellies	1	5
Liquorice plug ⎫ Liquorice rolls ⎭	3	15
Coconut rolls	3	20
Double sandwich	6	25
Single sandwich	10	35

The single and double sandwiches are normally bulk-mixed and added 'make weights', while the rolls, plug and non-pareil jellies are counted into each selection box.

11.9 Aerated confectionery: introduction

The most cost-effective food ingredient is the one that is obtained free of charge, irrespective of the quantity used; such an ingredient is air. Air is a safe ingredient that adds bulk to a product without increasing weight, giving a 'perceived value' benefit, an improved texture and an enhanced flavour.

Aerated food products can exhibit a whole range of textures depending on type of product, formulation, method of production and final density. Examples are:

Crunchy, crisp	Popcorn, honeycomb, meringues
Spongy, light	Swiss rolls, sponges, angel cake
Fuffy, chewy	Chews, nougat, nougatines
Mallowy, soft	Whippings, mallows
Creamy, smooth	Yoghurts, mousses, ice-cream

Aeration is used extensively in the confectionery industry to produce a range of products that includes chews, nougat, marshmallow, foam and pulled sugar in which the density ranges from 0.2 to 1.0 g/cm^3.

A foam is a suspension of gas bubbles (usually air) within a liquid, and confectionery foams can be produced by aerating sugar syrups, which can be stabilized by the addition of proteinaceous materials such as egg albumen, gelatin and milk protein. These stabilised foams may contain solid material, e.g. icing sugar, dispersed through the liquid phase, thus creating interesting variants.

A lot of energy is used to convert a liquid into a foam, and this process is carried out in a pressure whisk. The foam builds up slowly, with the formation of very large air bubbles initially. As the whipping continues these large bubbles are progressively broken down in size, until the foam reaches its optimum density with the finest bubbles. The formation of a foam depends on the speed and time of beating, and the amount of sugar present affects the increase in volume — high-sugar foam gives low volume but good stability, whereas a low-sugar foam gives high volume and poor stability.

11.10 Methods of aeration

Mechanical and chemical aeration are two methods of producing aerated products in the food industry, but mechanical aeration is by far the most common.

11.10.1 *Mechanical aeration*

The simplest example of mechanical aeration is the pulling of a high-boiled sugar, where the cooled mass, in a plastic condition, is mechanically kneaded. Air is incorporated into the mass, which becomes opaque, and the density drops from 1.5 g/ml to 1.1 g/ml. This density could be reduced even further by expanding the air bubbles within the mass, by applying a vacuum system to the process.

Mechanical aeration is used in the manufacture of products such as marshmallow and nougat, in which air is incorporated into the base syrup, either by a planetary beater at atmospheric pressure or by injecting pressurised air into a continuous pressure whisk, giving exact mechanical control over every variable, thus ensuring uniform quality and texture.

11.10.2 *Chemical aeration*

The making of bread, sponges and wafers depends on chemical aeration, but this method has a limited application in the manufacture of confectionery where the most common and well-known product is honeycomb crunch.

Honeycomb crunch is produced by the effect of heat on sodium bicarbonate within a high-boiled sugar mass. Carbon dioxide gas is released prior to immediate cooling and sets the aerated mass, making it suitable to cut into the required shapes, usually by a hot wire.

11.11 Marshmallow

The two most important ingredients in marshmallow are air and moisture. The air increases the volume and improves the texture, whereas the high moisture content, which can vary between 17 and 21%, controls the viscosity of the product and enables a large volume of air to be beaten into the mass, giving a density that can vary between 0.25 and 0.50 g/ml depending on the texture required.

Marshmallow is based on a foam in which the liquid phase has gelling properties; it is prepared by boiling a base syrup to a fixed concentration, cooling to a predetermined temperature and then adding the whipping agent prior to beating. The total process can be based on batch methods or a continuous method or a combination of processes from both methods.

Varying gelling agents can be used in the production of marshmallow, where textural considerations dictate the types of gelling agent used and the degree of aeration induced.

Egg albumen gives a light, softish gel.
Gelatin gives a rubbery, soft, but less light product.
Pectin, agar and starch all give short, soft-eating gels.

Egg albumen is the traditional gelling agent associated with the production of marshmallow, but, due to the requirement of a long shelf life, gelatin is now normally used, together with egg albumen when a quality product is required.

11.11.1 Batch marshmallow

A mixture of sugar, glucose syrup and invert sugar syrup is boiled to 115°C, cooled to 60°C, and transferred to a whipping machine. A solution of the required gelling agent is added, and the whole mass is beaten until the mixture is light and fluffy, when it is deposited into warm dry starch and conditioned in a warm room before demoulding.

11.11.2 Continuous marshmallow

A boiled mixture of sugar, glucose syrup and invert sugar syrup is continuously cooled to 66°C in a scraped-surface cooler, then a gelatin solution is continuously metered into the syrup stream as it passes to a continuous aerator. Air at high pressure is beaten into the mass, together with injected colour and flavour, and on extrusion the air cells in the mallow expand due to the pressure being reduced to that of the atmosphere.

The mallow ropes from the extruder pass onto a starched conveyor band, where they are cooled, cut into lengths by guillotine, coated with starch, tumbled in a rotary drum to remove the excess starch and then conditioned prior to packing.

11.12 Nougat

Nougat is basically an aerated high-boiled syrup containing fat that has been stabilised by the addition of a whipping agent. Typical whipping agents used in the manufacture of nougat are egg albumen, gelatin, milk protein or soya protein, which can be used in combination with starch or gum arabic.

The production of nougat can be adjusted to give a range of textures that can vary between a long-eating, chewy, non-grained product and a short-eating, soft, fine-grained product.

The texture of nougat is influenced by:

(1) The ratio of sugar to glucose syrup to invert sugar syrup.
(2) The final moisture content of the nougat base.
(3) The ratio of the liquid phase to the solid phase.
(4) The type of whipping agent used.
(5) The degree of aeration, which can vary between 0.8 and 1.0 g/ml.
(6) The quantity and type of additions, e.g. fat, nuts, cherries, etc.

Quality nougat of the white Montelimar type is made with egg albumen as the whipping agent. Honey is added to the syrup, and the additions include almonds, cherries and angelica. Other nougats, equally satisfactory but not of the same quality, are those based on a mixture of gelatin and egg albumen as the whipping agent, where the honey is replaced by invert sugar syrup and where the additions often comprise of hazelnuts, coconut, red and green jellies and honey flavour.

Nougat can be produced by either a batch or continuous method, but the batch method is considered to be a far superior system in terms of flexibility of production, textural consistency, the ability to absorb rework and the appearance after cutting.

The batch process consists of boiling a water, sugar and glucose syrup mix under vacuum to a moisture content of 8% at a temperature of 120°C. The vacuum cooker is used not only to reduce the time of boiling but also to produce a cooked syrup at a lower temperature — the higher the temperature, the longer the beating time.

The vacuum-cooked syrup is transferred to a robust and powerful atmospheric whipping machine that can operate on two speeds, low for mixing and blending and high for aerating. A gelatin solution is blended into the cooked mass before being aerated at high speed, when the density is reduced to 0.85 g/ml; fat, nuts, fruit and, if required, a small quantity of icing sugar to induce graining are then blended into the aerated product at low speed.

The nougat is discharged from the whipping machine into metal trays lined with rice paper and allowed to condition overnight. Here the induced fine grain can be developed in the product prior to cutting into the required shapes at a final water content ranging from 9.5 to 10.5%.

12 Tablets, lozenges and sugar panning

J. BEACHAM

12.1 Introduction

Tablets and lozenges are frequently confused. They are, however, manufactured by totally different processes. Lozenges are cut from a sheet of firm dough and dried to give a hard sweet with a rough surface. Tablets are made by compressing powder or granules in a confined space until the particles bond together. A tablet has a very smooth surface and is generally rather brittle. This chapter outlines the two processes.

Tablets are frequently used as centres for sugar-panned products, and the techniques of panning will be described later in this chapter.

12.2 Tableting

Tablets are formed by compressing powder in a die. The particles bond together under pressure and the compacted tablet is ejected from the die. Figure 12.1 shows the operation of a simple tablet press.

The die is filled volumetrically, excess material removed and the powder compressed between two punches. The lower punch ejects the tablet.

To form a tablet successfully, the powder must be free-flowing and yet be capable of bonding strongly under pressure. The bonds between the particles must be sufficiently strong to withstand the considerable force required to eject the tablet from the die, and the resultant compact must be hard enough to withstand handling and yet retain favourable 'mouthfeel'.

Certain powders already possess these characteristics and are termed 'directly compressible' materials. Other powders may be formed into tablets, but must first undergo a granulation stage.

12.3 Granulation

The aim of the granulation process is to produce a free-flowing material, suitable for compression. There are several ways of achieving this:

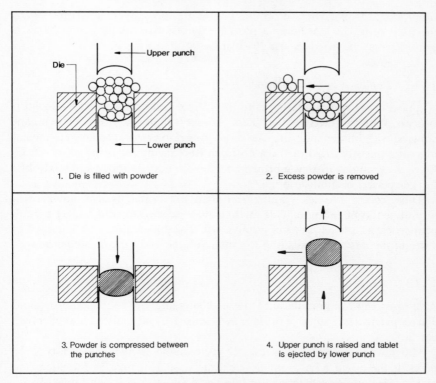

1. Die is filled with powder
2. Excess powder is removed
3. Powder is compressed between the punches
4. Upper punch is raised and tablet is ejected by lower punch

Figure 12.1 Operation of a simple tablet press (Leatherhead Food R.A. 1983).

12.3.1 Wet granulation

Wet granulation is suitable for most materials, but is expensive in terms of manufacturing space, time and energy consumption. The powder to be granulated is screened to a uniform particle size and mixed with a granulating solution until a firm dough is formed.

The granulating solution is a binder dissolved in water, which will glue particles together to form granules. Binders are materials such as gum arabic. gelatin, starches and alginates. It is important that mixing is thorough and that the correct amount of binder is added. Too much will cause the granules to be too hard, whilst too little will be insufficient to hold the powder particles together. The correct level of addition is such that the material may be compressed in the hand to form a ball which will not crumble or stick when broken apart.

The mixing may take up to 1 h and, when complete, the dough is roughly milled to aid the drying process. The granules are dried on trays for up to 24 h at 50–60°C. The temperature of the drying oven must not be too high, or the granules will case-harden and drying will be incomplete. There are several other methods of drying, including the use of rotary dryers, microwaves and fluidised beds, the last being a particularly effective method, as a batch of granules may be dried in just 20–30 min.

12.3.2   Fluidised bed granulation

A quicker way of granulating is to use a fluid bed granulator for the entire process. With this method, the bed of powder is fluidised in an air stream and sprayed with binder solution. The powder agglomerates into granules, which are subsequently dried in the air stream (the drying air being at 40–80°C). Once the granules are dry, lubricant and flavour may be added and mixed by a further period of fluidisation.

This process is quicker and easier than wet granulation, a batch being granulated in 60–90 min. This method may be used for optimising granule properties, as a wide range of granule size distributions may be obtained by varying the base materials and the rate, volume and type of binder added.

12.3.3   'Slugging'

A third method of granulation is termed 'slugging' or 'double compression'. This is particularly suitable for moisture-sensitive materials such as effervescent tablets.

The powder is fed into a large die (2–5 cm diameter), in a heavy-duty tablet press. If the powder has poor flow characteristics, it may be force-fed. The material is compressed, using flat-faced punches, into a rough tablet. This is done slowly to allow air to escape.

The tablets do not have to be perfect, as they are then ground down and recompressed. Little equipment is required for this process, but it is costly, as considerable wear occurs to the dies and punches due to the high compaction pressures necessary to form slugs. This method also depends upon the materials possessing some binding properties.

Since a binder is not added to hold the granules together, the resultant tablets tend to be softer than those which have been wet-granulated.

Many other methods of granulation are available, such as the use of pressure rollers for the precompression stage, agglomerating in a rotating pan and extrusion.

Regardless of the method of manufacture, the moisture content of the granules should be between 0.75 and 2.0%, however the optimum level must be determined for the individual recipe and tableting process. As the moisture content of the granules increases, so the tablets become softer. The tablets then harden during storage as a result of moisture loss.

After the granules have been dried, they must be ground to a suitable mesh for compression. The actual size will depend upon the base material and upon the diameter of the tablet being formed. The particle size distribution of the granules is very important. It should consist of mostly similar-sized granules, with a few larger particles and a few 'fines'. During the compression process, the particles rearrange in the die prior to bonding, and the fines fill in the small voids and reduce the porosity of the tablet.

Ideally, the granules should be spherical in shape, as this reduces interparticular friction and speeds up the compression stage. It is also important that the batches of granules are consistent. The bulk density of the granulate should be measured and must remain constant, otherwise die-fill and consequently tablet weight cannot be controlled.

Finally a lubricant is mixed with the granules. This is generally magnesium stearate at a level of 0.5–5.0%, depending on the base materials and method of compression.

12.4 Ingredients

12.4.1 *Base materials*

Numerous materials are available for tablet manufacture; some are available in a directly compressible form, whereas some require granulation. If a particular material does not possess all of the necessary properties for tablet formation, several materials may be blended together. Sucrose is available in directly compressible forms, which are expensive, but save on granulation costs. Sucrose can also be granulated, if required.

Fructose and dextrose may be compressed directly. Fructose tablets are soft and break easily. Sorbitol and mannitol are also available in directly compressible forms. The tablets have a cooling effect when dissolved in the mouth. During storage, sorbitol tablets are rather hygroscopic. Maltitol is available in a directly compressible form. The tablets melt slowly in the mouth. Maltitol may also be tableted in a granulated form.

Xylitol has a cooling effect and is also non-cariogenic. Its sweetening power is the same as sucrose. Xylitol tablets can be subjected to a thermal hardening process after manufacture.

12.4.2 *Binders*

The binder used to manufacture granules is not intended for holding the tablet together, although it does have an effect upon tablet hardness.

Typical binders are gums such as gum arabic, gelatin and alginates, but can also be starches, sugars or fats.

When using binders, it is important to use the correct amount of solution and to ensure a good mix with the base materials. The effect that the binder will have upon the final tablet must also be taken into account. Certain materials such as gelatin can cause hardening during storage. Binders are not necessary when the material is directly compressible.

12.4.3 Lubricants

Lubricants are added in order to overcome one of three possible problems.

A 'glidant' is added to a poor-flowing material to reduce interparticular friction and so improve flow characteristics; it may be added to directly compressible materials or granules. Suitable materials have a small particle size and, consequently, a large surface area which allows the glidant to form a coating around the particles of base material. Silica-type materials are glidants. The level of addition is critical, as above a certain level glidants have a detrimental effect upon flow properties.

Lubricants are added to coat the surface of the tablet and reduce the friction between the tablet and the die wall, thus increasing the ease of tablet ejection. Too much lubricant will reduce the bonding ability of the tablet, whereas too little can cause the tablet to bind in the die.

Lubricants may be added to the base material before compression, or prior to granulation. The latter method usually leads to better dispersion. Lubricants can be materials such as oils or fats, or more frequently magnesium stearate or stearic acid.

The third lubricant action is that of antiadherents, which reduce the likelihood of the tablet sticking to the punch faces and thus reduce the problem of 'picking; where part of the tablet is removed as the top punch is lifted. This problem is most likely to occur when using an intricately embossed or engraved punch face.

12.4.4 Disintegrants

If a tablet is required to dissolve in water, a starch which swells upon contact with water and breaks up the tablet may be added. This is best added prior to granulation.

In effervescent tablets, citric acid and sodium bicarbonate are included, as these cause tablet break-up. Such granules cannot be made by wet granulation, as water addition must be prevented.

12.4.5 Colours and flavours

12.4.5.1 *Flavours.* Tablets have a long shelf life and consequently it is essential that the flavouring is also stable for an equivalent period of time [1].

Liquid flavours can be added to powders and mixed in at the granulation stage, but considerable flavour loss occurs during drying. The liquid may be added to the dry granules or the directly compressible material, but as the flavour is spread over the surface of the granules the increased surface area exposed to the air makes the flavour susceptible to oxidation. A preferable method is to use powdered flavours, where the coating around the flavouring materials provides a protective covering.

The level of flavour addition to tablets is critical. The dose must also be related to the hardness of the tablet. A hard tablet which dissolves slowly in the mouth will require a higher level of flavour than a tablet which disintegrates rapidly.

Flavours most suitable for confectionery tablets are peppermint, or fruit flavours together with acid to enhance the fruit. Peppermint is especially suited to those tablets which dissolve in the mouth with a cooling effect.

12.4.5.2 *Colours.* Colours may be added at the granulation stage, however during drying water-soluble colours migrate to the surface of the granule and lead to mottling when compressed. It is preferable to use lake colours of a fine particle size which are mixed with the base material prior to compaction. It is important that the colour is well-mixed.

For direct compression materials, lake colours are used, as there is no suitable stage for the addition of a soluble dye.

Artificial colours are extremely light-stable and require no protection, but if certain natural colours are used the sweet may need protection from heat and light.

12.5 Compression

The compression process involves applying just sufficient pressure to a material to enable it to bind together and thereby form a firm compact.

Tablet presses range from single-punch presses to high-speed rotary machines with up to 75 sets of dies and punches. Figure 17.2 shows a Manesty Excelapress. This is a double-sided rotary tablet press, capable of producing up to 660 000 tablets per hour, depending upon the characteristics of the material being tableted.

In all processes, the same basic principle of compression applies. The die is filled with powder, the position of the lower punch being adjusted to alter the volume, and the excess powder is scraped away. The material is compressed either by the top punch being lowered or by both punches being squeezed together.

The pressure is maintained on the powder for a period of time (dwell time). The top punch is raised and the tablet ejected by raising the lower punch. When experimenting with any new materials, it is preferable to start by using a hand-operated single-punch press. Once the tablet can be formed in this way, the recipe may be slowly and carefully scaled up to a rotary press. It must be

Figure 12.2   Rotary tablet press (Manesty Machines Ltd.)

emphasised that no attempt should be made to run a new formulation on a rotary press operating at full speed.

It is very important to remember that the dwell times vary on different presses and at different speeds. This stage is important in the bonding process. If the dwell time is very short, as in the case of a high-speed press, bonding may not be complete and the tablet will break up. The degree of bonding is dependent upon the applied pressure, the dwell time of the applied pressure and the bonding force between particles.

Many shapes and sizes of tablet may be made by varying the shapes of the dies and punches. Figure 12.3 shows a selection of basic punch shapes.

The punch faces are highly polished to give a smooth surface to the tablet

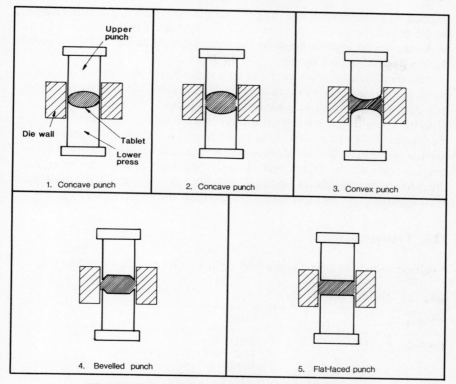

Figure 12.3 Basic punches creating a range of tablet shapes.

and to prevent sticking. A design or name may be engraved or embossed on the punch faces and the design will then be transferred onto the tablet.

During compression, the force applied to the tablet is considerable. It is important that the machine is set up properly and that the dies and punches are clean and correctly aligned. Up to 10 tons of pressure may be applied and considerable damage will occur if the punches are misaligned.

Care must be taken when using certain punch shapes, as concave punches tend to trap air in the tablet, which may subsequently break up; others leave the tablet with edges which are thin and fragile.

The volume and hence the weight of the tablets can be adjusted, as can the dwell time of the applied pressure. It is also possible to make multilayer tablets, produced with different colours, or even create a 'tablet within a tablet' by compressing a coating of one colour around a core of another colour.

12.5.1 Bonding during compression

Once the die is filled with material, the pressure is gradually applied. The first stage of compression is when the particles rearrange to fill voids in the die and trapped air is removed. Once the particles are no longer free to move about, further pressure causes fracture and elastic deformation. During the dwell time of the maximum applied pressure, the clean surfaces of the particles formed during fracture bond together.

If the dwell time is too short, it may be insufficient for the bonding process to occur. In this case either the machine must be slowed down or, if not already included, a glidant may be added to speed up particle rearrangement.

As the upper punch is removed, a stage of stress relaxation occurs, in which the internal stresses built up in the tablet relax, i.e. the 'elastic' portion of the particle movement. If these stresses are too great, the tablet will break up on ejection from the die. It has been shown that tablets continue to 'relax' and thus change dimensions for up to 100 days after manufacture. If the tablet has been sugar-coated, this can lead to cracking of the sugar shell [2].

12.6 Problem solving

Faults in tablets can be divided into eight categories (see Table 12.1).

Table 12.1 Common tableting faults

Problem	Cause
Capping	Trapped air Excessive compaction pressure Insufficient binder Moisture content Excessive elastic recovery of particles Incorrect machine settings
Laminating	As for capping
Picking and sticking	Granules too wet Improper lubrication Damaged punches

Binding	Worn die
	Lubricant failure due to:
	  (a) Operating conditions too hot/cold
	  (b) Insufficient or wrong lubricant
	Granules too wet
	Rapid expansion of tablet

Chipping and cracking	Damaged punches Incorrect punch settings
Pitting	Lack of fine granules

Mottling	Colour migration on drying of granules
	Lake colours
	  Particle size too large
	  Poor mixing

Variation in tablet weight, thickness and hardness	Incorrect machine settings Variation in bulk density of granules Poor flow of granules Poor mixing

12.6.1   Capping

Capping is a frequent occurrence in tablets. The weakest part of a compact is just below the top surface. When the tablet is ejected from the die, as the top portion emerges it may expand, causing a thin layer to separate from the top of the tablet in the form of a 'cap'. This can be caused by excessive compaction pressure, trapped air, weak bonding between particles as a result of weak granules (i.e. insufficient binder), excessive elastic recovery of the material, or poor machine settings.

Lamination is an extreme form of the capping problem, whereby the whole tablet separates into many thin layers.

12.6.2   Sticking and picking

Tablets may stick in the die during ejection. This can be overcome by the use of a lubricant or by adjustment of the moisture content of the granules.

Small portions of the tablet may be 'picked' off by the punches. This can be due to damaged punch faces or absence of an antiadherent material.

12.6.3   Pitting

A certain amount of fine particles is necessary to fill in spaces in the tablet structure; lack of 'fines' can result in the tablet having a pitted surface.

12.6.4   Mottling

The problem of mottling can occur in a tablet as a result of migration of water-soluble dyes during granule drying. When compressed, the colour is not uniformly distributed. Mottling also occurs where lake colours are incorporated, if the particle size is too large or as a result of poor mixing.

Another example of mottling is in effervescent tablets, where the particles of citric acid pick up moisture and dissolve, giving rise to dark spots and slight depression on the tablet. This can be caused by storing in high humidities, with inadequate protection from packaging.

12.6.5   Size and weight variation

Variation in bulk density of raw materials will affect the die fill and the dimensions and weight of the resultant tablet. It is essential that the bulk density is carefully controlled.

Secondly, if the material is not flowing evenly, the die fill will also vary.

12.7   Lozenges

Lozenges are made from icing sugar, which is mixed with a binder solution, sheeted, cut to shape and allowed to dry. Common types of lozenge are extra strong mints and medicated lozenges.

Whereas compressed tablets have a smooth, shiny surface, lozenges tend to have a rather rough finish, especially if they have been poorly manufactured and have distorted during the drying stage.

Compressed tablets are generally brittle in texture, in contrast to lozenges, which are very hard.

12.7.1 Composition [3]

Because the main ingredients of lozenges is icing sugar, the grade of sugar chosen will have a radical effect upon the final product. A fine-particle-size sugar must be used; the finer the particles, the better the texture produced. If any large particles are included, the final sweet will have a rough mouthfeel.

The next ingredients to consider is the binder. This is usually gum arabic, gelatin, gum tragacanth, or more often a blend. When used individually, the binders do have disadvantages. Gum arabic, used on its own, produces a very brittle sweet which breaks easily. Gelatin gives a poorer quality sweet, which tends to shrink and distort during drying. Gum tragacanth produces a hard, smooth lozenge, but is expensive.

To overcome texture problems and to reduce the raw material cost, a blend is more usually used as the binder.

Gum arabic is made up as a 50% solution with water; gelatin is soaked in twice its weight of water, and gum tragacanth is dissolved in seven times its weight of water.

12.7.2 Processing

Lozenge manufacture is a cold process. The icing sugar is loaded into a mixer such as the Z-blade type. The binder solution is strained before use and is gradually added to the batch and thoroughly mixed.

Binder solutions are prone to bacterial degradation and should therefore only be prepared in small quantities which will be used up on the same day.

After mixing, the lozenge mix should have a firm, doughy texture. If the mix is squeezed in the hand, it should stick together but not exude any water. If too much water is added at this stage, the dough will be difficult to handle and likely to crack during drying.

The flavours used for lozenges are frequently volatile and can be lost during the mixing process. For this reason, flavours are best added at the last possible minute, however it will still be necessary to add extra flavour to allow for losses.

Colours are also added during the mixing stage, but care must be taken not to add too much water.

As soon as the dough is mixed sufficiently, it should be unloaded from the mixer and loaded into the depositing hopper of the lozenge machine. If there is any delay, the surface of the mix will case harden and subsequently be mixed back into the main bulk of the dough, causing roughness in the final sweets. If a delay is unavoidable, the surface can be covered with damp cloths to prevent premature drying.

The dough is extruded from the hopper into a sheet which is passed through rollers until the desired thickness is obtained. The dough is then stamped, in order to cut out the lozenges, which pass onto trays, and the waste 'web' is reprocessed.

If the waste is handled quickly, it may be mixed directly into the feed hopper, but this cannot be done if it has started to dry out, as roughness will again be produced in the final lozenge.

12.7.3 Drying

The lozenges are spread in a single layer on trays and allowed to form a slight crust, prior to drying in an oven at approximately 35–40°C. The trays should be stacked in such a way as to allow efficient air circulation between them.

The sweets are dried until their moisture content is approximately 1.5%. This must be done slowly in order to reduce shrinkage and cracking, hence the relatively low oven temperature. The drying time should also, however, be as short as possible, certainly no more than 24 h and more normally 12–15 h. The sweets are turned during this period.

During extended drying, the flavour and colour of the lozenges deteriorate and the binders also degrade.

12.8 Sugar panning

Sugar panning is the process of building up a coating, layer by layer, on centres rotating in a pan. The coating may be hard or soft, depending on the thickness, sugar composition and method of manufacture. The resultant sweets are called dragées.

Originally, dragées were made in a horizontal pan, suspended over a fire by chains. The operator swung the pan by hand to coat the sweets with syrup, which was then allowed to dry.

Dragée pans have since developed into mechanically operated elliptical vessels, which rotate on an inclined shaft. One operator may control up to 10 pans at a time.

With demand for increased output and ease of manufacture, many fully automated plants are now available.

Sugar panning has always been considered an art, and certainly some skill and experience are necessary to produce good-quality work. However, there are some basic principles which can be used as a starting point, but it must be remembered that these are guidelines only. The exact recipe and process required to produce a particular sweet will depend upon the type of centre

Table 12.2 Basic comparison of hard and soft panning

	Hard panning	Soft panning
Coating texture	Hard	Soft
Shape of finished product	Same as centre	Poorly defined
Pan size	Large	Small
Speed of process	Slow	Fast
Processing temperature	Warm	Cool
Syrup type	Sucrose	Sucrose and glucose syrup
Method of coating	Sugar syrup allowed to crystallise by application of heat	Caster or powdered sugar added to 'mop up' moisture

used, the desired final texture and the equipment and conditions available within each factory.

There are two main categories of sugar-panned sweets: hard-panned and soft-panned.

Hard-panned confections have a hard, crystalline coating and include products such as sugared almonds, mint imperials, non-pareils (hundreds and thousands) and sugar-coated chocolate lentils and eggs. Soft-panned products have a soft texture, the most common example being jelly beans.

Hard panning is achieved by allowing suitable centres to tumble in a dragée pan. A sugar syrup is added, allowed to spread over the centres, then the excess moisture is evaporated. The frictional effect of the centres tumbling over each other allows the sugar to spread and crystallise in a thin, hard, even layer. Further coats are applied until the desired thickness of coating is obtained. Heat is generally applied to speed up the process. Since only a very thin layer of sugar is applied at a time, the process is very slow. Each layer is only 10–14 μm thick. The coating follows the contours of the centre, thus the finished product retains the same shape.

Soft panning applies a thick, soft coating to centres such as moulded jelly beans or chews. Rather than using heat to dry out and crystallise a sugar coating, soft panning uses a non-crystallising syrup made from all-glucose syrup or a sugar/glucose syrup blend which is applied to the centres and the excess moisture 'mopped up' with additions of caster or powdered sugar.

This is a cold process; the pan and the syrup are unheated and no drying air is used. It is also a fast process, and a thick coating can be built up in a very short time, although the well-defined shape of the centre is usually lost.

The basic differences between the two types of panning are summarised in Table 12.2.

12.8.1 Equipment

The equipment required for panning is essentially the same whether one is undertaking a hard or a soft panning operation.

A simple dragée pan is shown in Figure 12.4. The pan is an elliptical vessel made from copper or stainless steel. The diameter of the pan ranges between 3 and 5 feet; laboratory-scale pans of 12–18 inches are available. The size chosen will depend upon the process to be carried out and the firmness and size of the confectionery centres. Generally, larger centres such as almonds are coated in a large pan, whereas tiny non-pareils require a smaller vessel.

The pan is mounted on a shaft at an angle of 30° to the horizontal, but on certain pans this angle may be varied. Some machines rotate at a fixed speed whilst others are variable. The usual range is between 15 and 35 rpm depending on centre size and strength. Whatever the chosen speed, it must be sufficient to allow the centres to roll smoothly and continuously. Pans may be fitted with baffles, which increase the tumbling action, but care must be taken as damage may be caused to delicate centres.

The dragée pan may be heated, either electrically or by steam coils. Heating is only necessary for hard panning, although even then there are some centres which cannot be heated.

Hard panning also requires an air supply into the vessel. The supply must be capable of being readily varied, in both temperature and velocity. Ducting must also be supplied to remove humid air from the pan, to accelerate drying.

Soft panning does not require heating or ducting although it is a dusty process so some means of extracting excess dust is advisable.

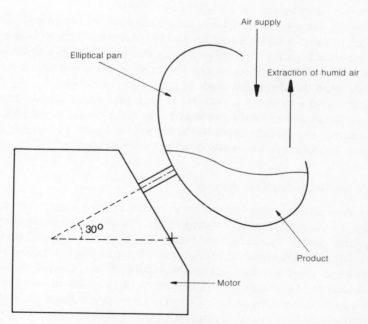

Figure 12.4 A simple dragée pan.

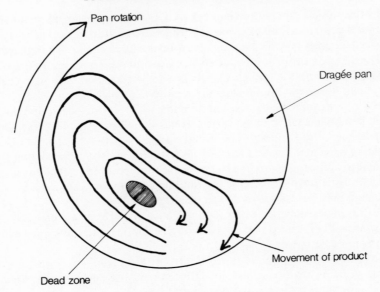

Figure 12.5 'Dead zone'.

For hard panning, the syrup may simply be ladled on by hand or a spray system can be installed.

Although a dragée pan is a fairly simple machine, its design will affect the product. In any pan which is rotating and full of centres, there will always be a dead zone (see Figure 12.5). This is towards the back of the pan and is an area where little tumbling motion occurs. The exact location and size of this zone depends upon the shape and angle of inclination of the pan.

There is also a tendency for centres to segregate according to size during panning. Small centres (and loose sugar) collect at the back of the pan, whilst large centres and clusters move to the front. During the panning cycle, the machine operator will frequently mix the sweets manually.

12.8.2 *Automatic panning systems*

Many automatic panning systems are available, ranging from a conventional dragée pan equipped with a timed spray system, to large-capacity fully automated plants. Typically, the systems comprise a horizontal perforated drum of up to 2000 kg finished-product capacity. Spraying of syrup and dosing of powdered sugar is carried out automatically and air is forced through the bed of centres. Hard and soft panning can be undertaken on suitable plants. Such automatic systems include Driam's 'Driacoater', Huttlin's 'Butterfly', Manesty's 'Accelacota' and Dumoulin's various IDA plants.

Selection of a particular plant will depend upon many factors, including the type of panning undertaken, the degree of automation required, the capacity and the amount of flexibility needed within the system.

Even in the fully automated systems, the panning process is based upon the same principles which apply to the traditional elliptical dragée pans.

12.8.3 Auxiliary equipment

In addition to the dragée pan, boiling pans are required for syrup preparation and separate dragée pans are necessary for polishing.

12.9 Hard panning

12.9.1 Pretreatment of centres

Suitable centres for hard panning include nuts, liquorice, chewing gum, tableted sweets and chocolate lentils. The centres must be sufficiently firm to be able to withstand their own weight when loaded into a pan and must not break up whilst tumbling.

Nuts should be sieved and then sealed to prevent oil from the nut migrating through the sugar coating and causing mottling on the surface. The nuts are dried overnight at 30–36°C. They are allowed to tumble in a dragée pan and a solution of 40–50% gum arabic is applied. Sufficient gum is added to form an even coating over the nuts. Once the gum starts drying and sticking slightly, a small quantity of wheat flour is added to dry the surface of the nuts and prevent them from sticking together. A second coat is usually applied. Once dry, the nuts are transferred from the pan into trays and allowed to dry overnight at about 38°C. The gum layer must be completely dry, otherwise moisture will migrate through the sugar coating.

It is sometimes useful to precoat other centres to improve adhesion of the sugar coating. This is of benefit when panning chewing gum, since the gum is water-repellent and it is often difficult to apply the first layers of sugar.

12.9.2 Engrossing

Engrossing is the process of building up the sugar layers. For hard panning, the engrossing syrup is made from sucrose alone. The more concentrated the sugar syrup, the faster the drying time will be. There are, however, factors which limit the strength of syrup which may be used. Sugar syrup concentrations may be quoted in degrees Brix or degrees Baumé. Table 12.3 provides a conversion. Generally, in hard panning, the concentration of the syrup will vary between 65 and 85° Brix (35 and 45° Baumé).

The larger the centre, the higher the sugar concentration that may be used; e.g. for almonds 77° Brix (41° Baumé), whereas for small centres such as non-pareils the syrup concentration is reduced to about 55° Brix (30° Baumé). An average centre may be coated with 70° Brix syrup (37° Baumé).

Table 12.3 Brix–Baumé conversion

Brix	Baumé	Brix	Baumé	Brix	Baumé	Brix	Baumé
50	27.3	63	34.0	76	40.5	89	46.7
51	27.8	64	34.5	77	41.0	90	47.2
52	28.3	65	35.0	78	41.5	91	47.7
53	28.9	66	35.6	79	42.0	92	48.1
54	29.4	67	36.1	80	42.5	93	48.6
55	29.9	68	36.6	81	43.0	94	49.0
56	30.4	69	37.1	82	43.4	95	49.5
57	30.9	70	37.6	83	43.9	96	49.9
58	31.5	71	38.1	84	44.4	97	50.4
59	32.0	72	38.6	85	44.9	98	50.8
60	32.5	73	39.1	86	45.3	99	51.3
61	33.0	74	39.5	87	45.8	100	51.7
62	33.5	75	40.0	88	46.3		

It must be remembered that syrups containing high percentages of sugar are prone to crystallisation. Such syrups should be prepared carefully, to ensure that no sugar crystals remain in the syrup when it is made and that it is kept covered during use, to prevent dust from seeding the surface. This is especially true of syrups used to coat chocolate centres, as the syrup is used cold and is more likely to crystallise. Syrups should be subjected to minimal agitation.

If there are any signs of crystallisation in the syrup, it must be discarded and fresh syrup prepared. It is also important that syrups are not held at high temperatures for long periods of time, as inversion of the sucrose will slow down drying and soften the casing.

Suitable centres are loaded into a dragée pan. Generally, a large pan is used for hard panning, as this increases tumbling action, but in the case of delicate centres a small pan would be used. The weight of centres will depend upon their texture; the harder the centre, the larger the load that can be panned. The larger the load, the greater the frictional forces developed, resulting in a better quality product. In most cases, the pan, its contents and the drying air which is applied are all heated to approximately 40°C. The syrup is also applied hot to improve dispersion and speed up drying. Higher temperatures will reduce panning times, but the resultant coating will be rough. In the case of chocolate centres, the pan and its contents must not be heated. This also applies to chewing gum, which will soften.

The centres are allowed to tumble, and a small quantity of syrup is added to the pan. The wetting must be just sufficient to coat all of the pieces evenly. It is important that the syrup addition is correct, as too much will cause the centres to stick together and an uneven surface coating will result; too little syrup, however, will not coat the pieces and will again produce an uneven surface.

The coating is allowed to dry until the first signs of dust formation become apparent. The second wetting is immediately applied and allowed to dry. (If the sweets are not sufficiently dried, the moisture will 'sweat back' later, however too much drying produces dust, which then sticks to the surface of the sweets.) This process continues until the desired thickness of coating is obtained. The last few applications of syrup should be diluted slightly to create a smooth surface, ready for polishing.

If at any time during the panning process the surface of the sweets start to become uneven, it is essential that it is rectified immediately. This is achieved by using a more dilute syrup to fill in the holes. This syrup must be used until the surface is again smooth. The engrossing process can then be speeded up by using a more concentrated syrup. Attempts to fill in holes by simply using more of the concentrated syrup will lead to increased unevenness.

Addition of 0.5–1.0% of glucose syrup or gum arabic to the sugar syrup will improve adhesion and reduce brittleness.

12.9.3 Non-pareils (hundreds-and-thousands)

Non-pareils are made from a medium-grade sugar (particle size 0.03–2.0 mm). The sugar is sifted to remove dust and fine grains and allowed to dry at 25°C overnight [4].

The sugar is loaded into a warm pan (about 40°C) and coated with small amounts of low solids syrup 55° Brix (30° Baumé). This must be done very slowly and carefully to keep the sugar running freely. As the sugar becomes sticky, a small amount of cornflour, wheat flour or powdered sugar is added to dry the surface. As the work grows, heat may be applied. From time to time, the grains must be removed from the pan and sieved to separate the different-sized grains. The last few wettings should be with syrup alone to provide a smooth surface.

12.10 Soft panning

The syrup used for soft panning should be approximately 77° Brix (41° Baumé). According to the texture required, the syrup may be all glucose syrup or up to 50/50 sugar and glucose syrup. It is important that the coating does not crystallise in the finished product, therefore a high proportion of glucose syrup is necessary. Before use, the syrup should be cooled to 38°C.

The dusting sugar is usually caster sugar, which is preferred to powdered sugar as it is less likely to clump and also distributes more evenly over the centres. The optimum particle size for the sugar is between 0.2 and 0.4 mm.

The centres are loaded into an unheated pan. Again, the weight of product depends upon the firmness of the centre. The pan is usually smaller for soft panning, as too much tumbling can cause the coating to pull away.

A wetting of syrup is applied, and as for hard panning it should be just sufficient to coat the centres. If too little syrup is added, the pick-up of the

Table 12.4 Factors affecting the panning process

Pan	Size
	Shape
	Angle of inclination
	Speed
Centres	Size
	Shape
	Texture
	Load in pan
	Sensitivity to heat
	Temperature
	Smoothness of surface
Syrup	Volume applied
	Rate of application
	Method of application
	Temperature
	Concentration
	Composition
	Viscosity
Dusting sugar	Quantity added
	Particle size
	Speed of application
Air supply	Temperature
	Velocity
	Relative humidity
	Extraction of damp air

dusting sugar will be uneven. Equally, too much syrup will cause clumping of the centres.

As soon as the syrup has spread, a charge of caster or powdered sugar is added. This must be sufficient to adhere evenly to the syrup, but an excess will run to the back of the pan and be picked up with the next syrup charge. If at any stage there is excess sugar in the pan, the centres must be removed and the sugar sieved out. If drying sugar is added too late, the syrup application starts to dry out by evaporation rather than by being dusted dry. This leads to a harder coating.

The centres are allowed to tumble until they no longer 'sweat', then the next layer may be added.

Often, only 3–5 coats are necessary to build up quite a thick coating. The top coats can be dusted with powdered sugar to give a smoother surface, followed by a few hard-panned coats using sugar syrup of 65° Brix (35° Baumé).

The more dusting sugar that is used, the harder the coating becomes, but it is important that the casing does not become too hard. Forced air must not be used as this dries the sweets too quickly.

12.11 Flavour and colour

12.11.1 *Flavour*

Flavours are generally added throughout the panning process. It is better to avoid oil-based flavours as these can migrate to the surface of the sweet and cause mottling. This can be reduced by blending the flavour with the panning syrup, together with a suitable emulsifier.

Cold-panned sweets are easy to flavour, but it must be remembered that with hot panning flavours may be lost. It is therefore advisable to avoid very volatile flavours for such products or increase the dosage accordingly.

In the case of soft dragées, any flavour added with the syrup will be 'diluted' when dusting sugar is added, so the dosage will need to be adjusted accordingly.

12.11.2 *Colour*

The surface of the dragées must be completely smooth before colouring is applied, as unevenness will result in varying thicknesses of colour layers and hence a mottled effect.

Water-soluble dyes may be used, but there is a tendency for the colour to migrate through the sugar coating as the shell dries out, giving a mottled appearance to the surface.

It is preferable to use a lake colour, which must be very finely divided. The colour is dispersed in sugar syrup and applied for the last 5–15 coats for hard-panned products, but is generally applied throughout the soft-panning process.

It is important that the colour concentration is constant for each application. The amount of colour added to the sugar syrup should be calculated on the basis of the dry sugar content. Any variations in syrup concentration to improve product texture will then be compensated for.

When colouring soft dragées, the colour strength must, as with flavour addition, be calculated to take into account the diluting effect of the powdered sugar.

Lake colours are also less susceptible than water-soluble dyes to fading during hot processes.

After the desired depth of colour has been achieved, two further coats of uncoloured syrup may be applied to 'seal' the colour. The last coat should not be allowed to run dry. The pan should be stopped just before any dust appears and left for about half an hour with the pan being 'jogged' (switched on briefly and then switched off again) frequently to prevent the sweets from sticking together. This should give the sweets a smooth, dust-free surface, ready for polishing.

The dragées are unloaded onto trays and allowed to dry overnight before being polished.

12.12 Polishing

Polishing both improves the appearance of dragées and provides a protective coating. It is essential that the sweets are fully dried prior to polishing, or the wax will smear.

Separate pans are used for polishing. These may be lined with wax and the dragées allowed to run until a shine develops. Beeswax can be used, but it is preferable to use a 50:50 blend of beeswax and carnauba wax. A small amount of cocoa butter may be added to prevent flaking.

Alternative methods of polishing include adding pulverised or micronised waxes to the sweets, where the frictional heat developed during tumbling melts the wax, and adding a ball of wax to run with the sweets and develop the shine. The wax addition is usually 0.05–0.1% of the batch weight.

Whatever the method of polishing, it is essential that the sweets and the polishing pan are dust-free and the dragées perfectly smooth to obtain a good finish.

A number of specially formulated polishes are available to suit particular products, but these are best evaluated by experimentation.

12.13 Additional panning techniques

Whilst hard and soft panning are two different techniques, giving rise to two different textures, there is no reason why a mixture of the two methods cannot be used.

If a syrup made from sucrose alone is applied to a product and then dusted with icing sugar, a hard coating can be built up more quickly. Unfortunately, the quality of the product will not be up to the standard achievable with straight hard panning, but by experimentation it is possible to obtain an acceptable finish.

Work has been carried out at Leatherhead Food R.A. using alginate to produce hard-panned products using soft-panning techniques [5].

12.13.1 Alternative sweeteners

Sucrose and sucrose/glucose syrup blends are generally used for panning, but it is also possible to use other sweeteners.

Dextrose has been successfully used for panning and has an appealing cooling effect which enhances peppermint flavours. Dextrose solutions of up to 85–87% solids can be used successfully for hot, hard panning. Dextrose is dissolved in water, cooked to 118°C and then allowed to cool. Dextrose syrups crystallise rapidly, and product drying times are reduced [6].

For soft panning, it is necessary to use a considerable quantity of glucose syrup to prevent crystallisation. High-maltose syrups are preferred to regular glucose syrup. A syrup consisting of 90 parts high-maltose syrup to 10 parts dextrose at 70% solids is suitable and is dried off using finely powdered dextrose.

Whereas with sucrose the dragées are allowed to dry between coats, the dextrose variant is allowed to run until the centre has just lost its 'wet' gloss.

Sorbitol syrups of 70% solids have been successfully used for panning [7].

12.13.2 Silvering

Silvered dragées are generally used as cake decorations.

Glass pans or conventional pans completely lined with sugar are suitable for silvering.

A gumming solution is prepared of three parts gelatin dissolved in one part 96% acetic acid. The solution is shaken and warmed until a clear liquid is obtained.

The centres are coated with gum solution and then added to a glass pan containing silver leaf (approximately 4 g silver leaf per kg of centres). The dragées are allowed to tumble until evenly coated. The pan is gradually vented to release the acid and dry the dragées.

The sweets are dried on paper-lined trays overnight to remove all traces of acid and are then polished with beeswax.

Acknowledgements

The author wishes to thank J.W. Hall for typing the manuscript and Chris Beacham for preparing the illustrations for this chapter.

References

1. H. Gremli, Confectionery Manufacture and Marketing 22 (6) (1985) 37.
2. M.E. Aulton, D.N. Travers and P.J.P. White, J. Pharm. Pharmacol. 25 (Suppl.) 79P.
3. Anon., Confectionery Production (Dec) 847.
4. Anon., Confectionery Production (1982) (Feb) 55.
5. A.G. Dodson, S.J. Wright, J. Beacham and D.M. Toler. Research Report No. 432, Leatherhead Food R.A. (1983).
6. R.F. Boutin, Manufacturing Confectioner 68 (1988) 70.
7. F. Devos, Manufacturing Confectioner 60 (1980) 26.

Further reading

J. Beacham, Scientific and technical survey No. 139, Tableting—A Literature Review, Leatherhead Food R.A. (1983).
J.S. Kitt, Panning problems—causes and remedies, Manufacturing Confectioner 68 (1988) 57.
K.W. Stock and A. Meiners, Silesia Confiserie Manual No. 2, Special handbook for dragée production, Silesia Essenzenfabrik Gerhard Hanke K.G. (1973).

13 Medicated confectionery and chewing gum

C.S. CUMMINGS

13.1 Medicated sugar confectionery

Medicated sugar confectionery encompasses formulations mainly for symptomatic relief of minor throat irritations, coughs, colds, respiratory tract congestions and allergies. Some stronger actives have other specific uses, and herbal extracts, vitamins, food supplements and antacids are also incorporated. Careful consideration is needed in logical selection of pharmaceutical combinations. Bases for dosage forms are hard-boiled candy including centre-filled, lozenges, gums, chewing (frappé) products, tablets, panned goods and chewing gums. Processing techniques limit the use of hydrolysable, temperature-degradable, highly volatile and large particle size, insoluble materials. Palatability and taste must be acceptable. Legislation restricts claims, advertising and label copy, and registration is usually necessary for general sale products.

Chewing gum is used for sustained release of actives. Sugarless formulations assist tooth and gum protection, re-enamelling and plaque reduction. Zinc salts in buccal cavity contact for cold protection and nicotine in smoking reduction therapy are patented. In gum, 'actives' incorporation and 'encapsulation' are restrictive.

Medicated sugar confectionery has evolved from the original tableting and panning techniques of the apothecaries' art, by taking on the mantle of science. Once the properties of sugar became known, the industry gradually developed, satisfying the needs of preparing acceptable, relatively inexpensive, easily obtainable and simple, portable medicated dosage forms. The later sophistication of confectionery equipment and the extensive research and development in the pharmaceutical actives field has allowed a specialised market segment to be expanded providing safe and effective products, many with well known brand-names having substantial marketing promotional support.

The most common forms of medicated sugar confectionery are manufactured in the high boiled sugar format followed by the vegetable gums, lozenges and sugarless product varieties.

13.2 High boiled sugar medicated confectionery

The manufacturing methods employed are similar to regular boiling techniques—continuous or batch—utilising plastic or depositing methods for forming and, for some products, centre filling [1]. Both sugar and sugarless technologies are available. The regular 'plastic' forming manufacturing uses a cooked sugars base in which sugar and glucose syrup (normally 42 DE, 43 Bé) are blended proportionately in ratios varying from 60 to 50 parts sugar and 40 to 50 parts glucose syrup (as received). The ratio is variable for different types of equipment to prevent sugar graining. The glucose syrup content can be varied with a sugar/glucose ratio of 100:60 using some fully continuous process. The sugar/glucose syrup ratio is a factor in the stability of the product particularly in hot humid climates where the preference is for lower moistures in finished product and a reduction in glucose quantity. Glucose syrup at 42 DE can have a variety of carbohydrate profiles relative to the method of conversion from starch. Specific enzymes can produce high-maltose glucose syrup with as little as 3% dextrose, with a viscosity suitable for depositing or plastic production methods [2]. This has the major advantage of reducing colour developed in processing and, since the higher oligosaccharides are carefully limited, allowing a suitable texture of cooked sugars for flavour, active, colour and acid addition. The cooling curve produced allows the transition of the cooked sugars batch from the soft to harder 'plastic' to be managed through the batch-rolling and forming die processes satisfactorily.

Various manufacturers have developed continuous and semicontinuous systems of batch weighing or proportionality blending of ingredients, followed by predissolving. Some systems are fully continuous from bulk raw materials handling to final product cooling. In small-scale manufacturing, dissolved syrup is usually prepared in steam kettles, but it is necessary to ensure that materials are accurately proportioned and consistently heated to the appropriate temperature. No crystals should be seen in the dissolved syrup.

Automatic weighing and metering systems require regular validation of accuracy by both physical checking and analytical means. Equipment suppliers have automatic systems capable of various recipe changes, microprocessor-controlled, linked to a low energy usage dissolving and cooking system. Bosch have a Solvomat design [3] where sugar is metered by a volumetric continuous system and glucose syrup by proportional geared pumping with ratios changeable by selective gear changes. Their latest weighing/batching equipment is microprocessor-controlled, and 'Gravimat' dissolvers equipment designs are much more energy-conservative and efficient [4]. Carle Montanari [5] also supply semiautomatic weighing and dissolving systems SZAC-linked to the cooker system.

Terr Braak [6] have developed the 'coolmix' system, a cold slurry made from a premix of water weighed into a tared container followed by sugar vibrated into the same vessel to formula requirement, followed by formula quantity of glucose syrup. The materials are continuously mixed together, then are dropped into a large reservoir, and the cycle repeats until sufficient material is available. The slurry is pumped via a ring main to the appropriate cookers and call-off from the ring main reduces the volume in the reservoir, which contains level sensors. Similar to other equipment, the system is microprocessor-controlled and ratios are easily reprogrammed. Different ratios for various products will require either separate coolmix weighing units or a system to add more sugar or glucose syrup to the coolmix from the ring main at another coolmix unit. 'Coolmix' is usually dissolved by pumping through the coil of a steam-jacketed heat exchanger or a 'Thermutator' [7]. Other types of heat exchanger, such as the pressure dissolver 118 energy-saving from Bosch or APV/Baker Perkins, dissolve the sugars premix with very low slurry water content to make a syrup of sugars prior to evaporation in the cooking system.

13.3   Third ingredient addition

At this stage of manufacturing, a third ingredient such as honey may be added. This can be warmed in its delivery drums on a suitable drum heater and pumped into a hot water-jacketed holding container, from which it can be proportionately pumped along with coolmix to the predissolving equipment. Alternatively, if a Solvomat unit is in use, the third ingredient pumping system will proportionately deliver the warm fluid honey into the dissolving chambers when the appropriate gear is used. About 8–10% honey can be added this way. If the honey solids are at the same total solids as the predissolved syrup from the coolmix system or similar, providing accurate proportional pumping is arranged, then it is sufficient to allow the honey delivery to enter the reservoir tank with the dissolved sugars syrup at the proportional rate and allow gentle mixing in the vessel. Similarly, a small amount of glycerin can also be added at this stage. However significant amounts will cause difficulties with the cooked sugars handling and plasticising, hence careful experimentation will be needed to determine the maximum amounts handleable with acceptable stability of finished product.

Usually the product will be vacuum-cooked, by either a batch process, continuous methods or possibly microfilm with or without vacuum.

If colour dye is to be utilised, this can be added, by colour stick or paste, at the mixing/kneading operation for batch products after cooking, carefully controlling the cooked sugar batch quantity by weight and the dispensing of colour sticks per batch [2]. Colour solution addition to the predissolved syrup prior to final evaporation is possible, but some dulling of the colour tone is inevitable in the finished product compared to colour addition at kneading on the batch line.

The colour solution addition is arranged by feeding into the dissolved syrup line just prior to the sugar syrup pump which feeds the syrup to the cooker evaporating coil. A linkage is required between the metering pump and the sugar syrup feed pump to ensure proportionality for any production rate changes. Infinitely variable pump stroke adjustment allows for formula variations.

Branne & Leubbe, Hughes/DCL micropumps or similar are useful for accurate dosage of colour, which is important for legislation reasons in countries where dye usage is limited to certain maximum concentrations, for compliance with product licences requirements, registration requirements, formula accuracy, normal quality consistency and consumer acceptability.

There are wide variations in colour dyes strengths and solubilities, and solutions must be made up well within the maximum solubility limits of the dyes. Sufficient hot water is used for dissolving, but the dye must not come out of solution when cool.

On continuous lines, it is possible to add colour after the cooking process, using in-line mixers. In this case, colour solutions need to be as concentrated as possible in order to minimise the water added to the cooked sugars. The sugars temperature will cause some evaporation of this moisture, but, depending on the line layout and design and whether volatile flavours are also added locally, some steam distillation will strip away some of the flavouring components and also may affect 'actives' by hydration or other reactions. Similarly if the formulation contains acids in solution, e.g. lactic, the moisture flash-off may have cumulative effects on the colour solution moisture and could cause unacceptable performance in the mixing and incorporation devices.

Channelling and spitting of the solutions may occur with poor mixing, particularly with in-line static mixers, resulting in flavour and colour running off the cooked sugars when they are presented to the continuous belt cooling systems. This results in product which is very inconsistent in flavour and appearance and may be totally unacceptable because of actives variability as a direct result.

Colour reactions can occur with certain actives and vitamins. The final pH of the product can cause dye to change colour in a way similar to chemical indicators. Some blue and red dyes are particularly susceptible, and previous laboratory-scale experimentation is seriously suggested before factory-scale formulation trials are planned.

Certain nature-identical or 'natural' colours are quite acceptable for use and may also provide other usage or claims for the products (e.g. β-carotene). Experimentation has shown some 'natural' colours have good light and heat stability, but others are less successful [8].

In Europe, all colour dyes used must conform to the EEC Food Colour Directive 78.25/EEC or the EEC Directive for Colours Used in Pharmaceuticals. For the USA, the use of colours approved and certificated by the Food and Drugs Administration (FDA) is mandatory. Other countries have their own regulations, but the specifications generally tend to follow the EEC and

FDA requirements. These colour requirements cover all manufactured types of formulations of medicated sugar confectionery.

If the actives are not a well-known and -used material defined by a Pharmacopoeia monograph, then a considerable amount of clinical and bioavailability data is needed. For each medicated formulation, previous experimentation and review of materials for interactions and stability is necessary before production, and detail has usually to be provided for registration, if necessary by local regulations.

The cooking equipment is generally provided with vacuum evaporation to allow low moisture retention products with good colour. Batch equipment usually allows evaporation down to about 2% minimum moisture (by Karl Fischer, equivalent to 1% weight loss on drying) with a usual 2.5–3.5% average level. Equipment is well-defined in literature [1–3, 9]. An interesting innovation is the Tower cooker from Terr Braak.

Evaporation temperatures are around 240°C with 26–28 mm Hg vacuum, and batch sizes can be up to 50 kg with batch cycle times from 2–3 min upwards. High-pressure steam is required at 90–120 psi. The batch of cooked sugars after collection from the cooker should be checked for weight accuracy and appropriate adjustments made. Visual checks for colour consistency and any carbon or foreign matter are made as the batch is transferred to the mixing slab.

Actives and flavour can be incorporated in batch proportion either by sprinkling over the surface of the gradually spreading batch on the slab and working in using a mixing stick (high-density polyethylene, polypropylene or similar—food-grade materials meeting materials in contact with food regulations), or by mechanical means. The actives may be of powdered consistency with fairly fine particle sizes, which usually melt in the candy base, or may be carried in a suitable food grade-approved solvent and added to the batch in a similar way as flavourings, but there are limits to the actives loading of the confectionery piece. Certain pharmaceuticals may have dosage limits up to 5 mg, others 15 mg or higher.

Ruffinati [10] have designed a batch collection bowl which takes the sugars from the vacuum cooker bowl to a fixed mixing unit which has rotary and static mixing arms to work in flavours, acids, colours, actives and pulverised salvage before transferring the mix to the kneading/tempering machines. Similarly a small Hobart planetary mixer can be utilised, in which case about 2–4 kg of pulverised hard-candy salvage is added to the bowl followed by batch quantity predispensed granulated or powdered acids, flavour and active. This is mixed at a suitable speed until components are sufficiently dispersed and then placed on the poured cooked sugars batch on the mixing slab. The edges of the batch are carefully folded towards the middle to form an envelope concealing the salvage mixture, then the batch is pushed on to a kneading machine for mixing and kneading automatically.

Many types of kneaders are available from Berke, Ruffinati, Otto Hansel,

Carle Montanari, etc. [11]. Care is required not to incorporate large air bubbles in the sugars batch during this operation, since this will cause a distorted-shaped product, which creates difficulties on automatic wrapping machines.

When the batch reaches a suitable texture, the kneading is stopped and, if required, the batch can be transferred to a pulling machine to create a different, satinised appearance product, depending on pulling cycles or time. This process helps in dispersion of actives, flavours and acids, particularly if very large inputs are formulated, whilst slightly reducing the density of the medicated high-boiled product. This process is advantageous in obtaining consistency when high concentrations of flavours and actives are needed in the product, since speed and timing of pulling cycles can be accurately controlled.

The product is formed by the usual batch-rolling and rope-sizing techniques. The rope formed is fed continuously into rotary or chain dies [12] in the usual way as for general high-boiled sugar confectionery, pressing out accurately shaped and sized pieces which are then cooled on a multitier air cooling unit.

The cooling operation should be located in an air-conditioned area with conditioned, cooling air drawn into the units at around 15°C, maximum relative humidity 30–45%, for efficiency, to preserve shape, and to help prevent surface stickiness of the confectionery. Alternatively, drop rollers such as HEMA [13] can be used. Regular piece weight checks are essential.

13.4 Continuous operations

Continuous operations can be utilised for certain confections where addition of actives is feasible either in liquid form or by accurate augering of powders and granules, etc. Continuous plants can be purchased as 'turnkey' operations or be built up as required. Some medicated confectionery manufacturers have designed their own equipment and converted batch lines economically into continuous processes.

Manufacturing techniques include vacuum boilings, microfilm evaporations, depositing or continuous 'plastic' forming. The Bosch automatic cooking line, with its patented, cooked sugar draw-off rollers from the vacuum chamber, has a continuous in-line mixing facility which can efficiently disperse colour, flavour and actives in solution. Actives in granular or powder form usually require addition in a way similar to granular or powdered acids by sprinkling across the lamina of sugars at the feed-point of the continuous, stainless-steel cooling conveyors. Accuracy needs verification, since process flow rates and active addition rates need to be carefully monitored.

Dispersion of active is critical, and the kneading and turning ploughs on the cooling belt assist in mixing the actives on the sugar's laminar surface. If the melting point of the 'active' is high, then checks should be made that the material is well dispersed before the 'rope' is formed at the batch roller prior to rotary or chain die-forming. Certain actives can be proportionately added to the syrup prior to cooking if temperature degradation does not occur and the products are water-soluble or can be carried in a suitable solvent. The process through cooking and forming will usually give good distribution of actives through the sugars, but regular checks on proportional metering must be made to ensure consistency.

All metering pumps and flow or mass-metering devices should be capable of simple on-line verification of performance and should be recalibrated when necessary. Similarly, product out-turn rates require regular verification to compare with actives and additives input rates. Computerisation of these functions is a major step forward in allowing the presentation of control and recent flow data from various in-line sensors. This can help detect trends and variations, although verification of these functions and the accuracy of data presentation requires regular monitoring to ensure compliance with good manufacturing practices. Simple on-line checks using calibrated sight-glass devices and timers will allow rapid checks of fluid materials flow. Similarly, collection and weighing of metered granular materials deliveries from on-line dosing units will verify accuracy of performance or problems contributing to lack of compliance which may be initially highlighted by chemical analysis of product.

13.5 Depositing high boilings

Another form of medicated high-boiled production uses continuous depositing techniques. Equipment is manufactured by APV Baker [14] and others. Actives and additives can be incorporated in identical ways as noted for continuous production. It is essential to have an efficient in-line mixing system (preferably not of the static type) which will carefully mix or comb in the dosed active ingredients into the cooked sugar feed prior to the depositing hopper, and it is usually necessary to utilise a liquid acid if acidification is required in the formulation.

Various problems can be encountered at the depositing hopper. Oil- or solvent-based materials can separate and float to the surface of the sugars, and if the sugars do no flow effectively through the hopper due to incorrect heat transfer, which causes viscosity variations, then variations in individual depositing pump volumes will occur, hence weight variation between confectionery pieces will be noted. Compliance to weight and the active ingredient content uniformity specifications is essential, since many formulations are based on milligram dosages per tablet rather than % wt/wt actives.

The variation in depositing quantity can also result in significant packaging problems. This is particularly important for confectionery in stickpack formats, where piece size tolerances are very precise to ensure good packaging performance within adequate overall combinational tolerances to ensure consistent pack lengths. Good hermetically sealed pack-ends are necessary to give pack protection against moisture ingress throughout the products' shelf life.

Individual depositing pumps should be set against data measured from performance trials where pieces are carefully sequentially removed in known order from the moulds after depositing. Weight and size statistical control charts or simple go/no-go gauges can be utilised to control tablet dimensions to specification once uniformity of individual pumps has been achieved. When considering depositing medicated sugar confection it is essential to consider processing temperatures and longer dwell-time effects on the active components of the formulation.

APV Baker has a 'double' depositer capable of providing a product with centre, by means of concentric pipe delivery from two hoppers, one containing shell, the other centre. The lower temperature for centre preparation and during processing is a feature which could be utilised for the more temperature-sensitive actives, but the centre can gain significant heat input when passing down the delivery pumping system pipe around the very hot shell pipe, before entering the mould. Since dosage of actives requires accuracy, it is necessary to ensure that the ratio between centre and casing does not vary between limits which will affect the final product.

Acidification on depositing lines usually requires the use of a buffered acid. Lactic acid with sodium lactate buffer, either 3:1 or 4:1, is usually used, however, the taste of lactic acid is not always suitable. The taste effect can be sharpened by the use of citric acid dissolved in the minimum of water with tripotassium citrate buffer salts or similar, blended into the buffered lactic acid. The amount of water used should be just sufficient to prevent recrystallisation of the salts, which could block delivery pipes and pumps. Excess water can cause stickiness of the final product, and a residual moisture level which is greater than necessary could result in long-term instability. It is difficult to incorporate more than the equivalent of 1–1.5% acidity in finished product using this type of acid solution, due to the excess moisture contribution to the finished product. The same constraints apply to liquid acid addition to the cooked sugars on automatic lines. On no account should the buffered acids be added in any significant quantity to the sugar syrup prior to evaporation in the cookers, since excessive inversion of the sucrose will occur. On the APV Baker Microfilm cooking process or Terr Braak system it is possible to inject buffered lactic acid solutions into the cooked sugar syrup just prior to the vacuum chamber. This overcomes the moisture retention problem, but the extent of sugar inversion should be carefully monitored.

As a general rule, the level of total reducing sugars in finished high-boiled product is acceptable up to 23% wt/wt, however at 25% wt/wt and above, serious stability problems are liable to occur. Sugarless depositing is possible using as a base sorbitol solution or blends of other bulk sugarless substitutes.

In this case, because of long set-up times, depositing into a continuous mould system is not always possible so individual plastic moulds are fed under a depositing hopper, and after filling are stacked in a conditioned area until the sorbitol or polyalcohols set into a supersaturated glass-like consistency, at which stage they can be ejected from the moulds. In some formulations, the sorbitol is seeded with up to 20% sorbitol powder to accelerate setting and crystallisation, whilst actives, essential oils and flavours are initially mixed in the molten supersaturated sorbitol solution prior to depositing. Certain countries have a maximum limit of sorbitol use and require a pack warning declaration, often as low as 25 g per day per adult due to the laxative effect.

In high-boiled confectionery medicated products, fluid centres have a use as a medium for simulating syrup dosage formulations, particularly for throat-soothing claims. Certain difficulties are immediately obvious, particularly in distribution of dosage between the boiled sugars shell and liquid, fluid or paste-type centres. Consistency in the quantity of the centre fill is important to ensure minimum variations of actives in finished pieces, and similarly minimum piece weight variation is critical. A consistent level of retention of actives in finished product is normally required, with the same percentage weight/weight retention in both the shell and the liquid centre, so that any variation in ratio between the shell and centre will have little effect on the total milligrams of active at the tablet weight specified. Liquid centres allow the use of actives which may be more temperature-sensitive and if used in the shell would require significantly more overages at input.

13.6   The 'Apollo' centre-filling line from Euromec

This machine [15] usually uses a chain-die system similar to the Strada from Carle Montanari, although a rotary die similar to the Bosch Uniplast system is available as an alternative. The line has a computer-controlled system to balance flows of liquid centre and shell feed, controlling filler pump, batch roller, rope-sizer die and cooling belt speeds exactly proportionately with microprocessor and sensors. Importantly, batch product cooked sugars which are coloured, flavoured and contain actives (if required) are tempered from the kneader, and should be fed into the batch roller around the centre-filler pipe by a side feeder which rolls the product into a candy slab about 30 mm thick for careful placement around the cone of candy in the batch roller. This helps remove hard and soft candy variations which could cause rope feed variations.

The centre-filler pipe in some installations is Teflon-coated on the outside, and design dimension and length are critical to performance. All centre-filler pipes require very regular lubrication on the outside surface which is in contact with the sugar shell. This is achieved by using an extended-nozzle oilcan containing an approved release agent, which is injected down the orifice formed by the candy at the wide end of the batch roller around the centre-filling pipe.

Depending on the manufacturing equipment type, the centre can range from an average 10% to 30% wt/wt or more of the tablet. Oval shapes can obviously contain more centre than 'square' or pillow-shaped products, and simple geometric calculations will easily explain why. Excessive centre can result in very thin shells which will not have sufficient strength to contain impact in transporting and pressures experienced in wrapping machines. Carle Montanari supply the Star 125 line [16] where up to 125 m per minute of centre-filled sugar rope is fed to a patented die, and has the special feature of microprocessor controls which allow infinitely variable machine speeds with balanced feeding from each individual unit of equipment. The die is particularly designed to allow up to 40% fillings.

13.7 The centre-filler hopper and pump unit

This requires precise control so as not to vary the centre temperature, and hence viscosity, which will affect centre-filling quantity. The pump should not pulse the centre, and reciprocating pumps are generally best avoided if high accuracy of flow is required. The geometric profile of the batch roller is also important to ensure adequate flow of cooked candy to the rope forming, with minimum variation and 'pulsing' caused by viscous drag and texture variations of candy, altering the rope-forming profile. The resulting unbalanced flow at the transfer from batch roller to rope sizer is a source of rope splitting and forming rope with no or little centre content. The flow of candy shell from batch roller through rope sizing and into the die-head must be as smooth and consistent in speed as possible to allow the least variation in centre fill, whilst the fluid centre flow should also be exactly matched to achieve the required percentage.

13.8 Bosch

Bosch have demonstrated a candy shell extruder with vertical batch roller feeding a WLS KM 400 or similar extruder linked with a 'P' series die. The centre-filling unit is controlled by computer which takes signals from the filled rope dimension by a patented scissor-sensing design. Feedback to a computer controller allows adjustment of speed rates between extruder and die to achieve controlled thickness of rope. Centre is injected into the large rope formed in the die end of the extruder through a concentric pipe which forms the centre opening of the 'pipe' of filled product or rope. A pressure-sensing device recycles excess centre to ensure consistency of quantity prior to final feed in the extruder. The accuracy of this system in delivering a fixed ratio of centre to casing should allow 'actives' dosing in either shell or centre separately to achieve pharmaceutical standards, without the difficulty of having to dose shell and centre equally, as in conventional centre-filling methods using pipe and batch roller. Bosch have also demonstrated a powder auger centre-filling line where the centre can be incorporated as a dry mass and automatically filled into the candy centre [3]. The actives can also be used as encapsulates to reduce bitter tastes.

Centre formulations using honey are particularly successful. Up to 90% or more of the formula can be honey. The viscosity can be reduced by adding up to 10% glycerin, and 'body' or more effective mouthfeel can be produced by maltodextrins.

If honey is not required, liquid or fluid centres can be prepared from syrups containing sugar, glucose syrup, sorbitol and invert syrup. Care in formulation is essential to ensure all granular/crystalline materials are dissolved in the syrup and sufficient solids are attained to provide absence of microbiological growth. The solids should generally be around 84–86% uncorrected Brix to prevent the sugar shell slowly dissolving into the centre, especially at the end-seals of the confection piece. Similarly, it is important in a fluid-centre product not to allow the sugar or crystalline components to crystallise out. Careful formulation balancing is required to achieve these conditions, but there are few published data referring to this.

Sometimes high-fructose syrups are used as a base as an alternative to honey. Sugarless formulae can be prepared, although the higher costs will result in premium-priced products. This is not an unusual feature, since the products are usually 'niche'-marketed in the premium sector since the products have a particular uniqueness and specialised marketability.

Flavouring of liquid-centre lines is not straightforward. If essential oils extracts are used, e.g. peppermint, eucalyptus oil, lemon oil, or other actives such as menthol, thymol, wintergreen, etc., the rate of release in the mouth when dissolving the tablet is critical to consumer preferences. As a guideline, from the shell, the normal flavour retention rates of 0.1–0.2% wt/wt after manufacturing are usually satisfactory, giving a sustained, pleasant flavouring/actives release. However, if the centre is dosed at this same level, this will result in almost instantaneous release which will be very unpleasant to the consumer and totally unbalance the flavouring effect of the product. Around 30–35% less flavouring inputs, and in some instances up to 60% less, is the recommended dosage for centres.

The hard candy shell may be flavoured with a different flavouring characteristic from the centre, however the flavourists' skills are necessary to achieve suitable tastes. Menthol is particularly useful because of both its taste and actives properties. Table 13.1 includes many well-known materials used in medicated confectionery which have therapeutic properties as well as flavouring impacts.

Table 13.1 'Active' ingredients and typical usage in medicated confectionery

Medicated or active ingredient	Typical confectionery products	Typical usage (in combinations signifies active is usually used with other actives)
Aqueous extract of marshmallow	Pastilles, gum products, high boilings	Herbal flavours Relief of catarrh, colds and cough symptoms
Ammonium chloride	Lozenges	Nasal decongestion in head colds, relief of catarrh and blocked sinuses in combinations
Amylmetacresol	Lozenges, high boilings	Throat infections
Aniseed oil Anisole	All forms of medicated confectionery	Flavouring Throat-soothing in combinations
Ascorbic acid Sodium ascorbate	High boilings, lozenges, gum products	Vitamin C supplements Cold relief
Benzalkonium	Lozenges, gum products	Sore throat relief Mouth infection Anaesthetic
Benzocaine	Lozenges, high boilings	Mouth and throat infections in combinations
Benzoic acid	Lozenges, high boilings	Sore throat relief in combinations
Benzoin tincture	Lozenges, high boilings	In combination for bronchial catarrh, coughs and colds relief
Blackcurrant-flavoured juices	All forms of medicated confectionery	Flavouring Throat-soothing, sometimes in combinations with vitamin C or glycerol
Camphor	Lozenges, high boilings, gum products, pastilles	Flavour Sore throat relief in combinations
Capsicin tincture	All forms of medicated confectionery, lozenges	Flavouring
Capsicin	Lozenges	In combinations for bronchial catarrh, coughs and colds relief
Cetyl pyridinium chloride	Lozenges, high boilings, liquid centres	Sore throats and irritations relief Pharyngitis and laryngitis in combination
Cherry extracts/juices	All medicated confectionery	Flavouring Throat-soothing, sometimes in combinations with vitamin C

Table 13.1 (*Continued*)

Medicated or active ingredient	Typical confectionery products	Typical usage (in combinations signifies active is usually used with other actives)
Chlorhexidine hydrochloride	High-boiled lozenges	Throat and mouth infections in combinations
Chloroform	Lozenges	Cough and sore throat relief in combinations
Cineole (from eucalyptus oil)	High boilings, lozenges, pastilles, gum products	Flavour Unproductive cough relief
Cinnamic acid	Pastilles, gum products	Cough relief in combination
Cinnamon leaf oil	Lozenges, gum products, pastilles	Sore throat relief Catarrh relief in combinations Flavouring
Clove oil	Lozenges, high boilings	Sore throat relief Flavouring
Codeine phosphate	Lozenges, pastilles, gum products	Cough and colds relief in combinations
Concentrated camphorated opium lind	Pastilles, gum products	Cough relief in combination
Coltsfoot extract	High boilings, lozenges	Cough, cold and catarrh relief Herbal products in combinations
Creosote	Gum products pastilles, lozenges	Catarrh
Dequalinium chloride	Lozenges	Mouth and throat infections in combinations Sore throats, pharyngitis
Dextromethorphan hydrobromide	Chewy products, high boilings	Cough relief
Diphenhydramine hydrochloride	Chewy products, high boilings	Cough suppressant
Domiphen bromide	Lozenges	Sore throats and husky voice relief
Ether	Lozenges	Cough, sore throat relief in combinations
Eucalyptus oil	High boilings, centre-filled products, lozenges, tablets, all forms of medicated confectionery	Cough and cold symptoms relief Decongestant Sore throat relief Slight antibacterial properties Flavouring
Extract of horehound	High boilings	Cough and cold relief Nasal decongestion in combination

Table 13.1 (*Continued*)

Medicated or active ingredient	Typical confectionery products	Typical usage (in combinations signifies active is usually used with other actives)
Extract of wild cherry bark	High boilings	Flavouring Cough and colds relief in combinations
Ginger oleoresin	Lozenges	Flavouring Cough, cold and catarrh relief in combinations
Glacial acetic acid	Pastilles, gum products	Cough relief in combination
Glycerol	High boilings, lozenges, gum products, liquid centres	Sore throat relief in combinations
Guaicol	Pastilles, gum products	Cough, colds and sore throat relief in combinations
Guaiphesin	Pastilles, gum products	Coughs and sore throat relief
Halogenated phenols	Pastilles, gum products	Coughs and sore throat relief
Hexylresorcinol	Lozenges, high boilings	Sore throat relief
Honey	Lozenges, high boilings, fluid centres	Throat-soothing
Iodine	Lozenges, high boilings	Throat infections
Ipecacuanha liquid extract	Pastilles, gum products	Cough relief
Juniper berry oil	Pastilles/lozenges	Flavouring Relief for coughs, colds catarrh, sore throat and nasal decongestion in combinations
Krameria dry extracts	Tablets	In combination with other actives—sore throat relief
Lemon oil	All medicated forms of confectionery	Flavour Combinations, sometimes with vitamin C
Liquorice extract	All forms of medicated products	Flavouring Throat-soothing
Linseed oil and mucilage	Lozenges	Cough and cold relief
Liquid squill extract	High boilings, lozenges, pastilles, gum products	Sore throat relief
Liquid tolu	High boilings	Cough and cold relief Nasal decongestion in combination
Menthol	High boilings, centre-filled products, lozenges, tablets, all forms, of medicated confectionery	Cough and cold symptoms relief Decongestant Sore throat relief Flavouring

Table 13.1 (*Continued*)

Medicated or active ingredient	Typical confectionery products	Typical usage (in combinations signifies active is usually used with other actives)
Methyl salicylate	High boilings, lozenges, liquid centres, pastilles, tablets	Flavour Sore throat, cough and cold relief in combinations
Myrrh	Pastilles, lozenges	Sore throat, coughs and catarrh relief
Oil cubebs	Pastilles, lozenges, high boilings, tablets	Flavouring
Papaverine hydrochloride	Pastilles/lozenges, gum products	Relief of irritating, unproductive cough in combinations
Peppermint oil	All forms of medicated confectionery	Flavouring Carminative
Phenol	Lozenges, high boilings	Throat infections
Phenylephrine hydrochloride	Lozenges	Nasal congestion in head colds Catarrh and blocked sinuses in combinations
Pholcodine	Pastilles, gum products	
Pine oil (pumilio)	High boilings, lozenges, pastilles, gum products, tablets	Flavour Cough and cold relief, nasal decongestion, sore throat relief in combinations
Pine oil (abietis and sylvestris)	Pastilles, lozenges, gum boilings	Catarrh relief and coughs in combinations
Potassium chlorate	Tablets	In combination with other actives—sore throat relief
Pseudoephedrine hydrochloride	Chewy products	Expectorant and upper respiratory tract decongestant in combinations
Squill vinegar	Pastilles, lozenges, gum products	Sore throat, cough relief in combinations
Terebene	Lozenges, pastilles	Sore throat relief in combinations
Terpine hydrate	Pastilles, gum products	
Terpineol	Pastilles, gum products	Coughs, colds and sore throat relief in combinations
Tincture of tolu	High boilings, lozenges, pastilles, gum products	Sore throat relief Catarrh relief Hoarseness relief in combinations Herbal products

Table 13.1 (*Continued*)

Medicated or active ingredient	Typical confectionery products	Typical usage (in combinations signifies active is usually used with other actives)
Tolu balsam	Lozenges, high boilings	Flavouring Herbal products Cough, cold and catarrh relief in combinations
Thyme oil	Pastilles, lozenges, high boilings	Flavour Sore throat relief Irritations, cough relief in combinations
Thymol	High boilings, pastilles, lozenges, gum products, tablets	Flavour Sore throats, cough and cold relief in combinations
Tyrothricin	Lozenges	Sore throats and irritation Pharyngitis, laryngitis
2, 4-Dichlorobenzyl-alcohol	Lozenges	Throat and mouth infections in combinations

Suppliers of herbal extracts for high boilings/gum products:

Emil Flachsman, Butzenstrasse 60, 8038 Zurich, Switzerland.
William Ransom & Son Ltd, 104 Bancroft, Hitchin, Herts, UK.
Potters Herbal Supplies Ltd, Douglas Works, Leyland Mill Lane, Wigan, Lancs, UK.
Dixa A.G., St Gallen, Switzerland.
Slater & Frith, Statham Road, Wroxham, Norwich, UK.
Pembroek b.v., PO Box 34, Industrieweg 3-22, 1230 aa Loosdrecht, Holland.
Dr Madis Laboratories Inc., S. Hackensack, New Jersey 07606, USA.
H. Finzelberg, Nashfolger, Koblenzer Strasse 44-54 5470 Andernach/Rhein, F.R.G.

In the shell or casing it is not unusual to have volatile losses from some actives with flavouring potential. For example menthol and eucalyptus oils need overages of 25–30% to achieve the desired residual content in any high-boiled candy base, either for hard-boiled candy pieces or for the shell of centre-filled products.

Other volatile and low boiling point actives will behave similarly and analytical determination of actives is required in preproduction development work to determine these levels. Blending these materials, including dissolving menthol or thymol in essential oils such as peppermint or eucalyptus then dispensing these in pulverised salvage for batch processing, will significantly reduce volatile losses.

Considerable attention has to be addressed to blends of flavouring materials which can be used with some actives, since strong dominant tastes and usually the bitterness of the actives has to be overcome. In cough and cold-relief products, cherry and lemon flavour are used in significant quantities, and a good-quality lemon oil blends well in taste with honey, and component flavours such as anis or anethole also combine well. Blackcurrant (cassis) and liquorice flavours are noted in many medicated confectionery formulations. A flavour producer has published detail of flavour 'bridges' to help overcome the actives bitterness and flavour fruitiness contradictions [17].

Herbal extracts are common in both high-boiled confections and gum products. Aqueous extracts of herbs are available in a wide variety, and many combinations have been used with other galenic materials. To introduce these products into the cooked sugars base, usually a premix is made with a solvent such as propylene glycol, with essential oils also combined. The ingredients are then mixed into the cooked sugars at the kneading stage, as previously mentioned for batch products. Alternatively, a solution in water is made of the herbal extracts, and the resulting premix can be added to predissolved sugar syrup continuously and proportionately, similar to colour solutions prior to the cooker evaporation coil. A disadvantage is that some piquancy of flavouring is lost by distillation effect with the evaporating moisture, but a good 'dry' non-sticky candy base incorporating the herb extracts is produced. Usually the candy base colour is brown after the addition of these ingredients, but acid-proof caramel can be added to the herbal premix to darken the final product appearance. Many herbal ingredients are found in gum products, with a significant proportion of formulations being 'sugarless'.

Vitamin C (ascorbic acid) can be introduced into medicated confectionery. Usually sodium ascorbate salt is dissolved in water and pumped into predissolved sugar syrup prior to cooking, similar to colour and herbal extract. A double-head pump will be useful for coloured product such as citrus-flavoured confections whilst proportionately adding vitamins supplement. An overage of about 20% is required calculated on a molecular basis as ascorbic acid. Up to 10% ascorbic acid crystals can be substituted for sodium ascorbate to provide some acidification, helping to develop citrus flavours. Care is needed to ensure that dwell-time processing is short and to avoid exposure of vitamin C to temperatures above 145°C since in the presence of other acids catalytic reactions occur, and above 145°C thermal degradation occurs with breakdown products culminating in furfural and carbon dioxide. Depositing is not recommended. It is also important not to mix colour dyes and vitamin C premix together for any extended length of time since reactions will occur, especially with some red colours. Freshly made colour and vitamin C solutions separately pumped into the dissolved sugars premix limits colours reaction time. Products containing up to 40 mg vitamin C per 1 g confection are seen on the European market.

When adding bitter active materials to confectionery it is necessary to choose bright strong flavours. A patented methodology in the USA prepares an adsorbate on materials such as magnesium trisilicate, with around 10% of medicament absorbed, and the bitterness effect is reduced. In very small particle sizes, these adsorbates can be added to the medicated candy without causing excessive roughness or soreness associated with insolubles when slowly dissolving the candy in the mouth. Addition of some therapeutic materials can cause slight mouth anaesthesia, e.g. diphenhydramine for cough suppression. Dextromethorphan is also used for coughs relief. Around 5–15 mg per tablet is the dosage form, however the FDA does define the amounts of these materials which can be used in the USA by means of specific end product use monographs. For example, the latest cough – cold monograph limits menthol to a minimum of 5 mg per 'lozenge' before claims can be made, and specific wording is required on the label noting instructions and warning [18]. Careful and logical selection of the formulations actives is necessary to ensure rational combinations that do not conflict, e.g. antitussives and expectorants in combination [19].

13.9 Salvage

Salvage usage requires controlled preparation. High-boiled medicated candy pieces which are mis-shapen, distorted or deformed can be pulverised and reused in the same batch manufacturing lot as the carrier for flavours, actives and acids. Provided good manufacturing principles of identification, lot labelling and keeping the pulverised product in clean-covered containers free from potential foreign matter contamination are used under strict quality assurance (QA) procedures, the usage is acceptable. If product from different 'lots' is used, this should be clearly indicated on manufacturing batch record forms. Clearly some pharmaceutical actives will preclude the re-use of salvage unless some effective way of removing the actives from solution made from the salvage, e.g. by neutralisation or carbon treatment, is arranged. Acids should be neutralised before sugar syrups are re-used, whilst carbon treatment or ion exchange will decolorise or deactivate some materials, leaving the sugars behind for re-use. Volatile flavours or actives for salvage may be evaporated during re-use of the sugar syrup at the sugars syrup evaporation.

13.10 Chewy medicated confections

Other types of product containing active ingredients can be found in chewy or frappé format and contain adsorbates of, for example, dextromethorphan or diphenhydramine, psuedoephedrine or other components. These manufacturing methods are normally patented. The products provide pleasant-tasting cough suppressants which chew out smoothly and dissolve away in the mouth. Similar products also contain antacids, calcium supplements or antibacterial preparations and provide a novel, soft-chew dosage form in an almost soft nougat consistency. Antacids without chalkiness and with pleasing peppermint flavours are already marketed using this technology. The manufacturing methodologies feature equipment and methods common to both chewy candy and chewing gum production, with individual pieces being formed on equipment, which is specifically modified.

13.11   Gum products

Gelatin and gum arabic starch-deposited gum products and non-starch-deposited gum products are useful bases for medicated confectionery. Manufacturing of the different bases is well documented in Lees & Jackson [20], Silesia [21] and equipment manufacturers' leaflets. Typical products contain actives from Table 13.1, but it is again worth noting that high-temperature processing is involved and volatile and heat-degradable substances are difficult to use. The stoving process causes significant losses of flavouring and volatile materials such as menthol and essential oils. Mainly base ingredients are manufactured from sugar glucose syrup, gum arabic (acacia), gum tragacanth, pectins, agars, starches and actives colours and flavours. Lozenges and paste products [22] are useful for slow actives release with some containing highly volatile materials such as ether and chloroform, which are added to the paste in much the same way as essential oil flavourings. An advantage of this manufacturing system is that non-water-soluble therapeutic actives can be utilised. Powders can be mixed proportionately into the pastes prior to extrusion/forming. Similarly, tablets of simpler therapeutic actives and panned goods are also on the market. Tablets are made by wet granulation, drying and tableting or from directly compressible mixtures, and contain salts, actives and in some cases low and high dosage levels of mineral water salts. Some sugarless (sorbitol) direct-compression tablets are available carrying up to 50 mg of some powder-form actives.

13.11.1   Chewing gum

Regular chewing gum manufacturing is documented in Refs 23–28.

Actives such as nicotine or fluorides are usually added in a strictly defined sequence in the gum mixer at the appropriate phase, usually just before solid sweetener addition or during the same towards the end of the mixing operation before flavouring and colouring (if required). The gum is formed into strips on typical Gimple machines, Togum or similar for rolling and scoring then packaging or pellet-sugar coating by panning for 'Chiclet'-type products. Chunk gums are extruded in rope form, conditioned continuously and cut and wrapped. WLS, G.D. and Rose Theegarten are typical manufacturers who can produce fully automated lines.

Sugarless gums usually require much more careful handling, and the proportioning of crystallising and anticrystallising phase ingredients is critical. These gums usually require a greater quantity of gum base and have different textural and elasticity properties during forming. The addition of actives is performed in a similar way to that used in regular sugared gums.

Teeth whitening, gum protection and plaque claims are made with patented usage of urea [30] and other compounds [31, 32]. The latest technology uses anhydrous gum formulations in which plasticity and softness are assured for much longer shelf-life periods than was previously possible. However, since the gums are much softer during manufacturing, significant storage in low-humidity conditions is necessary to condition the gum prior to packaging. The packaging material does not require as many protective properties, and the gums retain their soft chew. Sweetening can be enhanced using the latest approved intense sweeteners, but patented encapsulation is required to protect these materials and give good sustained release which is related to perceived flavour longevity. Encapsulation of the actives within the gum base during mixing can be problematical when sustained release is required during the chew out.

13.12 Packaging

Many styles of confectionery packages are noted in the marketplace from standard stickpacks in foil/paper/waxed laminates to highly specialised protectives laminates. Products are also twist-wrapped in waxed paper, polypropylene and coated cellophane or heat-sealed in foil or laminated plastics, forming pillow packs. Some dry products such as gums, pastilles or tablets, providing the protection required is attained, are packaged without further individual wrappings into either waxed or laminated coated paper bags formed into bags at the same time as a final cardboard carton is erected during the packaging operation. Some products have a useful 'Clic'-lock resealable lid device. Foil or extruded (PVDC) materials are also used for the bags. Some sugarless lozenges can be packed loose in lined cartons without any form of bag, but some formulations may be very hygroscopic.

Alternatively, twist-wrapped or pillow-packed products can be packed in flexible film bags in various materials and laminations, where the product quantity has been accurately preweighed by computer-controlled weighing systems such as those by Ishida Weighpack. Many well-known form-fill machines are available to produce the bags, and another format is blister packing. Weight control to ensure the requisite number of doses if products are sold by weight is essential to meet regulatory requirements.

13.13 Concluding remarks

In all cases of medicated confectionery manufacturing, pharmaceutical manufacturing philosophy is a prerequisite. The registration authorities usually require full documentation to be provided in product licence applications when any medicinal claim is made. In Europe it is not permitted to make medicinal claims for foodstuffs unless a medicines licence is obtained.

All raw materials must be identified by lot on receipt, simple identification tests performed, and records kept of analytical checks performed. Actives must be identified and either proforma analytical reports must be obtained from suppliers or a full analytical compliance check must be performed. Predispensing records for actives, flavours and colours premixes must be kept to allow traceability both forwards and backwards from raw material lot to finished lot or from consumer complaint to recall requirement. Master formulae are mandatory, and batch records should be kept for all lots manufactured with sign-offs for each addition of components by responsible operators.

Production should be subdivided into lots of units of manufacturing or by time sequence such as shifts in continuous production. Lots should be defined to allow identification of product by manufacturing line, time, period and date and thus allow trace-back through all stages of documentation to raw material lots used. At packaging the final product lot number should be capable of allowing complete trace-back of the lot history, including all analytical control checks performed on the product.

A positive release from quality assurance is also necessary. The complete QA system should involve the whole manufacturing system, and line operators should be responsible for their own appropriate on-line quality checks, which should be properly recorded.

For registered products the checks and controls are usually mandatory, but in the case of medicated confection manufacture it is not unreasonable to have these controls, since such products are ingested like medicines although regulated as foodstuffs. Proper quality assurance techniques should be used, since the liability for the products' safety and efficiency rests primarily with the manufacturer. A capable laboratory service is necessary to confirm product conformity to specification, and usually gas–liquid chromatography (GLC), high-performance liquid chromatography (HPLC) and specialized atomic absorption/UV spectrophotometry techniques are required to measure accurately actives in medicated sugar confectionery. Weight uniformity checks and actives content uniformity checks are normally performed using the published pharmaceutical methods.

Factories should operate good hygiene standards, well-maintained and supported by professionally qualified staff. Medicated confectionery products containing certain 'actives' may only be sold in pharmacies, and may require the presence of a pharmacist in the manufacturing operation for the dispensing and control of certain actives materials. Regulatory authorities usually demand a qualified quality assurance manager to be responsible for the signed release of medicated products after a thorough review of documentation for each manufactured lot.

References

1. L. Lachman, H.A. Lieberman and G. Richardson, Medicated Candies, *Drug and Cosmetic Industry*, **99** (1, 2, 3) (1966).
2. R. Lees and B. Jackson, *Sugar Confectionery and Chocolate Manufacture*, pp. 22, 164–5, Leonard Hill Books (Blackie & Son Ltd), Glasgow (1973).
3. A. Meiners, K. Kreiten and H. Joike, *Silesia Confiserie*, Manual no. 3, vol. 1/1, pp. 143–4 (1983).
4. *Ibid.* p. 167.
5. *Ibid.* pp. 178–82.
6. *Ibid.* pp. 194–7.
7. *Ibid.* p. 204.
8. C.J. Knewstubb and B.T. Henry, *Food Technology International*, Sterling Publications Ltd (1988).
9. B. Minifie, *Chocolate, Cocoa and Confectionery*, 2nd edn, AVI Publishing Company Inc., Westport, Connecticut (1980).
10. A. Meiners, K. Kreiten and H. Joike, *Silesia Confiserie*, Manual no. 3, vol. 1/1 (1983), p. 184.
11. *Ibid.* pp. 166, 180–1, 185–6.
12. *Ibid.* pp. 240–1, 244–5, 248–9, 250–3.
13. *Ibid.* pp. 257–9.
14. *Ibid.* pp. 226–9.
15. Nuova Euromec, PO Box 24057, Martinengo (BG) Italy, sales literature – Apollo centre-filling line brochure (1988).
16. A. Meiners, K. Kreiter and H. Joike, *Silesia Confiserie*, Manual no. 3, vol. 1/1 (1983), pp. 248–9.
17. Bush Boake Allen, Blackhorse Lane, London E17 SQP, UK, *Products for the Confectionery Industry* (sales brochure), medicated confectionery, pp. 57–61 (1988).
18. Federal Register vol. 52, no. 155, Aug. 12, 1987, FDA 21 CFR Part 341, Final monograph for OTC Antitussive Drug Products, Federal Register vol. 53, no. 17, Jan 27, 1988, FDA 21 CFR Part 356, Tentative final monograph Oral Health Care Drug Products for OTC Human use.
19. A. Morley, J. Blenkinsopp, J.R. Nicholls and J.L. Nicholle, Treating coughs. 1. Case studies in community pharmacy, *The Pharmaceutical Journal*, January 4 (1986).
20. R. Lees and B. Jackson, *Sugar Confectionery and Chocolate Manufacture*, Chapter 12, pp. 226–8, Leonard Hill Books (Blackie & Son Ltd), Glasgow (1973).
21. A. Meiners, K. Kreiten and H. Joike, *Silesia Confiserie*, Manual no. 3, vol. 2 (1983).
22. R. Lees and B. Jackson, *Sugar Confectionery and Chocolate Manufacture*, Chapter 14, pp. 286–95, Leonard Hill Books (Blackie & Son Ltd), Glasgow (1973).
23. *Ibid.*, Chapter 16, pp. 332–7.
24. A. Meiners, K. Kreiten and H. Joike, *Silesia Confiserie*, Manual no. 3, vol. 2, pp. 153–62 and 421–43.
25. Anon., The manufacture of chewing gum and bubble gum, *Confectionery Manufacturing Marketing*, May pp. 4–6, June, pp. 24–5, 28 (1988).
26. D. Fritz, a discussion and review of longer lasting flavours in chewing gums, Dragoco Report Flavouring Information Service **4** (1987).
27. R.K. Heinz, New taste sensations for chewing gum fans—extrusion technology for chewing gum production, *Int. Food Marketing and Technology*, March, pp. 6, 8, 9–11 (1988).
28. M. Muller, Production and flavouring of sucrose and sugar substitute chewing gums, *Confectionery Manufacturing and Marketing*, July/Aug, pp. 7, 9, 10, 12, 13, 14, 18 (1981).
29. F. Voirol, The evolution of chewing gum, xylitol and prevention of dental caries, Xyrofin Ltd, Basle.
30. G.B. Patent, GB 2174 902, a solid oral anticarciogenic chewing gum and lozenge.
31. USA Patent 619079 (June 11, 1984) and UK Patent GB 2179 536, improvement in the flavour of zinc supplements for oral use; GB Patent 2181 646, medicated chewing gum.
32. UK Patent 2180 157, anticalculus oral composition.

14 Centers, fondants, marzipan and crystallized confectionery

M.S. JEFFERY

14.1 Introduction

This chapter discusses the formulation, manufacture, use and quality control of those sugar confections which contain sugar crystals dispersed through the syrup phase. These include fondants, cremes, fudges and marzipan, particularly as used for the center of chocolate-coated confections.

The simplest and earliest confection used by man was honey, dating back over 3000 years ago. Honey is basically a syrup of dextrose, fructose and sugar dissolved in water, and has a 'straw'-like color and characteristic flavor. Normally honey is a clear liquid, but sometimes, when it is kept for some time, crystals appear in it, producing an opaque, pasty material. The crystals are those of dextrose, which has a lower solubility than sugar and often separates from the syrup.

This pasty, crystallized honey, familiar to ancient man, was the first 'fondant' used by him to sweeten his life. It is a 'dextrose fondant', whereas most of the fondants we use today are based on sucrose (or sugar). Nevertheless it has similar textural and physical properties to the sugar fondants.

Fondant is the simplest of crystallized sugar confections, consisting of sugar crystals in a saturated solution of sugar and other carbohydrates. Normally there is approximately 50–60% sugar crystals present in its structure mixed into the 40–50% of syrup. When other things are added to this simple confection, such as egg whip, color and flavor, another type of confection, a creme, is produced. Cremes are used extensively in boxed chocolates, and their manufacture and use are explained later.

A further complication is to add milk solids to the confection. During cooking characteristic flavors are produced by the Maillard reaction, as the sugar and milk protein react together to give caramel flavors. When this material does not crystallize, the resulting confection is called a caramel or toffee, but when sugar crystals appear in the syrup phase, a fudge is the result.

The chemistry of these confections becomes increasingly complex as more materials are added to the syrup phase. However, the physical properties have several things in common and are dependent on similar parameters such as composition of the syrup phase, its moisture content and the size distribution of the sugar crystals dispersed through the syrup. Each of these will be examined later.

14.2 Recipes

14.2.1 *Fondants*

The recipe of fondants is made up of three main elements:

(1) Sucrose which can come from sugar cane or sugar beet.
(2) Other carbohydrates: Corn syrup (or 'glucose') is most often used together with invert sugar.
(3) Water.

The percentages of these ingredients can be varied to give different taste and texture characteristics, depending on the use of the fondant. These can range from a high-sugar fondant of composition 80% sugar, 7.6% corn syrup solids, 12.4% water, to a low-sugar fondant of composition 57.5% sugar, 30% Glucose solids, 12.5% water.

The list of possible variations is endless because the properties depend also on the type of glucose solids, and whether they are low-DE (dextrose equivalent), high-DE, high in maltose, or high in dextrose, etc.

Other ingredients can also be added to alter the characteristics of the fondant, including:

Invert sugar solids
Glycerol
Sorbitol } All to lower the equilibrium relative humidity (ERH) of the fondant

Agar
Pectin
Gelatin
Carboxymethylcellulose } To control crystal size and texture

So the 'simple' confection, fondant, can be complex and give infinite variety.

However, there are several fundamental principles which should be taken into account in fondant formulations. Firstly, a fondant made of sugar alone will not keep because the solubility of sugar in water at 68°F (20°C) is only 67.7% and the water activity or ERH of this syrup is too high for good microbial stability. Yeasts and molds can be active in a syrup of this type, so that an all-sugar fondant is impractical.

It can be made practical by inverting some of the sugar by using either tartaric acid inversion or the enzyme invertase. Both of these methods have been used to convert a proportion of the sugar into dextrose and fructose, thereby increasing the concentration of sugars in the syrup phase and lowering its water activity.

Normally other sugars such as corn syrup are added to the recipe to increase the concentration of the syrup phase in a more controllable way. This ensures good shelf life, not only by eliminating microbial problems but also by minimizing the loss of moisture in the final confection. For the same reason humectants such as glycerol or sorbitol are sometimes added, especially when high water contents are required, for instance in a soft fondant center for a chocolate-coated unit. Addition of 1–2% glycerol would be normal, but this should generally be avoided if possible because of the laxative effects which can limit consumption.

14.2.2   Cremes

One of the main uses of fondant is in the manufacture of confectionery cremes, widely used for molding into centers for chocolate-coated boxed chocolates. Just as the 'simple' fondant can have an infinite number of recipes, so also can cremes. However, there are some common elements, in that cremes normally consist of three main ingredients:

(1) Fondant.
(2) Frappé or egg whip.
(3) Thinning or 'Bob' syrup.

together with color and flavor as desired.

The proportions of each of these elements can be varied to provide a spectrum of taste and texture sensations. This, coupled to the possible variations in the recipes and properties of each part, makes for a complex situation. Normally however the *fondant recipe* for molded cremes consists of three parts sugar to one part glucose solids with 12.5% water.

The *frappé* part normally consists of 1–2% dried egg albumen dissolved in a sugar, corn syrup and probably invert sugar syrup, which is then whipped with air to reduce the density from 1.3 to 0.2–0.4. This egg whip or frappé is used to give a light texture to the creme and a good white, opaque color suitable for adding color. The resulting colored creme has a bright, fresh color, pleasing to the consumer.

The *thinning* syrup or 'Bob' syrup is normally added to adjust the viscosity of the creme prior to molding, to make sure it can be deposited well without 'tailing' or producing molding defects. The recipe can be widely varied, but for simplicity can be the same as that of the fondant, except that normally the moisture content is higher, at approximately 15–20%. In certain processing applications the 'Bob' syrup can have exactly the same composition as the fondant and is used to reheat cool fondant to its depositing temperature, particularly in continuous creme-making plants using the 'Baker-Clay' process, which will be described later.

A typical deposited creme recipe is shown in Table 14.1.

Table 14.1 Recipe for orange creme

Fondant	60%	⎫
Frappé	10%	⎬ Moisture
Bob syrup	30%	⎭ content 14.0%
Color — Yellow color	⎫ As desired	
Flavor — Orange flavor	⎬	

Fondant composition
Sugar	66%
42 DE corn syrup solids	21.5%
Water	12.5%

Frappé composition
42 DE corn syrup solids	60%
Invert sugar solids	18%
Water	20%
Egg albumen	2%

Bob syrup composition
Sugar	64%
42 DE corn syrup solids	21%
Water	15%

14.2.3   *Fudge*

Fondant is also used in the manufacture of fudge. Fudge is a 'fondant' containing milk protein and fat, often butter fat, and having the characteristic flavor of caramel or toffee. The recipe of fudge can cover a wide range of textures from the hard 'snappy' texture of traditional Scottish cut 'tablet' with its very high sugar content, to the soft tender texture of chocolate-coated starch-molded units. Often an egg whip is added to give a light 'fluffy' texture similar to a soft creme. The common elements in a fudge recipe are:

(1) Sugar syrup.
(2) Sugar crystals.
(3) Milk protein.
(4) Fat—often dairy fat, but generally a hardened vegetable fat.

A typical hard fudge recipe of the 'tablet' type suitable for selling as an uncovered unit would be:

Sugar	45%
Corn syrup solids	7%
Full-cream, sweetened, condensed milk solids	40%
Water	8%
Salt and flavor as desired	

One for depositing and enrobing in chocolate would be as follows:

Sugar	35%
Corn syrup solids	12%

Full-cream, sweetened, condensed milk solids	30%
Hardened palm kernel oil	5%
Frappé solids	5%
Water	13%

Frappé recipe

63 DE glucose solids	60%
Invert sugar solids	18%
Egg albumen	2%
Water	20%

14.2.4 *Marzipan*

Marzipan is a favorite European confection and similar in some respects to the previous confections in that sugar crystals are present in its structure, giving a texture similar to a fudge. The characteristic flavor and texture of ground blanched almonds are added to give the unique confection so popular in France, Germany and Switzerland.

As with the other confections, recipes can vary over a wide spectrum from the firmer, extruded variety to a soft, tender texture found in deposited and starch-molded types.

With all of these confections it is difficult to cover recipe information adequately because the number of possible variations is limitless. However, the variables which have the greatest influence on the properties of the confections can be identified and means of controlling them outlined.

14.3 Variables affecting the properties of fondant

The key variables which affect the properties of fondant are described below.

14.3.1 *Moisture content*

The moisture content of a fondant governs its firmness: the higher the moisture content, the softer the fondant. It ranges from 10 to 15% with a norm of 12.7% and must be controlled in manufacture and in the marketplace. Poorly formulated fondants dry out with time and can become hard and 'chalky'. To avoid this the recipe must be designed to have a water activity or equilibrium relative humidity compatible with the environment in which it is to be sold or stored. It is impossible to cover all climatic conditions so that a good average has to be used which will vary from country to country or district to district. Normally an ERH of 65% is acceptable and designed for in the formulation.

14.3.2   The amount of sugar crystals present

The ratio of the amount of sugar in crystalline form to that in syrup form is also key to the properties of fondant. This is dependent largely on the *moisture content*, because the higher this is the less sugar will be crystallized and the more in solution and vice versa. However, it also depends on the presence and concentration of other carbohydrates in the syrup, such as glucose solids and invert sugar, which affect the solubility of sugar.

14.3.3   The concentration and viscosity of the syrup phase

As discussed earlier in the chapter, when sugar alone is dissolved in water it has a maximum concentration of 67.5% at 68°F (20°C). This syrup is thin in consistency as well as being unstable microbiologically. When corn syrup is added to the recipe the concentration of the syrup phase is increased, and the presence of gum-like dextrin higher sugars in the corn syrup also increases the viscosity of the syrup, changing the texture of the fondant. The thicker, low-DE glucoses with their higher dextrin contents give higher viscosity syrup, and higher DE glucoses a lower viscosity syrup, all other things being equal.

The addition of gelling agents such as agar can profoundly change the viscosity and texture of the syrup phase even more, but these are rarely used in fondants and cremes.

14.3.4   Crystal size of the sugar

The size of the sugar crystals is very important to both the texture and the rheological properties of fondant.

The human palate can detect particles above 12–15 μm in size, and anything below this tastes 'smooth'. In making fondant, crystal sizes below 15 μm are usually desired to give a smooth texture in the confection. However, often much coarser particle sizes are used to give a rougher 'sharper' texture which can be appropriate, for instance, in 'after-dinner' mints to help 'cleanse' the palate. In coarse fudge, such as tableted fudge, larger sugar crystals can be very desirable and complementary to the extreme sweetness of this high-sugar confection.

Sugar crystal size also affects the rheological properties of fondant. Because small crystals have a greater surface area than larger crystals for the same weight of sugar, the syrup in which the sugar crystals are dispersed has to 'wet' a larger surface area. Generally, the smaller the crystal size the more viscous the fondant. This will affect depositing properties to some extent, although syrup composition and moisture content have a much greater effect.

These same variables affect the properties of the other confections, but are more complicated as other things are added. So that with cremes the addition of egg albumen and air considerably changes the texture and mouthfeel of the confection. Similarly, milk protein and fat in fudge have a profound effect on taste and properties.

14.4   Basic steps in making the confections

This book is not designed to describe in detail manufacturing methods and plant, but to concentrate on *principles* of making confectionery. The basic steps or unit operations in making each of these confections are as follows:

14.4.1   *Fondant*

Fondant is made by:

(1) *Dissolving.* The sugar is dissolved in water and then the other materials such as corn syrup or invert sugar are mixed in. This produces a syrup of approximately 25% water and 75% dissolved solids.

(2) *Boiling.* The syrup is then boiled to a controlled temperature to give a material with a known moisture content. Under atmospheric boiling a normal fondant syrup will boil at 240°F (115°C), for a moisture content of 12.5%. However, this will depend on syrup composition to some extent and on atmospheric pressure. The higher the atmospheric pressure, the higher the boiling point for a given moisture content.

(3) *Cooling.* The supersaturated syrup is then cooled to a controlled temperature before crystallization of the syrup is induced. For fine (< 15 μm) crystals the syrup is cooled to 110–115°F (43–46°C) before mixing, and for coarser crystals temperatures of 170–190°F (77–88°C) can be used.

Normally the syrup is not mixed when being cooled, particularly on older fondant-making plant. With modern plant, control of mixing speed or 'shear rate' and cooling rate is used efficiently to crystallize the syrup to the required particle size distribution.

(4) *Mixing/crystallizing.* The next basic step is crystallizing by mixing or 'beating'. This induces the sugar to crystallize from the syrup, leaving the syrup saturated with sugar crystals dispersed through it.

The finished fondant is then ready for use in creme or for subsequent processing. Often it is stored in lidded pans in a store at 100°F to allow it to 'mature' before use. During storage small unstable crystals of sugar redissolve and then crystallize again on the large crystals, so that generally crystal sizes increase during this period. *If no moisture* is lost during storage, the fondant becomes more fluid as sugar crystal surface area becomes less. However, often moisture is lost and the stored fondant becomes thicker and more difficult to

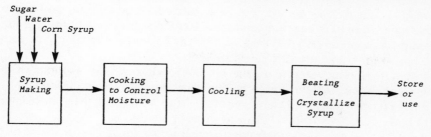

Figure 14.1 Unit operations in fondant making.

handle, as a dry 'crust' is formed. On modern continuous equipment this is avoided, as the fondant passes from making straight through to use.

A diagram showing these operations is shown in Figure 14.1.

14.4.2 Creme making

Creme making involves bringing together the three basic materials which make up the finished product, fondant, frappé and thinning (or 'Bob' syrup).

The fondant process is as outlines in section 14.4.1.

14.4.2.1 Frappé. The traditional method for making frappé involves:

(1) Dissolving powdered (spray-dried) egg albumen in water, normally using one part albumen to two parts of water.

(2) Dissolving sugar in water and mixing in corn syrup and invert sugar and cooking. Often sugar is not used in the recipe so it is only necessary to mix and cook the corn syrup and invert to the correct temperature to control moisture content (240°F, 115°C to 245°F, 118°C). The syrup is then cooled to 170–180°F (76–82°C).

(3) The egg albumen solution and syrup are mixed together and should be held at 170°F (76°C) for 10 min to pasteurize the solution, particularly to kill pathogens such as salmonella which can be present in albumen.

(4) The egg solution is then 'beaten' with air to reduce its density from 1.2–1.3 down to 0.3–0.4.

The resulting egg whip or frappé is then ready to be mixed with the fondant.

14.4.2.2 Thinning or 'Bob' syrup. The thinning or 'Bob' syrup is made simply by dissolving sugar in water, adding corn syrup and invert sugar, and cooking the mix to a controlled temperature, to give a controlled moisture content. This may be as high as 20% but is generally 13–14%. This material is then ready to mix with the other two bases.

14.4.2.3   *Final creme process.* For basic batch operation, the fondant has to be heated from its storage temperature of 100°F (38°C) to its depositing or use temperature of 160–190°F (71–88°C). This can be done in a mixing kettle with a hot-water or low-pressure steam jacket.

A more efficient way is to use the 'hot Bob' or 'Baker–Clay' method, which simply uses the 'Bob' syrup at its boiling temperature to reheat the fondant by mixing the two together. Often some of the syrup is held back to be added later to make a final viscosity adjustment prior to depositing.

The final stage is to add the frappé together with color and flavor, and to mix these into the fondant with minimum mixing to avoid deaeration of the whipped material and loss of flavor volatiles.

The finished creme should be at its depositing temperature of 160–190°F, which is crucial to its setting rate in the molding operation, and at the correct viscosity for good tail-free depositing.

Figure 14.2 shows a diagram of these operations.

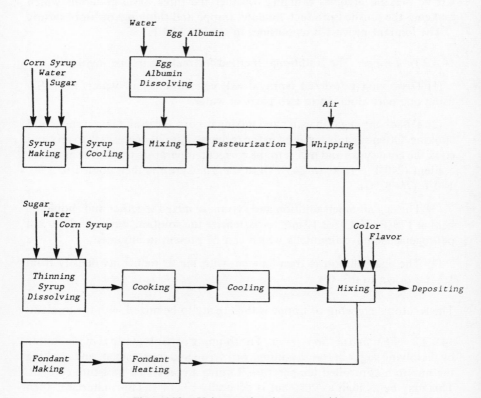

Figure 14.2   Unit operations in creme making.

14.4.3 Fudge making

Fudge making depends to some extent on the type of milk used in the recipe. If full-cream, sweetened, condensed milk is used or any liquid milk concentrate, then no reconstitution of the milk is required. If dry milk solids are used, such as skimmed-milk powder, then this must be *rehydrated* before being used in the recipe.

Any added fat such as butter oil or hardened palm kernel oil has to be emulsified into the milk syrup to avoid fat separation later, and normally an emulsifying agent such as glycerol monostearate (GMS) or lecithin is added to produce a stable emulsion.

The basic steps are as follows:

(1) *Emulsified milk preparation.* For sweetened condensed milk, fat is added together with GMS and then mixed with a high-shear mixer to emulsify the fat into the syrup. When milk powder is used it is dispersed in water at 120–140°F with a high-shear mixer, and fat with GMS is added to complete the emulsion.

(2) *Syrup preparation.* Sugar is dissolved in water in the normal way, and corn syrup or other sugars added to it to form the syrup. The emulsified milk is then added to this syrup and mixed well with it.

(3) *Cooking.* The mix of milk and syrup is then boiled to a controlled temperature to reduce the moisture content to the required level, depending on the type of fudge being made. This can range from 8 to 15%, from hard, tableted fudge to soft, chocolate-coated fudge.

During this cooking process, Maillard reactions takes place between the milk protein and reducing sugars in the syrup to give the characteristic 'caramel' flavor. The amount of flavor development depends on the type of cooker used and the length of cooking.

In batch kettles, sufficient flavor development normally takes place during the half-hour cooking process. In modern continuous cookers, residence times are much shorter and a second stage of caramelization is needed to develop sufficient flavor. The cooked syrup is held at its boiling temperature for 5–15 min to develop flavor in a 'caramelization' stage.

Another approach to flavor development is to 'precaramelize' the milk syrup by cooking it *under pressure* to raise its temperature above its boiling point *without* moisture loss. The caramelization reactions go faster at these higher temperatures and higher moisture contents, so that a more efficient continuous operation can be designed. In this, caramelization time can be as little as 30 s to reduce the amount of material held in the process. The method also gives better control of flavor development.

(4) *Cooling and crystallization.* The cooling and crystallization stage is similar to fondant in that sugar crystal size has to be controlled to avoid coarse 'sandy' textures, unless these are required.

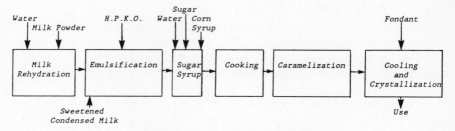

Figure 14.3　Unit operations in fudge making.

Usually fondant is added to the cooked material to provide fine sugar 'seeds' to control the crystal size in the finished fudge. The resulting material is then ready for sheeting, extrusion or depositing.

Figure 14.3 shows these operations.

14.4.4 *Marzipan*

There are a number of ways of producing marzipan centers to get the texture suitable for extrusion, sheeting or depositing. The common elements are:

(1) Producing a paste of blanched almonds, sometimes with the addition of cheaper apricot kernels. This involves grinding the kernels to release the oil and break down the fibrous structure with minimum loss of flavor volatiles.

(2) Making a sugar, corn syrup and probably invert sugar syrup, to a controlled moisture content.

(3) Mixing the syrup and almond paste together and then cooling and crystallizing the mix to produce controlled sugar crystals. Often, as with fudge, fondant is added to help control sugar crystal size.

Variations on this involve mixing granular sugar, corn syrup and invert with the almond paste and then refining it with a three- or five-roll refiner, as used with chocolate, to give the required sugar crystal size.

A key process is to deactivate enzymes and to pasteurize the almonds by proper blanching. Often steam treatment is best for this to raise the temperature of the nuts to 200–212°F (93–100°C) without excessive moisture pick-up. Hot-water blanching is also used effectively but can lead to excessive moisture pick-up by the nuts and loss of flavor.

As with fondant, the sugar solids in the syrup phase must give the syrup a water activity of no more than 0.70 for good stability.

Often antimold agents, such as sorbic acid, are added to improve stability,

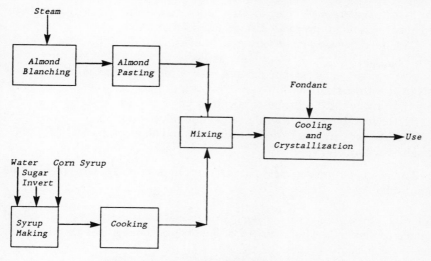

Figure 14.4 Unit operations in marzipan making.

but this is not recommended. Proper blanching and recipe control is preferred to give good stability.

A summary of the unit operations is shown in Figure 14.4.

14.5 Uses of fondant, cremes, fudges and marzipan

14.5.1 *Uses of fondant*

The main uses for fondant in confectionery are described below.

14.5.1.1 *In molded fondants.* The most popular type of molded fondant confections are crystallized fondants. These are often found in 'after-dinner' mints with the 'sparkling' appearance and clean refreshing taste they give. Crystallized fondants with fruit flavors and pastel colors are also found in boxed confections, and when half-covered with chocolate add visual interest to a boxed chocolate assortment.

'Crystallization' of the surface of the fondant is carried out by carefully immersing the molded fondants in a *supersaturated* solution of sugar in water and then leaving the units for 12 h. The sugar crystallizes from the solution, using the sugar crystals in the surface of the fondant as 'seed'. These surface crystals grow in size to give a strong 'skin' of large (100 μm plus) crystals which protect the confection from moisture loss, as well as enhancing the appearance.

The basic steps in crystallization are as follows:

(1) Dissolve sugar in water and cook to $74 \pm 2\%$ soluble solids, taking care

to avoid sugar crystals from splashes and around the rim of the kettle by frequent washing down with a small quantity of water.

(2) Cool the syrup *carefully* in a pan, avoiding crystallization of the syrup, to 90°F (32°C).

(3) Carefully immerse the fondants, on a wire tray, in the syrup, and cover the pan with a damp cloth to minimize evaporation.

(4) Leave for 12 h at room temperature, 70°F (21°C).

(5) Remove the units from the syrup and allow to drain.

(6) Transfer the units to a clean wire tray and allow to dry at 70°F (21°C), before packing.

Today semiautomated means of carrying out this operation on a large scale are available.

14.5.1.2 *In molded cream centers.*

Fondant is used extensively in molded creme centers of a whole variety of flavors and colors, and as centers for molded chocolate articles.

Creme centers can be molded by three main methods.

(1) Molding in starch impressions.

(2) Molding in rigid metal or plastic molds, by 'starchless' methods.

(3) As a center for a chocolate-molded article made by 'shell' techniques, or by 'single-shot' depositing.

14.5.1.3 *Molding in starch.*

The basic process is outlined in Figure 14.5 and involves:

Making impressions in starch.
Depositing the creme at 160–190°F (71–88°C) into the impressions.
Allowing the creme to cool and set with some drying on the surface.
Sieving the cremes from the starch.
Removing surface starch by air jets.
Enrobing the centers in chocolate.

Starch molding is a versatile but dusty method of molding. Important considerations are the moisture content of the starch, normally 5–7% for cremes, the cleanliness of the starch and impression board, and air conditions in the filled-board storage room.

The cremes set or firm up in the starch by:

(1) *Sugar crystallizing from the syrup phase:* The sugar crystals form 'bridges' between the creme crystals, giving firmness to the creme. It is important to understand that the rate at which the sugar crystallizes depends on the creme recipe, the depositing temperature, the cooling rate and the crystal size of the creme. The higher the sugar content in the recipe, the greater the setting rate, because other sugars such as corn syrup slow down sugar

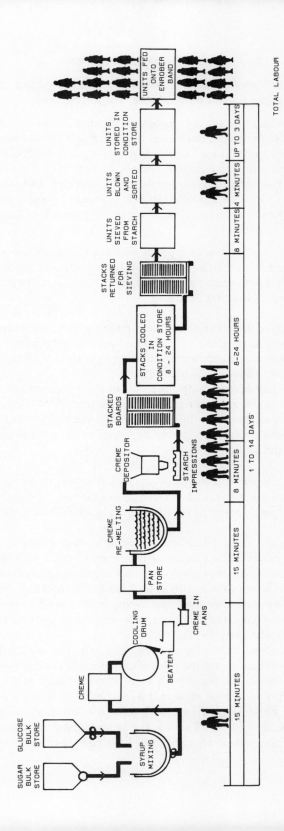

Figure 14.5 Creme making—old method.

crystallization. The higher the *depositing temperature*, the greater the super-saturation of the syrup phase and the higher the setting rate.

(2) *Cooling.* Cooling rate is very important, because if cold-air conditions are used, the cremes get cold quickly, but the syrup gets too *viscous* at these cold temperatures to crystallize, so that overcooling can be detrimental to rapid setting. The cooling rate depends on the cooling air temperature and flow rate and on the depositing temperature of the creme, and also on the starch temperature. Optimum cooling rate is important to good creme setting to allow proper crystallization and yet cool the center to enrobing temperature (75°F, 24°C to 80°F, 27°C).

(3) *Drying.* Drying of the center depends on the initial moisture content of the starch, the initial moisture content of the confection, its ERH, the temperature of the starch when the creme is deposited into it, the cooling air conditions, and finally the time in starch.

By optimizing each of these variables it is commercially viable to reduce the setting time of creme in starch to 1 h compared with the normal 8–12 h. This can make starch molding a much more efficient operation with better space utilization and more uniform product quality.

'Starchless' molding of cremes optimizes all of these parameters to enable the confections to set in 5–10 min and allow continuous 'straight-through' operation from raw materials to finished chocolate-coated cremes in 35 min. This is a very efficient operation, giving high-quality cremes automatically. Details can be found in Ref. 1.

14.5.1.4 *Centers for chocolate-molded articles.* Cremes make good, soft centers for molded chocolate, and very large brands use them in this way. Because the centers are contained in a shell or 'skin' of chocolate, they can be soft and 'runny'.

They are produced on a traditional 'chocolate shell' plant in which a chocolate 'film' is produced in a metal or plastic mold, filled with the creme, and then 'backed off' with chocolate, with suitable cooling between stages.

A more compact way of doing this is to deposit the chocolate and creme together through concentric nozzles, and timing each deposit to envelop the creme with chocolate. This is called 'single-shot' depositing and was developed by Cadbury Ltd in the early 1930s.

There are limitations in doing this, especially in the consistency and temperature of the creme and in the ratio of creme to chocolate, normally no higher than 40% creme, compared with shell-produced units at 50–55%.

Creme centers have also been produced by extrusion methods, particularly in the USA. Here a high-sugar creme, with sufficient 'stand-up' properties, is extruded mechanically and cut off with a wire to form small units. Invertase is included in the recipe, so that after the units have been covered by chocolate some of the sugar in the creme is inverted, increasing the sugar solids in the syrup phase and producing a soft creme. The variable inversion which can take place often leads to quality problems with this method of manufacture.

14.5.2 Uses of fudges and marzipan

Both of these confections are used for centers of chocolate-coated units as well as being eaten without coating.

They lend themselves to sheeting and cutting into units, or to extrusion into 'ropes' followed by cutting, and are often used in combination with other confection such as nougat or caramel, particularly in bar goods.

They can also be deposited into starch or starchless molds, or into chocolate shells.

14.6 Quality control in fondant cremes, fudges and marzipan

The critical quality parameters in these confections are described below.

14.6.1 Moisture content

The range of moisture content is approximately 8.0–15% and must be controlled by proper process control in the plant, and by auditing with analytical measurement, preferably 'on-line', to give operators the tools to measure this critical parameter.

There are three methods of measuring moisture content.

14.6.1.1 *Drying.* This is a direct method and involves weighing a small piece of the confection (5–10 g) and then drying it in a hot air, infrared or microwave oven to constant weight to give the difference and hence the moisture content. Short drying times and microprocessors have made this suitable for 'on-line' control because it is largely automated and certainly 'operator-friendly'.

14.6.1.2 *Chemical analysis.* The Karl Fisher method is standard for the industry, and gives accurate measurement ($\pm 0.1\%$) of moisture content, as long as the sample is properly dispersed in the titration medium. It is a *laboratory-based* method and needs laboratory training, so is more suitable for quality assurance and not 'on-line' control.

14.6.1.3 *'Near-infrared' techniques.* Instruments using near-infrared stimulation of a sample of the confection can be *calibrated* to measure moisture content very quickly and are increasingly being used 'on-line' to do so. Although they are normally a 'batch' instrument directed at a discrete sample of the confection, versions have been developed to give a continuous read-out of moisture content of a stream of the confection, e.g. an extruded rope. This is often used 'on-line' and can be used to *control* moisture content directly. The instrument must be calibrated *for the particular confection*, using Karl Fisher or drying methods.

14.6.2 *Soluble solids of the syrup phase*

Because the stability of the confection is dependent on having sufficient sugar solids in the syrup phase (no less than 75%), this is measured. It is done by pressing out a syrup sample from the confection and measuring its soluble solids on a sugar refractometer [2].

14.6.3 *Sugar crystal size*

As explained earlier, sugar crystal size distribution is critical to good taste and texture in these confections. It can be measured by:

14.6.3.1 *Optical polarizing microscope.* This is used by most companies and involves dispersing a small simple of the confection in an inert medium such as

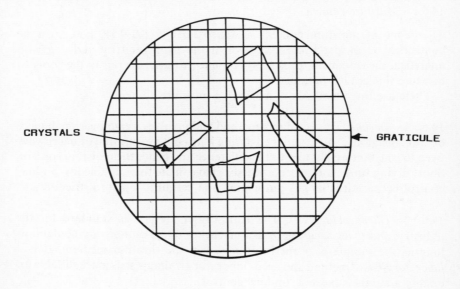

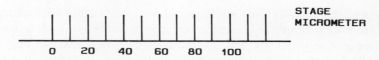

Figure 14.6 Particle size measurement—optical microscopy.

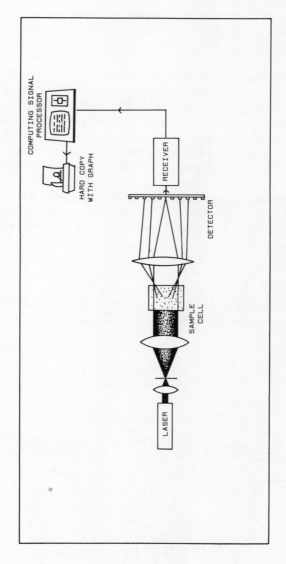

Figure 14.7 Light-scattering principle.

mineral oil and viewing it through a microscope fitted with a polarized light source and a graduated grid for measurement of particle size (see Figure 14.6). An estimate is made of the maximum particle size and average particle size.

Newer techniques involve the use of a computerized image analyzer, where the microscope image is fed to a computer which then automatically measures size distribution.

14.6.3.2   *Laser scattering method.* A low-power laser illuminates a sample cell containing a sample of the confection which has been dispersed in a medium of sugar-saturated isopropanol. The light scattered by the sugar crystals is focused onto a detector, which then measures particle size distribution accurately and automatically. The principle is shown in Figure 14.7, and a typical read-out is in Figure 14.8. This sophisticated method is generally laboratory-based and used in quality auditing.

14.6.3.3   *Electron microscopy.* The electron microscope can be used to give an image of crystals in fondant or other confections without disturbing its structure. This is more useful in development work on new processes than as a quality auditing tool.

14.6.4   *Fat content*

For fudges and marzipan fat content is important and can be measured analytically by solvent extraction in the Soxlet apparatus, essentially

```
| USER EXPERIMENTAL AND SAMPLE DETAILS                                          |
|-------------------------------------------------------------------------------|
| SAMPLED 3/2                                                                   |
| TESTED 4/20                                                                   |
| 2ND SHIFT 9:15 PM                                                             |
| 7 WEEK READING                                                                |
|-------------------------------------------------------------------------------|
|   RESULTS                                                                     |
|-------------------------------------------------------------------------------|
| RUN NUMBER= 22          TIME=03-16-10          LOG DIFFERENCE= 2.88           |
|-------------------------------------------------------------------------------|
| SAMPLE % VOLUME CONCENTRATION= 0.0241          BEAM OBSCURATION= 0.46         |
|-------------------------------------------------------------------------------|
|     SIZE      WEIGHT  |   WEIGHT IN BAND            |    LIGHT ENERGY          |
|   MICRONS     % UNDER |     MICRONS          %      | CALCULATED   MEASURED   |
|     188.0     100.0   |                             |                         |
|      87.2      99.9   |   188.0-    87.2     0.1    |    380         371      |
|      53.5      96.3   |    87.2-    53.5     3.6    |    630         628      |
|      37.6      84.9   |    53.5-    37.6    11.4    |    986         905      |
|      28.1      67.4   |    37.6-    28.1    17.4    |   1205        1203      |
|      21.5      45.9   |    28.1-    21.5    21.6    |   1545        1540      |
|      16.7      29.9   |    21.5-    16.7    15.9    |   1836        1836      |
|      13.0      19.9   |    16.7-    13.0    10.0    |   2040        2029      |
|      10.1      11.7   |    13.0-    10.1     8.2    |   2047        2047      |
|       7.9       7.5   |    10.1-     7.9     4.1    |   1943        1942      |
|       6.2       4.3   |     7.9-     6.2     3.3    |   1832        1814      |
|       4.8       2.9   |     6.2-     4.8     1.3    |   1670        1681      |
|       3.8       1.9   |     4.8-     3.8     1.1    |   1529        1518      |
|       3.0       0.3   |     3.8-     3.0     1.5    |   1463        1461      |
|       2.4       0.1   |     3.0-     2.4     0.3    |   1435        1432      |
|       1.9       0.0   |     2.4-     1.9     0.0    |   1469        1468      |
```

Figure 14.8   Read-out from a Malvern 3600 E type particle sizer. 90th percentile—44.7 microns, 50th percentile—22.8 microns, 10th percentile—9.2 microns.

laboratory-based, or by indirect methods. Indirect methods use near-infrared scanning as for moisture content calibrated by extraction techniques.

Nuclear magnetic resonance (NMR) instruments can be calibrated to give very rapid fat contents, and can be used 'on-line'.

14.6.5 *Density*

The density of the confections, particularly for 'fluffy' cremes or fudge, is important.

Normally this is measured on-line by weighing a known volume in a 'density cup'. It can also be measured in the finished confection by immersing a known weight of the confection in an inert liquid such as mineral oil and measuring the volume by displacement, and hence the density.

Other quality parameters, such as microbiological safety, taste, etc., are common to all confections in their importance and are not specific to these crystallized confections.

14.7 Conclusion

Fondants, cremes, fudges and marzipan have two things in common: they each contain *syrup* and each have sugar crystals dispersed through this syrup. The properties are largely governed by these two elements, and their control is crucial to quality and consumer acceptance. This chapter has sought to explain how this is done and to explain the influencing factors which are involved, so that recipe formulation and manufacturing techniques can be optimized for efficient operation.

Modern, high-output operation particularly requires this knowledge to convert the older, more 'forgiving' batch operations to more critical but controllable continuous operations.

References

1. M.S. Jeffery, Starchless moulding of confectionery centers, *Confectionery Production*, April (1969).
2. B.W. Minifie, *Chocolate, Cocoa and Confectionery Science and Technology* 1st edn., p. 356.

15 Countlines and cereal bars

P. MURPHY

15.1 Introduction

The origin of the term countline is somewhat obscure. It describes a category of confectionery products which are sold as individually wrapped units intended primarily for single-person consumption. In traditional confectioners, tobacconists and newsagents they are displayed and sold from the counter unit adjacent to the till. Their form is generally rectangular, although irregular, and they can mostly be held in one hand to eat. They consist mainly of sugar confectionery, cereal or biscuit centres covered in chocolate and range in eating characteristics from hunger-satisfying to light and indulgent. Fruit-based countlines such as fruit chew bars or fruit leathers (mainly sold in the USA) offer non-chocolate alternatives, and there are also some notable all-chocolate countlines available.

Most countlines are multicomponent and can be fairly complex in their make-up. As such, great care needs to be taken in the combination of the various component parts to ensure that they complement each other in texture, flavour and their physical behaviour, particularly equilibrium relative humidity (ERH).

This is the fastest-growing sector of the confectionery market, which has been helped by the recent 'snacking' trend, and countlines are frequently eaten as meal substitutes, particularly by teenagers. As such they are competing with the more conventional snack meals such as sandwiches, beefburgers, etc.

Cereal bars are a particular category of countlines and are classified in marketing terms into their own sector. They are presented in the conventional countline format and size and are characterised by consisting predominantly of cereals, nuts and fruit. Over the years cereal bars have evolved from the original hard and crunchy, to soft and chewy and finally to chocolate-covered soft and chewy products which closely resemble standard chocolate countlines. Consumption and availability have grown over the last 10 years. Previously they could only be purchased in specialist health shops, but today they are widely distributed in supermarkets and all major confectionery outlets. They have gained an acceptance in the consumer's eyes as being 'better for you' and good in nutritional terms. In reality, apart from the contribution of a small amount of dietary fibre, they offer little more (or less) than most chocolate countlines!

This chapter will look at the major component materials that are used in countlines and cereal bars and the manufacturing processes used for forming the products. Wafer- or biscuit-centred products are not included in this discussion.

15.2 Countline components

The components that have been used in countline products are many and varied and help to give the range of textures and flavours that give them their broad appeal. Table 15.1 gives a list of the components which have been used in countlines, although it is by no means exhaustive. It is interesting to note how a few materials appear regularly in the most successful products on the market.

15.2.1 *Chocolate*

The most common and popular type of chocolate for countline products is milk chocolate. It plays an important and dominant part in the eating sensation and generally makes up 30–50% of the products by weight. The viscosity is important for the control of weight on enrobing, although the firmness is not as critical as for moulded blocks, especially if there are cereals or nuts in the centre.

Recipes, methods of manufacture and handling techniques are given in detail in Ref. 1.

15.2.2 *Caramel*

Caramel is an integral part of many countlines, providing chew, moistness and flavour in the overall product. It may be present as a top layer, on top of nougat for example, as a sandwich between two layers of granola, or as a complete cover for a biscuit or extruded centre. Caramel may also act as a

Table 15.1 Countline components

Chocolate	Caramel
Nougat	Granola
Fudge	Marshmallow
Cereals	Fruit paste
Coconut paste	Biscuit
Wafer	Nuts
Truffle	Praline
Marzipan	Jelly

Table 15.2 Typical caramel recipe (parts by weight)

Ingredient	Caramel strips	Caramel casing
Glucose syrup (medium-DE)	100	200
Refined cane or beet sugar	60	68
Brown sugar		60
Hardened palm kernel oil	15	80
Egg frappé		
Butter		
Condensed milk, full-cream, sweetened		180
Condensed milk, skimmed	12	
Condensed whey	3	
Gelatin solution 140 Bloom (50:50)	5	
Salt	1	3
Peppermint oil	0.25	
Spearmint oil		
Vanillin crystals	0.02	0.02
Colouring		
Lecithin	0.5	
Boiling temperature	129°C (265°F)	125°C (257°F)

binding or adhesive layer for cereals or nuts. The texture is generally required to be fairly soft and not too chewy, and for economic reasons it is common for most or all of the butter fat to be replaced by vegetable fats and butter flavours. The introduction of whey proteins via various hydrolysed whey syrups or whey powders which are now commercially available can help to give the desired texture, as well as reduce costs. A typical recipe for a caramel for this application is given in Table 15.2.

Caramel may be manufactured by traditional batch processes, however it is more common and practicable for continuous cooking techniques to be employed, with the caramel being fed directly to the countline manufacturing plant (see Chapter 11).

15.2.3 Nougat

The large size of many countline products is as a result of the nougat component in the product. It is most commonly soft and tender with a short-grained texture. The traditional whipping agent employed is egg albumen, however a number of alternative materials based on soya or milk proteins are now available. These offer stability to high temperatures during processing and microbiological stability compared to egg albumen, although they may not always provide the same degree of whip or long-term stability in the product. The addition of various nuts (almonds, hazelnuts, peanuts), fruits, cocoa powder or malted milk powder contributes to a variety of textures and flavours. It is important that the nougat is fairly moist since it frequently

Table 15.3 Typical nougat recipes (parts by weight in each case)

	Chewy	Short	Grained
Syrup			
Cane or beet sugar	38.82	30.85	42.00
Glucose syrup	37.38	29.90	21.00
Water (sufficient to dissolve cane or beet sugar)			
Boiling temperature	124°C (255°F)	124°C (255°F)	138°C (280°F)
Frappé			
Powdered egg albumen	0.83	0.88	0.90
Maltodextrin	0.83	0.67	0.90
Glucose syrup	10.31	29.90	19.40
Water	8.50	4.00	9.20
Fat	3.33	3.80	3.60
Colour–flavour	3.33	3.80	3.60
Cocoa powder	—	—	1.50*
Icing sugar	—	—	1.50

*For grained batch add cocoa powder and icing sugar, with melted fat.

represents a large proportion of the final product which can be helped by the use of a high, 63-DE glucose syrup. Table 15.3 gives a typical recipe.

The manufacture of nougat is predominantly by use of continuous in-line pressure whipping equipment in conjunction with continuous cooking equipment. For detailed methods see Chapter 13.

15.2.4 Cereals

Crisped rice or other forms of extruded cereals contribute greatly to the crunch of the product and also help to reduce the density of the final bar. Without sufficient lubrication however, cereals can make the product a very dry eat. Moisture pick-up and hence loss of crispness can significantly affect the shelf life of the final product, hence considerable care needs to be taken in the formulation of other component parts of the countline.

15.2.5 Nuts

Almonds, hazelnuts or peanuts are most commonly used in the form of whole or kibbled pieces. They contribute flavour (depending upon the degree of roast) and texture to the overall eat. They are generally mixed into one of the layers or may be spread on top of the bar prior to enrobing, and thus give a rough appearance to the finished product. Coconut is used in a number of products in the form of a coconut paste.

15.2.6 Fruit

Fruit pieces may be incorporated, and these give additional moistness to the eat as well as flavour contribution. Fruits used as pieces are mainly raisins, apples or apricots in the form of either dehydrated or freeze-dried pieces. Fruits may also be incorporated in the form of a layer or sandwich as fruit pastes or jams.

15.2.7 *Granola (muesli)*

This is a general term used for a mixture of oats, crisp cereals, nuts and fruit, in varying proportions, which are used as the major components of cereal bars. These are bound together to form a matrix with either a predominantly fat-based wash or a cooked syrup consisting of various sugars, fat, milk and flavourings, e.g. malt.

Rolled oats, generally jumbo, are the mainstay of all cereal bars. Their positive contribution to the eat of the product, apart from minimizing cost, is debatable, since it is the oats which characterize many of the unpleasant textures that people recall about cereal bars. A correct balance of the proportion of oats in relation to the other ingredients such that the final eat in the mouth is not oats can be achieved. Sugar-toasting of the oats may be used to improve their eating characteristics and give additional crunch. The presence of lipase can be a problem in the subsequent development of soapiness in the product, particularly if coconut or other lauric fats are present.

The presence of nuts in cereal bars tends to increase the acceptability of the products and gives them a less 'mealy' texture.

Coconut in the form of flakes of various sizes is also a common inclusion. Care should be taken that the coconut is not too dominant, as it can be a cause of rejection of the product by those people who find it unpleasant.

The original hard and crunchy cereal bars consist of the above granola mixture compacted together, bound with a wash of fat, sugar and possibly cocoa powder for flavouring. If the correct fat is not chosen this can result in a greasy aftertaste and also problems of fat deposition on the bottom of the bar where excess has flowed through the cereal matrix.

The soft and chewy bars use a binding syrup which mostly consists of various sugars with the addition of fat, perhaps milk, and flavourings. The increase in the sugar content of the bars moves these soft and chewy bars closer in taste to standard countlines. The balance of the sugars is critical, as mentioned previously, in order to try and preserve the integrity and crispness of the cereals in the mix. Glycerol is frequently incorporated for that purpose.

Table 15.4 Cereal bar: a typical recipe (parts by weight)

Binding syrup	40
Oats	25
Crispied rice	10
Coconut	10
Almonds	10
Raisins	5

Malt extract, treacle, honey or other 'natural' flavourings may be added. A typical recipe for a cereal bar is given in Table 15.4.

The granola mix and the binding medium are mixed on either a continuous or a batch basis. Adequate coating of the dry ingredients by the binder is necessary to ensure the mass will hold together on layering. However it is important that overmixing does not occur, as this would cause the breakdown of the ingredients, especially the cereals, and subsequent loss of density of the layered product.

15.3 Manufacturing processes

15.3.1 Layering/slab forming

The majority of countlines and cereal bars are produced by a process of extrusion and layering.

Layering consists of forming sheets of the appropriate thickness and density of the component parts of the countline from which the individual bars may be cut. This was traditionally achieved by rolling out by hand on oiled slabs and cutting with a rotary wheel, the final density and compactness of the bar being highly operator-dependent. Subsequent equipment produced bars of more uniform consistency but with considerable pressure, such that the final product was very compact and dense. Nowadays continuous forming plants such as those by Sollich (Figure 15.1) or APV Baker produce extruded layers to a well-controlled density and thickness.

These can be used for a variety of materials including nougats and other

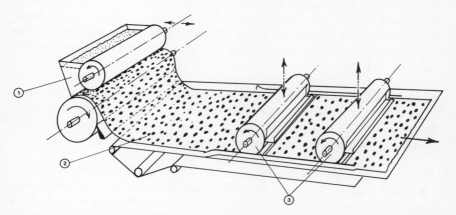

Figure 15.1 Sollich Conbar layering system. *1*, slab forming and closing machine; *2*, product slab; *3*, one to three compression rollers for final product height and density.

aerated masses, caramels, granolas, coconut and fruit pastes and fudge with or without the inclusion of ingredients. The exact combinations will vary depending upon product type, but the principle of the operation is as follows.

The material to be formed is fed via a hopper between cooled forming drums, and a sheet of the material extruded onto a belt. The speed of the drums and the take-off belt is critical to ensure that the material does not break up. The sheet then passes through a series of sizing/compression rollers in order to bring the layer down to the required depth and density. If a second component is to be added, e.g. caramel, the sheet passes under a second layering head where the material is deposited to the appropriate depth. Specially designed sprinkler units may be incorporated to sprinkle nuts, fruits or cereals directly onto the sticky caramel layer. After layering the product is generally cooled before forming into bars.

15.3.1.1 *Slitting, spreading and cutting.* The layers pass through rotary slitting knives which slit the sheet into bars of the appropriate width. As they are slit the bars are spread so as to be sufficiently far apart that they do not rejoin. The spread ropes of product are fed to a guillotine cutter where the bars are cut to the desired length. For soft cereal bars it may be necessary to spread after guillotining to prevent the ropes coming apart due to bending.

15.3.1.2 *Strip/rope forming.* For certain materials, such as fruit pastes, caramels and fudge, it is possible to form directly ropes or strips of the desired width and thickness from the layering head. After cooling these are then guillotine-cut to the required length.

15.3.1.3 *Sawing.* Hard cereal-based products may be cut into bars after cooling by the use of oscillating saw blades. The disadvantage with this process is the creation of considerable waste material in the form of dust, which needs to be reincorporated into the product. This form of cutting also gives a raw edge to the bar, which for cereal bars which are not to be covered in chocolate can look unsightly.

15.3.1.4 *Jet cutting.* A more recent form of cutting is the use of high-pressure water or oil jets. These have the advantage of reducing waste dust produced. However, care needs to be taken in the use of water jets for those products containing cereals, as these could be adversely affected by the water.

15.3.1.5 *Enrobing.* After forming and cutting, bars may be single- or double-enrobed depending upon the final chocolate cover required. In the case of some cereal bars they may pass through a bottom enrober only to be shoulder or half-coated (Figure 15.2).

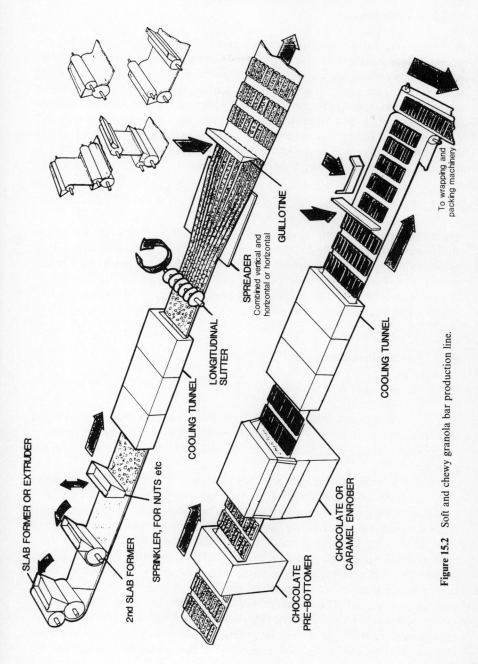

Figure 15.2 Soft and chewy granola bar production line.

SLAB FORMER OR EXTRUDER

2nd SLAB FORMER

SPRINKLER, FOR NUTS etc

COOLING TUNNEL

LONGITUDINAL SLITTER

SPREADER
Combined vertical and
horizontal or horizontal

GUILLOTINE

CHOCOLATE PRE-BOTTOMER

CHOCOLATE OR CARAMEL ENROBER

COOLING TUNNEL

To wrapping and packing machinery

15.3.2   *Coextrusion*

A more recent form of extrusion which has not been fully exploited for the production of countlines is the simultaneous extrusion from a cooker extruder of a partially or fully cooked outer tube of an expanded cereal base with a soft inner filling. This requires a special die-head which allows the filling to be injected as the cooked outer case is formed. Fillings tend to be fat-based, and as such if present in too large a proportion can give a heavy, overrich eat. Aeration of the filling may help to reduce this effect. The tubes are cut to the desired length after sufficient cooling in order to allow the filling to set and not flow out. The products may then be chocolate-enrobed or packed directly.

15.3.3   *Packaging*

The form of packaging for most countlines is a standard flow wrap. For many chocolate-enrobed products the wrap is required to protect from dirt, moisture and taint, and 'pearlised' film is frequently used. Unenrobed cereal products may require more protection, and in these cases more substantial laminates may be used. Gas flushing, although expensive, can be employed, to afford additional stability and protection.

15.4   Technical considerations

15.4.1   *Equilibrium relative humidity (ERH)*

The multicomponent nature of most countlines means that considerable care in their construction is necessary to ensure that interaction between the components is kept to a minimum, and as such maximises the shelf life of the product.

Cereals, biscuit, wafers and nuts are particularly vulnerable to moisture pick-up when in contact with relatively high-moisture materials such as caramels, nougats, etc., although interaction between the latter may also result in a change in product characteristics. In order to avoid these changes, recipes may need to be specially formulated to reduce the ERH. Table 15.5 gives typical ERH values of common components of countlines. If still further protection is necessary, an insulating/barrier layer of chocolate, or more commonly fat-based wash, may be necessary physically to separate the vulnerable material. This however will only be effective if complete with no cracks or pin-holes. Details of the theoretical calculation of the ERH of recipes are outlined in Ref. 2 or it may be practically measured using purpose-built instrumentation or the traditional method of desiccator and salt solutions.

Table 15.5 Typical equilibrium relative humidity (ERH) values of confectionery components

Component	ERH (%)
Crisp cereals	10–20
Biscuits	20–30
Caramels	45–55
Nougat	50–60
Fudge	60–70
Jellies	60–70
Marshmallow	65–75
Fondant	75–80

15.4.2 Texture and flavour

The component parts of countlines are commonly eaten individually as assortment sweets, straight lines or CBCLs. When presented together in a countline they need to be formulated and chosen carefully to ensure that they provide a balanced eat and are compatible in both texture and flavour. The individual parts, whilst each providing their own characteristics, should eat down together, and one should not be left at the end with one particular component. Their position in the bar is also important for a comfortable eat. It is not common for example, to find the caramel layer on the bottom of a countline!!

The flavours should all blend and none should dominate too much, except, perhaps, chocolate. If one thinks of the most successful countlines, these basic rules are well met.

15.5 Conclusion

Countlines offer to the consumer eating gratification in a variety of tastes and textures to suit a range of moods and eating occasions at an affordable everyday price. Their purchase is largely impulsive, and competition is strong, therefore efficient and cost-effective manufacture is imperative for a product to survive in the market.

Acknowledgements

Sollich/GmBH
APV/Baker

References

1. S.T. Beckett, *Industrial Chocolate Manufacture and Use*, Blackie & Son Ltd, Glasgow (1988).
2. R. Lees and E.B. Jackson, *Sugar Confectionery and Chocolate Manufacture*, Leonard Hill, Glasgow (1973).

16 Confectionery and extrusion cooking technology

D.J. VAN ZUILICHEM

16.1 Introduction

Among other applications, cooking extruders can be used to produce confectionery. Extrusion cooking technology is not new. Pasta products have been commonly extruded and shaped since the thirties and sausage has been produced for a hundred years on extruder-like equipment. The real novelty is that cooking extruder equipment is available to the food industry which allows a heating process to be introduced in which a controlled food, chemical or biochemical reaction takes places.

The chemical polymer industry started using extruder equipment in the forties with the so-called melting extruders based on design concepts of mixer compounders. The food industry discovered the cooking extruder in the fifties, and in the beginning used the equipment for the production of cooked and expanded snacks based on corngrits and other cereals. Most of the equipment used employed the so-called single-screw extruder concept. Twin-screw extruder equipment dates back to the sixties. A technological reason for the use of twin-screw extruders is the need for equipment capable of handling high viscosities, as they are known in confectionery, or to process low and high viscosities in a single recipe at the same time in one piece of equipment. Although most confectionery articles are unique, it is clear that the basic

Table 16.1 Generalised composition of some confectioneries

Ingredient	Product			
	Liquorices	Soft liquorice	Clear gums	Wine gums
Sucrose	+	+	+	+
Syrups	+	+	+	+
Starch	+	+	+	+
Wheat flour		+		
Block liquid	+	+		
Caramel	+			
NH$_4$Cl	+	+		
Additive		+		
Gelatins	+	+		
Water	+	+	+	+

components are sugar (sucrose), starch syrups (treacle) and starch or flours (see Table 16.1). At the same time water is always part of the recipe, and this is a reason for the selection of extruder equipment as an innovative tool in this area, since drying costs are responsible for a great deal of the price of the goods. Cooking extruders offer the possibility of processing confectionery goods at lower process moisture conditions compared with conventional processing, thus leading to attractive savings.

16.2 Problem description

In conventional confectionery processes, water is used to dissolve sucrose crystals at preset temperatures, as described by Honig [1]. The products are cast in corn starch and the water is removed to equilibrium conditions in order to give as long a shelf life as possible. For this operation careful and time-consuming drying is necessary at temperatures between 45 and 70°C. The low diffusivity constants for water in sugar-like materials determine the rate of drying.

It is clear that these methods are energy-consuming. It would be more attractive to develop a cooking method at which the water percentage is as close as possible to the moisture level of the end product (see Table 16.2). Such a wish may be fulfilled by the selection of an appropriate extruder for this

Table 16.2 Typical shelf life/moisture for some confectioneries

Product	Moisture (%)	Shelf life (months)
Chocolate		
Bakery	1	6–8
Milk	2	6–8
Pure	1	6–8
Toffees	6–7	8
Hard boilings	2–3	12
Agar gels	24	6–8
Cream	12–13	6
Whipped cream	6	8
Fondant	12	10
Wine gums	12	12
Soft gums	22	6–8
Fudge	7	5–6
Gelatine gels	22	6–8
Marshmallows (deposited)	12	4
Pastilles (soft)	18	4
Pastilles (hard)	11	18
Pectine gels	22	6–8
Tablets	1	18
Turkish delight	20	5
Liquorice	8–18	8–9

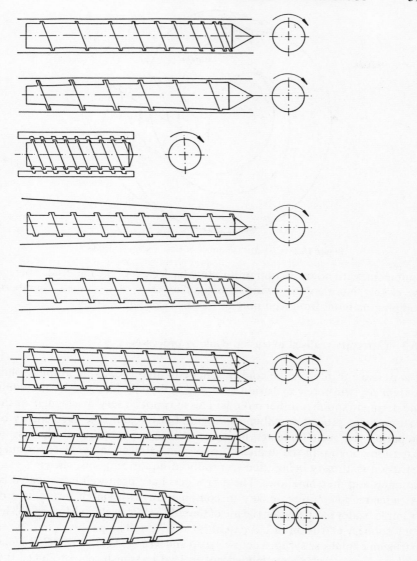

Figure 16.1 Existing food extruder models.

purpose. The available extruder designs can be divided into single- and twin-screw extruders (see Figure 16.1).

The twin-screw extruder designs consist of co-rotating and counter-rotating designs and closely intermeshing so-called self-wiping extruders. The most important difference between single-screw extruders and closely intermeshing twin-screw extruders is that single-screw extruders are so-called 'open channel'

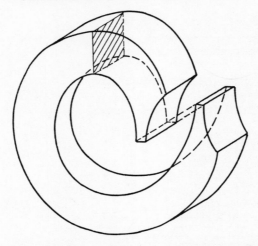

Figure 16.2 C-shaped chamber of a twin-screw extruder.

equipment, with no restriction prohibiting back-flow of the material, whereas the closely intermeshing twins consist of a series of C-shaped chambers, pumping material from feed port to the die (see Figure 16.2).

16.3 Currently realised extrusion cooking processes

It is possible to replace the conventional continuous cooking at high solids content by twin-screw extrusion cooking, optionally followed by moulding and drying in starch or other moulds. This may not be very spectacular, as the post-extruder process is still conventional, but the aim is to save energy by preparing the melt at lower moisture. Another possibility is the use of extrusion cooking in the manufacture of gum confectionery. Here forming-extrusion is already being used to produced liquorice, gums, chewing gum, caramels and marshmallows. These products have been well investigated by extruder manufacturers, mostly in combination with starch products. For example, Staley has patented the use of the cold-water swelling Miragel 463 for confectionery extrusion in US patent no. 4567055. The patent describes the extrusion of maltose syrup, fructose syrup and Miragel 463 at 121°C. Regular cold-swelling starches are claimed not to lead to translucent products. It is obvious that product development in this area is very possible and necessary, but the behaviour of the basic components in extruders should be understood.

16.4 Extrusion of starch

The commercially attractive starch sources are maize, potato, rice, manioc, wheat or sago. It is well known that starches have a gelatinisation temperature between 60 and 80°C (see Table 16.3).

Table 16.3 Gelatinisation of starches

Basic starches	Gelatinisation temperature (°C)
Corn starch	62–72
Potato starch	56–66
Wheat starch	52–63
Rice starch	61–78
Tapioca	58–70
Sago	60–72

Table 16.4 Starch composition

	Ratio (%)	
	Amylose	Amylopectin
Corn starch	24–26	74–76
Potato starch	22–23	Approx. 77
Tapioca	19–20	Approx. 80
Sago	20–26	74–80
Waxy maize	< 1	> 99

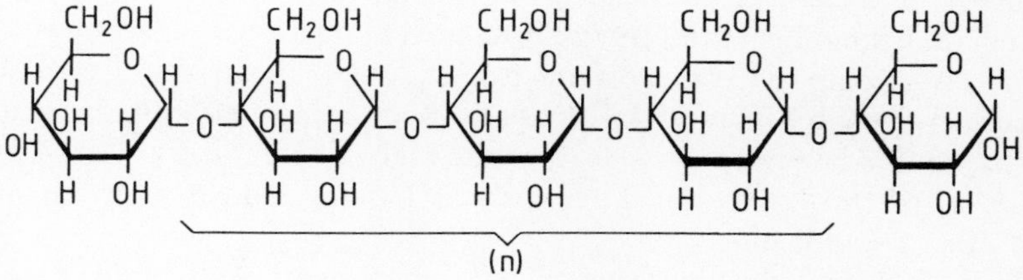

Amylose, α 1·4 glucan

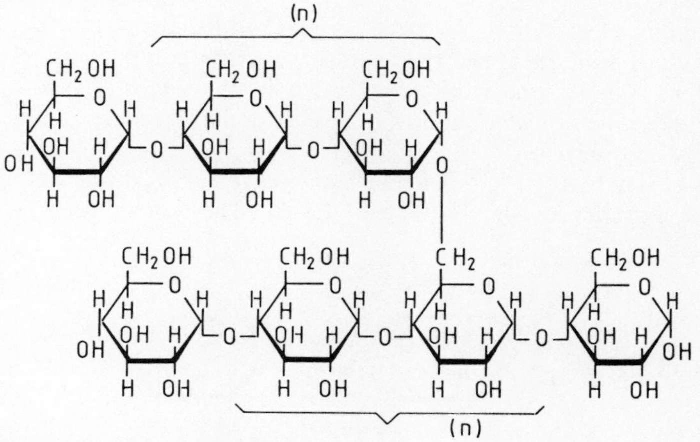

Amylopectin, α 1·4 and α 1·6 glucan

Figure 16.3 Structural formulae of amylose α-1,4-glucan and amylopectin α-1,4 and 1,6-glucan.

The composition of starches consists in most cases of amylose and amylopectin in a ratio of 1:4. An exception is waxy maize as shown in Table 16.4.

As shown in Figure 16.3 amylose consists of a chain of α-1,4 glucan elements. On the other hand, amylopectin shows a branched structure of α-1,4 and α-1,6 elements. The aim of an extruder when processing these polysaccharides is to damage cell walls of the starch particles, and to separate them by breaking or reducing the size of the molecular chain. For this purpose the product application is very important. For human consumption it is necessary, for reasons of digestibility, to gelatinise the starch almost completely; for animal foodstuff this is not the case as the ability of animals to digest partly gelatinised starches is much greater. For confectionery products the starch must be completely cooked.

16.5 Extrusion of dry sucrose crystals

Sucrose crystals are one of the most important components of the mixtures used in the confectionery industry. It is necessary to study the melting behaviour of sucrose in an extruder, as this stage offers the potential to save a considerable amount of the energy used in cooking.

Sucrose is composed of glucose and fructose units. The structural formula of sucrose is given in Figure 16.4. For application in the confectionery industry sucrose should be present as a clear melt at high temperatures (> 160°C) that can easily be cast in preformed maize-starch moulds and can easily be mixed with other components.

The extruded product must meet these requirements. At the same time it is necessary to know the possible degree of caramelisation caused by the high temperature levels in extruders. Further, one should also be aware of the possibility of inversion of sucrose, which means chemically that the disaccharide is split into the two monosaccharide components, glucose and fructose. Finally one will be interested in the viscosity developed in an extruder, which will determine the capacity of the extruder equipment and the energy consumption.

The extruder used by van Zuilichem *et al.* in 1985 [2] was a 50-mm single-screw extruder of the Battenfeld design. The screws used were of the

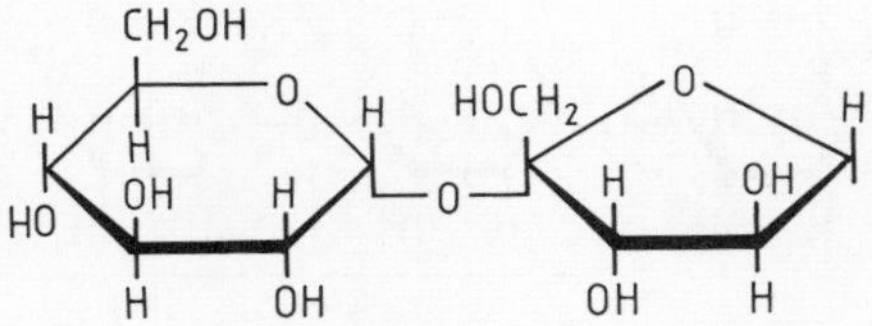

Figure 16.4 Structure of sucrose.

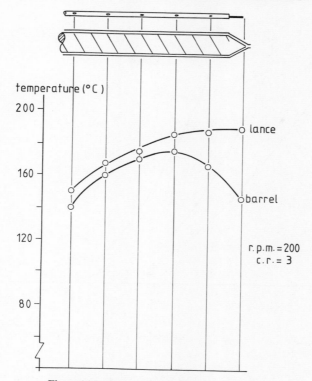

Figure 16.5 Temperature profile for sucrose.

compressing type, with constant pitch and compression ratios 3:1, 2:1 and 1.15:1. The sugar was supplied to the extruder by a simple vibratory metering device. At first a good temperature distribution had to be found in order to create a sufficient melting of the dry crystals. The necessary temperature profiles could be controlled very well, and an example is shown in Figure 16.5. It can be seen that the sugar is sheared on the screw side, resulting in a higher 'lance' temperature profile in connection with an extruder barrel profile going from 130°C, above 170°C, to 150°C at the barrel outlet. This temperature profile was measured at 200 rpm, with a screw compression ratio of 3:1.

An average throughput of molten sucrose is plotted in Figure 16.6 for screw compression ratios 3:1, 2:1 and 1.15:1 at 160–200 rpm. A maximum throughput of the melt of 60–70 kg/h resulted. A maximum throughput of over 90 kg/h proved to be possible at 200 rpm, using a 3:1 compression screw (see Figure 16.7). The molten sugar exhibited an amorphous structure and had lost its crystalline nature when it was sampled directly at the extruder die.

Of interest is the average specific power consumed in the above-mentioned trials. This is shown in Figure 16.8 for three different screw compression ratios. At compression ratios of 3:1 and 2:1, power consumption was low,

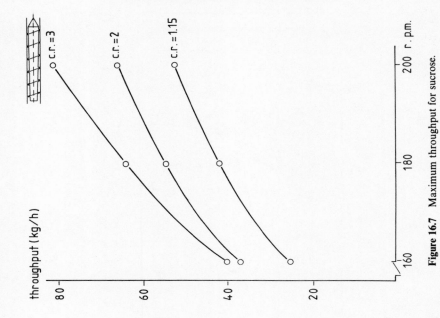

Figure 16.7   Maximum throughput for sucrose.

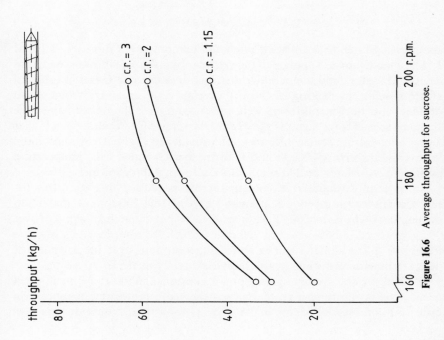

Figure 16.6   Average throughput for sucrose.

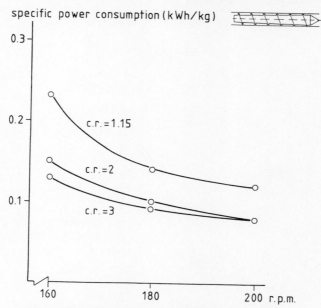

Figure 16.8 Specific power consumption for sucrose.

~ 0.1 kWh/kg. The lower compression ratio of 1.15:1 needed a specific power consumption of at least 0.15 kWh/kg. When motor power only is considered, the figures are much lower, in the region of 0.04–0.05 kWh/kg for screws with compression ratios of 2:1 and 3:1. The difference in power was consumed by the heaters that intermittently heat the barrel.

The melt must be produced at the higher rpm values in order to avoid scaling in the die and recrystallisation of molten sugar. The reducing ability of the sugar after this dry extrusion was measured by the method of Nierle and Tegge, and no considerable inversion could be determined in these circumstances.

Some colour measurements were also performed, using the standardised Icumsa method no. 4. Clear melts are produced when a steep temperature profile is applied at a cooled screw provided with a so-called mixing torpedo (see Figure 16.9). Colour ratings are below Icumsa 50. In this way a single-screw extruder can be used as a relatively economical melting tube for dry sucrose crystals.

16.6 Extrusion of sucrose–starch mixtures

In the confectionery industry many products based on starchy materials like rice, wheat and sometimes corn are used as candy bar fillers. In Figure 16.10 a

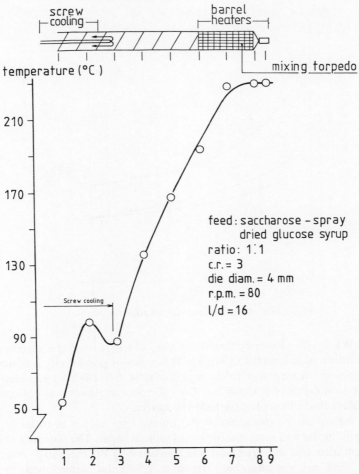

Figure 16.9 Temperature profile for dry saccharose–glucose mixtures.

temperature profile is given for a single-screw extruder processing a candy bar filler out of corn and sucrose in a ratio of 4:1. Such a product can still be handled by a single-screw extruder without difficulties. If the percentage of sucrose required is higher than 20%, then a twin-screw extruder is a good machine for such a product, as the forced flow for such a high-viscosity mixture is easily provided by the C-shaped chambers.

16.7 Extrusion of sucrose–syrup mixtures

The extrusion cooking of this type of mixture forms the basis of most confectionery products. Due to the unattractive viscosity of the starch syrups,

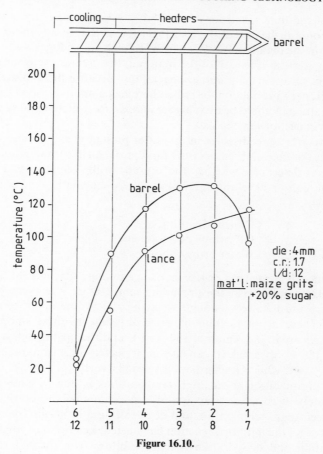

Figure 16.10.

a single-screw extruder will be unsuitable for such a job, but a closely intermeshing twin screw can easily be used.

In the conventional method of producing the melt from which hard-boiled sweets are formed, water is added to the other ingredients in a cooking vessel. The advantage of an extrusion cooker (EC) is that dissolution can be performed without the addition of any water. Thus by using an EC the time- and energy-consuming step of evaporation of the excess water can be obviated. A twin-screw EC is able to perform this function, as it has a large heat-exchange capacity combined with a favourable residence-time pattern. The positive forward transport mechanism together with the lateral mixing action of the screw result in a plug flow-like pattern combined with radial (interchamber) mixing. This results in a well-controlled, limited residence time, whilst at the same time a well-mixed material is processed.

Evidence for this plug flow character is given by Jager [3], who defined S as the ratio of the time taken for 16 and 84% of an injected tracer to pass a reference point at the end of the EC. Jager found that in a twin-screw EC S tends to be in the region of 0.3–0.5, which is a high value. Jager also explained that the greater the viscosity of the material, the greater the residence-time distribution, since viscosity induces back-flow. Because the material used in the confectionery production described here has a relatively low viscosity at EC temperatures, S could be even higher in this case, which implies even more favourable conditions in the EC.

The sucrose crystals dissolve in the water present in the glucose syrup. In this process the time and temperature (and pressure, in combination with the temperature) determine whether the crystals will disappear and whether undesirable colour development will occur. A schematic representation is given below:

$$\left.\begin{array}{l}\text{Time} \\ \text{Temperature} \\ \text{Pressure}\end{array}\right\} \Rightarrow \left\{\begin{array}{l}\text{Crystal dissolution} \\ \text{Off-colour development} \\ \text{Water evaporation}\end{array}\right.$$

The residence time must not be less than the minimum time needed to dissolve the crystals completely at the prevailing temperature. On the other hand, temperature must be low enough to avoid the formation of off-coloured products. There is no melting of sugar crystals involved since working temperatures are in the region of 130–150°C and the melting temperature of sucrose is 186°C. Shear effects can also be neglected since Brinkman numbers are below 0.001, while Graetz numbers are above 10^5.

Discoloration of sugars at high temperatures is due to caramelisation. Unfortunately there are no exact quantitative data available on the relationship between sugar temperature and degree of discoloration. The reason for this is that, once the initiating reaction has started, a complex of condensation, fragmentation and dehydration reactions follow. The starting reaction is known, however. Shallenberger & Birch [4] point out that colour formation begins with the 1,2-enolisation of a sugar-reducing end (see Figure 16.11). Since sucrose does not contain a reducing end, the colouring of the mixture considered here is most probably due to the glucose syrup. An experiment with material in test tubes heated in a temperature-controlled glycerine bath, sustained this view.

Tubes filled with glucose syrup discoloured to twice the intensity attained by

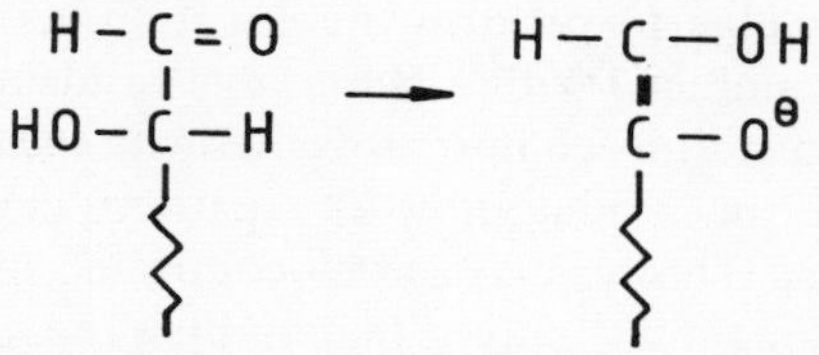

Figure 16.11   Schematic representation of the 1,2-enolisation of a sugar-reducing end.

tubes filled with a 1:1 sucrose–glucose syrup mixture, which indicates that the 50% sucrose in the latter tubes may be regarded as colour diluent. These tests also showed that colour development increases linearly with time and exponentially with absolute temperature. This means that the temperature is especially important. The test tube experiment showed that the reaction mixture should not be subjected to temperatures higher than 155°C for appreciable times.

The important question that must be answered is whether the bulk material flowing in an extruder will reach the temperature of the heated extruder wall. Van Zuilichem *et al.* [5] presented a calculation method for the mass temperature, which results in the following equation:

$$\varphi_{\text{wall}} = 5.71 \frac{(\rho^3 \lambda_m^4 c_p^2)}{\eta} \times N^{1/2} \times D_w D_s^{1/2} \times (T_w - T_m)_z \times z^{-1/2} \tag{1}$$

in which φ_{wall} = cumulative heat flow into the bulk material over length z (W), ρ = mass density (kg/m^3), m = mass thermal conductivity (J s^{-1} m^{-1} K^{-1}), c_p = mass heat capacity (J kg^{-1} K^{-1}), N = rotational speed of screws (revolutions per second, rps), D_w = barrel diameter (m), D_s = screw diameter (m), T_w = barrel temperature (K), T_m = mass temperature (K), z = distance along heated length of extruder (m) (with $z = 0$ at feed entrance) and η = bulk viscosity (N s m^{-2}).

This result needs to be corrected for the volumetric chamber filling degree U which is defined as the part of the volume of a C-shaped chamber that is actually filled with material.

$$U = \frac{Q_m}{2nNV_{\text{in}}\rho} \tag{2}$$

in which Q_m = mass flow (kg/s), V_{in} = volume of one C-shaped chamber at the entrance of the extruder (m^3) and n = number of screw channels. Multiplication by the factor U is necessary and can be done, although there is no linear relationship between the volumetric filling degree and the surface provided for heat exchange. However, since U is about 0.5 in the feed section of the extruder, the effective heat-exchange surface there is also about 0.5 of the total surface available, considering the circular geometry of the extruder. Thus, simple multiplication by U will hold in this case.

Including the heating supplied via the screws [6] and multiplying by the factor U, the following expression for the total heat flow into the bulk, φ_{tot}, can be constructed:

$$\varphi_{\text{tot}} = 11.44 \left(\frac{\lambda_m^4 c_p^2}{\eta \rho^3} \right)^{1/6} (D_w D_s + 2D_s)(T_w - T_m)_z \left(\frac{z^{1/2}}{2nV_{\text{in}}} \right) \left(\frac{Q_m}{N^{1/2}} \right) \tag{3}$$

Equation (3) can be differentiated with respect to z to obtain φ'_{tot}, the heat flow per unit (m) of linear distance from the feed point.

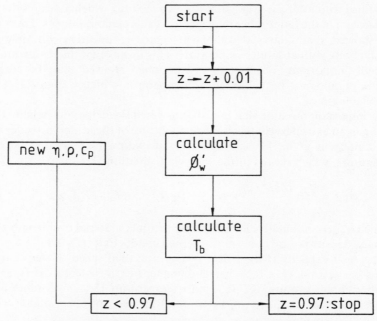

Figure 16.12 Scheme for calculating temperature development.

Next, the heat balance

$$\varphi'_{\text{tot}} = Q_m c_p \Delta T_b \tag{4}$$

is used, in which T_b is the rise in temperature of the bulk over an arbitrary small distance z along the extruder. For $z = 1$ cm,

$$\Delta T_b = \frac{0.01 \; \varphi'_{\text{tot}}}{Q_m c_p} \tag{5}$$

In this way the temperature development of the bulk along the extruder can be calculated for every centimetre, using the calculation scheme shown in Figure 16.12. In this way, a temperature profile of the bulk material in the extruder may be obtained (Figure 16.13). Corresponding heat transfer coefficients, α, are found to be in the region of 1000 W m^{-2} K^{-1}.

The conclusion is that only at high throughputs and high rotational speeds does the bulk temperature not reach the wall temperature. In other cases it may be concluded that the barrel temperature is reached quickly. The extruder is thus seen to be an effective heat exchanger.

The conclusion from the calculations is that the two determining factors are the operating temperature and the size of the sucrose crystals. It is obviously of crucial importance that the temperature of the bulk exceeds the saturation temperature for an 83.33% sucrose solution. The temperature may be lower

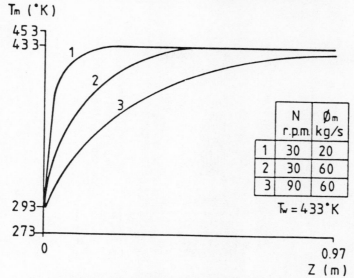

Figure 16.13 Temperature profiles of bulk in extruder.

when water is added or the ratio of syrup to sucrose is increased. However, when water is added, problems may be expected with excess water in the final product.

The size of the crystals is also very important. When the particle size is in the region of 0.1 mm, as is the case with icing sugars, the residence time in the extruder is amply sufficient to obtain a clear product. This calculation also shows that it will be difficult to produce a crystal-free product when normal-sized sugar crystals ($d_{p0} = 1$ mm) are used.

When the product leaves the extruder its pressure drops immediately and water evaporates from it, reducing its temperature. The temperature drop measured in this work is from 150 to 80°C, corresponding to a heat loss of

$$(150 - 80)c_p = 70 \times 2.5 \times 10^3 = 1.75 \times 10^5 \text{ J/kg}$$

Assuming that effectively all this heat goes in evaporating water from the product, with a latent heat of evaporation of 2250 kJ/kg, the water evaporated is

$$(1.75 \times 10^5)/(2250 \times 10^3) = 78 \text{ g/kg product}$$

The initial water content is 100 g/kg (i.e. 10%) and the final water content is thus 100–78 = 22 g/kg, or some 2%, which is the desired level in the product.

Tests have been performed with a Cincinnati Milacron CM45 twin screw EC. (For a drawing of conical screws similar to those used, see Figure 16.14.) The results of the test are shown in Table 16.5, T_{end} is the temperature of the bulk material just before it leaves the extruder. The feed end diameter of the

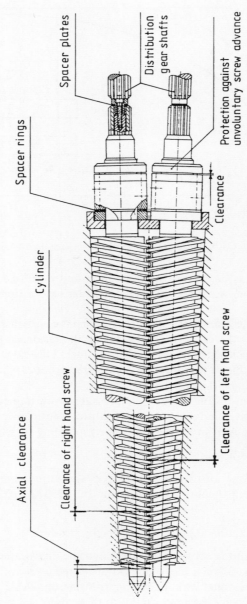

Figure 16.14 Example of a conical twin-screw extruder (Cincinnati).

Table 16.5 Results of extrusion test at different temperatures, through-puts and rotational speeds

$T_{barrel}(°C)$	$\varphi_m(kg/h)$	N (rpm)	T_{end}	Colour (I)	Water (%)	Crystallinity
140	20	40	139	54	3.5	—
140	20	60	138.5	43	3.2	—
140	40	60	138	41	3.5	—
130	20	40	129	39	5.3	—
130	20	60	128.5	38	5.0	—
130	40	60	127.5	30	5.1	—
130–140–150	20	40	142	82	3.1	—
130–140–150	20	60	140	58	3.2	—
130–140–150	40	60	136	47	3.2	—

screws is 90 mm, and the die-end diameter is 45 mm. The total length of screw is 970 mm.

The colour of the product was measured by the ICUMSA method no. 4, which essentially measures the light extinction at 420 nm. Water content was measured by the Karl Fischer method. Presence of crystals in the product was detected by use of a polarising microscope. A temperature profile of 130–140–150 means that the barrel temperature is 130°C at the feed section and then rises towards the end of the extruder to 150°C.

These tests confirm that the bulk material indeed attains the wall temperature. The product did not contain any sugar crystals, and there was little discoloration.

The water content of the product is low, considering that no special removal action was undertaken. If such were done, even lower values could be reached.

It is clear that the important factors are:

(1) For the dissolution of the crystals:
   The barrel temperature
   The size of the crystals at the entrance of the extruder.
(2) For the colour of the product:
   The final bulk temperature attained.
(3) For the water content of the product:
   The final bulk temperature attained.
   Any special provision for removal of water.

16.8 Coextrusion

Coextrusion is a redesigned process found in the bakery and confectionery industries. The coextruded product is mostly of the tubular type, in which the outer component is produced by a cooker extruder and the inner component is a pumpable product which will not flow freely at ambient temperatures. The two components are extruded simultaneously to produce a continuous filled tube, which is later cut to size. Earlier products on the UK market, like

Cadbury's Criss Cross and Mars Cornquistos, consisted of an extruder tube and a 'post-filled' centre. In the USA however Herschi produces a liquorice-type product which is die-dilled with a dried fruit containing chewable inner filling.

For each product development a number of problems have to be solved, including die design, recipe restrictions, pumping the filling, post-extruder processing and the cutting.

16.8.1   *Die design*

The best arrangement is to bring the centre filling over 90° in the extruded outer tube, giving the centre a more restrictive path but allowing the outer tube to be consistent. The outer tubing is mostly forced through a restriction formed by a number of small holes or by an annular ring. It is desirable to have the centre entry point as far away from the final die as possible, in practice a distance of about 40 mm. Be aware of the problems of manufacturing a die arrangement which will maintain the accurate gaps between centre die parts and the outers during the lifetime of the die.

16.8.2   *Size restrictions*

When the minimum dimension of the outer annulus is about 1 mm thick and a wall thickness of the centre tubing of 1 mm is also chosen, then the restriction will be clear. The outer easily expands to twice the diameter of the die annulus, giving way to a certain pumping area cross-section. It does not appear to be practical to work with a ratio greater than 10, giving a minimum inside diameter of finished product of about 10 mm, whilst the outside is about 14 mm. Reduction of the expansion can be achieved by changing the raw material properties and the product moisture. Multiple outlets are perfectly possible (see Demo APV-Baker at Interpack Fair Dusseldorf BRD in 1984) where 10 tubes were extruded simultaneously).

16.8.3   *Recipe restrictions*

Crisp extruded wheat-based outers can be directly produced in a twin-screw extruder at 5% moisture. A problem for the centre filling will be the equilibrium moisture content which will ultimately exist, but enough know-ledge is available from the biscuit, wafer and confectionery industry to develop attractive centre formulations for cheese, meat pastes, onion/nuts, caramel, gums, jellies and sugar/fat creams.

16.8.4   *Density influence*

If a round tube is extruded and filled, the weight of the centre will be two or three times that of the outer, which makes the centre dominant. This can be overcome by:

(1) Alteration of the cross-section after extrusion from circular tubing to a flattened cross-section.

(2) Addition of finely ground extruded and expanded starchy material to the centre filling, in order to reduce the density.

(3) Aeration of the centre filling, which reduces the density for a straight cream from 1.2–1.3 towards 0.7–0.8 kg/dm^3.

16.8.5   Centre pumping

Usually each tube produced by the twin-screw extruder is provided with its own metering pump, in order to match the weights in the two streams exactly. The temperature at which the cream is pumped depends on several factors. Very viscous creams may have to be preheated, but normally pumping at ambient temperatures would be preferred. For such a cream a typical temperature curve would be:

Hopper	22°C
Pump outlet	24°C
Die entry	25°C
Die exit	50°C
Post-die (60 s)	65°C

16.8.6   Post-processing

Several technological solutions are in use, such as rolling, the use of secondary dies, cooling provisions, drying and toasting. It should be mentioned that most products have a memory for the original die shape and more than one roller passage is needed for an alteration of the cross-section.

Since long secondary dies are impractical, these dies are in use only for outer recipes that set quickly. These dies must be adjustable, in much the same way that shaping jaws are used for flat-bread production. Since the outer tube cools faster than the inner centre, the outer tubing acts as an effective insulator. Nevertheless, in practice 2% moisture loss can be achieved by cooling.

For drying purposes warm air is suitable and will help to give a final texture to the outer tube. Finally, the products in the toasting section should be rotated in order to create an evenly distributed colour and taste.

16.8.7   Cutting

If closed product ends are needed the cutting/crimping device must be close to the die. If a symmetrical crimp is needed a pair of cutting rolls is essential. When the product ends are to be open, allowing the centre to be seen, then the tube must be set prior to the cutting, and at the same time the centre cream must be cool enough not to flow out.

It is difficult to see how the family of coextruded products will develop but product makers will handle this technology as a strong tool in the future.

16.8.8 *Process economics*

The advantages of using an extruder or a set of extruders for a confectionery product are, firstly, the ability to operate in a low level of moisture very close to the desired equilibrium moisture content of the final product and, secondly, the ability of the cooker extruder to shape and handle different component streams at distinct viscosity levels at the same time. If the extruders are operated by skilled people very attractive savings in manpower can be added to the savings in drying costs. Of course the recipe of the product will have a big influence on the savings, but even in the case of a simple hard-boiled candy savings of the order of 4–5 pence per kilogram of product can be achieved.

References

1. P. Honig, *Principles of Sugar Technology*, Elsevier, Amsterdam (1953).
2. D.J. Van Zuilichem, W.J. Tempel, W. Stolp and K. van't Riet, Production of high boiled sugar confectionery by extrusion cooking of sucrose liquid glucose mixtures. *J. Food Eng.* **4** (1985) 37.
3. Th. Jager, Residence time distribution in a twin screw extruder, *Internal Research Report*, Agricultural University, Wageningen (1983).
4. R.S. Shallenberger and G.G. Birch, *Sugar Chemistry*, AVI Publishing Co., Westport, Connecticut (1978).
5. D.J. Van Zuilichem, B. Alblas, P.M. Reinders and W. Stolp, A comparative study of the operational characteristics of single and twin screw extruders. *Proceedings Cost '91*, Athens (concluding seminar) (1983).
6. D.J. Van Zuilichem, W. Stolp and L.B.P.M. Janssen, Engineering aspects of single and twin screw extrusion of biopolymers. *J. Food Eng.* **2** (1983) 157.

Further reading

P.X. Hoynak and G.N. Bollenback. *This is liquid sugar*, Refiners Syrup Inc., New York (1966).
L.B.P.M. Janssen, *Twin-Screw Extrusion*, Elsevier, Amsterdam, New York (1978).
O. Levenspiel, *Chemical Reaction Engineering*, Wiley & Sons, New York (1972).
J. Van der Lijn, Simulation of heat and mass transfer in spray drying, *Dissertation*, Agricultural University, Wageningen (1976).
T.K. Sherwood, R.L. Pigford and C.B. Wilke, *Mass Transfer*, McGraw Hill, New York (1978).

17 Structure of sugar confectionery

D.F. LEWIS

17.1 Introduction

The texture and technological properties of confectionery products are to a large extent controlled by the structure of the product. This chapter aims to illustrate the structure of a wide range of sugar confectionery and explain how the control of structure leads to the ability to produce confectionery in an effective manner. Microscopy is essentially a visual science, and so the format of this chapter is one of few words and many pictures. The products considered are: toffee, starch gels, pectin gels, gelatin gels, boiled sweets, panned sweets, chews and coatings.

17.2 Toffee

The basic structure of toffee is that of fat droplets dispersed in a sugar matrix. The essential classification of the toffee is to a large extent controlled by the sugar matrix. Hence treacle toffee or butterscotch has a glassy sugar matrix with a very low moisture, whilst the caramel in a composite bar will have a more syrup-like sugar matrix. However, within each type of toffee the properties of different products will, to a large extent, be governed by the state of the fat droplets, and this in turn will be influenced by the protein in the recipe. In most toffee systems the fat is present as droplets of varying size along with a small amount of free fat. The free fat is a significant feature of the toffee and contributes to the mouthfeel and flavour of the toffee; if the fat is too well emulsified then the toffee may lack flavour. If the fat is too poorly emulsified then it may separate and lead to an oily or greasy mouthfeel.

In a normal toffee product using condensed milk or skimmed milk powder as the protein source the degree of emulsification is controlled by the interactions between the whey protein fraction and the casein micelles. During cooking the whey protein appears to form a membrane at the edge of the fat droplets and the casein micelles attach themselves to this membrane. The casein micelles make the membranes brittle, which leads to breakdown of fat droplets during cooking and stirring. This process is illustrated in Figure 17.1, which shows the premix, half-cooked and final product stages of a normal

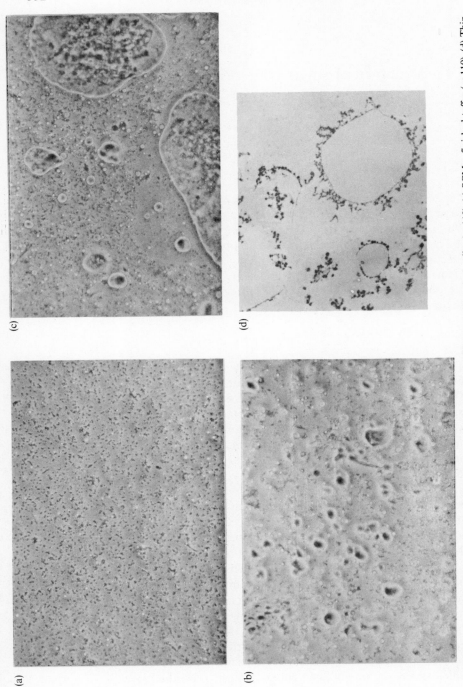

Figure 17.1 (a) Sweetened, condensed milk (SCM — premix (× 110). (b) SCM — half-cooked toffee (× 110). (c) SCM — finished toffee (× 110). (d) Thin section of a skimmed-milk powder (SMP) toffee showing whey protein membrane and casein miscelles attached (× 5000).

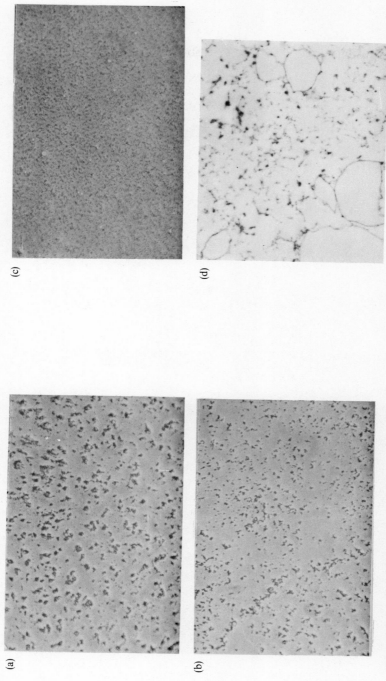

Figure 17.2 (a) Premix (× 100), (b) Half-cooked toffee (× 100), (c) Finished toffee (× 100), (d) 100% calcium-reduced skimmed-milk powder showing whey protein membrane and casein micelles distributed throughout the toffee (× 5000).

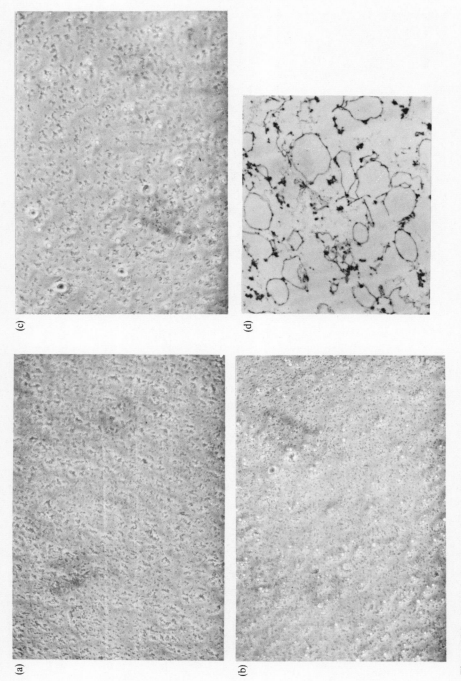

Figure 17.3 (a) Hydrolysed whey premix 90/90 (× 110). (b) Hydrolysed whey half-cooked toffee 90/90 (× 110). (c) Hydrolysed whey finished toffee (× 110). (d) Thin section of a whey toffee showing whey protein membrane.

toffee. The extent to which the fat droplets break down during cooking is seen to be related to the size of the casein micelles in the milk. If the calcium content of the milk is reduced by ion exchange then the result is small casein micelles in the milk, and this in turn results in a finer emulsion in the finished toffee. The various stages of cooking using a calcium-reduced milk are illustrated in Figure 17.2. In some cases various sources of milk can give rise to variation in the properties of the final toffee, and here the variation may be linked to the casein micelle size in the condensed milk. If a whey protein fraction is used with no casein fraction, then once again a very fine emulsion is formed in the finished product, as shown in Figure 17.3. The resulting toffee has a lower viscosity than normal and also shows some tendency to cold flow.

One of the problems encountered in toffee making is that of grittiness or roughness in the texture, and this can be caused by several structures. In some cases the protein may be poorly dispersed or may aggregate during cooking. Poor dispersion is a problem with some skimmed-milk powders, whilst toffees made by blending caseinate and whey proteins appear to be prone to aggregation of the protein. Figure 17.4 shows poorly dispersed skimmed-milk protein and aggregates in a caseinate/whey-based toffee. Sugar crystals can occasionally give rise to grittiness, and this is more likely in whey-based systems; more often however calcium salts (normally citrate or phosphate) give rise to this problem. The calcium salts are more frequently encountered in toffees made from condensed milk. Figure 17.4(a) shows some crystalline inclusions which can cause grittiness. In some toffees a mild roughness is encountered which cannot be attributed to any of the above causes, and in these cases excessive aggregation of the fat droplets into large discrete clusters appears to be the cause.

17.3 Starch gels

Natural starch occurs as starch grains which swell and take up water during cooking. The grains themselves contain starch in a crystalline state, and this causes the grains to be birefringent in polarised light; on cooking this birefringence is lost and amylose leaks from the grains. On cooling the extracted amylose forms a gel network. The other principal component of starch, amylopectin, remains in the grains, at least during moderate cooking. A natural starch gel consists of swollen (amylopectin-rich) starch grains held in a network consisting of amylose.

The gel properties depend on the state of both the starch grains and the network. Where the network is relatively weak and grains are solid, a short or brittle gel texture results. On prolonged cooking, as more amylose is extracted and the grains weaken, the texture becomes more elastic. The swelling of the starch grains during cooking causes a rise in viscosity, and this is sometimes used to monitor the progress of gelatinisation. On longer cooking and stirring

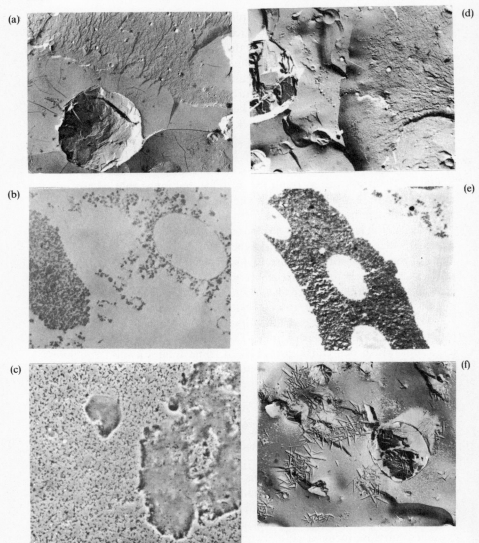

Figure 17.4 (a) Toffee made with skimmed-milk powder, freeze fracture. Note undispersed milk particle and fat globules. (b) Toffee made with medium heat-treated skimmed-milk powder, thin section. Note fat globule similar to those seen in (a) and milk powder particle (MP). Note also some fat globules with only a little casein associated with the membrane. (c) High-heat skimmed-milk powder (SMP)—premix. (d) Toffee made with SMP/whey to give a casein/whey ratio of 16:84, freeze fracture. Note undispersed milk particle and fractured fat globule (FG) which shows some signs of subdivision. (e) Toffee made with SMP/whey to give a casein/whey ratio of 16:84, thin section. Note undispersed milk protein particle. (f) Toffee made with 90/90 hydrolysed whey, freeze fracture. Note crystal clusters in toffee matrix; these needle-like crystals are probably dextrose. FG, fat globule; M, membrane, C, casein; CL, protein clump; CR, crystals; MP, milk powder particle; I, ice crystals; B, broken fat globule.

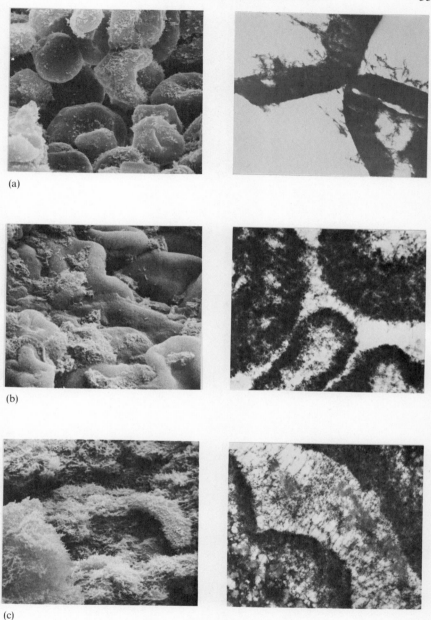

Figure 17.5   Ten per cent corn starch suspension (a, c, e, scanning electron micrographs; b, d, f, transmission electron micrographs). (a) Before peak viscosity (× 2000). (b) Before peak viscosity (× 10 000). (c) At peak viscosity (× 2000). (d) At peak viscosity (× 10 000). (e) Beyond peak viscosity (× 2000). (f) Beyond peak viscosity (× 10 000).

Figure 17.6 Ten per cent acid-thinned corn starch suspension. (a, c, e, scanning electron micrographs; b, d, f, transmission electron micrographs). (a) Before peak viscosity (× 2000). (b) Before peak viscosity (× 10 000). (c) At peak viscosity (× 2000). (d) At peak viscosity (× 10 000). (e) Beyond peak viscosity (× 2000). (f) Beyond peak viscosity (× 10 000).

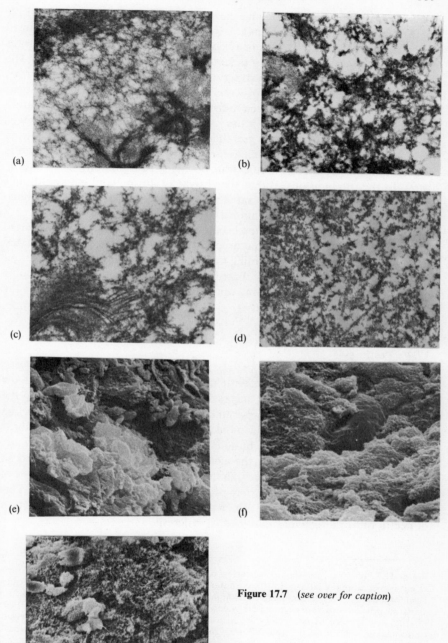

Figure 17.7 (*see over for caption*)

the swollen grains break down and the viscosity decreases again. This process of the swelling of the starch grains and the formation of a network by extracted amylose is illustrated in Figure 17.5, which shows starch gel structures resulting from different cooking times with 10% maize starch in water. The extent of swelling and amylose extraction is influenced by a number of factors, but especially the availability of water for the starch grains. In high-sugar systems, where starch is often used in confectionery products, the temperature at which starch grain damage occurs is rather higher than in simple aqueous systems. In many confectionery gels the production of a high viscosity during cooking is undesirable and modified starches are available which are known as thin-boiling starches. The modification, normally acid thinning or oxidation, weakens the starch grains so that they fragment during cooking and do not produce the viscosity rise associated with swollen grains. Figure 17.6 illustrates the breakdown of acid-thinned grains during cooking.

On storage the starch gels often become firmer, and this may be associated with weeping or syneresis. In microscopical terms this syneresis is associated with the amylose network becoming thicker as more amylose precipitates out of solution onto the gel network. These effects are shown in Figure 17.7. Some gums, such as locust bean gum, can interact with starch and reduce the tendency for syneresis to occur.

17.4   Pectin gels

High-sugar pectin gels produced with high-methoxy pectins are formed at low pH values. The key features of successful pectin gels are fully dispersing the pectin and achieving a moderately rapid setting rate. The gels form on cooling in several stages. Firstly, pectin molecules form into fibrils, then the fibrils aggregate into bundles and the bundles aggregate into a network, and finally more pectin aggregates onto the network. This process is illustrated in Figure 17.8. When the pH is too high then the gel does not set and the state of aggregation stops at the stage where pectin fibrils aggregate into bundles. This process is shown in Figure 17.9. When the pH is too low excessive aggregation of pectin onto the network can lead to syneresis.

Figure 17.7 (a) 10% corn starch suspension cooked to beyond peak viscosity (transmission electron micrograph × 20 000). (b) 10% corn starch suspension cooked to beyond peak viscosity, aged for 7 days at 5°C (transmission electron micrograph × 20 000). (c) 10% acid-thinned corn starch suspension cooked to beyond peak viscosity (transmission electron micrograph × 20 000). (d) 10% acid-thinned corn starch + 5% locust bean gum cooked to beyond peak viscosity (transmission electron micrograph × 20 000). (e) 10% corn starch suspension cooked to peak viscosity, aged for 7 days at 5°C (scanning electron micrograph × 2000). (f) 10% corn starch suspension cooked to beyond peak viscosity, aged for 7 days at 5°C (scanning electron micrograph × 2000). (g) 10% potato starch suspension cooked beyond peak viscosity, aged for 7 days at 5°C (scanning electron micrograph × 500).

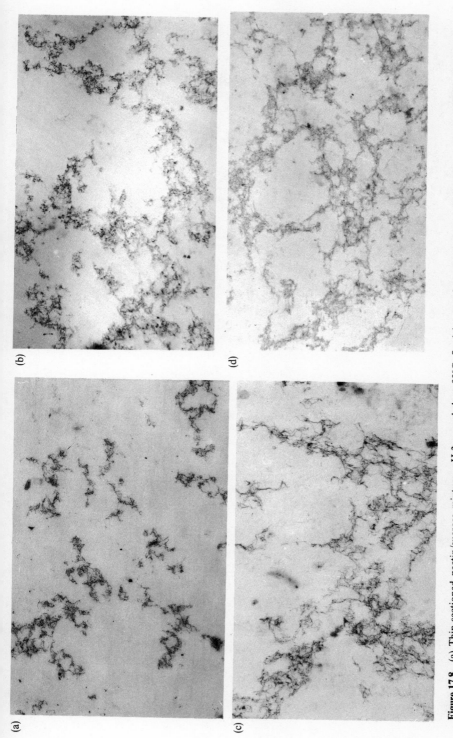

Figure 17.8 (a) Thin-sectioned pectin/sucrose mixture, pH 3, sampled at 90°C, fixed in uranyl acetate and ruthenium red (× 10000). (b) Thin-sectioned pectin/sucrose mixture, pH 3, sampled at 70°C, fixed in uranyl acetate and ruthenium red (× 10000). (c) Thin-sectioned pectin/sucrose mixture pH 3, sampled at 60°C, fixed in uranyl acetate and ruthenium red (× 20000). (d) Thin-sectioned pectin/sucrose gel, pH 3, sampled at 25°C, fixed in uranyl acetate and ruthenium red (× 20000).

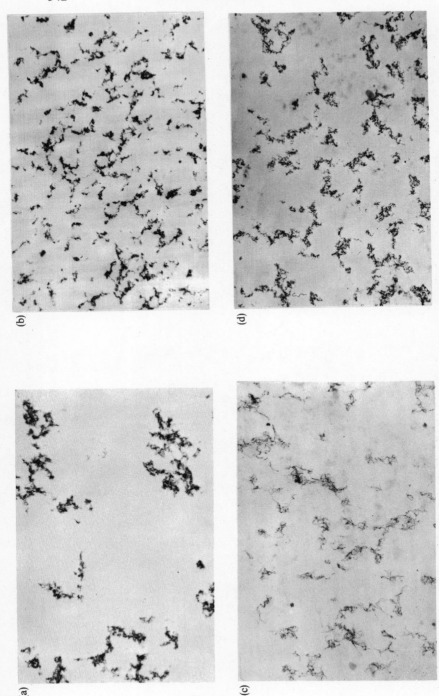

Figure 17.9 (a) Thin-sectioned pectin/sucrose mixture, pH 4, sampled at 70°C, fixed in uranyl acetate and ruthenium red (×10000). (b) Thin-sectioned pectin/sucrose mixture, pH 4, sampled at 90°C, fixed in uranyl acetate and ruthenium red (×10000). (c) Thin-sectioned pectin/sucrose mixture, pH 4, sampled at 60°C, fixed in uranyl acetate and ruthenium red (×20000). (d) Thin-sectioned pectin/sucrose mixture, pH 4, sampled at 25°C, fixed in uranyl acetate and ruthenium red (×20000).

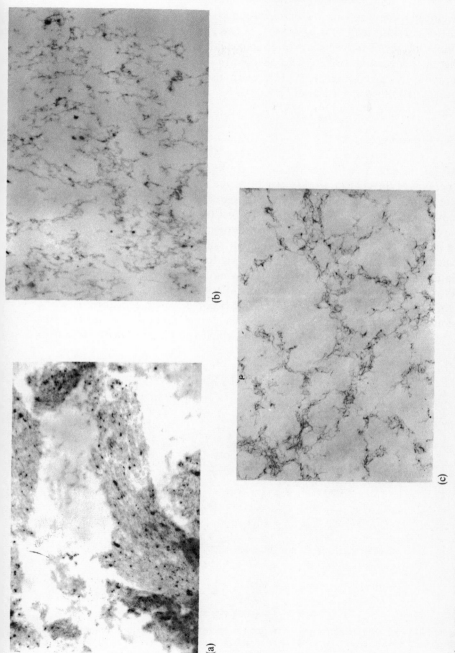

Figure 17.10 (a) Thin-sectioned pectin/glucose syrup (42 DE) mixture, pH 3, sampled at room temperature, fixed in uranyl acetate and ruthenium red (× 10 000). (b) Thin-sectioned pectin/glucose syrup (42 DE) mixture, pH 3, prepared with minimal stirring after addition of buffer, sampled at room temperature, fixed in uranyl acetate and ruthenium red (× 20 000). (c) Thin-sectioned pectin/glycerol gel, pH 3, fixed in uranyl acetate and ruthenium red (× 20 000).

Using glucose syrup instead of sucrose speeds up the process of aggregation, and this can also lead to a poor set—in this case the aggregation occurs so rapidly that the fibrils associate into separated tightly packed bundles and no coherent network is formed. The problem of too rapid aggregation can be countered by raising the pH slightly or by using a slow-release pH system. Figure 17.10 illustrates these effects.

17.5 Gelatin gels

Like pectin gels, gelatin gels form on cooling and rely on having a good dispersion of the gelatin. In this case however the setting process is naturally quite slow and the problems of too rapid aggregation are not normally encountered. The early stages of gelatin gel formation are less clearly seen microscopically, but may involve gelatin molecules reforming into a collagen-like structure. Collagen-like spindles can be formed from gelatin gels by treatment with enzymes, and it is interesting to note that, whilst acid pigskin gelatins tend to form long spindles showing collagen banding, acid ossein gelatins only form short, squat spindles. These structures are illustrated in Figure 17.11. As gelatin gels mature and become firmer, the fibre network becomes more compact, the temperature of storage and the 'Bloom strength' of the gelatin influencing the extent to which the fibre network develops.

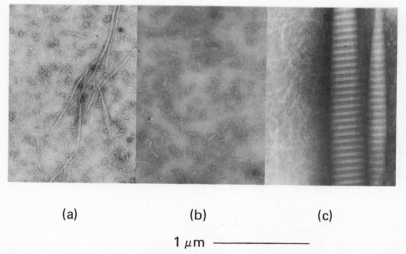

(a)   (b)   (c)

1 μm —————————

Figure 17.11 (a) Acid-prepared gelatin treated for 1 h with trypsin. (b) Lime-prepared gelatin treated for 1 h with trypsin. (c) Acid-prepared gelatin treated for 1 week with trypsin. All are negative-stained preparations from gelatin gels which have been disrupted using trypsin. Note increased size of spindles with prolonged trypsin treatment and different nature of aggregates in acid- and lime-prepared gelatins.

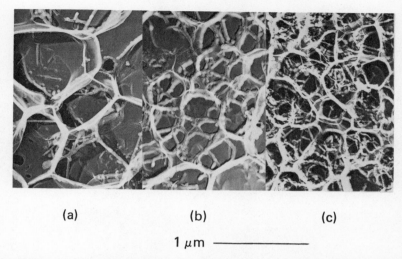

(a) (b) (c)

1 μm ─────────────

Figure 17.12 (a) 5% low-Bloom gelatin matured at 10°C for 5 h. (b) 5% high-Bloom gelatin matured at 10°C for 5 h. (c) 5% low-Bloom gelatin mature at 10°C for 48 h. All freeze-etched replicas. Note that a fibrous network has developed very much earlier in the high Bloom strength gelatin gel.

High-Bloom gelatins and lower temperatures tend to produce more compact networks. Figure 17.12 illustrates the network development in gelatin gels.

Gelatin is also used in the production of marshmallows, and in this case the foaming and gelling properties of the gelatin are required. In some cases it is possible to replace part of the gelatin with another protein, such as whey protein isolate. Here the whey protein isolate can take over the foaming characteristics of the gelatin, leaving the remaining gelatin to form a gel network.

17.6 Other protein gels

Gelatin is unusual amongst proteins in that it forms a heat-reversible gel on cooling. Most protein systems form non-reversible gels on heating. Particular examples which are used in confectionery products are egg albumen and whey proteins. In these proteins the gel is developed by aggregation into clumps, which attach to each other to form a three-dimensional network. These structures are generally pH-sensitive, and like pectin gels the rate of aggregation is critical: too rapid aggregation results in separation whilst too slow aggregation results in a weak gel. Figure 17.13 illustrates these effects.

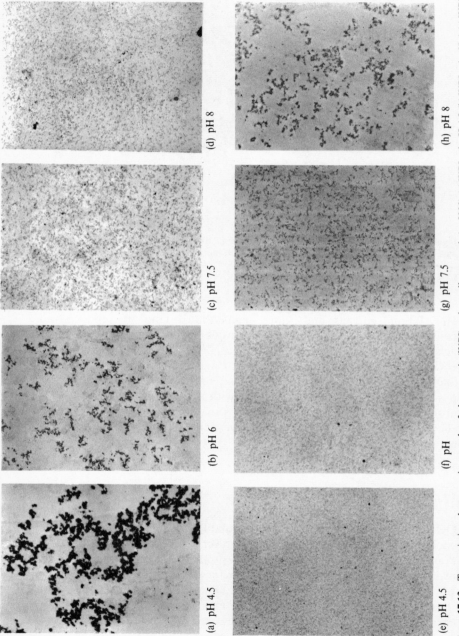

(a) pH 4.5   **(b)** pH 6   **(c)** pH 7.5   **(d)** pH 8

(e) pH 4.5   **(f)** pH   **(g)** pH 7.5   **(h)** pH 8

Figure 17.13 Transmission electron micrographs of whey protein (WPI) and egg albumen gels (× 5000). (a) WPI gel, pH 4.5. (b) WPI gel, pH 6. (c) WPI gel, pH 7.5. (d) WPI gel, pH 8. (e) Egg albumen gel, pH 4.5. (f) Egg albumen gel, pH 6. (g) Egg albumen gel, pH 7.5. (h) Egg albumen gel, pH 8.

17.7 Boiled sweets and pulled sweets

In microscopical terms boiled sweets represent the simplest confectionery product. When properly made and stored they consist of a glassy matrix with occasional flavour/colour and air inclusions. Graining can occur due to either poor formulation or storage, and this is seen as crystals growing out of one another (Figure 17.14). In some jelly products (e.g. jelly babies) it is desirable for a small amount of graining to occur at the surface of the sweet whilst the centre remains glassy. In these products small changes in ingredients or recipe can lead to the graining developing too quickly through the body of the sweet.

17.8 Panned sweets and coatings

Panning involves building up a layer of closely knit sugar crystals around the outside of a preformed centre. Producing a hard-panned coating is generally a lengthy process with many fine layers being applied and dried off. When more concentrated syrups are used to produce the coating, the crystals in the layer tend to be coarser. The normal process is to use more concentrated syrups at the beginning of the coating process and reduce the concentration towards the end in order to produce a finer finish. The essential structure of the panned coating is one of very tightly interlocked crystals, possibly held together by a very thin glassy or syrupy layer. In soft-panned products the sugar crystals are held in a firm gel matrix; these coatings can be applied much more rapidly. Alginate can be used to produce a hard-panned layer quite quickly; here calcium salts act to gel the alginate, which then acts as cement to hold the sugar crystals in the coating. The calcium salts may be derived from icing sugar or deliberately added. Coatings made with alginate generally need a few final coats of conventional hard panning to achieve a smooth finish.

17.9 Chocolate-flavoured couvertures

These are often used to coat nuts or other products, and an important characteristic of these coatings is their viscosity, which is controlled by the fat content and by the state of the non-fat components in the coatings. Milk-based powders are often used in these coatings, and different powders break down to different extents during manufacture of the coating. Calcium caseinate particles have a dense, compact structure which is not damaged much on processing and tends to produce a low-viscosity casting. Other milk products have highly aerated particles which fragment to give lots of fine particles and consequently lead to a higher viscosity in the coating. Figure 17.15 shows some of these powder particles and their breakdown products.

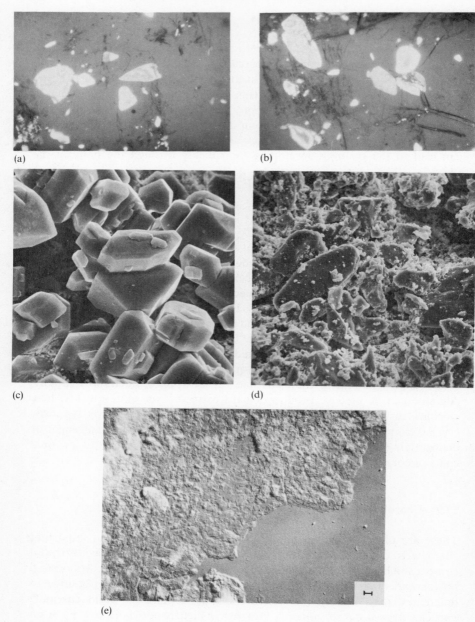

Figure 17.14 Micrographs of sugar crystals. (a, b) Light microscopy of crystals growing in extruded sugar glass (× 50). (c) Scanning electron micrograph of icing sugar (× 400). (d) Scanning electron micrograph of sugar crystals produced by shearing sugar syrup (× 400). (e) Growth of sugar crystals. A freeze-etch replica of an 80% sugar syrup. Note the packing of the aggregates into larger structures. Bar represents 1 μm.

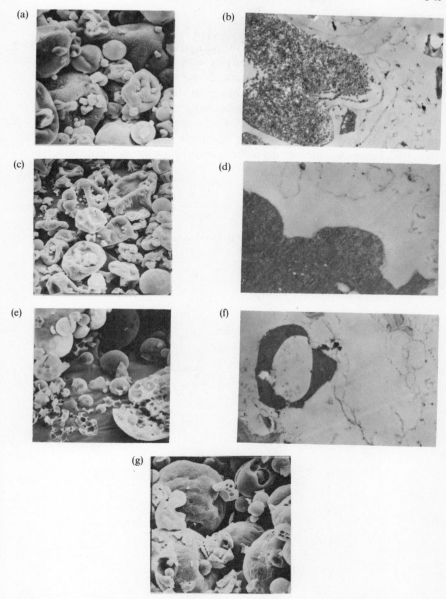

Figure 17.15 (a) Standard skimmed-milk powder (SMP) (scanning electron micrograph × 180). (b) Coating made with standard SMP (transmission electron micrograph × 3000). (c) Calcium caseinate powder (scanning electron micrograph × 180). (d) Coating made with calcium caseinate (transmission electron micrograph × 3000). (e) Calcium-reduced, potassium-replaced ultra-filtered SMP (scanning electron micrograph × 180). (f) Coating made with calcium-reduced, potassium replaced, ultrafiltered SMP (transmission electron micrograph × 3000). (g) WPC 35 powder (scanning electron micrograph × 180).

17.10 Concluding comments

This chapter has illustrated the wide range of structures found in confectionery items and has attempted to demonstrate how these structures relate to the overall performance of the products. Some mysteries still remain to be answered, many related to the state of sugar: How do different crystal shapes affect chewiness? What is the extent and character of 'amorphous' sugar? How do various gelling agents interact? These questions and many more will eventually be answered by a more complete description of confectionery structure. Emerging microscopy techniques promise much for the understanding of sugar technology.

Acknowledgements

The author wishes to thank the Food Research Association, Leatherhead, for permission to reproduce their photographs in this chapter.

18 Quality control and chemical analysis

I.M. BILLCLIFF and R.D. BULLOCK

18.1 Introduction

'*The better the quality, the greater the cost*'. For years, this supposition was thought to be valid, and indeed, where the quality control emphasis is on finished product inspection, then it will apply. Under this policy, insufficient attention is paid to the earlier parts of the process—out-of-specification materials are used, correct operating procedures are not followed, production operators are unaware of the standards they should be working to and therefore unaware of the process running 'out of control'; at the end of the manufacturing line reject product is sorted from that which, by chance, complies with the quality standards, and significant quantities of scrap are produced at appreciable cost to the company.

Under these conditions, when manufacturing management is under pressure to meet volume targets, a common remedial action is to increase the speed of the production line. Unfortunately, this generally results in the line becoming further out of control and generating even greater volumes of scrap.

The answer to the problem is to adopt the correct approach to quality control, that of *prevention* rather than cure, of controlling the whole manufacturing operation from raw materials through to despatch of finished product, the policy of getting it 'right first time' [1].

The confectionery industry involves selling taste, texture and appearance (or presentation), and quality efforts must be aimed at ensuring that these three parameters are up to standard. This objective is only achieved by adopting the above policy—by ensuring that only correct materials are used, that recipes are adhered to, that weights and manufacturing conditions are controlled and that procedures are correctly followed. By these means, scrap is reduced and manufacturing efficiency increased, thus improving profitability; the initial supposition is then seen to be fallacious and the opposite is, in fact, shown to be the case: *the better the quality, the lower the cost.*

18.2 Designer quality

The basic principles of quality control apply to all manufacturers, regardless of the end product. However, each company is unique in its operation, and the parameters critical to the quality of its products will differ from those of other companies, even within the same industry, depending on the products manufactured, the processes employed and the market sector within which the company operates.

Quality control procedures therefore need to be tailored to fit the requirements of each individual company, and indeed each manufacturing operation within the company. Hence the concept of 'designer quality'.

Quality must be 'designed' into a product as part of the development process; this starts with a product brief from marketing, which includes a definition of the quality standards. These are, therefore set by marketing, but *not* in isolation from other functions. It is absolutely crucial that all relevant managers are involved in this process, to ensure that they are not only aware of the standards required, but are also in agreement that the standards are achievable in practice.

Having defined the standards, it is the responsibility of each department to fulfil its role in ensuring that they are adhered to, from the procurement of materials by purchasing to the correct specification through to distribution, ensuring that products are stored and despatched to customers under the correct conditions. The role of the quality control department is to monitor all the activities involved, report variances from standard and then work in conjunction with the relevant departments to identify the causes of such variances, correct them and implement procedures to prevent recurrences.

There are thus two vital ingredients to the achievement of the correct quality standards. The first is *communication* between departments and the second is *cooperation* between departments. It is an absolute fallacy to believe that the quality control department is wholly responsible for product quality. Each department or section of the manufacturing and distribution process is responsible for the quality of its part of the operation, and must be held accountable for variances from standard within its sphere of activity. The quality control department is a service function, providing information and assistance to enable other departments to maintain the necessary standards.

18.3 Control of raw materials and packaging

'*Know your supplier*' is a very important maxim in ensuring the consistent quality of materials supplied. A good working relationship needs to be built up with suppliers; visits should be made to suppliers' premises to gain knowledge of their process capabilities and assurance that they will be able to supply to the required specification. Equally, suppliers should be invited to customers' premises, to become aware of the products and processes in which their materials are used and the difficulties caused by supplying material outside specification. Such reciprocal visits, and regular dialogue between technical staff, achieve a greater understanding between customer and supplier, the benefits of which are invaluable.

Specifications must be agreed between supplier and customer, with critical parameters defined, including conditions under which materials are to be delivered to prevent damage or contamination during transit.

Copy 1 **ORIGINATOR**

GOODS RECEIVED NOTE

GRN 6101

ORDER No.	
DATE RECEIVED	
ADVICE NOTE	
CARRIER	

SUPPLIER ____________________

Line	Item No.	Description	Supplier Lot No.	Stock Unit	Quantity Received	Location

Signature ____________________ Date ____________

Quantity Released ____________

Quantity Held ____________ Reason ____________

Quantity Rejected ____________

Signature ____________ Date ____________

LABORATORY TESTS

Test	Result	Specification

Signature ____________________ Date ____________

Figure 18.1 Goods received note.

18.3.1   *Receipt of materials*

On arrival at the factory, the first task is to ensure that the material is in a satisfactory condition to be unloaded from the delivery vehicle. In the case of bulk tanker deliveries, a sample should be taken and tested immediately, before allowing the material to be pumped into the factory's bulk storage tanks. Sacks and cardboard cartons of dry goods should be free of staples and metal fastenings, and containers which are damaged, heavily soiled or leaking should not be accepted. Deliveries of fruit and nuts require careful inspection and rejection of the consignment at the slightest evidence of infestation. Materials carrying any microbiological risk, such as skimmed-milk powder or cocoa powder, should be held in a separate isolation store, until shown to be uncontaminated.

No materials should be used in the factory until tested and released for use by the laboratory, and to facilitate adherence to this policy it is useful to operate a goods received note (GRN) system. The notes (Figure 18.1) are numbered consecutively and consist of four sheets. On delivery of a material, the stores supervisor completes a GRN, retains the top copy and sends the remaining three to the laboratory. After sampling and testing the delivery, the laboratory manager completes the forms, indicating whether the material is released for use or not, and returns one sheet to the stores supervisor, sends one to purchasing department and retains one for laboratory records.

18.3.2   *Sampling*

Correct technique is crucial to obtaining a representative sample of a delivery, and to ensuring that samples for microbiological testing are taken aseptically. Different lot numbers present in a delivery should be sampled and tested separately. Much has been written about the statistics of sampling, and to consider the subject in more detail the reader is directed to the official treatises—BS 6001 [2], BS 6002 [3] and the ICMSF sampling plans for microbiological testing [4].

18.3.3   *Testing*

Responsibility for ensuring that a material complies with specification rests squarely with the supplier, and the customer's laboratory should not find it necessary to perform a comprehensive range of quality control checks on a delivery. Critical parameters should, however, be tested routinely, together with checks which have commercial implications, e.g. solids content of glucose syrups or yield values on flexible packaging.

It can be useful to receive a certificate of analysis with a delivery, particularly for materials which carry a microbiological risk. By doing so, a lot of unnecessary testing may be eliminated, although it is still prudent to perform some tests on a random basis.

Analyses performed on raw materials are dealt with later in the chapter, but it is appropriate to discuss packaging testing at this juncture. This is a subject to which insufficient attention is often paid, which can be a false economy, since the efficiency of the packing operation can be dramatically affected by material which is outside specification, particularly when high-speed wrapping machinery is involved. It is recommended that the following tests be performed:

(1) Flexible packaging—yield, dimensions and coefficient of friction, with seal strength where appropriate.
(2) Foil laminates—yield and sealing temperature routinely, with a complete breakdown on a random basis.
(3) Waxed paper—yield, surface wax and total wax.
(4) Cartons, tins, etc.—fit of lid to base.
(5) All items—weight of a unit of wrap or pack, for tare purposes, and correctness of print and colour, and odour and taint, where appropriate.

The majority of sugar confectionery products are not normally associated with taint problems, but where this is a possibility, e.g. unwrapped toffee packed into cardboard cartons, then taint tests should be performd routinely on incoming deliveries. The procedure is to store the appropriate confection in a closed glass vessel, in the presence of the packaging, for 24 h, and then compare the taste with a control sample stored alone in a closed glass vessel for the same period of time.

The maintenance of correct storage conditions is very important and whilst most materials can be satisfactorily stored in a cool, dry, ambient warehouse, insulated to prevent excessive temperature variation, some items require special storage conditions, and adequate provision must be made for these, e.g. flavours requiring chilled storage, or packaging materials susceptible to drying out. Care must also be taken to ensure that materials are not kept in stores in excess of their normal shelf lives.

18.4 Process control

The primary requirements for adequate control of the manufacturing process are clearly defined recipes, manufacturing procedures and specifications. To control the process thoroughly, the principle of hazard analysis and critical control points (HACCP) should be utilised. In applying this, the process is analysed in detail, all operations which are critical to product quality identified, and appropriate controls introduced, e.g. weights, mixing times, temperatures, vacuum levels, steam pressures, etc.

Greater control of material usage can be achieved if minor ingredients are weighed up in a preparation area and dispensed to manufacturing departments in batch quantities. Fruit and nuts should be sorted to remove foreign matter and mouldy product, then passed through a metal detector before use. When premixes of bulk ingredients are produced in automatic equipment, samples must be analysed routinely to ensure that ingredients are present in the correct proportions.

In a batch process, all parameters can be controlled for each batch, which, in theory, should make all batches identical. However, in practice minor variations occur between batches and a continuous process will therefore lead to a more consistent product, as long as it is adequately controlled. Wherever possible, on-line checks should be automatic, e.g. temperature read-outs, although these need routine manual validation. On a continuous line, regular checks should be made on the levels of addition of ingredients which are pumped in, such as acid solutions, flavours and colours.

Apart from routine on-line inspection of product appearance, the following should also be checked:

(1) Weight—a regime for performing weight checks must be rigidly adhered to, and records kept on-line, using a chart as illustrated (Figure 18.2). This chart can be maintained either manually or automatically, via an on-line computer linked to a balance. To obtain an excellent commonsense guide to the use of control charts, the reader is directed to Frank Price's pragmatic approach to the subject [5].

(2) Dimensions—if weights are correct, then dimensions will also generally be correct, although this is not necessarily the case. Where large tonnages of regular-sized pieces are being produced, e.g. hard-boiled sweets for stick packs,

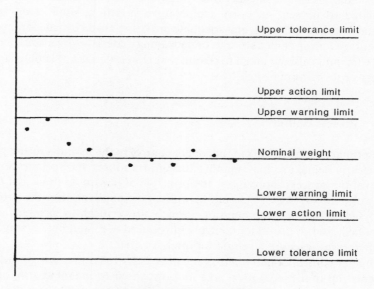

Figure 18.2 Weight control chart.

grading machines should be installed at the end of the line, to reject automatically undersize and oversize pieces.

(3) Metal detectors—the efficiency of these should be checked half-hourly, and records of test results maintained on-line, together with the action taken to rectify any faults.

The alternating of on-line checks between line operators and quality control staff helps to encourage communication and cooperation between the two departments.

18.5 Finished packs

Important attributes are general appearance, closures, correct data or batch coding and pack weights; inefficiency in this last-mentioned area can be extremely costly to a company. When packing to a set weight with an indeterminate number of pieces per pack, adjustments can, of course, be made during packing. This does not, however, detract from the importance of controlling individual piece weights during manufacture, since this has a bearing on the achievable pack weight. With a pack containing a fixed number of units, e.g. a presentation pack of pectin jellies, then weight control during manufacture becomes crucial.

In controlling pack weights, the first decision to be made is whether the line will pack to 'minimum weight' or 'average weight'. If the latter, then records of checks on finished pack weights must be kept, to satisfy legal requirements; these can vary from a simple manual record of five samples per half-hour from each production line, to a fully automated system with feedback to the weighing machine, which adjusts and controls the weights. Whilst the simple manual system will suffice, tighter weight control can be achieved by automating the system and taking many more weights than is possible manually.

The easiest way to achieve this is to install an automatic check-weigher on the packing line, which records pack weights, calculates the mean, standard deviation, etc., and prints a record for a given production period. This becomes expensive, however, when monitoring a large number of packing lines, when it is preferable to install a basic check-weigher on each line, all linked to a central computer which collects data from each check-weigher via an interface. The system is programmed to switch between lines, monitoring each for a short period, enabling sufficient data to be collected to allow pack weights to be finely controlled and 'give-away' reduced to a minimum.

18.6 Sensory evaluation

As the confectionery industry is selling taste, texture and appearance, great importance must be attached to the control of organoleptic quality. There are, however, a number of constraints to placing a major effort behind product tasting:

(1) Finished product is being tested, rather than control being applied to the process.
(2) The number of samples the human palate can taste in one session is very limited.
(3) Palate sensitivity varies during the day.
(4) Most products require 24 h from manufacture for the flavour and texture to mature.

Having said this, it is generally very useful to have information on organoleptic quality from the following sources:

(1) Routine daily evaluation by a panel of trained tasters
(2) On-line tasting by operators—this gives a more rapid feedback of any problems arising.
(3) Regular tasting by marketing management, to maintain their awareness of the standard quality levels of manufactured product, and provide an opportunity for comment against their perception of the product.

Sensory evaluation is very subjective, but becomes less so with correct training of the panel, a carefully considered questionnaire and the proper use of statistics. The technique of sensory profiling, developed in the UK by the Campden Food and Drink Research Association [6], is a useful step forward in this area and, as well as being a quality control tool, has a particular application in product development. Here, the desired attributes are initially defined, a theoretical profile is then built up, and the product is developed to match that profile.

18.7 Hygiene

The majority of sugar confectionery products are boiled to a temperature sufficient to kill any harmful bacteria present. However, surface contamination can always occur in the subsequent handling of products after they have cooled down, and thus products with lower solids levels, or which have not been boiled, can be subject to microbiological contamination. Good hygiene practices are therefore of paramount importance.

All aspects of food hygiene need to be covered in an induction training session for new employees, before they commence work. It may also be considered a wise precaution to have new employees stool-tested, to prevent a symptomless carrier of a pathogenic organism from entering the factory environment. Thereafter, this could be repeated once per year and after visiting any overseas country which may be considered a risk area.

On entering a production area, everyone should wash their hands, using a bactericidal soap, and then apply a sterilant, e.g. an alcohol-based rinse.

Wounds must be covered with an appropriate dressing, which must be readily visible and detectable by a metal detector. No jewellery, other than plain wedding rings or sleeper ear-rings, should be worn.

Each factory requires a fully documented cleaning schedule, defining the frequency of cleaning of every piece of equipment and working area, the chemicals to be used and the procedures to be followed. A manager responsible for hygiene should be appointed and adequate training for cleaning staff is essential, since the effort put into the job can be completely negated if correct procedures are not followed.

When maintenance work is performed in the factory, the area involved must be throughly cleaned afterwards, and any surfaces coming into contact with product should be sterilised with a terminal sanitising agent before production recommences.

Regular hygiene audits are necessary throughout the factory, paying attention to items such as housekeeping, cleanliness of machinery, surfaces and equipment, the risk of contamination by foreign bodies and any need for repairs or replacement, in relation to equipment or building fabric.

18.7.1 *Microbiological testing*

The number of incidents of microbiological contamination of foodstuffs is increasing rapidly, foods which were previously thought to be safe are increasingly found to be not so, and today's consumer is far more aware of the problem. New, rapid testing methods, e.g. Bactometer, are being introduced, which are more reliable and sensitive than traditional methods. Some testing is therefore considered necessary, and the extent to which this is required will be identified by the HACCP analysis. The following are recommended:

(1) The testing before use of any raw materials which may be considered a risk, or alternatively the receipt of microbiological certificate of analysis with the delivery.

(2) Routine swabbing of the factory to confirm the effectiveness of cleaning.

(3) Random swabbing of operators' hands, to ensure compliance with the hand-washing procedures.

(4) Testing of any finished products identified as being susceptible to contamination.

(5) Monitoring of cooling water systems for *Legionella*.

If testing is performed on site, then the microbiology laboratory should be physically separated from the factory, to prevent any risk of cross-contamination.

18.7.2 *Foreign matter*

At the very least, it is extremely unpleasant for a consumer to find foreign matter in a foodstuff. At worst, it can cause injury and be very costly to the manufacturing company in terms of compensation, lost reputation and consequent lost sales. Every precaution must therefore be taken to prevent this sort of contamination, and the following action is recommended:

(1) Sort fruit and nuts, and pass them through a metal detector, before use.

(2) Pass materials and mixes through sieves or in-line filters, at appropriate stages in the process.

(3) Keep wooden pallets out of processing areas.

(4) Debox raw materials before they enter processing areas.

(5) Prevent glass from entering the factory; protect all lights and ensure all internal windows are of Perspex.

(6) Keep paperclips, staples, drawing pins, etc., out of the factory.

(7) Ban smoking on site, with the possible exception of designated areas within the canteen.

(8) Provide maintenance engineers with containers in which to place nuts, bolts, washers, etc., when working on-line.

(9) Do not permit 'tape engineering', i.e. repairs effected with adhesive tape, string, etc.

(10) Regularly inspect conveyor belts for fraying edges and trim or replace as soon as necessary.

(11) Pass product through metal detectors as late as possible in the process, ideally as finished packs.

(12) Employ a reputable firm of specialists to provide a comprehensive pest control service.

(13) Keep doors shut and screen any windows which need to be opened.

The list is not exhaustive, but covers the main points.

18.8 Legislation

Compliance with food legislation, with regard to composition and labelling, must be built in at the development stage, taking due account of any export requirements. With the increasing complexity of legislation relating to foodstuffs, it is frequently necessary to seek advice on the matter, either from a specialist consultant, or from a trade or research association; the authors have found local trading standards officers very willing to advice on the legality of labelling. Whilst legislation is continually changing, it is perhaps worth noting that the current list of Acts with which the confectionery manufacturer has to comply is as follows:

Medicines Act 1968—for medicated confectionery only
Trade Descriptions Act 1968
European Communities Act 1972
Trade Descriptions Act 1972
Food Act 1984

Weights and Measure Act 1985
Food and Environment Protection Act 1985
Single European Act 1986

There are a host of statutory instruments associated with the above Acts, all of which are available from HMSO.

18.9 Chemical analysis

The main purposes of chemical analysis are to ensure that raw materials are to specification and finished product is of the correct composition and will have the required keeping qualities. Of the raw materials used, granulated sugar, glucose syrup, fats (including butter), condensed milk, nuts, acid and flavours need to be monitored (see Table 18.1). Finished product may require analysis for sugars present, moisture content, acid content, fat and protein levels and, in the case of medicated products, levels of active ingredients. The laboratory may thus be called upon to perform a wide range of analyses and, in doing so, a number of precautions must be taken.

Table 18.1   Tests applied to raw materials

Raw material	Parameter	Potential problem
Sugar	Particle size	Handling/processing difficulties
	Dampness	Clumping in silo
	Clarity of solution	Foreign matter
	Protein content	Foaming when boiling
Glucose syrup	Clarity/colour	Foreign matter
	Per cent dextrose	Incorrect grade
	Foam index	Foaming when boiling
	Total solids	Buying excess water
Fats	Slip point	Incorrect grade
	Free fatty acid content	Rancidity in product
Condensed milk	Taste	Off-flavours
	Viscosity	Handling difficulties
	Total solids	Buying excess water
Nuts	Free fatty acids	Rancid flavour
	Aflatoxins	Carcinogenicity, noncompliance with legislation
Acids	Particle size	Poor distribution in product
Flavours	Taste	Wrong flavour to product

18.9.1 Laboratory practice

It is essential that all reagents are standardised and all instruments calibrated, as necessary. Specific responsibilities for equipment maintenance, cleaning and calibration should be assigned to laboratory technicians, with these activities recorded.

Analyses performed should be clearly documented and results clearly and concisely reported. When numerous analyses are performed routinely, the authors have found it extremely useful and time-effective to use preprinted sheets for this purpose.

The laboratory manager should perform internal audits to ensure that all procedures are being correctly followed and all safety requirements being rigidly adhered to.

18.9.2 Sugar analysis

Various techniques are available for the analysis of sugars, the major components of sugar confectionery products. The traditional methods of reducing sugar analysis by Lane & Eynon [7] and polarimetry, with subsequent inversion and reanalysis, enable sucrose, glucose and invert sugar systems to be analysed [8], and are widely used. These are, however, being superseded by the more modern methods of gas–liquid chromatography (GLC) and high-performance liquid chromatography (HPLC) [9].

To perform GLC analysis, the carbohydrates must be quantitatively converted to volatile derivatives, which must be stable at column temperatures. Although accurate, the method is time-consuming, and HPLC is thus the current widely used technique. With this method, the liquid mobile phase is pumped through a narrow-bore column (typically 0.01 inch) under high pressure (typically 2000 psi), most commonly into a refractive index detector. Using an ion-exchange column in the calcium form, and water as solvent, oligosaccharides in glucose syrup up to Dp4 may be separated, and mannitol and sorbitol may be separated from dextrose. With an amino column and 75:25 acetonitrile:water as solvent, fructose, dextrose, sucrose, maltose, lactose and glycerine all separate, but mannitol and sorbitol coelute with dextrose (Figure 18.3). Using a 62:38 ratio of acetonitrile:water, oligosaccharides up to Dp8 can be separated.

Other rapid methods include the YSI industrial analyser (Figure 18.4), which uses an immobilised enzyme, on a membrane, to generate hydrogen peroxide in the presence of a specific sugar. The quantity generated is measured by an electrode and the sugar concentration is displayed in terms of mg/dl, within 60 s. Membranes are available for dextrose, lactose and sucrose determinations.

The authors have developed a novel method of determining dextrose in glucose syrup, using the Exactech blood glucose meter. This cost-effective

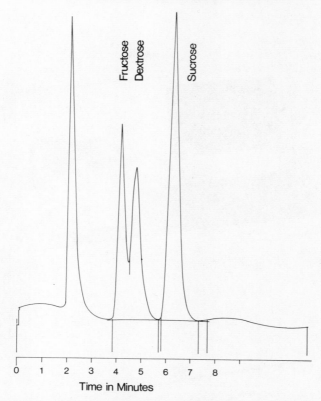

Figure 18.3 Analysis of sugars. Column, Rosil NH$_2$, 250 × 4.6 mm; solvent, 75:25 acetonitrile:water, 1.6 ml/min; refractive index detector.

method uses a disposable biosensor, specifically sensitive to dextrose, which is viscosity- and temperature-dependent. The sample is prepared in 0.05 M KCl at 20°C, as the method requires a source of chloride ions. Results are produced within 30 s, with no instrument set-up time required, and correlate well with those from the YSI analyser.

18.9.3 *Moisture content*

This has a major effect on the keeping qualities of sugar confectionery, and although generally regulated by accurate temperature control (and vacuum control where appropriate), still needs to be checked occasionally. The method used depends on the moisture content and physical state of the sample, and is generally either loss on drying, total solids by refractometry or Karl Fischer titration.

Loss on drying is a simple but time-consuming method, and finished

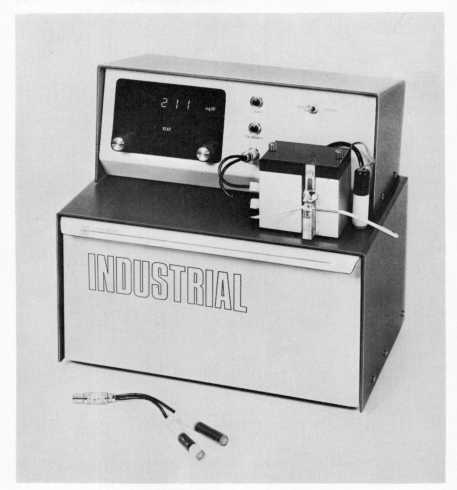

Figure 18.4   YSI industrial analyser.

products have to be dispersed in an inert matrix before drying, which is generally done in a vacuum oven.

Refractometry is used for higher moisture content products, e.g. jellies, for which a direct reading may be taken if the sample is clear, or fondants, for which a 50% solution is prepared, and the reading doubled. Corrections are necessary if sugars other than sucrose are present [10], and also for temperature [11].

Karl Fischer titration is an invaluable method for sugar confectionery products, the KF Turbotitrator with a working range of 5–100 mg of water being the most useful variant for difficult samples. After calibration of the instrument, the sample is dissolved, using 7:3 methanol:formamide for fat-free confectionery or 3:2:1 formamide:methanol:chloroform for fat-containing confectionery, and titrated automatically, using modified Karl Fischer reagent [12].

18.9.4 Protein

The Kjeldahl [13] method is the standard for protein determination. Nitrogen present is converted to ammonium sulphate by sulphuric acid, using selenium and copper as catalysts. After diluting and making alkaline with sodium hydroxide, the ammonia is distilled off, collected in standard acid solution and estimated by titration. The total nitrogen present is then calculated, and from this the protein content is arrived at by using an empirical factor. Foaming, due to carbohydrates present, can cause difficulties with this method, and the analysis is lengthy.

A simple method for protein determination in milk products is the formol titration. Amino acids present are reacted with an excess of neutral formaldehyde, and the resulting stronger acids estimated by titration. However, variable results can be obtained.

The method of dye-binding depends on the reaction of the sample with an appropriate dye at low pH, producing an insoluble protein/dye complex. After centrifugation, the decrease in absorbance of the supernatant liquid, compared with the original dye, is measured spectrophotometrically. Calibration against the Kjeldahl method is necessary, but the analysis takes only 20 min. Although purported to be inaccurate if caramelisation has occurred, the authors have developed a method for use with toffee, using amido black at pH 2.3, the results of which correlate well with those from the Kjeldahl method.

18.9.5 Fat analysis

Confectionery fats are mainly triglycerides of long-chain saturated or unsaturated fatty acids. The standard tests performed on fats are listed in Table 18.2. These give a good insight into general fat quality, but if comparing two differing fats a more specific analysis may be required. A GLC triglyceride

Table 18.2 Standard tests performed on fats

Parameter	Analysis	Expected values
Degree of unsaturation	Iodine value [14]	Variable—80–200
Melting temperature	Slip point [15]	Variable
	Clear point	Not greater than 36.4°C
Oxidative rancidity	Peroxide value [16]	Not greater than 10
Hydrolytic rancidity	Free fatty acid content [17]	Not greater than 0.7% as oleic

profile is useful here [18], since each fat produces a distinctive 'fingerprint' (Figure 18.5), in which peaks can be separated for carbon numbers in the range 30–58.

Alternatively, fatty acid methyl ester (FAME) analysis also gives a 'fingerprint' of the fatty acid components, after hydrolysis of the triglycerides. This is standard IUPAC methodology [19], producing peaks for carbon numbers in the range 14–22.

Total fat content is determined by Soxhlet extraction, the traditional technique taking 4–5 h, since an acid hydrolysis stage is required to release partly bound fat. However, modified, more rapid, extraction systems are now available, and the authors use a modification of the Fosslet method. The Fosslet fat analyser extracts fat from the sample with perchlorethylene, in a reaction chamber containing a heavy brass weight sliding on a spindle. Incomplete extraction, due to complexing of the fat, can occur, but this is overcome by adding 2 N HCl and, after reacting, adding plaster of Paris to take up the aqueous phase. This modification also speeds up the subsequent

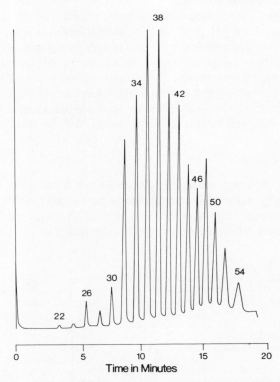

Figure 18.5 Chromatogram of hydrogenated palm kernel oil. Column, 0.5 m × 2.5 mm; packing, 100/120 CasChromQ with 3% OV-1; temperature programme, 200–355°C, rising by 10°C/min.

filtration step, producing a very clear filtrate, and gives very accurate results in the analysis of toffees and caramels.

18.9.6 *Aflatoxins*

The standard method is that of the Tropical Products Institute but is very time-consuming. HPLC, using a fluorescence detector, produces quantitative results, but the detector is rather expensive. Monoclonal antibody research has, however, led to the development of test kits, which preferentially adsorb aflatoxins onto minicolumns containing specific antibodies, e.g. the Aflatest 10 kit. After elution from the column, the aflatoxins are absorbed on to fluorosil tips, for quantification against supplied standards in a UV viewing cabinet, or, alternatively, may be differentiated by HPLC.

18.9.7 *Viscosity*

This may be measured by U-tube, falling ball, cup or torsional viscometers, but the simplest method is the digital rotational viscometer. After adjusting the sample temperature, the instrument takes an instant reading, displaying the result in poise.

18.9.8 *Particle size*

The simplest methods are either by determining the retention on standard sieves or by microscopy. Other methods are available for fine materials, but are either tedious or expensive.

18.9.9 *Acid content*

This is determined simply by dissolving the sample in water and titrating against standard sodium hydroxide solution, using either an indicator or pH-meter to determine the end-point. Where mixed acids are present, care must be taken to use the correct calculation factor.

18.9.10 *Modern methods*

Nuclear magnetic resonance (NMR) uses the absorption of radiofrequency energy by hydrogen nuclei in a powerful magnetic field. It is specifically tuned to hydrogen, and can therefore be used to measure parameters such as water content, in the absence of fat, or fat content of dry materials, e.g. chocolate. It may also be used to determine the solid:liquid ratio in fats at different temperatures, from which the performance of different fats can be predicted, in a particular product.

Near-infrared (NIR) is a technique which enables the very rapid determination of fat, protein and moisture content in a sample. A very high sample throughput can be maintained, but for each analysis 100 standards of known composition are required to calibrate the instrument.

18.10 Conclusion

It can be seen that a great deal of thought and effort is involved in ensuring the correct quality standards throughout the whole manufacturing operation, from acquisition of raw materials through to maintaining the correct conditions of storage and distribution. The use of HACCP is extremely valuable in identifying the control checks required, which include a diversity of on-line tests and laboratory analyses; the latter range from dry physical testing and classical wet chemical analysis to sophisticated, modern, instrumental techniques. As more consumer questions are raised, and an increasing number of statutory requirements introduced, the total quality control role will become greater.

Assistance in meeting these demands, and ensuring satisfactory quality, can be obtained by the application of BS 5750 [20], the UK national standard for quality systems. This can be applied to any company, large or small, and sets out the requirements to establish, document and maintain an effective and economic quality system. When first introduced, it was felt to be irrelevant to the food industry, but a few pioneering food manufacturers have now achieved registration to the standard, and it is increasingly seen to be just as relevant to the food industry as to engineering. Indeed, supplements are being drawn up by two independent quality assurance organisations, which interpret the standard specifically for food manufacture.

Finally, achievement of the required quality standards is entirely dependent on the people involved. A company's quality policy must be defined by the chief executive and communicated throughout the organisation, so that everyone clearly understands it; management at every level must then be consistent in its application. The single most important criterion in ensuring that products meet the required standard is, therefore, attitude, since: *quality is everyone's responsibility.*

References

1. F. Price, *Right First Time*, Gower, London (1984).
2. BS 6001: Part 1, Specification for sampling plans indexed by AQL for lot by lot inspection (1972), Part 2, Specification for sampling plans indexed by LQ for isolated lot inspection (1984).
3. BS 6002, Specification for sampling procedures and charts for inspection by variables for percent defectives (1979).
4. ICMSF *Micro-organisms in Foods*, vol. 2, *Sampling for Microbiological Analysis: Principles and Scientific Applications*, 2nd edn, Chapter 23 (1986).

5. F. Price, *Right First Time*, Chapter 3, Gower, London (1984).
6. D.H. Lyon, *Technical Memorandum 264*, The technique for the characterisation of flavours of canned carbonated soft drinks by sensory analysis methods, Campden Food and Drink Research Association (1981).
7. J.H. Lane and L. Eynon, *J. Soc. Chem. Ind.* **42** (1925), 32T.
8. E.M. Chatt, *Analytical Methods for Sugar Confectionery*, Leatherhead Food RA, Res. Rep. No. 17 (1949).
9. P.R. Smith, C.J. Blake and D.A. English, *Determination of Sugars by Gas–Liquid Chromatography, High Pressure Liquid Chromatography and Enzymic Methods*, Leatherhead Food RA, Res. Rep. No. 285 (1978).
10. ICUMSA, *Report of the Proceedings of the 11th Session*, Paris (1954).
11. International Correction Table 1936, *Int. Sug. J.* **39** (1937) 225.
12. P.R. Smith and P.I. George, *Technical Circular No. 385*, Leatherhead Food RA (1968).
13. R.B. Broadstreet, *The Kjeldahl Method for Organic Nitrogen*, Academic Press, London (1965).
14. BS 684, Section 2.15 (1981).
15. BS 684, Section 1.3 (1976).
16. C.H. Lea, *Proc. Roy. Soc. Lond. B* **108** (1931) 175.
17. BS 684, Section 210 (1976).
18. C.W. Hammond, *Analysis of Oils and Fats*, Chapter 3, Elsevier, Amsterdam (1986).
19. International Union of Pure and Applied Chemistry (IUPAC), *Standard Methods for the Analysis of Oils, Fats and Derivative*, 6th edn, Part 1 (Sections I and II), Pregamon Press, oxford (1979).
20. BS 5750, Part 2, Quality Systems; specification for production and installation (1987).

19　Wrapping, packaging and shelf-life evaluation

C. NELSON

Over the years sugar confectionery packaging has been developed based on the requirement to fulfil two major criteria: firstly, to provide a visual impact, or marketing appeal, making a product unique, identifiable and distinct from its competition; secondly, to provide environmental protection for the confection in order to present the consumer with a product in the form in which it was manufactured. Historically both of these became necessary as the market for each confection widened and the time between manufacture and consumption increased.

Few of us can be left without a recollection of a tin of sweets or a candy dispenser or a regular bag of goodies weighed out across the counter. Robert Opie in his book *Sweet Memories* [1] provides a nostalgic look at the marketing and advertising developments undertaken by confectionery manufacturers on their packaging in an attempt to bring their products to the consumer's attention in an increasingly competitive market.

Many confectionery firms either maintained a local, loyal clientele or ran a fleet of vans carrying freshly produced goods, only returning once their full complement was sold. This meant in all likelihood that no more than a week elapsed between production and consumption, ideal for environmentally sensitive confections, which remained tender and fresh. Some of the local brand loyalty still remains; however, due to the changing nature of shopping, with the need to compete nationally both as brands and in private label outlets, products have been forced into a requirement for longer shelf life, increased handling and distribution, and consequently modified forms of packaging.

This can be most clearly seen in consideration of the increasing influence of the multiple grocery sector at the expense of the traditional, local, confectionery–tobacconist–newsagent outlets. This too has changed the shape of the market in packaging terms, away from bulk-packed goods requiring weighing out towards prepacked, preweighed forms suitable for presentation on supermarket shelving. The one obvious exception to this is the ever-popular pick and mix market. More recently, the wrapped products have been joined by unwrapped displays with an imaginative variety of dispensers to ensure avoidance of hand contact. The other major influence from the major grocery chains has been the requirement for a consistent, specified, quality-guaranteed product. This has pushed manufacturers to better understand their processes and packaging, maintain their hygiene standards during production and hence minimise the risk of a quality problem being unexpectedly identified.

19.1 Immediate wrapping of confectionery goods

Listed below are a number of reasons, technical and commercial, for the wrapping of confectionery goods.

19.1.1 *Control of the deterioration of the confection*

Confectionery deteriorates over time through a number of physical or chemical processes, namely: exposure to heat, movement of moisture to or from the product, exposure to light, mould or yeast growth, taints or odours and mechanical damage [2].

The major fault identified in the majority of sugar confectionery is the recrystallisation of sucrose from the finished product. This results in either *graining* or stickiness or, given time, both—caused by the modification of the surface viscosity through the picking up of moisture from the atmosphere. Hence the principal factor which requires control to maximise the lifetime of the product is the *moisture level*. This is achieved by packaging which maintains the environment at the *appropriate equilibrium relative humidity* (the relative humidity at which the product neither gains nor loses moisture). This consequently keeps the confection in the condition as at manufacture.

Paine & Paine in *The Handbook of Food Packaging* [3] have tabulated the effects of humidity on various types of sugar confectionery and the equilibrium relative humidity (ERH) of a range of common products. These tables are reproduced in part below (Tables 19.1 and 19.2).

Table 19.1 Effect of humidity on various types of sugar confectionery

Type of confection	Deterioration caused	ERH
Boiled sweets	Graining and stickines	Below 30
Toffees	Graining and stickiness	Below 30
Gums and pastilles		50–65
Liquorice paste goods	Stickiness, growth of moulds	55–65
Turkish delight	and yeasts	60–70
Fruit jelly goods		60–75
Cream-paste goods	Fairly stable at ambient UK	65–70
Marshmallow	conditions	65–75
Marzipan		70–85
Fondant cream	May dry out or grow mould	75–85
Jam		75–85

Table 19.2 Equilibrium relative humidity of various kinds of confectionery

Type of product	Average values	ERH of typical specimens	Usual limits
Jam	Measured 77 Calculated 78		5–82
Fruit jellies	Measured 76 Calculated 75	59, 67, 72	59–76
Turkish delight	Measured 66 Calculated 64	65, 70, 61, 64	60–70
Marshmallow	Measured 72 Calculated 72	69, 68, 71 69, 68, 71, 66, 82, 63	63–73
Liquorice	Measured 64 Calculated 65	66 65, 55, 53, 56, 62	53–66
Gums and pastilles	Measured 60 Calculated 55	61, 64 60, 62, 61, 53, 53, 57	51–64
Toffee	Measured 47 Calculated		Below 48
Boiled sweets	Measured 28	30, 29	Below 30
Fondant cream	Measured Calculated		75–84
Marzipan	Measured 68 Calculated 69	83*, 77*	Approx. 70
Cream paste	Measured 65 Calculated 65	67, 68, 68	65–70

*For use by bakers.

The appropriate packaging materials which will protect the various types of confectionery are selected to ensure limited movement of moisture to or from the confection. The various types of wrapping and some common materials are given consideration later in this chapter.

19.1.2 *Separation of individual sweets*

Immediate wrapping of products provides a means of separating individual sweets, protecting them from mechanical damage through contact with their immediate neighbour during the rigours of distribution.

19.1.3 *Presentation*

Ever-developing printing techniques are allowing for greater originality in design and format to give identification of goods and catch the consumer's eye. This is particularly important when the customer is presented with such a huge choice of confections in present-day pick and mix outlets.

19.1.4   *Trend towards natural colours in confections*

Natural colours are largely more light-sensitive than their synthetic counter-parts and the choice of opaque materials would be important where such colours are used.

19.1.5   *Cut and wrap*

In certain instances—and perhaps not intentionally—wrapping immediately following forming (cut and wrap) may provide a support for a relatively mobile confection while it cools, avoiding undue distortion. This can be evidenced with certain softer toffee products, where a more tender eating recipe can be utilised than with a different means of forming.

19.2   Legislation

Before proceeding to consider the types of immediate wrap, the materials used and some of the characteristics associated with the choice of those materials for a particular task, it is appropriate to consider the current legislation covering the packaging which comes in contact directly with a foodstuff.

In the past in the UK there was no direct legislation on the packaging itself; the law enforcement agencies relied on the food laws such as the Food Act 1984 and more recently the Consumer Protection Act 1987, which made it an offence to sell food unless it is safe and of the 'nature, substance and quality' demanded by the consumer. This includes components which may have migrated from packaging into the food and are either toxicologically harmful or cause a deleterious effect on the organoleptic properties of the goods.

The components covered by this legislation include both volatiles, which may have been left from an incomplete packaging manufacturing process, and non-volatiles, those which migrate from the contact material into the product.

In 1979 a Statutory Instrument No. 1927 (1978) was introduced, which provided framework regulations such that under normal conditions of use any migrating constituent must not endanger human health or deteriorate the taste and aroma of the food. This was supplemented by voluntary codes of practice such as the BPF-BIBRA 'plastics for food contact applications'.

1987 saw the introduction of Statutory Instrument No. 1523 (1987) which retained the title of 'Materials and articles in contact with Food Regulations' but consolidated Statutory Instrument No. 1927 (1978) and its two amend-ments. This however only regulated two plastics, namely PVC and regen-erated cellulose films (RCFs) with particular reference in the second of these to the migration of *mono- and diethylene glycol* (MEG and DEG). These are plasticising agents used in the manufacture of RCFs and are an example of a more recently publicised concern, first aired in Germany, where positive migration into sweets was identified. The EEC is formulating—in preparation for the harmonisation of legislation in 1992—a new directive which will extend categories of controlled substances based on positive listings of those substances which can be used in the manufacture of a wider range of plastic packaging, including the monomers, antioxidants, stabilisers, slip agents and antistatics.

The methodology for the analysis of the total migration of components into a foodstuff is currently being developed at PIRA Leatherhead, the Packaging Industries Research Association [4]. In parallel it is being assessed for its usability as a tool in an industrial setting.

The most relevant aspect to sugar confectioners will be the pick-up of taint or odour in the fat phase of products such as toffees or chocolate-centred/coated goods. The simulants at present used to test for this are olive oil, sunflower oil or a synthetic triglyceride, and this test is proving the most likely to give unreliable results. The use of laminates, as is common, also demands a test for single-surface migration and requires additional care and attention.

The coming years will see further legislation implemented, which may cause additional procedural costs and require the introduction of new methods by packaging manufacturers and users.

19.3 Characteristics of materials against which selection is made

Covering the technical intricacies of all applications would be impossible within the scope of this chapter, but the material used should be selected on the basis of a combination of the criteria and properties listed below.

19.3.1 *Immediate-wrap type*

Double-fantail twist wrap (most common).
Bunch wrap.
Fold wrap—both envelope fold and open-point fold.
Pleat wrap.
Sachet wrap.
Basket wrap.
Miniwrap (individually flow-wrapped).
Combination of the above, e.g. heat seal and single fantail for the wrapping of a number of product pieces together.
Multiwrap (e.g. chewing-gum balls).
Blister pack (medicated confectionery).

Strip-packed (e.g. flat lollipops).

Tubed (Smarties).

Form filled and sealed (VFFS) for normally unwrapped product due to size or texture such as gums and jellies.

Stick packs (fruit gums/pastilles/extra-strong mints).

Other novelty packaging (Christmas, Easter, etc.).

Travel tins/travel pots.

19.3.2 *Properties of the available materials*

This will involve some or all of the following:

Gas barrier—water vapour and oxygen permeability.

Heat sealability.

Light barrier.

Plasticity.

Twist retention (twist wrap).

Dead-fold retention (fold wrap).

Scuff resistance (resistance to abrasion on passing through wrapping machine).

Retention of static electricity.

Transparency or opaqueness.

Sparkle.

Printability.

19.3.3 *Moisture sensitivity of the confection*

Consideration of the varying degrees of moisture sensitivity has been previously covered in this chapter.

19.3.4 *Price and availability of materials*

A change to new or different materials to achieve a task similar, or the same, as that already achieved by a well-established or proven material is instigated for three major reasons.

(1) Major price advantage seen through improved material yield (i.e. a material with similar properties and of a similar base price per tonne but which can yield more wraps per tonne) or a lower base price.

(2) A marketing demand to improve presentation of a product through printing modifications not possible on a given material (e.g. new techniques such as metallisation, pearlisation).

(3) Introduction of new-technology wrapping machinery able to handle different materials.

19.4 Twist wrapping

The most common format for the immediate wrapping of sugar confectionery is twist wrapping. There are two materials in various forms which are used in this country for the majority of all twist wrapping, these being:

Regenerated cellulose films (RCFs)
Waxed papers or tissues, either directly printed or laminated to plain/embossed foils.

Historically, waxed papers would have been utilised first and been the sole twist wrapping material until the introduction of regenerated cellulose films in the 1930s. Since that time RCFs have dominated the market for boilings and as overwraps to toffees wrapped first in a foil-laminated paper understrip. Paper has remained, however, the primary wrapping material for toffees and fudges.

19.4.1 *Regenerated cellulose films*

At the time of writing cellulose films remain the major material supplied for twist wrapping sugar confectionery in the United Kingdom. This has been the case for nearly fifty years. It exhibits the following properties and characteristics:

(1) It is a naturally generated material from wood pulp and has been readily available.

(2) It is transparent, glossy, flexible and able to form a barrier to oxygen.

(3) It can be adequately plasticised to provide a suitable twist and hold its twist-retention properties.

(4) It is largely polyvinyl dichloride-coated (PVDC), which provides excellent barrier properties and a good surface on which to print.

Until recent years the nitrocellulose-coated cellulose film sufficed for the majority of confectionery applications. This material—which was given the nomenclature MS—was the subject of close scrutiny during the scare associated with the migration of MEG and DEG from RCFs into confections. The use of these components as plasticisers in RCFs is now being regulated under European law, as highlighted earlier in this chapter. MS film has further been questioned on the possible migration of phthalates from nitrocellulose coating, a possibility which is legislated against in a number of overseas markets. The need for standardisation of materials within an organisation has led to the almost total replacement of MS film with MXXT.

MXXT is the standard nomenclature used to describe cellulose film PVDC-coated on both sides. This coating is laid on either as an aqueous suspension, in which case it is given the suffix 'A', or in a solvent solution, in which case the suffix is 'S'.

One of the most common specifications as in use at present is 340MXXT/S. The 340 refers to there being 340 g of material in 10 m². This greater sample size—rather than utilising g/m² (gsm)—allows for greater accuracy of weight over the larger area.

The rather clumsy nomenclature mentioned above is in the process of being replaced by a rather more simple alternative, where MXXT/S will be referred to as XS. The X here will imply 'coated', and the S solvent application of that coating.

The PVDC coating of cellulose not only provides the barrier properties as required, it also has advantages in printability. The MS material, having waxes in the coating, required that the ink system be designed to break through these waxes in order to find a suitable bonding surface. The smooth PVDC coating provides a totally adequate printing surface, giving the opportunity to apply new and developing ink technologies.

The aqueous-coated cellulose film MXXT/A has the advantage of behaving more like its forerunner MS, and can be used where a higher temperature product requires wrapping. This is due to the higher heat-seal threshold imparted to the material as a result of its coating by the aqueous method.

The future possible competitors to cellulose films are covered in the section following 'Waxed papers' below.

19.4.2 *Waxed papers*

Waxed papers would certainly have provided the earliest means of individual twist-wrapping of sugar confectionery. Only with the advent of RCFs was this monopoly overturned, although, on the whole, this is not as yet the case for toffees and fudges. It is appropriate at this point to consider why this might be. The prime reason is likely to be the grease factor associated with the fat-inclusive toffee and fudge recipes, suppliers preferring not to present their customers with an apparently greasy product. Secondly, many manufacturers have found that films have not displayed the same holding properties as papers, reducing the distortion of the product being wrapped. No conclusive explanation of this has ever been proffered, but it may be due to the insulating properties of the wax in the material.

As price advantages of alternatives put increasing pressure on manufacturers, alternatives to waxed papers are likely to be sought with increasing vigour. The most popular paper in use at the moment is a metallised wax paper. Its popularity is mainly due to its up-market presentation. This is increasingly important in a pick and mix market, which is static in standard toffees and fudges.

More recently, understrips, made from a foil-backed wax paper, have been replaced by metallised or strip-metallised cellulose films, the latter giving a similar, though cost-beneficial, finished look. The benefit arises both from increased yield of the wrapper and increased efficiency as a result of the reduction in difficulties encountered by dual-material feed systems and reel changeovers.

Standard specifications for finished wax papers would follow a pattern similar to that shown below:

(1) Foil-backed waxed paper:

Base paper	37 gsm	Opaque twisting GIP (glazed imitation parchment)
Humectant	1–2 gsm	Normally a sorbitol-based plasticiser for the paper
Foil	8–9 gsm	
Wax	10 gsm	

This provides a finished weight of *c.* 57 gsm.

(2) Plain printed waxed paper:

Base paper	37 gsm	Opaque twisting GIP
Humectant	1–2 gsm	
Wax	13–14 gsm	

This provides a finished weight of *c.* 52 gsm.

In applications where *metallised papers* are required, a base paper of around 42–44 gsm metallised GIP would replace the opaque twisting GIP in (2) above.

Should heat sealing be required, the wax chosen for the specification must be appropriate.

Embossed foil-laminated wax papers are utilised for the fold wrapping of certain products, e.g. butterscotch, which also utilise small contact points of heat-sealing wax to prevent the product from unwrapping in further handling, and to assist in providing improved integrity of the finished wrap.

19.4.3 *What does the future hold?*

As noted earlier, changes in materials and their appearances are being encouraged by (1) price advantage in a highly competitive market, (2) marketing requirement for a more noticeable product and, rarely, (3) any major technical advantage. The last of these advantages and its rarity as a development reason owes a lot to the average age of confectionery wrapping equipment in the UK. Often the competition being offered into the well-established twist wrapping market is found to run poorly, if at all, on the equipment installed within the purchasing organisation. Investment in newer wrapping machines designed to handle alternative materials may generate the opportunity to implement the introduction of cost-effective wrapper changes. So what is available?

As we have already seen, metallisation and strip metallisation of cellulose films have already provided one avenue in the replacement of waxed papers as understrips.

As immediate competitors to cellulose films two plastics are projected into the frame. These are (1) *PVC* (polyvinylchloride) and (2) *polypropylene*. The polypropylene discussed here is cast polypropylene, as opposed to oriented polypropylene, which is used for flow wrapping or similar applications.

In the UK—unlike Japan, Italy or France—PVC has not readily caught on. The majority of the PVC offered in the UK is Italian-produced and maintains an advantageous price only due to subsidisation at source, an advantage partly offset by UK tax demands. Comments above about the ability of installed equipment to run PVC are relevant here, and an additional process is required to coat with an antistatic lacquer.

The requirement for an antistatic lacquer is also true for polypropylene, but it is highly probable this will provide the greatest opportunity for a cost-driven change for the future. Polypropylene, combined with equipment capable of running it, has a major yield advantage and, given a period of investment in new equipment for the wrapping of confectionery goods, it may herald a major change in development emphasis.

Both plastics provide excellent printing surfaces and allow further inventiveness on the part of the technologists. For example a recent, though expensive, development has been the production of an ink from a suspension of metallised film. This allows for spot metallisation of product, where previously only full or strip metallisation had been possible. Pearlisation and other techniques available to the plastics industry give great opportunity for variation of the finished look. However, it is worthy of note that the wrapping of hot sweets may cause problems with heat-sensitive plastics. As to wax papers and their future, it has already been seen that they are no longer being used as understrips, specifically, to the author's knowledge, for applications with fudges. Already available as a development is a coated translucent paper, the translucent paper replacing opaque twisting GIP, waxed on one side only. This has the advantages of a good wax-free surface for printing, high gloss, better yield, wax saving, and somewhat improved runability. This still provides a suitable response to the 'grease factor'.

It is likely however that a plastic film opaquely coated could also provide a similar suitable response. If the wax does play a role as an insulator, perhaps a wax-coated film will provide an avenue for development.

A move towards a plastic-based twist wrap could provide a significant cost benefit to an industry which needs to capitalise on every opportunity in order to survive in a contracting market. However, lack of investment in wrapping machines may well prove to be an obstacle to this process of development.

19.5 Secondary packaging of confectionery

19.5.1 *Bulk packaging*

Bulk confectionery is sold into outlets where it will be weighed out in front of the customer into a bag or other container. Much of this now finds its way into the larger pick-and-mix outlets, where the customers select their own mixture of displayed wrapped sweets. Recently there has been a rise in the number of specialist sweet-retailing outlets. Both of these continue to grow, to some degree at the expense of the original corner shop confectionery, tobacconists and newsagents (CTNs). Having said that, the latter is more and more served via confectionery wholesalers as manufacturers find it increasingly difficult to support a full CTN salesforce.

There has also been an upsurge in demand for unwrapped pick-and-mix, focusing on gums and jellies in their ever-varied and often repellent shapes and sizes, through foam products, to the higher priced chocolate-coated confections. This has put pressure on manufacturers and retailers to provide hygienic dispensing and display methods for these goods.

Bulk packaging falls into three major categories:

(1) Plastic jars, now replacing the older tradition of glass, containing 5–7 lb of sweets.

(2) Seven-pound or 3-kg twist-top or pillow-packed plastic bags supplied two, four or six to an outer containing a dagger card for display purposes, product description and ingredients list.

(3) Cartons containing anything between 1 and 3 kg or 7 lb of product ranging from minimally marked brown or white cartons for market sales outlets through to five- or six-colour printed cartons for under-counter display purposes.

It is worth noting that *legislation* allows for the sale of product in bulk form by its gross weight as long as this is declared on the pack, e.g. saying 7 lb including wraps. This is allowable in view of the weighing to be done later in front of the customer. This legislation also allows for a percentage weight of the bag into which the product is weighed as part of the goods bought.

There continues to be debate in LACOTS (Local Authorities' Committee on Trading Standards) as to the role played by the wrapper in the 'goods' which are being purchased. Many confectioners argue that sweets cannot be supplied without the wrapper and hence should be included as part of the total product weight. Trading standards officers in general are not totally happy with this view and prefer, in any instance, that the actual weight of the sweet is determined in a weighed pack. This has further relevance in relation to average weight legislation when considering prepacked goods.

19.5.2 *Prepackaged items*

Prepackaged confectionery is found in shapes and forms ranging from vertical form-filled and sealed (VFFS) bags, through cartons and acetates, to more novel or adventurous packaging, often combining a variety of packaging media, designed for Christmas and Easter seasonal ranges.

Prepacked items, i.e. those items which are sold to a retailer to pass on to the customer in their manufactured form, are well legislated for in the Weights and Measures Act 1979. This declares that there must be a net weight declaration on the pack, and should only one weight be given it is assumed to be net of all wrapping materials. Legally therefore all check-weighers operating an average or minimum weight should be set with a tare to compensate not just for the packaging but also for any immediate wrapper included within the pack.

As mentioned above, LACOTS may well review the current legislation, recommending that a percentage wrapper weight should be allowed for immediately wrapped confectionery in prepackaged goods. However, this is purely speculative.

There has been a very large increase of the market sector involving prepacked bags (VFFS) with the involvement with the grocery trade and motorway service and garage forecourt facilities. This demand is largely being met by the use of reverse-printed single-web oriented polypropylene films of around 50 μm. These prepacks often have a window to display the product and are very flexible as far as design is concerned.

Surface-printed polypropylenes do not give the same gloss appearance as their reverse-printed equivalents, and some manufacturers have been unwilling to transfer unwrapped confectionery into a reverse-printed film, lacquered internally, to ensure avoidance of the risk of possible migration of components from the ink into the product. Transfer to this type of packaging would provide a major cost advantage compared with sandwich-printed laminates currently in common use.

Examples of these laminates would be the ICI-supplied polypropylenes C28/C22 laminated together or a cellulose film with a plastic partner such as 315 MXXT/S laminated with a 25 μm PVC. The films will always be fin-sealed to provide compatible surfaces for heat sealing. Should cold seal be used a fin seal would also be required.

Certainly the greatest growth has been seen in the use of pearlised or opaque polypropylene, which has provided an up-market presentation package at a reasonable price. On-going developments in ink systems are also providing other means of changing the image of plastic packaging. Examples would be (1) the technique of pearlesence, providing a finish similar to a pearlised material but allowing for a display window, or (2) polychromatic inks creating the image of metallisation, again allowing for windows in a design.

Prepacked bags in the market range in size from small medicated sweets such as Fisherman's Friend or Victory V through to 1 lb packs of confectionery found in certain major retailers.

Legislation requires that all confectionery with a life time of less than 2 years must be marked with a best before end date to identify its normal shelf life. Products with a shelf life in excess of this time scale do not require a best before end date but most manufacturers do have a policy of adding a code to all their products.

19.5.3　Display cartons for stick- and roll-packs

This is a sector in which are found fruit gums, fruit pastilles, extra-strong mints, wine gums, Polos, Refreshers and a significant number of individually wrapped boiled sweets and medicated lozenges, e.g. Tunes, Hall's Mentholyptus, Hacks, Lockets, Glacier Mints. The attraction of this pack has been the ability to keep such a product in a pocket or handbag without depositing the entire contents out after first opening, as often occurs with prepacked bags.

These stick-packs or roll-packs are usually packaged in foil-laminated papers overwrapped with a printed paper label, as in the case of fruit pastilles or Polos, or in a printed-foil, laminated waxed paper alone, e.g. Hacks or Tunes. To provide an end seal, three methods are adopted, namely (a) twist-finished ends, (b) dead-folded ends or (c) folded and heat-sealed ends, relying on the wax as the sealant, which is laminated into the paper, migrating through the tissue when heated and setting when cooled.

19.6　Outer packaging

Outer packaging required for confectionery needs to take into account the susceptibility of the various types of confectionery to crushing and deformation. This is particularly important where a generic bag, printed on-line, is used to supply a wide range of products. Here the variety of densities of the confections and the tendency of twist wrapping to settle during transit makes the rationalisation of outers a more complex task, and care should be taken in the selection of outer dimensions.

Coverage of the whole area of outer packaging, its selection and quality control is outside the scope of this chapter.

19.7　Evaluation of product shelf-lives

Evaluation of the shelf-life is normally undertaken organoleptically to identify the point at which an unacceptable level of deterioration is passed. Table 19.3 shows the shelf lives normally associated with sugar confectionery products.

At production of preliminary product samples, a number are wrapped in the appropriate packaging medium and stored for evaluation at intervals after the expected product shelf life. This shelf-life evaluation can be accelerated using the following well-established technique:

10°C above ambient doubles the rate of ageing.
20°C above ambient quadruples the rate of ageing.

Of course, the second of these is only for product and packaging which does not melt or shrivel under higher temperature conditions, i.e. not pectin jellies.

Table 19.3 Normal product shelf lives

Product type	Normal shelf-life (months)	Comments
High boilings < 2.5% water	12	
Centered high boilings	9	Normally in excess of 3.5% moisture and material available in centre to encourage graining
Lozenge paste products	> 24	Normally < 0.5% moisture
Hard-panned	24	Except nut centres
Soft-panned	6	Normally hygroscopic. Tend to be centre-dependent in ability to absorb free glucose in coating
Jelly beans	9	
Toffees	9	
Centred toffees	9	Less if softer
Soft cream paste	6–9	< 7.5% moisture
Liquorice allsorts	6–9	
Liquorice	Up to 12	
Gums and jellies	6–12	Dependent on recipe and finished moistures

19.8 Quality assurance of packaging

With the increasing pressure from, particularly, the major grocery outlets, manufacturers are being encouraged to ensure that suppliers of packaging materials provide well-specified and quality-assured packaging. The prime role for a confectionery manufacturer will be therefore to test the key operational and quality parameters of the material.

In the majority of instances these will be

(1) Grams per square metre of material (gsm). This is important if the material is being bought by weight, ensuring that adequate yield is being achieved.

(2) Detection of residual solvents and taint. This is normally conducted by one of three methods:

(a) By smell.

(b) Gas–liquid chromatography of a sample from the head space above a stored piece of packaging in a bell jar. The normal acceptable level is a maximum of $30 \, mg/m^2$ of material, of which no more than 10 mg can be ketones.

(c) The chocolate test. Forty-eight hours' incubation of a sample of chocolate in the space above $1 \, m^2$ of packaging at $25°C$ in a bell jar. This is tested by taste panel against a standard, a similar sample of chocolate incubated in an otherwise empty container. The samples are ranked on a scale of 1–4, where 2 + is the maximum acceptable score. It is possible to accelerate this test slightly by incubation at 32°C. Though this method is at slight variance with the British Standard, it is a commonly used test.

(3) Print stability and resistance to abrasion. This is done on a Patra rub tester giving 40 rubs at 2 lb/square inch.

(4) Print quality. Visual examination under standard lighting.

In more established packaging laboratories the following should also be able to be tested:

Seal strength for heat seals.
Burst strength.
Tensile strength.
Tear strength.
Twist retention.
Moisture vapour resistance.
Cobb size test for paper bases giving level of absorption of moisture caliper for cartons.

Sadly, much quality assurance is based on the ability of a material to run during production. Materials are often considered suspect when static electricity, cutting knife quality and machine wear all become a function of runability, particularly in the case of twist-wrap materials.

Further detailed information is available on the standard testing of packaging materials from packaging publications, British Standards Institute and PIRA Leatherhead.

References

1. R. Opie, *Sweet Memories*, Pavilion Books, London (1988).
2. C.R. Oswin and L. Preston, *Protective Wrappings*, Cann Publications.
3. F.A. Paine and H.Y. Paine, *A Handbook of Food Packaging*, Blackie & Son Ltd, Glasgow (1983).
4. P.A. Tice, PIRA Leatherhead, *Packaging Magazine*, October (1988).

20 Sugar confectionery in the diet

E.M.S. EDMONDSON

Confectionery is a food which provides pleasure, the popularity of which is demonstrated by the large number of people who regularly purchase these food items.

20.1 Confectionery in society [1]

Confectionery is often given as a gift because of the pleasure it bestows and because its ready portability makes it easy to send long distances. Confectionery in one form or another has been given as presents for many years, and carries with it connotations of luxury and indulgence. It also makes a pleasurable experience more pleasurable (e.g. a visit to the cinema or a trip to the seaside).

For children, confectionery is an important part of games, in part because of the interesting colours and shapes and partly as it is something that can be shared as a gesture of affection, which of course is not only limited to children. In order for the confection to be shared, it needs to either be in individual pieces or able to be broken up easily.

With changes in eating patterns and the move away from formalised eating regimes, meals are more often consumed 'on the way', so the portability and long shelf life of confectionery makes it a useful adjunct to this style of eating.

The use of confectionery to supplement or replace other food is seen by many as degrading our diet. This demands serious attention. The following sections are therefore devoted to the dietary, as distinct from the social, role of confectionery, and to the criticisms made of it.

20.2 Confectionery as food

20.2.1 *What is food?*

Food is any solid or liquid which when swallowed can supply any of the following:

(1) Material from which the body can produce movement, heat or other forms of energy.

(2) Materials for growth, repair or reproduction.

(3) Substances necessary to regulate the production of energy or the processes of growth and repair.

The components of foods which have these functions are called *nutrients*. The *diet* consists of those foods or mixtures of foods in the amounts which are actually eaten. A good diet will provide adequate amounts of all the nutrients without harmful excesses, from a wide range of foods. (For additional nutritional background see Refs. 2 and 3.)

Most foods contain more than one nutrient, but no food except mother's milk contains all of the nutrients in the right balance. Therefore, it follows that there is a place in the diet for all foods—including confectionery. There are no such things as 'good foods' or 'bad foods', but there are, of course, 'good' or 'bad' diets. If the balance of nutrients is wrong, this will lead to ill-health.

20.2.2 *Energy*

Energy provides the ability to do work, and therefore means more than just vigorous activity. It can be derived by the body from carbohydrate, fat, protein and alcohol. In the body energy is released gradually from these materials, by a series of steps, each carefully controlled by enzymes. This energy is used to perform muscular work, to maintain body temperature, and for essential bodily functions such as breathing, heart beat, etc. A considerable amount of energy is lost as body heat.

The energy content of food is measured in kilocalories (kcal or Calories) or kilojoules (kJ).

20.3 Nutrients

The following types of nutrients may be present in foods:

Carbohydrates provide the body with energy, and may also be converted into body fat.

Fats provide energy in a more concentrated form than carbohydrates and may also form body fat.

Proteins provide amino acids for growth and repair. They can also be converted into carbohydrate and used to provide energy.

Minerals are used in growth and repair, and help regulate body processes.

Vitamins help regulate body processes.

Water. Like oxygen from air, this is essential for life although rarely considered as a food or nutrient. However it comprises about 65% of the body's weight and is the medium or solvent in which almost every bodily process takes place.

Dietary fibre (roughage). In contrast to the nutrients described above, dietary fibre is a mixture of materials which are indigestible in the small intestine and are not absorbed into the body; instead they add bulk to faeces. This property is considered to be beneficial to health, although fibre can also decrease the absorption of certain minerals.

One kilocalorie is roughly equal to 4.186 kJ. One gram of either sugars or starches provides 3.75 kcal (15.6 kJ) of energy; 1 g of protein gives 4 kcal (16 kJ); 1 g of fat gives 9 kcal (37 kJ); 1 g of alcohol 7 kcal (29 kJ). To give some idea of what energy needs are in practical terms, each of the activities listed below requires about 300 kcal (1255 kJ).

   2 h golf.
   45–60 min tennis.
   30–40 min football.
   1 h walking at 4 mph.
   3 h watching television.
   5 h sleeping.

This amount of energy is provided by:

   1 lb (454 g) of potatoes.
   2 pints (1.14 litres) of beer.
   $\frac{3}{4}$ pint (430 ml) of full-cream milk.
   65 g filled chocolate bar.
   60 g chocolate biscuit.
   70 g fruit chews (14 bite-size pieces).

It should be noted that the amount of energy required for different activities varies greatly from one individual to another.

20.3.1   Carbohydrates

There are three major groups of carbohydrates in food: sugars, starches and cellulose and related materials. All are compounds of carbon, hydrogen and oxygen only and their chemical structures are all based on a common unit (nearly always glucose). The units can be linked together in different ways and in different numbers, and classification of the carbohydrates depends primarily on the number of units, which can vary from one to many thousands. Sugars and starches are a major source of food energy throughout the world, and cellulose is one of the major constituents of dietary fibre.

20.3.1.1   *Starch* Starches are polysaccharides (many sugars) composed of variable numbers of glucose units linked together to form both straight and branched chains (amylose and amylopectin respectively). They exist in granules of a size and shape characteristic of each plant source. In this form they are insoluble in water and essentially indigestible if eaten raw. When heated or cooked in the presence of water the starch granules swell and eventually gelatinise. They can then be more readily digested. In contrast, dry heat can make a small part of the starch more resistant to digestion.

All starches are broken down to their simple sugar (glucose) components in the process of digestion before being absorbed and used for energy.

20.3.1.2 Sugars

Monosaccharides (simple one-sugars). Glucose (dextrose) occurs naturally in fruit and plant juices and in the blood of living animals. Most carbohydrates are converted to glucose during digestion. Glucose can also be manufactured from starch by the action of enzymes.

Fructose occurs naturally in fruit and vegetables and especially in honey. It is the sweetest sugar known.

Galactose does not occur in the free state but forms part of lactose.

Disaccharides (two sugars). Sucrose is a combination of glucose and fructose. It is found naturally in sugar cane, sugar beet and in many fruits and vegetables such as carrots. Common table 'sugar' (whether white or brown) is sucrose.

Maltose is a combination of two glucose units. It is formed during the breakdown of starch by digestion and when grain is germinated for the production of malt liquors such as beer.

Lactose occurs only in milk and milk products. It is a combination of glucose and galactose. It is less sweet than sucrose or glucose.

Oligosaccharides (several sugars). These are most commonly found in the diet as glucose syrups which result from the partial hydrolysis of starch. They are mixtures of glucose, maltose and several more complex longer sugars chains. They are used in sugar confectionery, soft drinks and jams.

All carbohydrates when absorbed by the body provide similar amounts of energy. They are all metabolised in essentially the same way. Health concerns associated with carbohydrate consumption will be addressed under criticisms of confectionery. Some 50% of energy should be from carbohydrate.

20.3.2 Fats

Fats in the popular sense are familiar to everyone as the visible fat of meat and in the form of vegetable oils and butter. It is less well known that many other foodstuffs which are not obviously fatty also contain appreciable amounts of fat. Fats are a more concentrated source of energy than carbohydrates and are the form in which most of the energy reserve of animals and some seeds is stored.

Like carbohydrates, they are compounds of carbon, hydrogen and oxygen, but the proportion of oxygen is lower.

Fats comprise complex mixtures of substances called 'triglycerides'. Each triglyceride, in turn, comprises three fatty acids linked to one glycerol (glycerin). The difference between fats is their different fatty acid combination.

When fats are eaten, these links are broken and the component fatty acids and glycerol reassembled in different form in different parts of the body. Many, but not all, of the different fatty acids are interconvertible according to the human body's requirements. A few fatty acids are essential (and therefore known as 'essential fatty acids') and must be present in the diet if good health is to be maintained.

Dozens of different fatty acids are found in nature. They differ in the number of carbon atoms and 'double bonds' which they contain.

Saturated fatty acids have no double bonds and this makes them stable. Examples are palmitic and stearic acids, which are major constituents of hard fats such as lard, suet and cocoa butter. Butyric acid is present in small amounts in milk fat.

Unsaturated fatty acids have one or more double bonds which can react with air and make the fat go rancid. The more unsaturated the fat, the more liquid it will be at room temperature (oils). Unsaturated fatty acids can be changed into saturated fatty acids and into a mixture of *cis* and *trans* monounsaturated acids by controlled treatment with hydrogen (hydrogenation). This happens when liquid oils are hardened.

Monounsaturated fatty acids have one double bond. Oleic acid occurs in most fats but is especially predominant (70%) in olive oil. *Trans* isomers of oleic acid are found in hard margarines and in small amounts in milk, cheese, beef and lamb.

Polyunsaturated fatty acids. Examples are linoleic (with two double bonds), which occurs in large amounts in vegetable seed oils such as maize, soya and sunflower seeds, and in small amounts in some pork and poultry fat. Linolenic acid (with three double bonds) occurs in small amonts in vegetable oil, especially linseed oil. Arachidonic acid (with four double bonds) occurs in very small amounts in animal fats. It can be formed in the body from linoleic acid. Fatty acids with even more double bonds occur in fish oils prior to hydrogenation.

Linolenic, linoleic and arachidonic acids are 'essential fatty acids'.

Fats are a concentrated energy source for the diet, as well as providing essential fatty acids and carrying fat-soluble vitamins. However, because of the concerns that a high-fat diet may contribute to an increased risk of cardiovascular disease, it has been recommended that not more than 35% of energy should come from fat, and no more than 15% energy from saturated fat [4]. These recommendations do not apply to children under 5 years of age.

20.3.3 Protein

Superficially, proteins are less obvious as a group than carbohydrates and fats, although most people nowadays know that meat, fish, eggs and legumes are good sources. To the biochemist they comprise a very large group of substances with only two properties in common: they are characteristic and essential components of all living cells, and they consist of 'amino acids' linked together. Amino acids all contain carbon, hydrogen, oxygen and nitrogen. Many also contain sulphur, and some contain phosphorus. There are only 22 of them, plus a few rare ones, found in nature. However, there are very large numbers of proteins formed from various arrangements of these amino acids. This explains the diversity of proteins, e.g. egg white and human hair are both mainly protein although with very different properties.

In humans, proteins are essential for growth and maintenance. The entire body, except the skeleton, is mainly protein of one kind or another. Protein must be produced in the diet, but any excess is used for energy. When protein is eaten, it is broken down into its constituent amino acids, which are later reassembled in the form and location required. As with fatty acids they are interconvertible by the body except for the eight so-called 'essential amino acids'. These eight essential amino acids for adults are: isoleucine, leucine, lysine, methionine, phenylalanine, threonine, tryptophan, valine. Another amino acid—histidine—is essential for growing children.

Between 10 and 15% of energy in the diet should come from protein. This should be from a variety of sources to ensure a good mixture of amino acids. If more protein is eaten than is needed for growth and maintenance, the excess is used for energy. This is wasteful: protein is less plentiful in the world than carbohydrate and fat. If the excess is very large the effects may even be harmful. Protein provides 4 kcal/g.

20.3.4 Vitamins

Other substances are necessary for life, although in minute amounts only. These substances are the so-called 'vitamins'. They have no common feature. The better known ones are listed below. There are others, less well-defined, and more may await discovery.

Vitamin A (retinol) is essential for tissue development. It provides the basis of the pigment responsible for dim-light vision. Deficiency causes night blindness. Rich sources are liver, carrots, dark-green vegetables, fish liver oil, eggs, butter and margarine.

Vitamin B₁ (thiamin) is involved in the transformation of carbohydrate into energy. Deficiency causes beri-beri, a disease characterised by inflammation of the nerves, found among populations subsisting largely on highly milled rice. Rich sources of vitamin B and the other vitamins in the 'B' group are milk, offal, pork, fruit, vegetables, cereals, eggs, nuts.

Vitamin B₂ (riboflavin) is essential for the utilisation of energy from food. Deficiency causes dermatitis, particularly sores in the corner of the mouth. Offals and fortified cereals are good sources of riboflavin.

Vitamin B₃ (niacin, nicotinamide) is also used for utilisation of food energy. Deficiency causes pellagra, a disease found among maize-eating populations, with dark scaly skin symptoms. Milk and eggs have high niacin equivalents.

Vitamin B₆ (pyridoxine) is required for protein utilisation and formation of haemoglobin. Meat, fish, eggs, cereals and vegetables are good sources.

Vitamin B₁₁ (folic acid) and vitamin B₁₂ are both required for fundamental metabolic process. Deficiency causes various types of anaemia. B₁₂ is a mixture of cobalt-containing materials which do not occur in vegetables. Folic acid occurs in offals and raw, green, leafy vegetables.

Vitamin C (ascorbic acid) is a multipurpose vitamin involved in collagen, synthesis of certain hormones and metabolism of some amino acids. Deficiency causes 'scurvy' characterised first by bleeding gums and, later, more extensive bleeding. The richest sources of vitamin C are fruit and vegetables.

Vitamin D (cholecalciferol) is required for bone formation and maintenance. Deficiency causes rickets, a disease characterised by bone deformation. It is unique in that it can be formed by the body following exposure to sunshine. Rich sources are liver, fish oil, butter and margarine.

For some reason, the discovery of vitamins caught the public's imagination and they are sold in great quantities, mostly to people who do not need them. The normal diet of western societies contains ample vitamins. Deficiency is rare, except occasionally of vitamin D among immigrants from Asia to less sunny areas.

20.3.5   *Minerals*

Minerals are as necessary as vitamins. Their most important functions are:

(1) As constituents of bones and teeth.
(2) As soluble salts which help to control body fluid composition.
(3) As essential adjuncts to many enzymes and other proteins such as haemoglobin.

Those listed below are needed in greatest amounts in the diet, and together with sulphur (part of some amino acids) may be considered the major minerals. However, many other 'trace minerals', such as cobalt, copper, chromium, fluorine, iodine, manganese, selenium and zinc, are equally essential, although needed in very small quantities. Excess amounts of these can be toxic.

Calcium is required for skeleton building, conduction of nerve impulses, muscle contraction, blood clotting. Deficiency causes rickets. Rich sources are milk and cheese, sardines, white bread, watercress.

Phosphorus is required for skeleton building and the transformation of food into energy. Good sources are milk and milk products, meat and meat products, bread, cereals.

Magnesium is also required for food–energy transformation and bone formation. Magnesium is especially abundant in vegetables as it is an essential constituent of chlorophyll.

Sodium is required for conduction of nerve impulses and for maintaining the correct composition of body fluids. One of the main sources of sodium in food is salt.

Potassium is needed for similar purposes to sodium, but sodium and potassium are not interchangeable: both are needed. Many sources in the diet include vegetables, meat and milk.

Iron is an essential component of haemoglobin, the red substance in the blood which carries oxygen from the lungs. Rich sources of iron are meat, liver, eggs, dark-green vegetables, peas and beans.

20.4   What food does: how it provides energy, growth and maintenance

During digestion, which takes place in the stomach and upper intestine, the following transformations occur. Carbohydrates are broken down into simple sugars, glucose, fructose or galactose; proteins into amino acids; fats into fatty acids plus glycerol. These simple breakdown products are absorbed via the wall of the small intestine. The simple sugars, amino acids and some of the fatty acids go to the liver.

Glucose does *not* go into the general circulatory system directly. It is converted in the liver into a starch-like substance called glycogen. The liver can accommodate about 400 g of this. It is broken down again to release glucose into the bloodstream as and when needed. It thus serves as a reserve stock. Even during starvation, this reserve is never entirely depleted. Subsidiary stocks of glycogen are held in the muscles, available for immediate use.

Glucose is one of the two main sources of energy (the other one is fat). The level of glucose in the bloodstream is kept within narrow limits, about 80–120 mg/100 ml, by the action of two hormones, insulin and glucagon. These work in opposite directions—insulin mediates the building up of glucose into glycogen, while glucagon mediates glycogen breakdown. These limits are not exceeded except under pathological conditions. The best known of these is diabetes, when the body either produces insufficient insulin or does not utilise its insulin properly. In consequence the blood glucose level rises too high, and if unchecked would lead to coma and death.

People vary a great deal in the efficiency with which they convert carbohydrate (and fat) into energy, and this may partly explain why some people seem to be able to eat a great deal without getting fat. It has also been claimed that some people can burn off excess energy in the form of heat via 'brown adipose tissue' ('brown fat'). This does happen with laboratory animals, but its occurrence in man is less certain [5].

Amino acids circulate in the bloodstream and their level rises greatly after a high-protein meal. They constitute the so-called 'amino acid pool' and serve as the raw material for the growth and repair of body tissues. If more protein is eaten than is necessary for this purpose, the surplus is converted into forms which can be used for energy.

Fatty acids and glycerol, after absorption into the body, are quickly reassembled into fats and circulate in the form of minute droplets coated with protein. Deposits are laid down in the muscles as a ready source of energy and in other tissues (to excess in the obese) as a reserve stock.

As already mentioned, glucose (derived from glycogen) and fatty acids (derived from fats) are the two primary sources of energy. Glucose may be utilised either aerobically (i.e. requiring oxygen) or anaerobically (i.e. not requiring oxygen). Fatty acids can only be used aerobically.

Weight for weight, fat provides more energy than glycogen, but glycogen provides it faster. Glycogen used aerobically provides it fastest of all, but this is limited by the rate at which oxygen can be transported from the lungs to the muscles.

One or other of these routes predominates according to circumstances and requirements [6]. Fat is the main source during rest and mild activity, glucose via the anaerobic route during brief vigorous activity, glucose and fat, both aerobically, during prolonged activity. Switches from one energy route to another are controlled by a hierarchy of hormones and enzymes. Thus in an emergency extra energy is made available by adrenaline (the 'fight or flight' hormone) which overrides the hormone insulin. Training improves the efficiency of fat utilisation and increases oxygen capacity.

20.5　What is a healthy diet?

As noted above, a healthy diet contains all of the necessary nutrients, without harmful excesses, from a wide variety of foods. The healthy majority of people eat the foods which suit them and which, as individuals, they prefer. Their diet provides sufficient nutrients for their needs.

Healthy eating need never be boring. It is normal and natural to enjoy what we eat and drink. Although those people with specific health problems may need to be more careful about what they eat, favourite foods have a place in

Table 20.1　Contributions of macronutrients to a healthy diet [4,7,8]

	Percentage of energy
Protein	10–15
Fat—total	< 35
Saturated fat	< 15
Carbohydrate	> 50–55

Table 20.2　Recommended daily allowances

		UK [9]	EEC [10]	Codex [11]	USA [12]
Vitamin A	µg	750	1000	1000	1000
Vitamin B$_1$ (thiamin)	mg	1.2	1.4	1.4	1.4
Vitamin B$_2$ (riboflavin)	mg	1.6	1.6	1.6	1.6
Niacin	mg	18	18	18	18
Folic acid	µg	300	400	400	400
Vitamin B$_{12}$	µg	2	3	3	3
Vitamin C (ascorbic acid)	mg	30	60	60	45
Vitamin D	µg	2.5	5	5	—
Vitamin E	µg	—	10	10	15
Vitamin B$_6$ (pyridoxine)	mg	—	2	2	2
Biotin	mg	—	0.15	—	—
Pontothenic acid	mg	—	6	—	—
Calcium	mg	500	800	800	800
Iodine	µg	140	150	150	130
Iron	mg	12	12	14	10
Phosphorus	mg	—	800	800	800
Magnesium	mg	—	300	300	350
Zinc	mg	—	15	15	15

anyone's diet, given adequate variety, balance and moderation. This can of course include confectionery.

The elements of a typical healthy diet for the average adult are summarised in Tables 20.1 and 20.2. The micronutrient recommendations vary considerably (and often unjustifiably) between different countries.

The macronutrients are given as a percentage of energy, whereas the recommended daily allowances for micronutrients are in absolute amounts. The values are given for a typical moderately active adult. None of these values is definitive, and there are continual debates about the validity of any set of dietary goals or recommendations. The evidence for setting them is not well established or conclusive in most cases. For example, the UK DHSS defines RDAs for micronutrients as 'the average requirement plus a margin of safety'.

20.5.1   Confectionery as part of a healthy diet

In most people's minds, food is eaten primarily for sustenance, and only incidentally for pleasure and confectionery primarily for pleasure and only incidentally for sustenance.

How real is this distinction? Everyone expects food to be pleasant as well as nutritious, and significant effort goes into making it so. Confectionery, even if eaten primarily for pleasure, is acknowledged as having value as food even though it often tends to be under-rated.

The nutritional contribution of confectionery products is based entirely on the ingredients used. These are normal household ingredients and the percentage of these used by the UK confectionery industry is given in Table 20.3

The average nutritional contribution of confectionery to the total UK diet is shown below [13].

Energy	6%
Protein	1.5%
Fat	5%
Carbohydrate	9%

Table 20.3   Usage of major ingredients in confectionery expressed as a percentage of total food industry usage [13]

	Usage in confectionery (%)
Sugar	14.4
Glucose	30.3
Cocoa	82.5
Milk	3.9
Oils and fats	7.4
Dried fruit	3.9
Nuts	33.0

Table 20.4 Table of nutritional profiles per 100 g for typical categories of products*

	Energy kcal	kJ	Protein (g)	Carbohydrate (g)	Fat (g)	Dietary fibre (g)	Calcium (mg)	Iron (mg)	Thiamin (mg)	Riboflavin (mg)	Nicotinic acid (mg equivalents)
Confectionery											
(1) Boiled sweet	327	1397	0	87.3	0	0	5	0.4	0	0	0
(2) Fruit gums	172	734	1.0	44.8	0	0	360	4.2	0	0	0
(3) Liquorice allsorts	313	1333	3.9	74.1	2.2	—	63	8.1	0	0	0.7
(4) Pastilles	235	1079	5.2	61.9	0	—	40	1.4	0	0	0
(5) Peppermints, compressed	350	1590	0.3	99.2	0.5	0	2	0	0	0	0
(6) Toffees, mixed	430	1810	2.1	71.1	17.2	—	95	1.5	0	0	0.4

* Most of the data are taken from Ref. 14. This is supplemented with data supplied by individual manufacturers.

This represents a typical confectionery consumption of 240 g per person per week—35 g per person per day.

These figures are average and, of course, approximate. Some individuals eat less, some more. There is no evidence that current confectionery consumption is detrimental to health, and there is no reason why confectionery cannot be eaten as an enjoyable part of a healthy balanced diet.

20.5.2 *Nutritional content of sugar confectionery*

The nutritional values of some typical sugar confectionery items are given in Table 20.4. None of the products listed contains more than trace amounts, if any, of vitamins C or D. All foods are subject to some variability in nutrient content, reflecting differences in ingredients, recipes and cooking methods.

20.6 Nutrition labelling

Nutritional information about products is a useful adjunct in helping consumers to compile a healthy diet. This is now being given on many packs in the form of nutrition labelling, and it requires that manufacturers can describe the nutritional profile of their products. A typical example is given in Table 20.5 according to the government guidelines for layout (see also Figure 20.1). There are two routes to this information, either by calculation using a detailed recipe together with published nutrient values for the individual ingredients or by chemical analysis of typical finished product samples.

20.6.1 *Calculated nutritional data*

A calculation has the advantage of relative speed (once the reference tables are available), reduced costs, and no requirement for specialist analytical resources. There are however several limitations.

(1) Published nutrient data values are needed for all the ingredients in the

Table 20.5 Typical nutrition information on sugar confectionery products

Nutrition information	
Each pack gives you:	
Energy	220 kJ/51 kcal
Protein	0 g
Carbohydrate	13.4 g
Fat	0 g

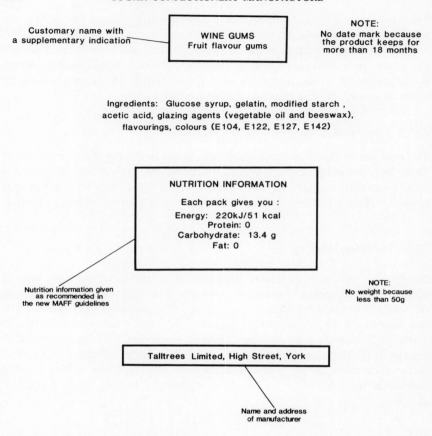

Customary name with
a supplementary indication

WINE GUMS
Fruit flavour gums

NOTE:
No date mark because
the product keeps for
more than 18 months

Ingredients: Glucose syrup, gelatin, modified starch ,
acetic acid, glazing agents (vegetable oil and beeswax),
flavourings, colours (E104, E122, E127, E142)

NUTRITION INFORMATION

Each pack gives you :
Energy: 220kJ/51 kcal
Protein: 0
Carbohydrate: 13.4 g
Fat: 0

Nutrition information given
as recommended in
the new MAFF guidelines

NOTE:
No weight because
less than 50g

Talltrees Limited, High Street, York

Name and address
of manufacturer

Figure 20.1 Typical information found on sugar confectionery governed by 'Food Labelling Regulations (1984)'.

recipe. In some cases data may be available directly from the ingredient suppliers.

(2) 'Seasonal' variations in values are not accounted for, e.g. milk fat varies from summer to winter.

(3) Processing can influence the final nutritional content of the product. This is particularly relevant for higher temperature processes and is especially applicable to vitamins, which are not thermally robust nutrients.

20.6.2   *Analysed nutritional data*

Analytical values from a representative sample of finished products will provide the most accurate nutritional data. The samples need to reflect as many potential variables as possible, such as manufacturing process extremes, raw material variations, and the shelf life of the product if it is comparatively long.

The analysed values reflect one recipe only, and any future recipe development may trigger a need for further analysis. On the other hand, analysis only requires samples of product, and no detailed recipe knowledge.

Most laboratories will use published standard methods for their analysis.

20.6.3 *Which nutrients are needed?*

The commonest format for nutritional declaration is that from the international *Codex Alimentarius* [11], which requires declaration of the so-called 'Big 4', i.e. energy, protein, carbohydrate and fat. There are usually opportunities to declare further nutrients, but these four are the basic minimum.

Vitamins and minerals are usually only declared if a significant quantity is provided in a portion or a typical day's intake of the product. Significant is typically defined as 5% of the RDA [11]. RDAs do vary from country to country, so it is important to confirm the appropriate values.

20.6.4 *Development of nutritional content*

The following worked example will serve as a model.

Calculation. A detailed recipe is needed to work from. The recipe for basic fudge (to make approximately 1 kg) is as follows:

Granulated sugar	850 g
Milk	300 ml
Butter	120 g
Vanila extract	2 tsp

(1) From standard tables of nutritional values [14,15], the macronutrients supplied by each ingredient can be calculated. Values are usually provided per 100 g of ingredients, and in the above recipe the density of milk (1.03 g/ml) is used to give an accurate weight of $300 \times 1.03 = 309$ g. Sucrose is a disaccharide which provides 5% more carbohydrate when it is expressed as a monosaccharide. Minor weight ingredients like concentrated flavours, emulsifiers, etc. are usually considered insignificant for nutritional calculations. The nutritional values of the ingredients of basic fudge are shown in Table 20.6 (for 1 kg).

(2) In order to progress accurately to the final percentage values of fat, protein and carbohydrate it is necessary to know the final weight of product and its final moisture content. (The recipe suggested 1 kg approximately.) Assuming it did produce 1 kg (i.e. final moisture is 1.5% approximately) of fudge, the nutritional value would be fat 11%, protein 1.1% and carbohydrate 86.5%.

(3) From these percentage totals for fat, protein and carbohydrate, the

Table 20.6

	Fat (g)	Protein (g)	Carbohydrate (g)
850 g sugar	0	Trace	850.00
309 g milk	11.74	10.20	14.52
120 g butter	98.4	0.48	Trace
1279g	110.1	10.7	864.5

Table 20.7   Kilocalories per gram (kilojoules per gram) of macronutrients

	Fat	Protein	Carbohydrate	Alcohol	Organic acid	Sugar alcohols
UK	9 (37)	4 (17)	3.75 (16)	7 (29)	—	—
EEC	9 (37)	4 (17)	4.0 (17)	7 (29)	3 (13)	2.4 (10)
Codex	9 (37)	4 (17)	4.0 (17)	7 (29)	3 (13)	—

energy value can be calculated. Standard conversion values have been assigned and are usually found in legislation. The values can be given as kilocalories or kilojoules. 1 kcal (Calorie) is equal to 4.186 kJ. Different values are used, depending on the origin of the data (Table 20.7).

Applying these values in Table 20.7 to the fudge recipe above gives

Fat	99.0
Protein	4.4
Carbohydrate	340.1 (sucrose re-expressed as monosaccharide using 100 g ⟶ 105 g; 90.7%)
Total	444 kcal or 1856 kJ

Using the same procedure, the vitamin and mineral content can be calculated from standard tables.

Attention to units is needed as some values are quoted in mg, and some in μg per 100 g of ingredient:

$1\,mg = 1 \times 10^{-3}\,g$
$1\,\mu g = 1 \times 10^{-6}\,g$

Since vitamins are heat-sensitive, the true vitamin content is likely to be less than that calculated if substantial ingredient processing has occurred.

Analysis. Representative samples need to be analysed for macronutrients:

Fat (%)
Protein (%) (usually nitrogen × 6.25 or nitrogen × 6.38 for milk)

Moisture (%)
Ash (%)

Although carbohydrate should be analysed directly, in some cases it can be calculated 'by difference' (i.e. 100 minus the sum of the above). If the samples have a significant fibre content, then this should be measured and subtracted from the available carbohydrate, prior to calculating the energy value. Energy is calculated as outlined above.

Micronutrients. Vitamins and minerals need to be specified for analysis. Since analysis can be expensive, it is worthwhile considering the type of ingredients in the recipe and selecting the micronutrients which are likely to be present. If a full micronutrient breakdown is needed for a dietitian's use, as opposed to nutritional labelling purposes, then a complete analysis may be essential.

For declaration of micronutrients, it may be necessary to confirm that the product serving size or likely daily consumption will contribute more than 5% of the RDA for that micronutrient.

Representative samples. As raw materials vary with season, supplier source etc. ensure that the samples analysed are typical of a range of production. Ageing will also influence nutritional values—especially micronutrients—and this should also be accounted for in sample selection.

Method of analysis. There are standard reference methods for most nutrients. Ensure that the method used is acceptable in law.

20.7 Labelling sugar confectionery

Specific, legal requirements for labelling food products, including confectionery, exist in most developed countries. In the EEC, these are usually derived from a horizontal directive on food labelling (79/112). It is essential to check the prevailing labelling requirements for an export market prior to committing the packaging. The major elements of the label are presented in Figure 20.1. There may be other national requirements which should be provided. These are subject to change and should be reviewed regularly.

The primary objective of labelling is to provide consumers with appropriate information in order to choose a product. The primary elements of EEC labelling for packaged goods are:

(1) *Name of food.* Legal/customary name—this is either the name which is specified in law or that which is generally recognised for that product e.g. barley sugar, fudge. It is not the brand name.

The name has to be sufficiently accurate to inform a consumer of the contents, without misleading. If it is appropriate, an indication of the state of product is needed e.g. dried, frozen.

(2) *Ingredients list.* This lists the ingredients (including additives) in decreasing order by weight as they are added to the mixing bowl. Water is declared, at the appropriate place in the order, only if there is more than 5% added water in the final product. However 'glucose syrup', as a declaration, embraces its associated water.

The names used in an ingredients list should generally be those which would be used to sell the ingredient on its own.

Additives generally need to be prefixed with a functional category and followed by their specific name or number. For example, colour E124 or colour Ponceau 4R. The major exception is flavourings, which only need the category name.

The proposed full list of additive categories in the EEC includes colours, preservatives, antioxidants, emulsifiers, emulsifying salts, thickeners, gelling agents, stabilisers, flavour enhancers, acids, acidity regulators, anticaking agents, modified starches, sweeteners, raising agents, antifoaming agents, glazing agents, flour treatment agents, firming agents, humectants, sequestrants, enzymes, bulking agents, propellant and packaging gases.

Processing aids and additives which serve no technical function in the final product can be omitted from ingredients lists.

(3) *Best before dates* or indication of minimum durability, may be required. The format is usually:

'Best Before: day   month   year'

for products which have more than 6 weeks' shelf life.

(4) *Manufacturer/packer/seller.* The name and address of one of these is required. Sufficient detail is required to enable a consumer to make successful contact.

(5) *Country of origin* may be required if by omitting it a consumer could be misled.

(6) *Instructions for use and/or storage* are rarely applicable to sugar confectionery, but should be stated, if necessary.

Special emphasis. If labelling includes phrases which place special emphasis on an ingredient which characterises the food, then the minimum percentage of that ingredient must be given, either next to the name of the food or in the ingredients list. Similarly, a low content claim triggers a maximum percentage declaration.

Field of vision. A product with a 'best before' date must give it such that it is legible in the same field of view as the name of the food. If a weight mark is given, then this too should be in the same field of vision.

Weight marking. This may be required depending on the type and product size. For example, in the EEC, packaged sugar confectionery only needs a weight mark between 50 g and 10 kg.

The average weight system applies in the EEC, and full details should be sought from specific references. The details are extensive. Weight marking rules for multipacks and seasonal/fancy goods vary from country to country.

Claims must be true and not misleading to a consumer. In some countries they may be governed by laws or codes of practice.

Medicated confectionery. Cough and throat sweets, etc., which carry a medicinal-type claim describing relief of symptoms, may need to be considered under the Provisions of Medicines Act. These products may require manufacturing and product licences from the authorities depending on the claims being made for them.

20.8 Confectionery and the critics

In a society where speech is free, everything will be criticised, and there is no reason to expect confectionery to be exempt.

Nutrition probably generates more emotion than any other branch of science. The amount of information about nutrition is awesome, and much of it is inconsistent. The various confectionery trade associations usually have experts whom they can call upon to help member companies who have to face criticisms of their products.

20.8.1 *Obesity*

In any discussion of obesity it is necessary first to settle the question 'what is normal?' A mathematical relationship between the height and weight of adults who were judged to be of normal build was first suggested in 1869 by Quetelet in his *Physique Sociale*. Quetelet showed that weight was roughly proportional to the square of the height, so that the index W/H^2 (weight in kg, height in metres) was roughly the same for all adults of 'normal' build, no matter whether they were short or tall. Normal weight as judged by Quetelet and defined by his index coincides with what is medically and in our culture aesthetically pleasing. This is between 23 and 25. The Quetelet index for various weight categories is given in Figure 20.2 [5].

20.8.2 *Additives*

Confectionery is sometimes criticised as being 'full of additives', without further comment, as if this were sufficient condemnation in itself.

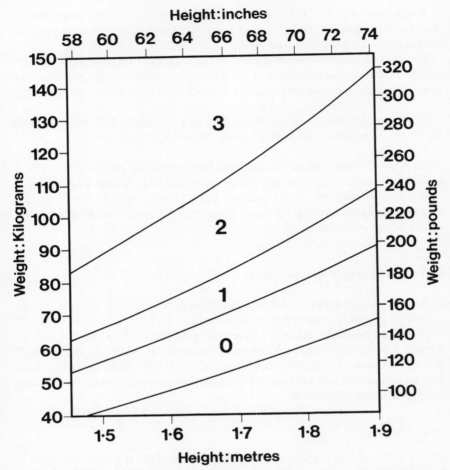

Figure 20.2 Quetelet index for different height–weight groups 0, < 25; 1, 25–29; 2, 30–40; 3, > 40.

Why are additives used in food? They are used to keep food safe and fresh, sometimes to improve its stability, appearance or flavour. Additives are not new. Salt, sulphur dioxide (by way of burning sulphur) and acetic acid (as vinegar) for preservation, spices for preservation and flavour, saffron for colour, vanilla for flavour and so on have all been used since ancient times, and none of these has any food value of its own.

Why are additives often condemned? There seem to be several reasons. They are thought of as chemicals (as indeed they are) and as such are sinister in the minds of some. This is understandable, because not everyone appreciates that all food consists entirely of chemicals. They often have unfamiliar names, and unfamiliarity breeds suspicion. There is nothing reassuring about 'gamma-tocopherol' (an additive used as an antioxidant) on a label unless you happen to know that it is the name of a substance which also occurs as a normal and beneficial component of many natural, unprocessed foods.

They are suspect because many of them are synthetic. Of these, some are identical with natural ingredients, others are truly artificial. It is not unreasonable to be cautious about substances which have no counterpart in nature, but the authorities who regulate their use *are* extremely cautious. Strict safety and need criteria are applied by international authorities before additives are permitted for use. These can be multitiered from international bodies such as the FAO/WHO Joint Expert Committee on Food Additives (JECFA); the EEC Scientific Committee for Foods (SCF); and national authorities such as the Food Advisory Committee of MAFF and DHSS in the UK.

The criteria of safety are often so strict that, if applied to natural components of foods, many food items such as rhubarb, mustard and certain kinds of beans would have to be banned.

Lastly, additives have been held responsible for various disorders, including allergic reactions and hyperactivity. These are sometimes ascribed to all additives as a group, sometimes to single ones. The attribution of a specific disorder to all additives as a group is baffling, since they have no common feature. It is also totally unsupported by any evidence.

There are certainly cases reported of allergies to some individual additives, but these are far fewer and less well documented than allergies to traditional foods, e.g. eggs and milk. It is an unfortunate fact that probably every component of food, whether new or old, natural or artificial, will cause an allergic reaction in somebody. There is no reason to single out additives.

To put allergy to additives in context, the incidence of intolerance to various items in Great Britian is outlined in Table 20.8. A more recent study [16] has shown that, whilst 15% of the population reported allergy to additives, only 0.0–0.23% could be demonstrated in double-blind trial.

However, for those who are sensitive or intolerant, it is best to read the ingredients list carefully and avoid any products as necessary.

20.8.3 *Hyperactivity or hyperkinesis*

The word 'hyperactivity' is fairly new, although the condition is not. It refers of course primarily to children who instead of being docile and lovable are

Table 20.8 Incidence of intolerance in Britain (population 56 million)

(1) Benzoates (food preservative)	0.05% (25 000)
(2) Tartrazine (food colour)	0.06% (30 000)
(3) Aspirin	0.4% (200 000)
(4) Cow's milk protein	over 1.5%
(5) House dust mites	over 10.0%

'hostile and aggressive'. Some articles in the popular press extend this to include violent crime at all ages. A favourite theory is that hyperactivity is a consequence of diet, with sugar and additives as the culprits.

The idea that hyperactivity might be an allergic reaction goes back to 1945, but its attribution to food additives (amongst other things) dates from 1975, when the 'Feingold diet', additive-free and low in sugar, became well-known, and accounts of its beneficial effect on uncontrollable children, delinquent adolescents and criminal adults have multiplied. However, rigorous examination of the effects of the 'Feingold diet' in properly controlled scientific experiments has shown benefit with a small proportion of children only.

The issue is clouded by differences in criteria which account for the difference between the incidence of hyperactivity reported in the UK and the US—0.1% and 10% respectively.

A serious difficulty in getting at the truth of the matter lies in the fact that the hopes, fears, and general demeanour of observers, especially if they are parents, may themselves influence behaviour as well as their interpretation of it. This has been shown to happen even in experiments with laboratory animals when the customary 'double-blind, cross-over' procedure was not used.

Scientific studies (as opposed to anecdotal or testimonial evidence) led to the conclusion that a very small proportion, probably less than 5%, of *hyperactive* children respond to an additive-free diet in which all additive-containing food, not merely confectionery, is eliminated [17]. Sugar has not been shown to have any adverse effects on behaviour. If anything, it has been shown to have a calming effect [18].

20.8.4 *Dental caries*

The belief that confectionery rots the teeth is widespread, long-standing and deeply rooted. It is probably the most serious criticism that confectionery has to face.

Dental caries is one of the most common diseases in the world today. It results from the fermentation of carbohydrates by bacteria in the mouth to produce acid. The bacteria, particularly *Streptococcus mutans*, are in the plaque which surrounds the uncleaned surfaces of the teeth [19–21]. Here acid is produced which attacks the tooth enamel and gradually dissolves (or demineralises) it. This demineralisation process is offset by the repair process known as remineralisation. The balance between demineralisation and remineralisation determines whether caries will actually occur.

20.8.4.1 *What foods are involved?* Bacteria on teeth can produce acid whenever any fermentable carbohydrate food is eaten. Natural or added sugars found in food and cooked starches, which are broken down by amylase (an enzyme in the saliva) to form glucose, are all involved [22–27]. There are similar amounts of acid formed following ingestion of confectionery or an apple. A banana or raisins can cause as many caries as bread or a chocolate bar.

Potential food cariogenicity is not determined by carbohydrate content alone. There are cariostatic components in some foods (e.g. cocoa, milk proteins and cereals) which will reduce their tendency to cause caries.

Retention of a food in the mouth is also important. However, contrary to popular opinion, foods such as caramels and cakes, which are perceived to be sticky, tend to clear from the mouth faster than many other foods not generally associated with stickiness, e.g. bread and raisins [28].

20.8.4.2 *Frequency of food intake* It is not what one eats but how often one eats that is related to the development of caries. Every time a carbohydrate food is eaten, acid is produced which can cause demineralisation. Greater time between acid attacks allows remineralisation to occur [29, 30].

There is a consensus that frequent eating of carbohydrate foods is contributory to the development of dental caries, but no one has determined how many eating occasions a day are 'safe'. Research is needed to establish the interactions of frequency with oral hygiene and use of fluoride. There is an increasing view that, provided the use of fluoride is optimal and oral hygiene adequate, frequency is less important [31, 32], and that as many as 6–8 acid challenges per day can be tolerated [33].

20.8.4.3 *How important is diet?* In the UK, the percentage of 5-year-olds with tooth decay fell from 73% in 1973 to 48% in 1983 [34]. This has been mirrored or exceeded in several countries [35–37]. It is generally accepted that the major factor has been the increased use of fluoride in water, toothpastes or mouth rinses. This decrease has not been associated with any significant reduction in sugars ingestion or in snacking.

It appears that the remineralising influence of fluoride can outweigh the demineralising effect of carbohydrate in the diet.

20.8.4.4 *Control of caries* The disease can be controlled:

(1) By reducing the number of bacteria on the teeth by frequent and thorough brushing as well as professional cleaning.

(2) By application of fluoride in its various forms, which strengthens tooth enamel and makes is less susceptible to decay.

(3) By avoiding constant nibbling of carbohydrate foods. Sensible snacking can be tolerated.

Nearly all foods contain carbohydrate including apples, bananas, bread, pasta, raisins, sugar, confectionery, etc. It is believed by some researchers that reducing the frequency of eating any one of these foods is unlikely to have a significant effect unless that food forms the bulk of the diet.

A British Market Research study indicated that, on average, food or drink is taken 6.7 times a day. Fermentable carbohydrate was eaten on 97 and 96% of all eating or drinking occasions of 5- to 12-year-olds and 13- to 17-year-olds respectively. Confectionery [38] made up only 15% of these occasions. On this basis, it is therefore unlikely that reducing confectionery in the diet would make any significant difference to oral health. Rather it would require a dramatic alteration in eating patterns or the application of alternative preventive treatments. The latter are more likely to be successful, as dietary manipulations are notoriously difficult to achieve, even in cases of life-threatening disease.

20.8.5   *Other criticisms*

Many of the criticisms of sugar confectionery are based on the criticisms of sugar *per se*. In this context it is worth noting that several recent reports on sugars in the diet have given sugars (as currently consumed) a clean bill of health [39–42], with the exception of their role in dental caries. These reports together covered such issues as sugars and coronary heart disease, diabetes, behaviour, gall stones and hypertension, renal stones, obesity.

20.9   Conclusion

Confectionery does provide an enjoyable contribution to a healthy diet. There is no reason why, used sensibly, it should not continue to do so.

References

1. A. James, Confectionery as a cultural symbol: an anthropological approach. Paper presented to IOCCC General Assembly, Vienna, October 1988.
2. MAFF, *Manual of Nutrition*, HMSO, London (1985).
3. R. Passmore and M.A. Eastwood, in Davidson and Passmore, *Human Nutrition and Dietetics*, 8th edn, Churchill Livingstone, Edinburgh (1986).
4. DHSS, *Diet and Cardiovascular Disease*, Committee on Medical Aspects of Food Policy, Report of the Panel on Diet in Relation to Cardiovascular Disease, Report No. 28, HMSO, London (1984).
5. J.S. Garrow, *Treat Obesity Seriously. A Clinical Manual*, Churchill Livingstone, Edinburgh (1981).
6. C. Williams, *Nutrition in Sport. Proceedings of the National Symposium, London*, D.H. Shrimpton and P.B. Ottoway, Shaklee (UK) Ltd. (1985).
7. DHSS, *Recommended Daily Amounts of Food Energy and Nutrients for Groups of People in the UK*, DHSS Report No. 15, HMSO, London (1979).
8. Royal College of Physicians, *Medical Aspects of Dietary Fibre*, Summary of a report of the Royal College of Physicians of London, Pitman Medical, London (1981).
9. Food Labelling Regulations, S1.1305, HMSO, London (1984).
10. EEC Proposal for a Council Directive on Nutritional Labelling 489 final—SYN 255 rules CDM (88).
11. *Codex*, 18th Session Codex Food Labelling, March 1985.

12. National Academy of Sciences, National Research Council (1974).
13. Cocoa, Chocolate and Confectionery Alliance, *Confectionery and Nutrition*, p. 15 (1985).
14. A.A. Paul and D.A.T. Southgate, eds., *McCance & Widdowson The Composition of Foods*, 4th edn. HMSO, London (1978).
15. *Handbook of the Nutritional Contents of Foods*, USA (1975).
16. E. Young, S. Patel, M. Stoneham, R. Rona and J.D. Wilkinson, The prevalence of reaction to food additives in a survey population. *J. Royal Coll. Phys.* **21** (4) (1987) 5.
17. E.A. Taylor, Childhood hyperactivity. *Br. J. Psychiat.* **149** (1986) 562.
18. D. Benton, *Dietary Sugar, Blood Glucose and Behaviour*, A review of the literature prepared for CCCA (1984).
19. P.H. Keyes, The infectious and transmissible nature of experimental dental caries. *Arch. Oral Biol.* **1** (1960) 304.
20. F.J. Orland, J.R. Blayney, R.W. Harrison, J.A. Reyniers, P.C. Trexler, R.F. Ervin, H.A. Gordon, and M. Wagner, Experimental caries in germ-free rats inoculated with enterococcus. *J. Am. Dent. Assoc.* **50** (1955) 259.
21. F.J. Orland, Oral environmental factors in experimental rat caries, in *Advances in Experimental Caries Research*, American Association for the Advancement of Science, Washington DC (1955).
22. M.E. Jensen, C.F. Schachtele and P.J. Polansky, In dwelling pH electrodes: Analysis of human dental plaque responses at different sites, in *Foods, Nutrition and Dental Health*, vol. 3, ed. J.J. Hefferen, Pathotox Publishers Inc., Illinois (1981).
23. S.A. Mundorff, J.D.B. Featherstone, A.D. Eisenberg, N. Espeland, C.P. Shields, and M.E.J. Curzon, Cariogenicity of Foods: Rat study. Paper presented at the 1985 IADR/AADR annual meeting held at Las Vegas, March 1985.
24. A.J. Rugg-Gunn, W.M. Edgar and G.N. Jenkins, The effect of eating some British snacks upon the pH of human dental plaque. *Br. Dent. J.* **145** (1978) 95.
25. R.M. Stephan, Changes in the concentration on tooth surfaces and in carious lesions. *J. Am. Dent. Assoc.* **27** (1950) 718.
26. J.M. Navia, and H. Lopez, Rat caries assay of reference foods and sugar containing snacks. *J. Dent. Res.* **62** (1983) 893.
27. M.E. Jensen and G.F. Schachtele, The acidogenic potential of reference foods and snacks at interproximal sites in human dentition. *J. Dent. Res.* **62** (1983) 889·
28. B.G. Bibby, Foods and dental caries, in *Foods Nutrition and Dental Health*, vol. 1, eds. J.J. Hefferren and H. Keohler, Pathotox Publishers Inc., Illinois (1981).
29. B.E. Gustafsson, C.E. Quensel, L.S. Lanke, C. Lundqvist, H. Grahnen, B.E. Bonow and B. Krasse, The Vipeholm dental caries study. The effect of different levels of carbohydrate intake on caries activity in 436 individuals observed for five years. *Acta Odont. Scand.* **11** (1984) 232.
30. K.G. König, P. Schmid, and R. Schmid, An apparatus for frequency-controlled feeding of small rodents and its use in dental caries experiments. *Archs. Oral Biol.* **13** (1968) 13.
31. L.M. Kerebel, M.T. Le Cabellac, G. Dasulsi, and B. Kerebel, Report on caries reduction in French school children 3 years after the introduction of a preventive program. *Comm. Dent. Oral Epidemiol.* **13** (1985) 201.
32. J. Klimek, H. Prinz, E. Hellwig, and G. Ahrens, Effect of a preventive program based on professional teeth cleaning and fluoride applications on caries and gingivitis. *Comm. Dent. Oral Epidemiol.* **13** (1985) 295.
33. J.M. Ten Cate, and Y.M. Simons, PH-cycling, a useful technique, now being automated. ORCA, Angers, 6–9 July P88.
34. R.J. Anderson, G. Bradnock, J.F. Beal, and P.M.C. James, The reduction of dental caries prevalence in English schoolchildren. *J. Dent. Res.* **61** (special issue) (1982) 1311.
35. J.A. Brunell, and J.P. Carlos, Changes in the prevalence of dental caries in US schoolchildren, 1961–1980. *J. Dent. Res.* **61** (special issue) (1982) 1346.
36. H. Kalsbeek, Evidence of decrease in prevalence of dental caries in the Netherlands: An evaluation of epidemiological caries surveys on 4–6 and 11–15 year old children, performed between 1965 and 1980. *J. Dent. Res.* **61** (special issue) (1982) 1321.
37. G. Koch, Evidence for declining caries prevalence in Sweden. *J. Dent. Res.* **61** (special issue) (1982) 1340.
38. British Market Research Bureau, *British Food and Drink Survey*, CCCA, London (1985).

39. FAO/WHO, Joint meeting. *Expert Report on Carbohydrates in Human Nutrition* (1980).
40. FDA, US Food and Drug Administration Task Force, *Report on Sugars and Corn Sweeteners* (1986).
41. FDA, US Food and Drug Administration GRAS status of sugars and corn sweeteners, *Federal register*, November 1988.
42. BNF, British Nutrition Foundation Task Force report on sugars and syrups (1987).

Appendix: Glossary

Alkalising A treatment used during the manufacture of cocoa powder to give particles better suspension properties when they are used in a drink. (Commonly known as the Dutch process.)

Amorphous Not having a distinct crystalline form.

Balling Formation, when sieving a powder, of balls which cannot pass through the mesh.

Baumé scale A scale devised for convenient hydrometer reading which can be related to concentrations of sugar solutions.

Blanch (*v.*) To clean away the skin of nuts by scalding with hot water.

Blocking (of powder) Compression of a powder to produce a non-flowing mass.

Bloom Fat or sugar on the surface of the sweet giving a white sheen or, sometimes, individual white blobs.

Bloom grade Measure of the strength of a jelly determined on a Bloom gelometer.

Brake Twin adjustable rollers used to reduce the thickness of confectionery products.

Brix scale A scale with the same purpose as the Baumé scale.

Buffer Salt used to minimise small changes in acidity, and acidity arising from the addition of other ingredients.

Cacao Botanical name referring to the tree, pods and unfermented beans from the pods.

Candy (*v.*) To preserve fruits by immersing them in syrup thereby increasing their sugar content.

Caramel (in boiling) A stage reached during the boiling of sugar syrup.

Carbohydrate spectrum. The hydrolysis of starch with either acid or enzyme yields a glucose syrup containing a variety of molecular species ranging from dextrose (DP_1) through maltose (DP_2) and maltotriose (DP_3) and on to the higher molecular fractions (DP_n). The quantitative spread of such fractions within a glucose syrup is known as the carbohydrate spectrum, and can be very distinctive depending on the type of syrup and the control of reaction conditions.

Chew (*n.*) The 'mouth feel' of a confection during mastication.

Chocolate Drink made from crushed cocoa beans developed by the Aztecs.

Chocolate liquor Another name for cocoa mass.

Chocolate mass(e)   May refer to either cocoa mass or partially processed chocolate. In this book, masse is used exclusively to mean partially processed chocolate (to avoid confusion with cocoa mass).

Cocoa   Traditionally the manufactured powder used for drinks or food manufacture. At present, it often refers to fermented beans in bulk.

Cocoa butter   Fat expelled from the centre (kernels or nib) of cocoa beans.

Cocoa butter equivalent   Vegetable fats which are totally compatible with cocoa butter and can be mixed with it in any proportion.

Cocoa butter replacer   Vegetable fats which may be mixed with cocoa butter but only in a limited proportion.

Cocoa liquor   Another name for cocoa mass.

Cocoa mass(e)   Cocoa nib ground finely to give a liquid above 35°C (95°F). Cocoa mass is used in this book for all except origin liquor, as mass is used in the official EEC regulations.

Cocoa powder   Cocoa nib with some of the fat removed and ground into a powder.

Conche   A machine in which the chocolate is kept under agitation, so that the flavour is developed and the chocolate becomes liquid.

Confectioner's glucose   Obsolete term for glucose syrup.

Corn syrups   Glucose syrup can be manufactured from multi cereal sources to give various corn syrups.

Corn syrup   USA term for glucose syrup.

Countline   An individual unit normally purchased singly and eaten by the consumer in informal surroundings, e.g. Mars Bars.

Couverture   Legal use, high-fat (i.e. over 31% cocoa butter), normally high-quality chocolate. In this book, these are referred to as high-fat couvertures. Common UK use as biscuit-coating chocolate, often containing other fats.

Crack   Stage in boiling sugar syrup.

Crumb   Intermediate material in the milk chocolate making process, composed of dehydrated milk, sugar and cocoa mass.

Dextrose equivalence (equivalent) (DE)   This is a broad indicator of the extent of hydrolysis. It represents the total reducing sugar value of the starch hydrolysate expressed as a percentage of the reducing value of pure dextrose. The DE is calculated on a dry basis.

Dextrose/glucose   Chemists describe the monosaccharide obtained from the complete hydrolysis of starch as D-glucose. Our industry historically calls this monosaccharide dextrose; glucose is used to describe glucose syrups with a DE above 20 obtained by the controlled hydrolysis of starch.

Dietetic chocolate   'Chocolate' made for people with special dietary requirements, e.g. diabetics.

Doctor (sugar) A sugar ingredient which represses the crystallisation of sucrose by raising total saturation concentration.

DP$_n$ Means 'dextrose polymer', the suffixed number indicating the number of anhydroglucose units in the molecule; thus DP$_1$ is dextrose, DP$_2$ is maltose etc.

Dress (v.) To restore a piece of equipment, such as a roller, or an ingredient, such as starch, to its original specification.

Drop Variety of high-boiled sweet product on a drop roller.

Dusting A coating on confection of icing sugar, fine sugar crystals or anti stick powders.

Engrossing In panning, the building up of a sugar coat on centres.

Enrober Machine for coating sweet centre with chocolate, by pouring molten chocolate over it.

Enrobe (v.) To cover a confectionery centre with a coating of chocolate.

Extra hard crack Stage in boiling sugar syrup.

Fat Term for a greasy look to a confection, due to excessive inversion of sucrose during boiling.

Fat bloom Development of unstable fat crystals on the surface of chocolate.

Feather Stage in boiling sugar syrup.

Fermentation A process in which cocoa beans are treated such that chemical change is brought about by enzyme action. This usually involves removing the beans from the pods and placing them in covered heaps for an extended period.

Flow Term used generally for the flow behaviour of a confection.

Foam Beaten mixture of a whipping agent in water.

Formers Series of horizontal rollers arranged to form boiled sugar syrup into thin rope.

Frappé Whipped mixture of foaming agent in sugar syrup.

Fudging Unplanned crystallisation of sugar in a confection.

Gel (v.) To form a jelly.

Gelling agent A material which promotes gelling.

Glass An amorphous 'rigid liquid' arising when cooling takes place so rapidly that crystallisation does not occur.

Glaze (v.) To coat a confection with a solution which, on drying, produces a high gloss.

Glu A corruption of term 'glucose syrup'.

Graining Unplanned crystallisation of sugar in a confection.

Hard crack Stage in boiling sugar syrup.

Husk   A shell round the nib or kernel.

Inversion   Breakdown of sucrose into its two constituent sugars.

Invert sugar   Mixture of approximately equal parts of dextrose and laevulose.

Kettle   Steam jacketed warming or boiling pan.

Large ball
Large pearl   } Stages in boiling sugar syrup.
Large thread

Leaching (of sugars)   Transfer of sugar or starch from one confectionery type into another.

Leakage   Seepage of syrup from a coated confection.

Lecithin   Class of organic compounds similar to fats but with molecules containing nitrogen and phosphorus. Used in chocolate as a surface-active agent to improve its flow properties.

Light crack   Stage in boiling sugar syrup.

Lipid   Generic term for oils, fats and waxes.

Liquid sugar   Commercial mixture of sugars offered in syrup form.

Maltodextrin   Obtained from the controlled hydrolysis of nutritional saccharides, a maltodextrin is a concentrated purified solution (or the dried product thereof) with a DE of less than 20.

Massecuite   Mixture of boiled syrup and sugar crystals.

Medium crack   Stage in boiling sugar syrup.

Microniser   Device for the radiant heating of cocoa beans to loosen the shell.

Mogul   Machine for depositing confectionery mixtures into impressions formed in starch or in rubber mats.

Non-Newtonian liquid   A liquid whose viscosity varies according to the rate at which it is stirred (sheared).

'On the turn'   Change of a boiled sugar mass from the plastic to the glassy state.

Origin liquor   Cocoa mass manufactured in the country of origin of the beans.

Outer   Box containing a number of retail units.

Pearl   A stage reached during the boiling of sugar syrup.

Plastic state   The semi-labile state of high-boiled sugar syrup during cooling.

Plastic viscosity   Relates to the amount of energy required to keep a non-Newtonian liquid moving once it has started to move (*see also* yield value).

Polymorphism   The existence of the same substance in more than two different crystalline forms.

Press cake   Compressed cocoa powder after removal of cocoa butter.

Pulling   Repeated folding of high-boiled sugar syrup, carried out on the revolving arms of a pulling machine.

Reducing sugars   All the sugars obtained from the hydrolysis of starch are termed reducing sugars because they are reducing agents. Their ability to reduce alkaline copper sulphate (Fehling's solution) to cuprous oxide, is widely used in their quantitative determination.

Refiner   Roll mill, often with five rolls, used to grind solid chocolate ingredients. In some countries it also refers to machines for changing the flavour of cocoa mass. This is not used in this context in this book.

Rope   Rod of cooked sugar syrup produced on a forming machine.

Sand (*v.*)   To coat confections with icing sugar or fine sugar crystals.

Seeding   Addition of a small amount of crystals ('seed').

Small ball ⎫
Small pearl ⎬ Stages in boiling sugar syrup

Snap   Breaking characteristics of a .confection.

Soufflé   Stage in boiling sugar syrup.

Sugar bloom   Development of fine sugar clusters on the surface of chocolate.

Sweat (bleeding)   Appearance of droplets of moisture or sugar syrup on the surface of a confection.

Temper (*v.*)   To process chocolate so that any crystallisation of fat occurs in a stable modification.

Temperer   A machine for cooling/heating chocolate to form stable fat crystals.

Thread   Stage in boiling sugar syrup.

Tray off   To remove confections on to a holding tray.

Weeping   Same as *sweat*.

Wetting   Charge of syrup added during sugar panning.

Whip   To beat a syrup mixture so that air becomes entrapped.

Whipping agent   Products which promotes the formation of stable whips and foam.

Winnowing   The separation of a light material from a denser one by blowing air over them. In the case of cocoa, the shell is blown away from the cocoa nib and collected separately.

Yield value   Relates to the amount of energy required to start a non-Newtonian liquid moving (*see also* plastic viscosity).

Index